Desisting from Crime

CLARENDON STUDIES IN CRIMINOLOGY

Published under the auspices of the Institute of Criminology, University of Cambridge; the Mannheim Centre, London School of Economics; and the Centre for Criminological Research, University of Oxford.

Recent titles in this series:

Repair or Revenge?: Victims and Restorative Justice
Strang

Policing World Society: Historical Foundations of International Police Cooperation
Deflem

Accountability in Restorative Justice
Roche

Bouncers: Violence and Governance in the Night-time Economy
Hobbs, Hadfield, Lister, and Winlow

Policing and the Condition of England: Memory, Politics, and Culture
Loader and Mulcahy

The Criminological Foundations of Penal Policy: Essays in Honour of Roger Hood
Zedner and Ashworth (eds.)

CCTV and Policing: Public Area Surveillance and Police Practices in Britain
Goold

Prisons and their Moral Performance: A Study of Values, Quality, and Prison Life
Liebling

Constructing Victims' Rights: The Home Office, New Labour, and Victims
Rock

Desisting from Crime

Continuity and Change in Long-Term Crime Patterns of Serious Chronic Offenders

Michael E. Ezell
and
Lawrence E. Cohen

OXFORD
UNIVERSITY PRESS

OXFORD
UNIVERSITY PRESS

Great Clarendon Street, Oxford OX2 6DP

Oxford University Press is a department of the University of Oxford.
It furthers the University's objective of excellence in research, scholarship,
and education by publishing worldwide in

Oxford New York

Auckland Bangkok Buenos Aires Cape Town Chennai
Dar es Salaam Delhi Hong Kong Istanbul Karachi Kolkata
Kuala Lumpur Madrid Melbourne Mexico City Mumbai
Nairobi São Paulo Shanghai Taipei Tokyo Toronto

Oxford is a registered trade mark of Oxford University Press
in the UK and in certain other countries

Published in the United States
by Oxford University Press Inc., New York

First published 2005

British Library Cataloguing in Publication Data
Data available

Library of Congress Cataloging-in-Publication Data

Ezell, Michael Eugene 1973–
Desisting from crime : continuity and change in long-term crime patterns of serious chronic offenders / Michael E. Ezell and Lawrence E. Cohen.
p. cm. — (Clarendon studies in criminology)
Includes bibliographical references and index.
ISBN 0–19–927381–2 (hard cover : alk. paper)
1. Juvenile delinquency—United States. 2. Juvenile justice, Administration of—United States. I. Cohen, Lawrence E. II. Title. III. Series.
HV9104.E995 2005
364.36′0973—dc22

2004023569

ISBN 0–19–927381–2

1 3 5 7 9 10 8 6 4 2

Typeset by Newgen Imaging Systems (P) Ltd., Chennai, India
Printed in Great Britain
on acid-free paper by
Biddles Ltd., King's Lynn

General Editor's Preface

Clarendon Studies in Criminology aims to provide a forum for outstanding empirical and theoretical work in all aspects of criminology, criminal justice, penology, and the wider field of deviant behaviour. The Editors welcome excellent PhD work, as well as submissions from established scholars. The series was inaugurated in 1994, with Roger Hood as its first General Editor, following energetic discussions between Oxford University Press and three criminology centres. It is edited under the auspices of these three criminology centres: the Cambridge Institute of Criminology, the Mannheim Centre for Criminology at the London School of Economics, and the Oxford Centre for Criminology. Each supplies members of the Editorial Board.

Michael Ezell and Lawrence Cohen's book, *Desisting from Crime: Continuity and Change in Long-Term Crime Patterns of Serious Chronic Offenders*, makes an outstanding contribution to developmental and life-course criminology. The authors take a detailed and critical look at the 'age–crime curve'—a robust but aggregate criminological finding that has paradoxically suffered from insufficient exploration. There is both substantial continuity and significant change in offending patterns. Juvenile offenders often persist in offending well into adulthood, but a large number do not. The etiological explanation of this relationship between youthful and adult criminal offending patterns is, as the authors demonstrate, 'actually very complex'. The authors consider these important criminological questions eloquently and in detail, drawing on comprehensive longitudinal data from three independent samples of serious chronic youthful offenders dealt with by the California Youth Authority. They explore whether there are discrete groups of offenders with different crime patterns hidden in this curve, and just how stable individual differences are in the propensity to commit crime over the life course. In so doing, the authors provide an empirically precise test of several leading criminological theories. They show that '*change matters significantly* in the lives of offenders'—even among those who are most persistent. They provide important evidence that longer prison sentences do nothing to reduce recidivism, and that it is possible that 'three strikes' sentences imprison serial offenders at the point in the age–crime curve when 'most no longer appear to pose a danger to public safety'. This book constitutes a highly readable and carefully constructed account of both continuity in offending, and of pro-social behavioural change.

The editors welcome this important addition to the *Clarendon Studies in Criminology* series.

Alison Liebling
Cambridge, August 2004

To my wife, Liz, for the wonderful continuity she has brought to my life, and to my daughter Sabrina for the wonderful change she has already brought to my life

M.E.E.

To my best friend and God-daughter, Michele Felmlee-Gartner

L.E.C.

Acknowledgements

This book's 'trajectory' began about ten years ago and has undergone significant amounts of change over that time period. During that time period, many people encouraged and facilitated our endeavor to publish this book, and we wish to acknowledge and thank these people. The data collection for this study was made possible by grant No. 98—CE—VX—0026 to the California Department of the Youth Authority and the University of California at Davis from the National Institute of Justice. The data collection was facilitated through the cooperation of the Research Department of the California Department of the Youth Authority. The aid of Lee Britton, Rudy Haapanen, and Norm Skonovd in collecting and cleaning the data is gratefully acknowledged. Hernaldo Baltanado, Randy Bonnell, Kim Dochterman, Karla Haber, Kasie Lee, Kathleen Medina, and Hunter Moje worked diligently to code the data employed in this study. The authors also wish to thank Tony Brown, Jean Bottcher, Diane Felmlee, Ken Land, Bill McCarthy, Phil Morgan, Angela O'Rand, Ken Spenner, and the anonymous book reviewers for their helpful and insightful comments on earlier drafts. Our editors at Oxford, Gwen Booth and Louise Kavanagh, helped us mold this manuscript into its current form, and we thank them for their help. We also thank Lynn Childress for her excellent copy-editing of the manuscript and for helping catch our errors before this book went into print. Finally, the authors wish to emphasize that the views and opinions expressed in this study are solely theirs and do not necessarily represent the views and opinions of the National Institute of Justice, the California Department of the Youth Authority, the University of California at Davis, or Vanderbilt University.

Contents

List of Figures

1

Looking Forward

Criminologists generally agree that age is one of the strongest predictors of criminal activity and that a disproportionately large share of offending is committed by those who are in the age range between mid-adolescence and young adulthood (Farrington 1986). In fact, the relationship between age and crime is one of the most robust empirical findings in criminology, or as Hirschi and Gottfredson (1983: 552) state, 'this distribution thus represents one of the brute facts of criminology.'

When criminologists speak of the relationship between age and crime, they usually are referring to the 'age–crime curve'. The aggregate age–crime curve (which is computed by dividing the total number of arrests of individuals of a given age by the total population size of the specific age) indicates: (1) a sharp increase in the arrest rate in the early teen years; (2) a peak age of arrest in the late teen or early young adult years (depending on the crime type); and (3) a decrease in the rate of arrest over the remaining age distribution. Graphically, the distribution of arrests over the age range resembles the lognormal or gamma probability density functions, distributions characterized by both a peak and a long right tail (see Britt 1992).

Consider, for example, the two panels in Figure 1.1 that contain the aggregate age–crime curves for both violent and property FBI Index crimes in 1980, 1994, and 2000.[1] Although there is some parametric invariance in these age–crime curves (i.e. the mean, mode, skew, and kurtosis are not identical in each year), the general age–crime relationship described above can be readily seen. In each of the panels and for each year, crime rates dramatically increase in

[1] Violent Index crimes include murder and non-negligent manslaughter, forcible rape, aggravated assault, and robbery. Property Index crimes include burglary, larceny theft, motor vehicle theft, and arson.

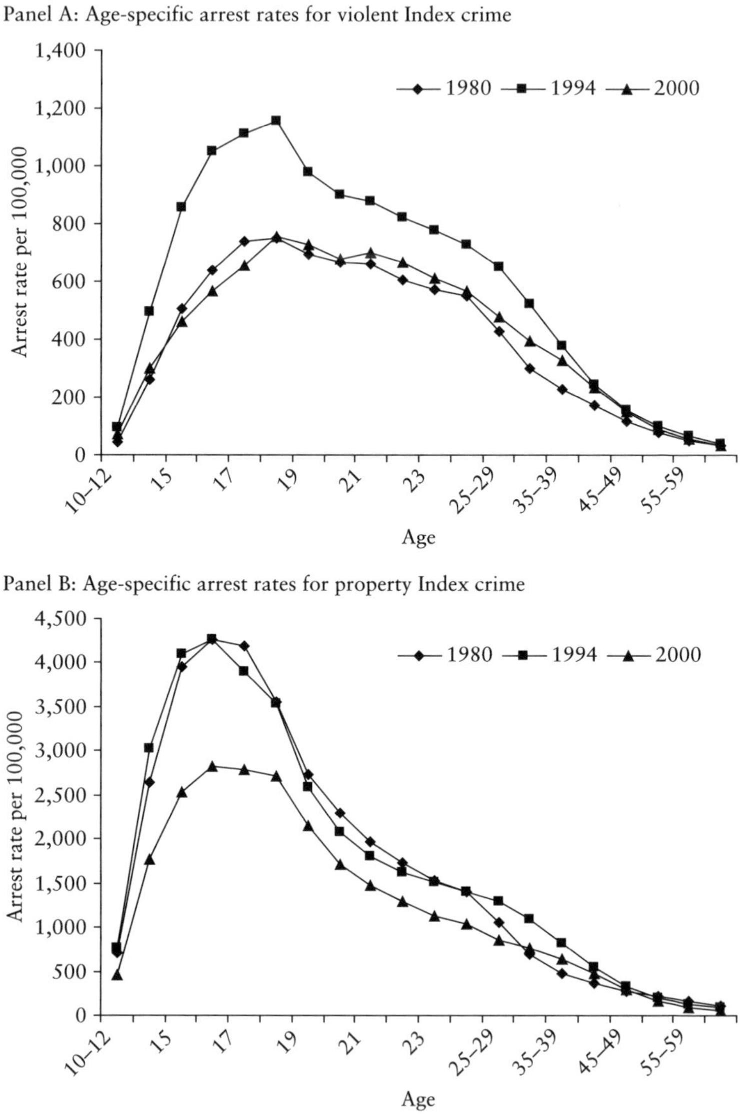

FIGURE 1.1. Violent and property aggregate age–crime curves in the United States in 1980, 1994, and 2000.

Source: Adapted from H. Snyder, *Juvenelie Arrests 2000* (Washington, DC: Office of Juvenile Justice and Delinquency Prevention, 2002).

early adolescence, peak in late adolescence or early adulthood, and then continually decrease over the remaining age distribution. Further evidence of the relationship between age and crime can be found in studies that analyze data relating crime rates to aggregates of various sizes. These studies consistently report that, overall, the age distribution of any population is inversely related to its crime rate (Cohen and Land 1987; Hirschi and Gottfredson 1983; Steffensmeier and Harer 1987; Steffensmeier *et al.* 1989).

Beyond that basic description, however, the relationship between age and crime is the fundamental source of many controversies in criminology, controversies that have sometimes led to rather rancorous debates between researchers. According to Lauritsen (1998: 127), 'Few substantive issues in criminology have been more contentious than those raised by the study of age and crime. While most social scientists agree that the aggregate age–crime curve reaches a peak during late adolescence and declines rapidly thereafter, there are ongoing debates about the theoretical meaning of this "brute fact".'

This study, which employs the use of three samples of serious chronic youthful offenders, examines three key questions regarding the relationship between age and crime: (1) are there two (or more) discrete groups of offenders with distinct age–crime curves concealed within the aggregate age–crime curve; (2) how stable are individual differences in the propensity to commit criminal acts across the life course; and (3) does the relationship between offending at one time period and a subsequent period endure when time-stable individual differences in criminal propensity are controlled?

The 'Great Debate' Concerning the Age–Crime Curve

Beginning in the mid-1980s, the discipline of criminology witnessed what Vold, Bernard, and Snipes (1998: 285) have called the 'Great Debate' concerning the relationship between age and crime. This debate involved a dispute over whether one finds the same relationship between age and crime with individual-level data as that which is observed when analyzing aggregate data. Two main factions formed within this debate—one represented by Hirschi and Gottfredson (1983; Gottfredson and Hirschi 1986, 1988, 1990) and the other by Blumstein and his colleagues (Blumstein and

Cohen 1979, 1987; Blumstein *et al.* 1986; Blumstein, Cohen, and Farrington 1988*a*, 1988*b*; Farrington 1983, 1986).[2]

Hirschi and Gottfredson (1983) contend crime is everywhere inversely related to age at both the individual and aggregate levels of analysis. Thus, the relationship between age and crime is deemed to be invariant; all people, everywhere, within any historical period (and with both official statistics and self-report data), tend to commit less crime as they age regardless of offense type. Hirschi and Gottfredson argue that age-specific offense rates increase dramatically from age 10 until age 17, and then continually decrease thereafter. In addition, Hirschi and Gottfredson (1983: 565, 578–9) emphasize that the decrease in offending with age occurs regardless of the offender's criminal propensity (i.e. no matter whether the individual's criminality is high or low). Thus, they expect that (after the peak years) the rate of offending will decrease with age, even among those serious and/or chronic offenders who are still criminally active.

Blumstein and his colleagues, on the other hand, argue that age is not inversely related to criminal offending at the individual level of analysis among *active offenders*. Blumstein and his colleagues concede that both participation in criminal activity and the incidence rates of offending vary inversely with age *at the population level*. However, they contend that Gottfredson and Hirschi confuse changes in participation and incidence rates with changes in the frequency of *individual* offending among active offenders (often referred to as lambda). While Gottfredson and Hirschi argue that incidence rates decline because there is a decrease in *frequency of offending* by active offenders, Blumstein *et al.* argue the incidence rate declines because there are *fewer* active offenders as age increases. Thus, it is the effect of offenders beginning (*onset*) and terminating (*desisting*) their criminal careers that is largely driving the shape of the age–crime curve. In short, Blumstein and his colleagues argue that as long as offenders are active, they will continue to commit crimes at a relatively constant rate independent of their age. If this is true, it has profound implications for crime control policies as the incapacitation of active offenders would significantly reduce the crime rate.

[2] Piquero, Farrington, and Blumstein (2003) present an excellent and detailed history of the criminal careers approach to explaining crime patterns (and research based on this approach), as well as detailing the debate between Blumstein and colleagues and Gottfredson and Hirschi.

Certainly, one of the major points that Blumstein and his colleagues are trying to convey is that the shape of the age–crime curve could be the result of a process other than offenders simply committing fewer crimes as they age, and thus, that caution is imperative when offering explanations for the empirical shape of the age–crime curve. More specifically, they indicate that the age–crime curve is driven by two processes: participation rates and incidence rates. A change in either one of these rates affects the empirical shape of the age–crime curve. Still, their argument, which has been made repeatedly, is that as long as offenders are active, they will continue to commit crimes at a relatively constant rate independent of their age. As Farrington (1986: 218) notes, 'they [Blumstein and his colleagues] have consistently argued that the individual crime rate or incidence of offending [lambda] is constant during a criminal career and that changes in aggregate crime rates reflect changes in prevalence.' In addition, Farrington (1986: 189) himself argues, 'age–crime curves for individuals do not resemble the aggregate curve since incidence [lambda] does not change consistently between the onset and termination of criminal careers.' Indeed, recently Farrington (1997: 365) argued that a '30 year old offender commits offenses at roughly the same rate as an 18 year old offender, although offenders are more prevalent in the population of 18 year olds than in the population of 30 year olds.'

Brame and Piquero (2003: 108) recently noted, 'a key issue is whether individual age–crime curves vary primarily in terms of the overall volume of offending or whether the aggregate age–crime curve is a mixture of micro-level curves that vary widely in shape,' while Farrington (2003: 226) noted in his discussion of contentious issues facing developmental and life-course criminology that information is lacking with respect to 'how much there are distinctly different behavioral trajectories.' In other words, the primary source of contention between various researchers still concerns the causes of the inverted-J shape of the age–crime curve, but the specific disagreement has shifted somewhat from purely focusing on whether the relationship between age and crime is constant among 'active offenders.'[3] Recent issues related to the relationship between age and crime focus on three key questions: (1) how stable or unstable are individual differences in criminal behaviour across the

[3] Chapter 3 reviews the evidence from longitudinal studies of criminal offending patterns over time.

life course; (2) are there two discrete groups of offenders in the offender population, each with their own age–crime curves that differ from the overall aggregate curve, but which when aggregated together produce the observed overall curve; and (3) is there a significant relationship between criminal activity at adjacent ages (or periods) after controlling for persistent differences in the propensity to offend? Although these issues are sometimes treated as mutually exclusive, they are actually highly interconnected and can all be viewed within the bounds of the long-standing 'paradox of persistence' phenomenon in criminology (Cohen and Vila 1996).

The Paradox of Persistence

The 'paradox of persistence' refers to the consistent finding that when looking *in reverse* (or *retrospectively*) researchers find that most adult criminal offenders were juvenile delinquents, yet when looking *forward* (or *prospectively*) in the lives of juvenile delinquents researchers find that most delinquents do not go on to become adult criminal offenders (see e.g. Blumstein *et al.* 1986; Caspi and Moffitt 1992; Cernkovich and Giordano 2001; Cline 1980; Gove 1985; Loeber and Le Blanc 1990; McCord 1980; Robins 1978; Sampson 2000; Sampson and Laub 1993, 1997; Tracy and Kempf-Leonard 1996). An oft-cited quotation from Robins (1978: 611) perhaps best summarizes the issue: 'adult antisocial behavior virtually requires childhood antisocial behavior, yet most antisocial children do not become antisocial adults.' Thus, on the one hand, there is a considerable amount of continuity in behavior over time, evidenced by the fact that few, if any, criminologists would argue with the statement that the presence (and/or frequency) of delinquent criminal activity during childhood and adolescence is one of the best, if not the best, predictor of adult criminality. Yet, at the same time, the relationship between juvenile and adult criminal activity is not a deterministic one, and a number of juvenile offenders are able to escape the criminal lifestyle and do not become 'career criminals.' In other words, there is both continuity and change (discontinuity) over time, and while this is a relatively straightforward (and some might argue simple) statement, the etiological explanation of this relationship is actually very complex. This relationship, in fact, is the source of a key theoretical controversy in the discipline of criminology (Cohen and Vila 1996): how can one simultaneously explain the sources of both continuity and change in criminal behavior over time? Any valid explanation of the sources of continuity and change (discontinuity) in criminal offending patterns must consequentially produce an explanation that is consistent with the observed shape of the age–crime curve and account for whether offending at adjacent ages is causally related after accounting for individual differences in the propensity to offend.

Explaining the Paradox of Persistence

Three broad theoretical explanations have been proffered to explain both the paradox of persistence and the shape of the age–crime curve: (1) population heterogeneity, (2) state dependence, and (3) the dual taxonomy approaches. According to the population heterogeneity explanation (in its purest form), continuity and change in criminal offending patterns over time are explained entirely by *time-invariant differences* in a latent proneness to engage in criminal activity. Population heterogeneity theories are sometimes called *latent trait* theories because they posit that there is variation across the population on a persistent, underlying or *latent* variable that explains crime (Nagin and Farrington 1992*a*, 1992*b*; Nagin and Paternoster 1991). This latent variable is argued to be either unmeasured or poorly measured (Cohen and Vila 1996). According to the population heterogeneity position, all offenders follow the same age–crime curve and all offenders are argued to decrease their offending over time. The individuals who have higher levels of the latent variable, however, will engage in criminal activity earlier in life, persist in committing criminal acts further into adulthood, and commit criminal offenses at a higher rate at all points in time. Individuals lower on the distribution of latent propensity, on the other hand, are argued to begin offending later in life, end their offending earlier in the life course, and commit offenses at a lower rate at all points in time. In other words, continuity and change is explained entirely by between-individual differences in latent criminal propensity. The association between criminal activity at any two points in time (e.g. two adjacent ages) is argued to be caused by the latent propensity, and controlling for the underlying differences in propensity eliminates any relationship between crime at any two points in time. Gottfredson and Hirschi's (1990) self-control theory is arguably the leading population heterogeneity theory.

A pure state dependence explanation, on the other hand, argues that the *propensity to engage in crime is malleable* over the age distribution. Continuity in criminal activity arises as a result of the negative cumulative consequences of earlier criminal activity and/or continued engulfment in the 'criminal lifestyle', whereas change results from experiencing positive events that can potentially mitigate one's criminal propensity (e.g. getting married or obtaining a good job). The shape of the age–crime curve is derived from the fact that criminal propensity is variable over the life course and is at its highest levels in the mid- to late adolescent years. An important proposition of state dependence arguments is that criminal activity at one point in time is *causally* related to criminal activity at a later point in time. The age-graded theory of informal social control proposed by Sampson and Laub (1993) is often considered as an example of a state dependence theory.[4]

A third primary theoretical perspective, the dual taxonomy explanation, argues that the criminal offender population is comprised of two empirically distinct offender categories, each with its own etiological explanation. In dual taxonomy approaches, there is a larger group of offenders who only engage in criminal activity during adolescence, while the second smaller group is 'life-course persistent' in their criminal activity. Thus, since the aggregate age–crime curve mixes these two groups together, it takes on its observed shape. The change is the result of desistence by the 'adolescent-limited' offenders, whereas continuity results from the continuing criminal activity of the 'life-course-persistent' group (Moffitt 1993, 1997). According to this stream of theoretical thought, the association between criminal activity at two points in time is argued to be spurious for the life-course-persistent group, and causally related for the adolescent-limited group. The dual taxonomy theory of Moffitt (1993, 1997) is an example of this type of theoretical approach.

[4] As described in the next chapter, the age-graded theory of Sampson and Laub (1993) is better described as a 'mixed' theory that allows for both state dependence and enduring individual differences (Nagin and Paternoster 2000). The primary assumption of this theory, however, is that criminal propensity can be changed as a result of changing levels of social control over the life course, and thus it is generally referred to as a theory of state dependence.

Overview of the Study

As noted above, this study examines three key, often controversial questions. These questions will be examined using arrest data from the serious youthful offender population, a population of offenders that is rarely included in examinations of the issues addressed in this study. To date, research has largely ignored the empirical question of whether or not serious youthful offenders are a homogeneous group or a heterogeneous bunch of groups with differential rates and trajectories of criminal activity across the age distribution.[5]

The remainder of this study will proceed in the following manner. In Chapter 2, we present a more comprehensive description of the population heterogeneity, state dependence, and dual taxonomy perspectives, with special emphasis on the self-control theory of Gottfredson and Hirschi (1990), the age-graded theory of informal social control proposed by Sampson and Laub (1993), and the dual taxonomy theory of Moffitt (1993).

In Chapter 3, we review the extant empirical literature on the topics of concern in this study. The specific hypotheses examined in this study are also presented in Chapter 3. In Chapter 4, we describe the California Youth Authority (the source of the samples used herein), the state agency responsible for housing the most seriously delinquent/criminal youthful offenders in that state.

The data and statistical methods employed in this study are described in Chapter 5. More specifically, the data utilized herein are three samples of individuals released on parole from the California Youth Authority in fiscal years 1981–2, 1986–7, and 1991–2. The sources of data and variables used in the analyses are described in this chapter. Chapter 5 concludes with a brief

[5] Previous research too often treats this group of serious offenders as a homogeneous group (especially in terms of the continuity of their behavioral patterns) because they only comprise a very small fraction (<6%) of general population samples (e.g. birth cohort samples, school samples). They are usually treated as a homogeneous group via a binary variable (usually labelled 'chronic', 'serious', and/or 'persistent' offenders on the basis of making some often *ex post facto* cut-off point) and then are compared against the low-rate offenders and non-offenders. Sampson (2000) criticizes this static, between-individual research (which produces conclusions indicating high-rate offenders have elevated risks of continuity in offending relative to non-chronic offenders) because it tends to reify the fixed categories and neglects the nature and extent of within-individual change.

description of the statistical methods employed in this study, namely the finite mixture or semiparametric random effects models of Nagin and Land (1993; Land and Nagin 1996; Land, McCall, and Nagin 1996; Nagin 1999), as well as parametric random effects panel methods.

We present a descriptive summary of the three data sets in Chapter 6. This chapter includes a description of the characteristics of the cases (e.g. ethnicity, gang membership, and drug abuse), the age at first criminal arrest, the types of offenses the individuals in the samples were arrested for perpetrating, their adult incarceration experiences, and the mortality patterns of these individuals.

The results of the substantive analyses are presented in Chapters 7 and 8. Chapter 7 presents the results from applications of the Nagin and Land (1993) finite mixture model to each of the three samples. The results in Chapter 7 are, in turn, used to investigate the age–crime curves for distinct 'latent classes' of offenders who share a similar age-specific offending trajectory, with an emphasis on examining whether the relationship between age and crime is invariant across the latent classes. Also, the latent classes derived from the application of the finite mixture models in this chapter will form the basis for subsequent analyses in Chapter 8 that test whether there is a relationship of past to subsequent criminal activity after controlling for unobserved or 'hidden heterogeneity' (Land and Nagin 1996).

The methodological approach used in Chapter 8 is the multimethod approach described by Bushway, Brame, and Paternoster (1999), who recommend using several different statistical models (each with different assumptions) to estimate the relationship between past and subsequent criminal behaviour. This is critical because recent research suggests that conclusions arrived at in some previous empirical investigations of this issue could possibly be method-specific, thereby bringing into question the robustness and reliability of the prior findings. To the degree that one can robustly replicate the findings using different methods that have different assumptions, one can be more assured of the existence of the estimated effect (Bushway, Brame, and Paternoster 1999). Similarly, replicating findings across multiple samples would lend further support to the robustness of any observed effect.

The final chapter, Chapter 9, discusses the main findings of this study as evidence in support of or contrary to the hypotheses described in Chapter 3. Chapter 9 then concludes with a discussion of the limitations of this study, policy implications, and directions for future research concerning the topic of continuity and discontinuity in criminal offending patterns.

2

Crime Over the Life Course: The Empirical Implications of Three Theories

As noted in Chapter 1, this study focuses on several issues central to the continuity and discontinuity of the criminal careers of serious youthful offenders across the age span. This chapter focuses on the theoretical frameworks guiding this study and consists of four main sections. First, the general population heterogeneity, state dependence, and 'mixed' explanations of criminal behaviour will be described. The next three sections contain discussions of three specific theoretical perspectives (one from each framework): Gottfredson and Hirschi's (1990) general theory of crime, Sampson and Laub's (1993) age-graded theory of informal social control, and Moffitt's dual taxonomy theory (1993). Attention will focus on how each theoretical perspective accounts for the processes of continuity and discontinuity in criminal offending patterns, the relationship between age and crime, and the relationship between past and subsequent criminal activity.

It is important to note at the outset that this study does not test the specific causal structures of a particular theory or set of theories, but rather it presents an empirical evaluation of the precise longitudinal implications of three leading criminological theories. Thus, this study is best viewed as providing evidence either supporting or refuting the direct empirical implications of each of these theoretical perspectives. To date, these implications have remained largely untested among the serious youthful offender population.

Population Heterogeneity and State Dependence

As indicated in Chapter 1, etiological explanations concerning continuity in criminal behaviour over time are broadly defined in terms of their basic presumption of either population heterogeneity and/or state dependence processes. Heckman (1981*a*: 150) sharply describes the distinction between the two processes:

> One [explanation] is that individuals who experience the event are altered by their experience in that the constraints, preferences, or prices (or any combination of the three) that govern future outcomes are altered by past outcomes. Such an effect of past outcomes is termed structural state dependence. A second explanation is that individuals differ in some unmeasured propensity to experience the event and this propensity is either stable over time, or if it changes, values of propensity are autocorrelated. Broadly defined, the second explanation is a consequence of population heterogeneity.

Drawing heavily on the 'urn schemes' analogies presented in Heckman (1981*b*) and Nagin and Paternoster (1991, 2000), this section explicates the basic principles of both the population heterogeneity and state dependence explanations as they pertain to crime.

To begin, assume that each individual in the population has an urn containing red and blue balls. The balls represent an individual's propensity to engage in crime and pro-social activities, respectively. Over time, individuals pick balls (i.e. event trials) and replace the balls in the urn (i.e. sample with replacement). Further, allow a red ball to represent the commission of a crime, while a blue ball represents engaging in a conventional 'pro-social' activity. The proportion of red balls in an individual's urn represents their criminal propensity. Thus, individuals with greater proportions of red balls in their urns have greater propensities to engage in criminal activities, whereas individuals with more blue balls have greater propensities to engage in 'pro-social' behaviors (Nagin and Paternoster 2000: 120).

Population Heterogeneity

Consider first the population heterogeneity urn scheme. According to this scheme, individuals are assigned urns, and the initial constellation of red balls to blue balls *varies across urns in the population*; in other words, there is population heterogeneity with respect to the mix of red and blue balls in individual urns. The critical assumption of the population heterogeneity argument is that for any given individual, once an urn is assigned, the proportion of red and blue balls is considered *fixed across time* or *time-invariant*. Individuals draw and replace balls over time, but neither red nor blue balls are added to or extracted from a person's urn.

Given the assumptions of sampling with replacement and the fixed nature of red and blue balls in any given urn, the odds of drawing a red ball or a blue ball *never* changes for each individual across the lifespan. Accordingly, some individuals in the population simply have a greater chance of drawing a red ball (because they have more red balls in their urn). Given the assumption of sampling with replacement, each draw from the urn is statistically independent of the prior draws in the sense that drawing a red ball does not increase (or decrease) the odds of drawing another red ball at the next draw. In retrospect, however, the knowledge of an individual's past experience of drawing red balls will certainly be highly predictive of the odds of a future drawing of a red ball. For example, an individual who has never drawn a red ball will be unlikely to draw a red ball in the future. Conversely, an individual who has only picked red balls in the past is highly likely to continue picking red balls in future trials. Why is this so? According to the population heterogeneity perspective, the correlation between past and future draws is simply determined by the initial mix of red and blue balls in one's urn.

As Nagin and Paternoster note (2000: 121), 'the predictive power of past events is entirely due to the *initial distribution* of red and blue balls in the urn' (emphasis in original). The observed correlation between past and subsequent criminal activity is deemed to be entirely due to the initial distribution of red balls in the urn. Since the probability of picking a red (or blue) ball is constant over time (i.e. from trial to trial), continuity in behavioral patterns (criminal or pro-social) is simply a consequence of the initial propensity to engage in those behaviors (i.e. the initial odds of drawing a red or blue ball). The correlation is not causal, but rather it simply (and spuriously) reflects the initial distribution of balls in the urns.

Under the assumption that it is not possible to see directly inside the urn to count the exact number of red and blue balls, past counts of red balls drawn can be used as an indicator of a given individual's latent criminal propensity. Naturally, the greater the number of trials observed (i.e. the longer the length of follow-up period in a study of criminal behaviors), the more accurately one could measure the latent propensity variable.

State Dependence

Using the same urn analogy, the pure form of state dependence differs from the population heterogeneity explanation on two key assumptions. First, all individuals are initially assigned identical urns with the exact same number of red and blue balls. Second, while individuals still sample with replacement, under state dependence assumptions the number of red and blue balls is malleable over time. The critical assumption of the state dependence perspective is that the selection of a given ball results in the addition of one or more balls of the same color to the individual's urn. Thus, if one selects a red ball, that drawn red ball is replaced and additional red balls are deposited in the individual's urn. In other words, the commission of a criminal act (i.e. the selection of the red ball) is argued to causally increase the odds of future criminal acts as the additional red balls increase the proportion of red balls in the individual's urn. The same process is assumed to occur for the selection of a blue ball; engaging in a conventional or pro-social activity is argued to increase the odds of future such activities.

Thus, the state dependence position views continuity in behavior as resulting from the fact that after the event of picking a ball of a given color, the odds of picking that color increase in the future because of the additional balls added to the urn. In other words, the proportion of red and blue balls is considered to vary over time and to be causally related to past events. Thus, the observed correlation between past and subsequent criminal activities is argued to be genuinely causal in nature rather than spuriously due to the initial distribution of red and blue balls. Thus, one can see why population heterogeneity theories are often referred to as *static* theories, while theories assuming a state dependence process are often referred to as *dynamic* theories (Paternoster *et al.* 1997). The key proposition of a state dependence theory, then, is that events have consequences, and those consequences can either increase or decrease the likelihood of future criminal behavior:

> The state dependence position adopts the view that: (1) criminal behaviors may subsequently open up new opportunities for other criminal activities while closing off opportunities for noncrime, and (2) some noncriminal behaviors may subsequently open up opportunities for other noncriminal

behaviors while closing off criminal opportunities.

(Nagin and Paternoster 2000: 125)

In other words, criminal propensity can be significantly reduced over the life course by continued involvement or investment in pro-social activities (Nagin and Paternoster 1993, 1994).

The Mixed Perspective

While in their pure forms population heterogeneity and state dependence theories are diametrically opposed explanations, they are not mutually exclusive processes (Nagin and Paternoster 2000; Sampson and Laub 1997). That is, theories can both allow for population-level heterogeneity in the initial distribution of criminal propensity, while also allowing for consequences to result from engaging in criminal activity. As Sampson and Laub (1997: 155) state, 'to assume that individual differences influence the choices one makes in life (which they certainly do), does not mean that social mechanisms emerging from those choices can then have no causal significance.' Indeed there is a growing consensus in the field of criminology that persistent individual differences must be incorporated into any valid theoretical explanation of criminal behavior, since it has become clear that 'there are persistent differences across individuals in the rates of offending over time' (Land and Nagin 1996: 164). Whether those persistent differences are the 'be all and end all' of explaining crime and exactly how stable they are over time is a fundamental debate in criminology (Paternoster, Brame, and Farrington 2001).

In the next three sections, the theories of Gottfredson and Hirschi, Sampson and Laub, and Moffitt are discussed.[1] A key distinction between each of these theories is in their different explanations of the stability of antisocial tendencies over the life course. The question of stability has direct implications for explaining the shape of the age–crime curve. Thus, particular attention is focused on each theory's explanation of continuity in crime and its corresponding explanation of the age–crime relationship.

[1] Even though both Sampson and Laub's (1993) age-graded informal social control theory and Moffitt's dual taxonomy theory are conceptually distinct theories, each integrate elements of both population heterogeneity and state dependence propositions into their explanations.

Gottfredson and Hirschi's General Theory of Crime

In their book, *A General Theory of Crime*, Gottfredson and Hirschi (1990) explicate their population heterogeneity theory centered around the notion of self-control.[2] This theory has profound implications for sociological explanations of crime because it challenges the basic fundamental premisses of most sociological theories (Cohen and Vila 1996; Nagin and Paternoster 1994), and thus is highly deserving of both empirical testing and critical evaluation.

To begin, Gottfredson and Hirschi say that their theory is 'meant to explain all crimes, at all times, and for that matter, many other forms of [risk-taking] behavior that are not sanctioned by the state' (1990: 117), which is why they refer to their theory as a *general* theory of crime. Gottfredson and Hirschi place the concept of self-control as the centrepiece around which nearly every 'fact' of crime can be organized and explained, including continuity in crime, the age–crime relationship, the gap between male and female involvement in criminal activities, the disproportionate involvement of minorities in criminal activities, the role of peer groups, why pro-social activities are negatively correlated with criminal activity, and why criminal offenders tend to engage in a constellation of non-criminal yet similarly risk-taking behaviors that are 'analogous to crime' (e.g. alcoholism, drug abuse, smoking, excessive speeding in an automobile, automobile accidents, and promiscuous and unprotected sexual activity).

Crime versus Criminality

One of Gottfredson and Hirschi's primary theoretical contributions is their argument for distinguishing between crime and criminality as a necessity for understanding the etiology of crime. They argue that the failure of positivistic etiological explanations to make this distinction renders most theories of crime seriously flawed in the conceptualization of their dependent variable (Gottfredson and Hirschi 1990: 144). In short, for Gottfredson and Hirschi, crime

[2] Wilson and Herrnstein (1985) have proposed another well-known population heterogeneity theory. Wilson and Herrnstein's theory is more strongly rooted in the biological and constitutional determinants of criminal propensity, including the presence of a genetic predisposition (see Cohen 1987 for a brief review). Their theory has longitudinal implications similar to those of Gottfredson and Hirschi's theory.

refers to the behavioral acts that people engage in, whereas criminality refers to the individual's propensity to engage in crime.

To be consistent with the 'characteristics of ordinary crimes', Gottfredson and Hirschi define crime as 'acts of force or fraud undertaken in the pursuit of self-interest' (1990: 15–16). According to them, crimes are (1) simple behavioral acts that involve immediate gratification and satisfy ordinary and universal desires; (2) provide few long-term benefits to the actor and cause pain and suffering to the victim; and (3) are exciting, risk-taking behaviors that can be committed by every individual in society without specialized knowledge, training, or prior learning (Gottfredson and Hirschi 1990: 89).

While most criminological theories try to explain the 'causes of crime', they fail to clearly conceptualize their dependent variable. By distinguishing between crime and criminality, Gottfredson and Hirschi remove the confounding preoccupation with the 'acts of crime' from the real theoretical question of criminality—explaining the propensity of some individuals to engage in crime. This focus on the actor clearly sets the stage for the central mechanism they employ to explain criminality: self-control.

Criminality and Self-Control

To describe the type of individual most likely to repeatedly engage in behaviors fitting their definition of crime, Gottfredson and Hirschi offer a *control theory*. They posit (like all control theories) that people, in the absence of some 'controlling' force restraining or preventing them from satisfying their immediate desires, are free to commit crimes (Vold, Bernard, and Snipes 1998).

According to Gottfredson and Hirschi (1990: 90–1), individuals who repeatedly commit criminal acts 'will tend to be impulsive, insensitive, physical (as opposed to mental), risk-taking, short-sighted, and nonverbal.' The authors note that the above characteristics are the precise traits of individuals with low levels of self-control. Thus, their theory posits that the inclination to commit criminal acts in the pursuit of self-interest is a function of an individual's lack of self-control. Importantly, they argue that those characteristics are positively correlated and tend to coalesce within certain individuals and to *persist* throughout the life course.

Stated succinctly, individuals are assumed to vary in their propensity to use force and fraud as a means of fulfilling their own self-interests and/or obtaining resources; this varying propensity is what Gottfredson and Hirschi refer to as *criminality*. People have varying degrees of criminality because there is a population variation in the level of self-control. People with high levels of self-control have low levels of criminality, whereas individuals with low levels of self-control have high levels of criminality.

Again, the authors also argue that their theory explains not only criminal acts, but other 'analogous' behaviors as well (e.g. alcoholism, drug abuse, and automobile accidents). Individuals with low self-control tend to engage in a wide variety of risky acts consistent with the definition of 'crime.' Further, individuals with low self-control also have difficulty, for example, obtaining and keeping employment, maintaining friendships with spouses and others, completing educational endeavors, becoming effective parents, staying healthy, and keeping long-term financial commitments. In other words, low self-control does not enhance the quality (or longevity) of life and severely restricts the potential to have or build positive social relationships. As Gottfredson and Hirschi (1990: 96) argue, 'Social life is not enhanced by low self-control and its consequences.' If the propensity to engage in crime is a consequence of low self-control, the obvious question is: what are the causes of these varying levels of self-control? According to Gottfredson and Hirschi, levels of self-control arise largely from family teaching and child-rearing practices. Effective child rearing includes the following three components: (1) the parents must adequately monitor the child's behavior; (2) deviant behavior must be recognized when it occurs; and (3) deviant behavior must be consistently and fairly punished when it is recognized (Gottfredson and Hirschi 1990: 97). These three external controls on the child's behavior when employed consistently by effective parents eventually become internalized in the child through the process the authors call 'socialization.' Effective socialization develops the abilities to delay gratification, empathize with others, and to sacrifice personal needs for the well-being of others. In the absence of effective parenting/socialization, individuals fail to develop the self-restraint necessary to resist pursuing one's self-interest in the easiest, quickest manner possible; or as Gottfredson and Hirschi (1990: 88) pointedly state, 'money without work, sex without courtship, revenge without court delays.'

Considering both the concepts of crime and criminality together, Gottfredson and Hirschi claim to have produced an internally consistent argument by making their conception of crime congruent with their conception of criminality: 'people who commit crimes are assumed to possess traits that reflect the nature of those acts' (Barlow 1991: 233). However, this internally consistent result has been criticized as tautological because their conception of low self-control is defined by the very behaviors assumed to be indicators of low self-control. For example, Akers (1991) argues that until measures of self-control are operationalized independent of the behaviors said to reflect low self-control, the theory will remain tautological. In their defense of this criticism, Gottfredson and Hirschi (1993: 52–3) retort, 'the charge of tautology is in fact a compliment; an assertion that we followed the path of logic in producing an internally consistent result' and that non-tautological theories will produce definitions of crime and criminality that are 'independent of one another.'

Explaining Continuity and Discontinuity in Crime

A crucial proposition of Gottfredson and Hirschi is that criminal propensity is set very early in life (generally by around the age of 8), and that the degree of self-control instilled at that point will remain relatively stable throughout the remainder of the life course. From their perspective, the failure of socialization processes to instill adequate levels of self-control is extremely difficult to overcome in later life, and, similarly, high levels of self-control, once attained, cannot be easily unravelled. The authors clearly favor the position that it is easier to initially instill higher levels of self-control than it is to change the amount of self-control already instilled, and thus they ultimately contend that criminality is largely determined and intractable by around the age of 8 (Gottfredson and Hirschi 1990: 106–8). They do, however, admit that an individual's level of self-control is somewhat flexible over time. They attempt to reconcile the discrepancy between the notion of self-control (criminal propensity) as a time-stable trait, on the one hand, and allowing for the possibility of it changing over time, on the other hand, in two ways. First, Gottfredson and Hirschi assert that changing from lower to higher levels of self-control is perhaps possible, but extremely unlikely because the pre-existing low level of self-control and all of its consequences essentially overwhelm the odds of such change. Second, Gottfredson and Hirschi (1990: 107) argue that while 'socialization continues to occur throughout life' for everyone in the population, the relative position one occupies on the self-control distribution scale in the population continues to remain stable throughout life. In other words, they assume that while socialization may continue throughout the life course, 'the rate at which socialization continues to occur is approximately the same for everyone' (Nagin and Paternoster 2000: 122).

In sum, the relative positions of individuals with respect to the distribution of self-control present in the population at approximately the age of 8 will be equal to the relative distribution of criminality present in the population at age 20, age 30, age 40, and so on. In the words of Gottfredson and Hirschi (1990: 107), 'differences between people in the likelihood that they will commit criminal acts persists over time.' Barlow (1991: 235) refers to this as the 'stability postulate.'

It is important to point out that Gottfredson and Hirschi's argument of time-invariant individual differences in criminal propensity after age 8 essentially discredits nearly all modern positivistic theories of crime from the disciplines of psychology, economics, and sociology.[3] If that assumption is true, then experiences in later childhood, adolescence, and adulthood are essentially irrelevant to crime causation, and an individual's educational, economic, social, and psychological experiences are immaterial to explaining criminal involvement (Nagin and Paternoster 1994). Moreover, Gottfredson and Hirschi argue that all of those experiences are, in fact, determined by initial levels of self-control and thus none will have any effect on criminal behavior after one controls for this initial level of self-control. Thus, they argue that individuals *self-select* such conventional experiences, meaning that they will select or choose educational, economic, and social experiences that are entirely consistent with their level of self-control (Benson 2002).

For example, individuals with low self-control are uncomfortable in structured environments and do not perform well in school or traditional jobs that involve rote tasks. As a result, individuals with low self-control tend to do poorly in school and conventional work

[3] It is worth noting that Gottfredson and Hirschi's conceptualization of economic theories of crime (e.g. Beccaria 1963; Becker 1968) as 'positivistic' appears to be at serious odds with the main theoretical propositions of positivistic criminology (see e.g. Cohen and Land 1987; Jeffrey 1972; Vold, Bernard, and Snipes 1998) and stands in contrast with their earlier descriptions of economic theories of crime as distinct from positivistic theories (Gottfredson and Hirschi 1987*b*).

environments, often leave school before graduating and are unable to retain employment, and search for alternative environments that do not advocate following rules or being punctual, orderly, attentive, and quiet for extended periods of time. Parallel arguments are made by Gottfredson and Hirschi for the inverse correlation between criminal activity and the variables of marital stability and parental investment. The negative but significant correlations between crime and these events/experiences are entirely spurious and due to a lack of self-control itself. Thus, from Gottfredson and Hirschi's perspective, individuals with low levels of self-control *self-select* or sort themselves over the life course into life experiences and choices (crime, non-marriage or bad marriages, ineffective parenting, high unemployment, low educational attainment, and frequent drug and alcohol abuse) that are consistent with their deficient level of this underlying characteristic or latent trait (Nagin and Paternoster 2000).

Explaining the Age–Crime Curve

If the propensity to engage in criminal activity is constant throughout life, how can Gottfredson and Hirschi explain the shape of the age–crime curve, especially the apparent sharp decline in crime after late adolescence? To get around such seeming incongruity, they draw on their initial distinction of crime and criminality and argue that criminality only predisposes people to engage in crime in the face of available criminal *opportunities*. In the absence of opportunities, criminal propensity is just that, criminal propensity. Individuals with high degrees of self-control will rarely commit crimes, even in the presence of opportunities, whereas individuals with low self-control will use force or fraud to pursue their own self-interest at a relatively high rate in the face of such opportunities to do so. The implication of their argument is that because of age roles, structural factors, and perhaps even biological processes, the opportunities to commit criminal acts tend to decline with age. Thus, since criminal propensity remains fixed across time, the authors clearly rely on a host of different social forces that lead to a 'reduction in exposure to criminal opportunities, that, on average, decline as activity patterns change with age', to explain the age–crime relationship (Cohen and Vila 1996: 131). It has been argued that Gottfredson and Hirschi are not exactly as clear as they could be on this topic (Cohen and Vila 1996; Tittle 1995).

For the purposes of this study, though, Gottfredson and Hirschi's critical argument concerns 'age invariance' and its longitudinal implications. Their age-invariance argument, originally presented in their *American Journal of Sociology* article 'Age, Crime, and Social Explanation' (Hirschi and Gottfredson 1983), posits that the relationship between age and crime is 'inherent, invariant, and inexplicable' (Tittle and Grasmick 1998: 309). They claim that whether one uses self-report offense data or official police or court records of arrest, the data suggest that all people, everywhere, and within any historical period, tend to commit fewer crimes as they age. The authors argue that if the relationship between age and crime is invariant and *all* individuals commit fewer crimes as they age, then age is actually irrelevant to the study of crime and no sociological, psychological, or economic variables that covary with age (e.g. employment, marriage) can explain this 'age effect' (Greenberg 1985; Tittle and Grasmick 1998).

Because this is such a controversial argument, with far-reaching implications for both the explanation of and the proper methods for the study of crime, we consider their argument in further detail here. The authors have made it clear in several expositions of the invariance argument (Gottfredson and Hirschi 1986, 1987*a*, 1990; Hirschi and Gottfredson 1983, 1985, 1988) that they believe the shape of the age–crime curve is relatively robust across persons, groups, cultures, and time periods. All sources of data suggest that individuals will have their greatest involvement in criminal activity during the late adolescent years of life and offending will decline thereafter. The implication of this argument is that even individuals with vastly different life circumstances and experiences will have similarly shaped age–crime curves across the life course (Greenberg 1985). However, Greenberg (1985: 8) notes that if the age–crime curve results from the effects of social processes that develop with age, then those processes should affect 'different groups differently, breaking the uniformity of the relationship between age and crime across groups.' Gottfredson and Hirschi assert, however, that crime declines regardless of whether individuals experience such events as employment, completion of schooling, and marriage, an argument that directly counters the explanations of life-course researchers such as Sampson and Laub (1993) and Marxist-oriented criminologists such as Greenberg (1985).

Again, we reiterate that the key implication of Gottfredson and Hirschi's invariance argument that we are concerned with here is that the *differences between individuals are said to persist over time*. Both the relative differences of criminal propensity (criminality) and relative group differences in criminal offending (crime) should endure throughout life. Group differences in criminal offending histories reflect 'no more than group variation in the propensity to commit offenses at any point in the life course' (Shavit and Rattner 1988: 1459). Thus, the only explanation needed is why some individuals/groups have higher rates of involvement in crime at any given point in time compared to other individuals or groups. For Gottfredson and Hirschi, of course, this pattern is due to the different levels of self-control distributed throughout the population. Tittle and Grasmick (1998: 314) provide an excellent summary of the invariance argument of Gottfredson and Hirschi on this point: 'variations in criminal behavior between those with different degrees of self-control at any age will be similar to such differences at any other age, even though the absolute amount of crime by everybody changes over the life cycle in conformity with the inverted-J curve.'

The implications of the age-invariance argument are profound and far-reaching. If the relationship between age and crime is invariant and between-group differences that exist at one point in the age–crime curve continue to exist at any other point in the age–crime curve, then only a single time point is necessary to measure the criminality of any group. To quote Gottfredson and Hirschi (1987*a*: 592), 'if there is continuity over the life course in criminal activity (or its absence), it is unnecessary to follow people over time.' Following individuals across time merely provides redundant information (available at any point in cross-section) at a hefty price because longitudinal research is vastly more expensive to conduct than is cross-sectional research (Gottfredson and Hirschi 1987*a*).[4]

If Gottfredson and Hirschi are wrong, however, and there are different criminal offending trajectories in the population that do not follow the overall aggregate age–crime curve, then it is

[4] Sampson (1992: 546) critiques Gottfredson and Hirschi's argument that longitudinal data provide no empirical benefits to the study of crime (over cross-sectional research designs) and thus wastes research money. Sampson contends that 'such data are necessary to verify the core assertions of their theory regarding stability and the lack of change across the life course.'

absolutely necessary for researchers to follow individuals over time to determine not only the actual empirical shape of their crime trajectories, but also if any events or experiences help explain the different trajectory shapes. If crime is a social event that takes on different meanings across the life course, then it is necessary to study trajectories of criminal offending as dynamic processes that unfold over time, with a particular emphasis on whether trajectories of crime are linked or interrelated with trajectories in other social, economic, psychological, and perhaps even biological domains of life (Benson 2002; Greenberg 1985; Hagan and Palloni 1988).

Explaining the Relationship of Past to Subsequent Criminal Activity

This discussion of Gottfredson and Hirschi's self-control theory concludes by describing their position on the relationship of past to subsequent criminal activity. Recall that their self-control theory uses a population heterogeneity argument in which they argue that the correlation between past and subsequent criminal activity is merely a spurious correlation due to an unmeasured (omitted) variable—level of criminal propensity. It is a classic 'variant of the familiar "omitted variable" bias argument' (Nagin and Paternoster 1991: 166). In their view, individuals with high criminal propensity tend to commit crimes very frequently, including at adjacent ages and/or time periods, while individuals with very low criminal propensity rarely commit criminal offenses. Thus, there will naturally be a high correlation between criminal offending measured at two different time points. The high correlation, however, is argued to arise from the unmeasured variable denoting the level of criminal propensity. If the authors' argument is correct, then including a variable to measure criminal propensity in an equation should eliminate the significant relationship between past and subsequent criminal offending. According to Gottfredson and Hirschi (1987*a*: 594), 'subsequent delinquency cannot be predicted among groups homogeneous on current delinquency.' Their assumption that criminal propensity is time-invariant is absolutely critical to their argument, for 'if they were not enduring, the [population heterogeneity] theories could not explain the positive association of past to subsequent criminality' (Nagin and Farrington 1992*a*: 237).

Sampson and Laub's Age-Graded Social Control Theory

In contrast to Gottfredson and Hirschi, Sampson and Laub (1993) present an age-graded theory of informal social control that focuses on the *changing/malleable* strength of social bonds over the life course. Their theory draws heavily on the main principles of the life-course perspective in sociology (Elder 1985; Riley 1986). Before proceeding to a discussion of their theory, we first present a brief theoretical backdrop describing the life-course perspective.

The Life-Course Perspective

The life-course perspective is both a conceptual and a theoretical perspective (Elder 1992). As a theoretical perspective, the life course is 'a theoretical orientation for the study of human development that incorporates temporal, contextual, and processual distinctions' (Elder 1996: 31). As a concept, the life course refers to 'the interdependence of age-graded trajectories, such as work and family, that are subject to changing conditions in the larger world, and to short-term transitions, ranging from birth to school entry to retirement' (Elder 1996: 35). The life-course perspective envisions aging and development as a process that continues throughout life (Riley 1986).

Two key theoretical concepts of the life-course perspective are *trajectories* and *transitions*. A trajectory is a longitudinal pathway of linked states within a major domain of life (e.g. social, psychological, or biological states) (Benson 2002; Elder 1985; Sampson and Laub 1993). For example, individuals have educational trajectories, marital trajectories, physical and mental health trajectories, criminal offending trajectories, and employment trajectories, to name just a few. Trajectories are long-term patterns of behavior that often exhibit both change and stability, depending on whether they are interrupted by transitions (Sampson and Laub 1990).

Transitions are life events that represent discrete changes of state; they evolve over shorter periods of time and are embedded in trajectories (Elder 1985; Sampson and Laub 1990, 1992, 1993). Some examples of transitions include graduating from high school, getting married, or obtaining a job. Some transitions act as 'turning points' because they serve to redirect or change the course of the trajectory (Elder 1985; Sampson and Laub 1993). The long-term view of trajectories implies a strong connection (i.e. continuity) between behaviors in childhood and adolescence, and between behaviors in adolescence and adulthood, but the short-term view implies that trajectories can be modified by transitions and even *redirected* by turning points (Laub *et al.* 1995).

One of the central premisses of the life-course perspective is that trajectories in different domains of life tend to be interconnected because of the 'interplay' of trajectories: changes or transitions in one domain of life are often associated with changes in other domains. In other words, trajectories can have reciprocal effects on one another (Elder 1985). Indeed, it is this interlocking nature of trajectories that allows for change. Other key premisses or themes of the life-course perspective include the idea that aging and development cannot be separated from the historical time and place in which it occurs, also known as the principle of contextualism (Dannefer 1984; Elder and O'Rand 1995), that the timing of events or the age at which the events occur is crucial for determining the effects of those events on individuals (the life-stage principle), and that our lives are linked or embedded in the lives of individuals around us (the linked-lives principle) (Elder 1985, 1996). Clearly, those who study the life course consider the acquisition of longitudinal data as imperative to any research design.

In the criminological literature, the life-course perspective is considered one branch of what has become known as 'developmental criminology' (Vold, Bernard, and Snipes 1998). The term 'developmental criminology' refers to 'within-individual changes in offending' and a major interest of this theoretical paradigm is the documentation and explanation of longitudinally dynamic patterns of offending from childhood through adulthood (LeBlanc and Loeber 1998: 117). According to Loeber and Stouthamer-Loeber (1996), there are three main goals of developmental criminology: (1) describing within-individual changes in offending patterns over the life course; (2) developing etiological explanations of the longitudinal patterns of offending; and (3) examining the impact of transitions on patterns of offending. On the basis of these three goals, Sampson and Laub's theory definitely qualifies as a developmental theory, for it focuses precisely on these three goals.

In their book, *Crime in the Making: Pathways and Turning Points through Life*, Sampson and Laub (1993) formally proposed their age-graded theory of informal social control. The authors embarked on this theoretical exposition to move criminologists past their preoccupation with adolescence by demonstrating the importance of explaining variation in criminal behavior over the entire life course. As Sampson and Laub note, they were interested in bringing 'both childhood and adulthood back into the criminological picture' (1993: 7) because sociological criminology 'has not come to grips with the link between early childhood behaviors and later adult outcomes' (Sampson and Laub 1990: 609). It was of special concern to Sampson and Laub to confront and reconcile the 'paradox of persistence' phenomenon discussed in Chapter 1.

Varying Informal Social Control over the Life Course

Sampson and Laub (like Gottfredson and Hirschi) posit a control theory that assumes people will normally often commit crimes in the absence of some 'controlling' force that restrains or prevents them from engaging in these acts to satisfy their desires. It is the source or locus of the 'controlling' force that is the quintessential difference between the two theories. To Gottfredson and Hirschi, the locus of the constraining force is a time-invariant internalized force (self-control) that is fixed after early childhood, whereas for Sampson and Laub, the constraining forces (informal social controls) dynamically vary across the life course. Sampson and Laub argue that crime is more likely to occur when an individual's bond to society is weak or broken and, ironically, their theory draws heavily on Hirschi's (1969) classic 'social bond' theory. According to Hirschi (1969: 16), 'delinquent acts result when an individual's bond to society is weak or broken.' The bond is comprised of various attachments, commitments, involvements, and beliefs that when present constrain the individual from attempting to satisfy desires, wants, and needs through illegal means. Although Hirschi's theory was originally constructed in static terms, Sampson and Laub provide a dynamic interpretation of the theory that allows the strength of social bonds to vary over time (Sampson and Laub 1997). Such a dynamic conceptualization of changing social bonds over individual lifetimes fits perfectly with the life-course perspective.

Utilizing the life-course perspective then, Sampson and Laub differentiate the life course by age or life stages and argue that the critical institutions of formal and (especially) informal social control vary across these stages. To Sampson and Laub, the key explanation of differential crime patterns across the life course is the varying amount of informal social control present in childhood, adolescence, and adulthood. Over the life course, the key institutions responsible for varying levels of social control are:

- family, school, and peer groups in childhood and adolescence;
- higher education, vocational training, work, and marriage in young adulthood;
- work, marriage, parenthood, military service, and investment in the community in subsequent adulthood (Sampson and Laub 1990).

More importantly, Sampson and Laub emphasize the 'role of age-graded informal social control as reflected in the structure of interpersonal bonds linking members of society to one another and to wider social institutions (e.g. work, family, school)' (Laub *et al.* 1995: 93). Like Durkheim ([1897] 1951), Sampson and Laub define social control as the ability of a social group to regulate the behaviors of its members according to its accepted norms and values. Their crucial argument is that the most important sources of social control are actually the informal social bonds that *emerge out of or from* role relationships established for purposes other than social control. Thus, it is not the variability of age-graded social institutions themselves that serves to induce conformity, but rather it is the informal, interpersonal bonds between people that serve to link individuals to those institutions; informal social control is not maintained merely by having a teacher, parent, spouse, or child present.

The theory of Sampson and Laub thus highlights the quality of interpersonal relations between individuals (e.g. parent–child, student–teacher, and husband–wife) as a form of *social investment* or *social capital* (Coleman 1988, 1990), which is created when relationships of interdependence serve to facilitate action and provide social and psychological resources for those individuals to utilize (Laub *et al.* 1995). There are two critical points associated with the 'social investment' argument of Sampson and Laub.[5] First, it is not simply the occurrence of an event (e.g. getting married or

[5] Nagin and Paternoster (1993, 1994) make a similar theoretical argument in their discussion of personal capital and personal control. They argue that the social bond is a developmental 'investment' process whereby individuals who make investments in personal capital are, other things being equal, less likely to engage in criminal behavior because of their stake in conformity. Nagin and Paternoster note that

obtaining a job) per se that serves to reduce the likelihood of crime and deviance, but rather it is the strength of interpersonal ties in the relationship that dictates the negative, neutral, or positive benefits of the relationship (Laub, Nagin, and Sampson 1998; Sampson and Laub 1990, 1997). Although turning points are frequently envisioned as positive events, negative turning points can redirect a trajectory onto an even more 'maladaptive path' (Rutter and Rutter 1993: 244; Sampson and Laub 1997). For example, a male adult criminal who marries a female and has an unstable, conflict-riddled marriage may actually increase his rate of criminal activity. Second, because social capital is an investment process that develops over time, it is expected that the effects of the investment will also be gradual and accumulate over time. Thus, desistence from criminal activity is better viewed as a developmental process whereby one gradually reduces involvement in criminal and deviant activities over time, rather than 'going cold turkey' (Laub and Sampson 2001; see also Bushway *et al.* 2001; Nagin and Paternoster 1994).

Sampson and Laub's theory of informal social control rests on three main themes (Laub *et al.* 1995; Sampson and Laub 1993). First, informal social controls derived through the social bonds to family and school inhibit delinquent activity during childhood and adolescence, and these two social control mechanisms mediate the effects of background structural (e.g. poverty) and individual factors (e.g. family disruption). During childhood, informal social control largely derives from family processes: monitoring and supervising behavior, consistent application of discipline, and attachment between the parent and child. During the adolescent years, schools are added to the list of important social institutions, as well as peer groups and the juvenile justice system.

Second, Sampson and Laub stress the importance of continuity in behavioral tendencies over the life course. Antisocial behavior during childhood and adolescence predicts negative adult outcomes

individuals differ with respect to their inclination to make investments in other persons, institutions, and conventional activities, or in the words of the authors, individuals differ in their 'discount rate' (i.e. how they weight present consumption versus future consumption). Yet, the authors argue (and found support for in their study of college students) that even individuals with high discount rates can benefit (in terms of reduced criminal activity) by making investments in their social capital (which they call personal capital). This argument is congruent with the argument of Sampson and Laub.

in a variety of life domains (e.g. adult crime, incarceration, frequent unemployment, and marital instability). Third, even in the presence of a pattern of stability in behavior across time, salient life events (turning points) associated with social ties to the adult institutions of informal social control (attachment to the labor force, cohesive marriage, military service) can serve to modify or redirect trajectories of criminal offending, *regardless of prior individual differences with respect to criminal propensity*. Stated more pointedly, 'childhood pathways to crime and deviance can be significantly modified over the life course by adult social bonds' (Sampson and Laub 1990: 611).

Explaining Continuity and Discontinuity in Crime

According to Sampson and Laub, continuity and discontinuity are the result of two processes. First, they agree with Gottfredson and Hirschi that there are individual differences with respect to criminal propensity and that the self-selection argument cannot simply be dismissed. Thus, Sampson and Laub do agree that part of the observed patterns of continuity in criminal behavior results from persistent individual differences in criminal propensity and that low self-control tends to be relatively stable for periods of time (Laub and Sampson 1993: 306; Sampson and Laub 1997: 155). However, they completely disagree with Gottfredson and Hirschi that persistent individual differences rooted in early childhood are the end of the story. They take exception with Gottfredson and Hirschi's assertion that individual differences in crime propensity persist over time and that social processes and experiences during adolescence and adulthood have no ability to alter patterns of criminal behavior. Rather, Sampson and Laub argue in support of a process of state dependence, which for better or for worse is also responsible for patterns of both continuity and change in crime. This is why their theory is best described as a 'mixed' theory, allowing for both population heterogeneity and state dependence effects (Nagin and Paternoster 2000).[6]

[6] To make this point more emphatic, consider the following quote of Laub and Sampson (1993: 306): 'the cumulative continuity of disadvantage is thus not only a result of stable individual difference in criminal propensity, but a dynamic process whereby childhood antisocial behavior and adolescent delinquency foster adult crime through the severance of adult social bonds' (see Bernberg and Krohn 2003 for a recent empirical examination of this issue).

To start, Sampson and Laub (1992: 73; 1993: 21) argue that levels of criminal propensity can change over time as a direct consequence of life events and social processes that modify the strength of one's social bonds. Of course, state dependence is a 'double-edged sword' that can serve to either reduce or increase the strength of one's social bonds, and which thus could either increase or decrease the likelihood of future participation in crime and deviance. They posit that criminal involvement at any point in time can weaken or sever the social bond through a process known as *cumulative continuity* (Caspi *et al.* 1993; Sampson and Laub 1993). Cumulative continuity refers to the process whereby the consequences of behavior at one point in time serve to directly influence both opportunities and behavioral choices at later points in time. 'Cumulative continuity is generated by the negative structural consequences of delinquency for life chances' (Sampson and Laub 1993: 124). From Sampson and Laub's (1997) viewpoint, social processes that result from criminal activity, including negative labelling effects, tend to channel individual traits such that people with low self-control often have a diminishing social bond to the social order as a direct *consequence* of criminal activity. Criminal behavior early in life tends to evoke repressive social responses that serve to further weaken the individual's social bond and make future crime and deviance more likely (Sampson and Laub 1997: 144, 154).

In other words, there is a 'closing down' of future conventional opportunities or 'closed doors' that leave fewer options for a conventional life (Caspi and Moffitt 1993; Moffitt 1993). As Laub and Sampson (1993: 306) note, 'delinquency incrementally mortgages the future by generating negative consequences for the life chances of stigmatized and institutionalized youths.' Over time, the effects of cumulative continuity build into a process known as *cumulative disadvantage* (Dannefer 1987) such that escape from the criminal lifestyle becomes increasingly more difficult.

Yet, Sampson and Laub point out that even though the process of cumulative continuity (state dependence) encourages continuity in behavior, change can and frequently does occur because things can get better (even for persistent chronic offenders), just as they can get worse (Nagin and Paternoster 2000). Thus, they contend that desistence from crime can occur to the degree that there is a positive shift in the social bond between a repeat offender and the sources of informal social control, which in adulthood are argued to come primarily from marital cohesion and attachment to the labor market. In other words, qualitative changes in the social bond can occur during adulthood, and the social capital resulting from experiencing positive transitional life events or turning points can help build other conventional relationships that both further strengthen social bonds and simultaneously decrease criminal propensity. Sampson and Laub argue that positive adult experiences can increase an individual's stake in conformity, as well as provide further opportunities to experience other sources of informal social control. In sum, both stability and change are often embedded in adult life events, which can modify the propensity to engage in criminal and deviant behavior (for better or for worse) despite the level of the individual's prior criminal propensity.

Sampson and Laub have also criticized the casual operationalization of the concepts of 'continuity' and 'stability.' For example, Sampson (1998) questions a recent study of continuity in criminal careers, aptly titled *Continuity and Discontinuity in Criminal Careers* (Tracy and Kempf-Leonard 1996), for defining continuity in crime as anyone with one juvenile arrest before age 17 and at least one arrest between ages 18 and 26. Sampson (1998) finds a contradiction between the authors' conclusion that 'continuity was by far the most likely transition' because individuals with an arrest as a juvenile were more likely to be arrested as adults, while the same authors simultaneously report that two-thirds of the individuals with arrests as juveniles were never arrested as adults. Sampson (1998: 1150) notes, 'some readers might reasonably interpret this pattern as discontinuity imposed on an aggregate pattern of normative stability' that entirely ignores the amount of within-individual change that actually occurred among two-thirds of the juvenile delinquents. Sampson and Laub (1992) have argued that this concept of 'normative' or 'relative' stability serves to reify the concept of stability such that there is a misconception about the amount of within-individual change that is taking place over time (see also Cline 1980; Loeber and Stouthamer-Loeber 1998; Sampson 2000). As Sampson (2000: 712) has recently argued, 'despite aggregate stability, that is, there is far more heterogeneity in criminal behavior over time within-individuals . . . change is near ubiquitous.'

In essence, the key theme of Sampson and Laub's theory is the 'theoretical commitment to the idea of behavioral malleability across the life course and the focus on the constancy of change' (Laub and Sampson 2001: 44–5). This has important implications for the explanation of both the shape of the age–crime curve and the relationship between past and subsequent criminal activity.

Explaining the Age–Crime Curve

Sampson and Laub's theory of age-graded informal social control can be used to explain the observed age–crime curve. Recall that Gottfredson and Hirschi see the general decline in crime with age as occurring for all individuals largely due to maturational processes and reductions in criminal opportunities (presumably as a result of aging). Sampson and Laub, on the other hand, see the general decline in crime with age as a result of 'institutional forces associated with employment, marriage, prison, and former military service that affect bonds to conformity in adulthood' (Cohen and Vila 1996: 144). Thus, the rapidly increasing offending rates in the mid- to late teen years can be viewed as a weakening of the social bond as individuals enter adolescence, a period of time when their social bond with their family/parents is strained and they are not yet experiencing the changes in the social bond that generally occur with the positive transitional events of adulthood.[7] As adolescents enter adulthood and experience the informal social control from their investments in marriage, parenthood, and work, crime becomes less attractive due to risks that have accrued through the formation of attachments and commitments of adult life. Thus, the decrease in offending is not due to 'inexorable aging of the organism' (Gottfredson and Hirschi 1990: 141), but results from the strengthening of the social bond that often accompanies movement into the various adult roles and responsibilities (Cernkovich and Giordano 2001: 372).

Sampson and Laub (1990, 1992, 1993) are especially critical of the stability and invariance hypotheses of Gottfredson and Hirschi (1990), arguing that such hypotheses are a classic example of the ontogenetic fallacy described by Dannefer (1984). According to Dannefer (1984), the ontogenetic fallacy refers to attributing an outcome solely as a consequence of a pre-existing personal trait of the individual rather than recognizing that the outcome is actually

[7] Tittle (1988) made a similar argument for the shape of the age–crime curve using the social bonding theory of Hirschi (1969).

the result of interactions between the *social environment* and the personal trait. Dannefer's (1984: 106) argument, directed at biological and psychological models of adult development, was that 'sociological research and theory provide the basis for understanding human development as socially organized and socially produced, *not only by what happens in early life*, but also by the effects of social structure, social interaction, and their effects on life chances throughout the life course' (emphasis added). Sampson and Laub (1990: 612) reiterate that many sociological theories of crime (such as pure state dependence arguments) are problematic because they ignore the developmental consequences of the events and processes of early childhood and are excessively fixated on the adolescent years.[8]

Building on the comments of Dannefer (1984), Sampson and Laub (1990: 609) argue that their model is 'sociogenic' because it explicitly incorporates not only individual differences, but also acknowledges how salient life events in adulthood play an important role in determining the amount of change in an individual's criminal offending trajectory over time. Sampson and Laub challenge the invariance argument because it cuts at the core conceptual foundations of the life-course perspective on several fronts, especially the presumption that time and place matter in the lives of individuals (Benson 2002). The invariance argument posits that trajectories do not vary even as social conditions change, which is a direct attack on the principle of contextualism discussed above. As Laub and Sampson (2001: 44) note:

> Life-course accounts embrace the notion that lives are often unpredictable and dynamic and that exogenous changes are ever present. Some changes in the life course result from chance or random events, while other changes stem from macrolevel exogenous shocks largely beyond the pale of individual choice (e.g. war, depression, natural disasters, revolutions, plant closings, industrial restructuring). Another important aspect of life-course criminology is a focus on situations—time-varying social contexts—that impede or facilitate criminal events.

[8] Baltes and Nesselroade (1984: 842), in response to Dannefer's (1984) article, criticized sociological theories of adult development for overemphasizing the 'intra-individual plasticity (modifiability)' of individuals and for explicitly ignoring the developmental consequences of the 'first half of life.' Sampson and Laub's mixed theory (allowing for both state dependence and population heterogeneity processes) can be viewed as incorporating the critical arguments of both Baltes and Nesselroade (1984) and Dannefer (1984).

Explaining the Relationship of Past to Subsequent Criminal Activity

Before moving on to the dual taxonomy theory of Moffitt, a final comment is in order concerning the implication of Sampson and Laub's theory for the relationship of past to subsequent criminal activity. Their use of the concept of cumulative continuity is a state dependence argument, whereby past criminal activity increases the likelihood of subsequent criminal activity as a result of its weakening the individual's social bond to society. As Sampson and Laub (1997: 144) state, 'the state dependence component [of our theory] implies that committing a crime has a genuine behavioral influence on the probability of committing future crimes.' Therefore their theory predicts a persistent significant effect between past criminal activity and subsequent criminal activity even after controlling for persistent (unobserved) heterogeneity.

Moffitt's Dual Taxonomy Theory

According to the general theories of Sampson and Laub (1993) and Gottfredson and Hirschi (1990), a single theory of crime is applicable to all individuals in the population, and offenders are merely *different in degree*; variations in criminal offending patterns over time are explained purely by variation in the key theoretical constructs of each theory, but the same theoretical explanation applies to all individuals (Dean, Brame, and Piquero 1996; Paternoster and Brame 1997; Paternoster *et al.* 1997). Moffitt (1993, 1997), on the other hand, proposes a *typological* theory of criminal behavior based on the presumption that offenders are *different in kind*, with each 'kind' or type requiring a separate, distinct etiological explanation. In the words of Gibbons (1982: 219), the adage 'different strokes for different folks' explains the core assumption of any typological theory of criminal behavior. Typological theories of crime have a long-standing history in the field of criminology, but the basis for creating the distinct categories or typologies of offenders has changed from differentiating offenders on the basis of offense type (e.g. property offenders, violent offenders, and sex offenders) or skill level (e.g. professional thief versus amateur thief) to more recently differentiating offenders on the basis of broader behavioral categories and/or longitudinal pathways/trajectories of criminal behavior across the life course (Loeber, Farrington, and Waschbusch 1998).

Moffitt's dual taxonomy theory is an example of this recent brand of typological theoretical expositions and was posited by Moffitt as a direct response to the paradox of persistence findings. Moffitt's theory proposes two distinct, unique groups of offenders in the population: 'life-course-persistent' offenders and 'adolescent-limited' offenders.[9] Moffitt argues that each of these offender types follows a distinctly different longitudinal trajectory of criminal/antisocial behaviour and that the explanation for each trajectory must use variables that are proximally related to the shape of each offending trajectory. Moffitt proposes one trajectory consisting of individuals who begin offending early in life and then consistently engage in criminal/antisocial activities across adulthood, whereas the other trajectory does not begin offending until the onset of adolescence and then confines or limits their offending largely to the adolescent years (i.e. desists by early adulthood). During adolescence, both of these groups are actively offending and Moffitt argues that it is difficult to separate the two groups of offenders using only a cross-section of data; longitudinal data is absolutely necessary to separate out the two distinct groups (Moffitt 1993, 1997).

Since these offender types are argued to be distinct, the causes of their criminal activity must explain why their offending begins and then either persists (life-course-persistent) or desists (adolescent-limited), and the relevant predictors of each type must be proximally related to their predicted offending trajectory (Paternoster and Brame 1997; Paternoster *et al.* 1997). Like the theory of Sampson and Laub, Moffitt's theory is a mixed theory incorporating both population heterogeneity and state dependence processes; however

[9] Patterson and colleagues (Patterson 1995; Patterson and Yoerger 1993; Patterson, DeBaryshe, and Ramsey 1989; Patterson *et al.* 1992) have presented a theory that similarly divides the population into two groups, labeled 'early starter' and 'late starter' groups. Similar to the distinction between the theories of Gottfredson and Hirschi (1990) and Wilson and Herrnstein (1985), both of these theories present theoretical explanations that have identical longitudinal implications about continuity and discontinuity in patterns of offending, the relationship between age and crime, and the relationship between past and future criminal activity. Paternoster and colleagues (Paternoster and Brame 1997; Paternoster *et al.* 1997) have noted that there is a great deal of similarity between the two theories even in terms of the theoretical exposition of each offender type, but that the etiological explanations of each are not entirely identical.

each process is hypothesized to operate on only one of the distinct offender types (Nagin and Paternoster 2000). In Moffitt's theory, a set of dynamic, state dependence variables is responsible for the offending patterns of the adolescent-limited offenders, whereas a set of static/population heterogeneity variables is responsible for the criminal behavior of life-course-persistent offenders (Paternoster and Brame 1997).

The Life-Course-Persistent Group

The life-course-persistent group, as defined by Moffitt, accounts for roughly 4 to 9 per cent of the male population who (as the name suggests) begin offending early in life (prior to the onset of adolescence/puberty) and persistently engage in criminal/antisocial activities over the duration of the life course.[10] Because of this group's early and persistent criminal behavior, Moffitt grounds her theory of the life-course-persistent offender type (hereafter referred to as LCP) using factors present very early in life (i.e. proximal to the start of their offending).

The life-course-persistent group consists of individuals who during the early formative years of life are faced with neuropsychological deficits caused by their mother's drug use during pregnancy, poor prenatal nutrition, complications during delivery, pre- and post-natal exposure to toxic agents (e.g. lead), and/or child abuse/neglect shortly after their birth. The neuropsychological deficits leave the 'vulnerable and difficult infant' with early deficits in cognitive functioning, emotional reactivity, and verbal and social skills, as well having a generally 'difficult' temperament that results in the child being irritable, inattentive, impulsive, aggressive, having poor judgement, and low self-control. According to Moffitt (1997: 18), 'children with neuropsychological problems evoke a challenge to even the most resourceful, loving and patient families.'

Unfortunately, however, these difficult children are generally born into families that do not have the social, psychological, and/or

[10] Patterson's theory (Patterson 1995; Patterson and Yoerger 1993; Patterson, DeBaryshe, and Ramsey 1989; Patterson *et al.* 1993) of the 'early starter' is more heavily grounded in the effects of poor parenting as largely responsible for producing this class. Poor or ineffective socialization clearly plays a definitive causal role in both theories. More importantly, both theories agree that by the end of childhood, this class of individuals has been formed and there is little that can be done to change their offending propensity thereafter.

financial resources or the parenting skills necessary to deal with the unruly, difficult child. Thus, Moffitt argues that these neuropsychological deficits (i.e. personal traits) then reciprocally interact with environmental variables that serve to further exacerbate the child's already difficult personality as a result of being socialized in a criminogenic home environment (Moffitt 1997: 18). Parents with difficult children tend also to have often suffered neuropsychological deficits and difficult temperaments themselves, resulting in ineffective and counterproductive parenting. As a result, 'the juxtaposition of a vulnerable and difficult infant with an adverse rearing context initiates risk for the LCP pattern of antisocial behavior. The ensuing process is a transactional one in which the challenge of coping with a difficult child evokes "a chain of failed parent–child encounters"' (Moffitt 1993: 682). By the end of the childhood years, the socialization process has broken down and failed, resulting in an individual with a strong, time-stable proclivity to engage in various criminal and antisocial activities (e.g. serious violent offenses, property offenses, drug offenses, and sexual promiscuity) across the remaining duration of the life course. The interaction of a problem child with problem parents is the nexus of the LCP offender.

While the theoretical propositions related to the LCP offender are often characterized as static because of the time-invariant nature of the criminal propensity of such offenders after childhood, it is important to note that the theory is a dynamic theory in the early, formative childhood years (Paternoster *et al.* 1997). However, by the end of childhood, Moffitt argues that the option for future changes in the antisocial propensity of LCP individuals is limited because: (1) they fail to successfully engage in or learn pro-social alternatives to their antisocial behavior as a direct consequence of their neuropsychological deficits that make it extremely unlikely they will perform well in school or pro-social activities (i.e. self-selection), and (2) they become increasingly ensnared in the criminal/deviant lifestyle as a direct result of the consequences of engaging in such activities (cumulative continuity). Interestingly, Moffitt describes LCP individuals in terms very similar to Gottfredson and Hirschi's description of a low self-control individual, and thus it is not surprising that Moffitt echoes sentiments similar to Gottfredson and Hirschi with respect to the poor odds of LCP individuals changing their behavior over time (Cohen and Vila 1996; Paternoster and Brame 1997; Paternoster *et al.* 1997).

The ineffective socialization of the LCP offenders (a consequence of the interaction of the personal traits and criminogenic environments in which they are raised) produces individuals destined to fail in virtually all aspects of their family, academic, and interpersonal lives who are likely to engage in criminal activities throughout their entire lifespan. For example, in contrast to Sampson and Laub's proposition that marriage and job ties can decrease the offending propensity of *any* offender, Moffitt argues that LCP individuals will simply select both jobs and wives that serve to support rather than change their antisocial lifestyles (assuming they can relate to jobs and wives at all). In other words, these transitional life events do not function as turning points in the life courses of LCP individuals according to Moffitt. Thus, by the beginning of adolescence, the lives of LCP individuals are dominated by a static process that resulted from a dynamic process that began at (or before) birth. Their propensity to engage in criminal and antisocial behavior is therefore hypothesized to be 'tenacious across time and in diverse circumstances' (Moffitt 1997: 24). LCP offenders have trouble getting along with individuals in any social setting in which they find themselves, and further, they engage in impulsive, aggressive antisocial behavior in all social settings as children, adolescents, and adults. As Paternoster *et al.* (1997: 237) describe this group, they 'are "bad apples" who exhibit significant deficits in early childhood socialization and rarely get back on track.'

The Adolescent-Limited Group

The second offender type in Moffitt's dual taxonomy theory is the adolescent-limited offender group (hereafter referred to as AL). The AL offender type is the near ubiquitous offender group, and in a statistical sense, their behavior is entirely normal in modern society. Individuals in this offender group only offend for a very short period of time, and that period of time is *limited* to the adolescent years.[11] They begin offending in early adolescence (around ages 14–15), commit offenses that are less serious in nature

[11] Patterson's theory (Patterson and Yoerger 1993; Patterson, DeBaryshe, and Ramsey 1989; Patterson *et al.* 1993) of the 'late starter' is heavily grounded in the causal effects of 'family disruption' variables. Family disruption variables (such as divorce) are said to decrease parental supervision, which in combination with accessible delinquent peers, provides the social setting for excursions into antisocial and delinquent activity.

compared to those committed by the LCP group, and have all but ended their criminal offending patterns by the end of adolescence. According to Moffitt (1997: 16), individuals following the AL trajectory of criminal offending 'have no notable history of antisocial behavior and little future for such behavior in adulthood.'

Importantly, and in stark contrast to the generalized offending pattern of the LCP offender type, this group of offenders engages in 'situation-specific' behaviors. In some situations they may well behave in a criminal or antisocial manner, while in other situations they may show no such tendency to engage in such behaviors. According to Moffitt, their tendency to engage in criminal/antisocial behaviors is the result of dynamic variables that represent changes in local life circumstances that shift or alter the reinforcement contingencies (i.e. costs and benefits) of engaging in such behaviors. Given that their offending patterns are hypothesized to be entirely bounded by the adolescent years, the causal factors for this group must be proximal to these ages and account for both the start and stop of their offending patterns. For the AL group, Moffitt emphasizes the importance of dynamic variables that rapidly evolve over a short period of time (the years of adolescence). Moffitt's argument is that changes in these variables lead the AL individuals into starting their offending, and changes in these variables will also be responsible for extinguishing their offending behavior.

The AL group of offenders, unlike the LCP group, is hypothesized to lack any underlying, persistent criminal propensity and to have been effectively socialized by their parents. So why do they offend at all? According to Moffitt, individuals in the AL type engage in criminal activity as a result of the strain-inducing *maturity gap* that exists between biological and social maturity.[12] In all modern societies, adolescents occupy an ambiguous status between childhood and adulthood, leaving them in 'five-to-ten year role vacuum' (Moffitt 1997: 26). For example, adolescents want to have their own families (or at least engage in frequent sexual activity) and their own places of residence, but they are socially admonished to complete their schooling trajectories prior to beginning their families of procreation or establishing their own housing. As Moffitt (1997: 26) states, 'they want desperately to establish intimate bonds with

[12] Greenberg (1977, 1985) provides a similar sociological 'strain' explanation for the age–crime curve.

the opposite sex, to accrue material belongings, to make their own decisions, and to be regarded as consequential by adults... [they are] chronological hostages of a time warp between biological and social age.'

Eventually, the strain of the cognitive dissonance caused by the maturity gap leaves the adolescents looking for an alternative means to obtain the resource they so desire: mature status. Moffitt (1993: 686) argues that the AL group of offenders engages in a process of *social mimicry* in order to obtain the desired resource: 'Social mimicry occurs when two animal species share a single niche and one of the species has cornered the market on a resource that is needed to promote fitness. In such circumstances, the "mimic" species adopts the social behavior of the more successful species in order to obtain access to the valuable resource.'

Members of the AL group view the behavior of the LCP offender groups as the embodiment of mature status. LCP offenders resist and fight the powers of authority, they smoke, drink, have sex, are frequently truant from school, often have (stolen) cars, attorneys, and offspring, and generally go about making decisions concerning when and what they will do regardless of what other people want them to do (i.e. they act independently). Thus, members of the AL group begin to mimic the behavior of the 'more successful species' (the LCP group) in order to obtain access to the valuable resource (mature status). In essence, the AL group emulates the behavior of the LCP group because their lifestyle resembles the experiences of adulthood rather than childhood.

It is important to note that access to delinquent peers is one of the most critical dynamic variables in the explanation of the AL offending pattern, as there must be behaviors to emulate or mimic. Essentially, Moffitt argues that first a few AL boys mimic the behaviors of the LCP individuals, more AL boys join in, and eventually a critical mass is obtained in which offending during adolescence is near ubiquitous. Moffitt argues this access to delinquent peers can be as simple as watching the LCP offenders 'at work' from a distance. Mimicry need not involve exchanges of affection (which LCP offenders are presumably incapable of anyway) or actual direct communication.

In sum, Moffitt's explanation of the causes of AL offending is that engaging in criminal/antisocial behaviors allows these individuals (who are trapped in the maturity gap) to have access to mature status and all of its resulting power, privilege, and resources. During the adolescent years, delinquent/criminal behavior holds 'symbolic value as evidence that teens have the ability to resist adult demands and the capacity to act without adult permission' (Moffitt 1997: 31). The independence and maturity symbolized by delinquent acts is so intrinsically rewarding to the AL individuals that it reinforces the delinquent behavior while they are trapped in the maturity gap. Thus, criminal activity is likely to be followed by subsequent criminal activity in this group because the perceived rewarding consequences of engaging in criminal activity (i.e. obtaining mature status) serve to reinforce the behavior itself.

As members of the AL group near the end of the adolescent years, however, they begin to desist from their criminal offending for two reasons: (1) eventually the perceived rewarding properties of delinquent activities are outweighed by the severe negative costs and consequences (i.e. incarceration) associated with continued engagement in such activities (i.e. the reinforcement contingencies change); and (2) the members of this group begin to obtain access to the valuable resource of mature status through more conventional routes (parenthood, employment) that they did not have access to, but desired, during the adolescent years. Thus, as the AL offenders exit the maturity gap, they begin to desist from committing criminal/delinquent acts because 'they realize that continued participation in crime could threaten their newfound and long-awaited autonomy' (Moffitt 1997: 35).

AL offenders, unlike their LCP counterparts, are able to effectively desist from committing crimes and delinquent acts for three primary reasons. First, unlike the LCP offenders, the AL offenders still have family, occupational, and marital opportunities that they could lose if they continue to engage in criminal activities. Second, the AL offenders are assumed to have no underlying criminal propensity, and thus they do not have the usual characteristics associated with that criminal propensity such as poor social skills, poor academic performance, the inability to forge and keep close relationships with other individuals, and low self-control. Because their antisocial and criminal activity did not begin until adolescence, they were able to avoid accumulating these negative personal characteristics and are still eligible for post-secondary educational and occupational training opportunities, have good marital prospects, and able to obtain desirable jobs. In short, AL offenders have both good and available options for change, and have the personal characteristics that allow them to take advantage of the pro-social opportunities that become available in early adulthood.

Finally, because their antisocial and criminal activity began at a later age than the LCP offenders, the process of cumulative continuity operated for fewer years for AL offenders. This is especially true, since the AL offenders are hypothesized to engage in less serious offenses (e.g. theft, vandalism, drug and alcohol offenses) that do not carry the same severe consequences as the serious offenses in which the LCP offenders are hypothesized to be involved. Moffitt acknowledges that some AL offenders, however, will become ensnared in the damaging consequences of their criminal activities (e.g. incarceration, drug addiction) and that these offenders will have a more protracted period of desistance, even into early adulthood.

Explaining Continuity and Discontinuity in Crime

Moffitt began the exposition of her dual taxonomy theory with the explicit goal of accounting for both the shape of the age–crime curve and the paradox of persistence. Moffitt's account for the paradox of persistence (e.g. adult criminal behavior is best predicted by criminal activity during the juvenile years, but most juvenile offenders do not become adult offenders) is that the aggregate mixture of the two offender types is responsible for this finding. One of the offender types, the LCP group, is responsible for the pattern of continuity, while the other offender type, the AL group, is responsible for the change or discontinuity in criminal offending patterns. Since the LCP group begin their offending at an early age and continue offending well into adulthood, 'continuity is the hallmark of the small group of life-course-persistent antisocial persons' (Moffitt 1993: 679). The AL group, on the other hand, begins offending during early adolescence and desists shortly thereafter, and thus discontinuity is the hallmark pattern of this group. Since one group is characterized by a pattern of continuity (LCP) and the other is characterized by a pattern of discontinuity (AL), longitudinal data should be able to empirically separate or tease out the two different groups of offenders.

Explaining the Age–Crime Curve

In a manner identical to her explanation of the paradox of persistence, Moffitt argues that it is the mixture of the two hypothesized offender types that makes the age–crime curve assume its observed shape. Indeed, Moffitt argues that her typology 'addresses the shape of the curve of crime over age . . . by drawing attention to two trajectories concealed within the curve of crime over age' (Moffitt 1997: 11–12). The upward surge of the curve results from the increasing participation rates of the AL group, whereas the downward surge results from the patterns of desistance of this group. Given that the members of the AL group are assumed to greatly outnumber the LCP group, their offending patterns are argued to dominate the shape of the curve, while the small number of LCP offenders are responsible for composing the childhood and adulthood offenders in the tails of the curve.

Again, the implicit assumption in this argument is that upon empirically separating the two hypothesized groups, one should find two distinct trajectories: (1) the criminal offending trajectory of the LCP group should be relatively flat because they are hypothesized to engage in criminal activities across the life course at a relatively constant rate (i.e. they do not desist); and (2) the offending trajectory of the AL group should show a strong upward surge at the beginning of the adolescent years and a similar downward surge at the end of the adolescent years (and which may extend into young adulthood as a consequence of the AL offenders who become more ensnared in the consequences of their criminal activity). To be clear, Moffitt (1993: 695) is adamant that age is not a predictor of subsequent criminal activity *within* the LCP group (because they engage in criminal activity at a persistent rate), whereas age is a strong predictor of future criminal activity of the AL group (because of their trajectory's bounded dependence on the adolescent years).[13]

[13] According to Moffitt (1993: 695), the variables that predict membership in the LCP offender type are 'health, gender, temperament, cognitive abilities, school achievement, personality traits, mental disorders (e.g. hyperactivity), family attachment bonds, child-rearing practices, parent and sibling deviance, and socioeconomic status, *but not age*' (emphasis in original). For the AL type, Moffit hypothesizes that 'individual differences should play little or no role in the prediction of short term adolescent offending careers. Instead the strongest predictive factors should be knowledge of peer delinquency, attitudes toward adulthood and autonomy, cultural and historical context, *and age*' (emphasis in original).

Before concluding this section, it is important to re-emphasize that one of the key assumptions embodied in the dual taxonomy theory of Moffitt is that the heterogeneity of criminal offending across the life course can be decomposed into two discrete groups of offenders (and two only) with distinctly different age–crime curves. Theoretically, because we are dealing in our sample with serious repeat offenders, we should not find an AL group among our data. On the other hand, if several groups of LCP offenders were to be uncovered in a study, this would cast serious doubt on the empirical validity of any theory that advocates a 'dual taxonomy' approach to the explanation of criminal offending. In Chapter 3, we review the results of previous empirical investigations that present evidence on this assumption. For now, we note that these studies all shed considerable doubt on the claim that the aggregate age–crime curve can be adequately and sufficiently decomposed into only two discrete offender groups. This empirical result is very important for two primary reasons. First, Moffitt, in fact, discursively presented her theory by largely drawing on a number of cross-sectional epidemiological studies and she has not yet (to the best of our knowledge) presented a longitudinal analysis clearly showing that two groups are adequate to explain criminal offending patterns across the age distribution.

Second, and perhaps more importantly, the dual offender types described by Moffitt are frequently used in empirical applications for both interpreting results and completing analyses on the two 'offender groups' after dividing the sample into two groups (which are then labelled LCP and AL) solely on the basis of age of onset (see, e.g., Aguilar *et al.* 2000; Cernkovich and Giordano 2001; Dean, Brame, and Piquero 1996; Ge, Donnellan, and Wenk 2001; Klevens *et al.* 2000; Mazerolle *et al.* 2000; Piquero and Brezina 2001; Piquero *et al.* 1999; Scholte 1999). If there are more than two offender groups, analyses and interpretations based on this dual taxonomy distinction are not only of questionable theoretical import, but they also are at risk of being potentially misleading. If populations/samples cannot be neatly and discretely divided into two groups (especially arbitrarily on the basis of age of onset), then completing analyses on two groups (derived on the basis of age of onset) is likely to do nothing other than reify the dual offender categories as if they actually exist in the offender population. In Chapter 7 of this study, we present empirical results from the application of recently developed statistical models that allow one to test this empirical assumption of the dual taxonomy theory (see also Nagin 1999).

Explaining the Relationship of Past to Subsequent Criminal Activity

The dual taxonomy theory of Moffitt has two implications regarding the relationship of past to subsequent criminal activity, one implication for each offender type. First, for the LCP individuals, the correlation between past and subsequent criminal acts should be largely nonexistent *within this group* (Paternoster and Brame 1997). These individuals, as a result of their poor socialization, engage in criminal activities persistently across time due to their time-invariant propensity to engage in such acts. Thus, there is a natural correlation between past and subsequent criminal acts, but it is *spuriously* due to their underlying propensity that predisposes them to consistently engage in these behavioral acts. For the AL individuals, there is an opposite expectation that there will be a strong *causal*, state dependence effect resulting from both the consequences (i.e. ensnarement into the lifestyle) and benefits (i.e. the positive reinforcement contingencies of achieving mature status) of engaging in criminal activity. Thus, the dynamic reinforcement contingencies and possible ensnarement consequences of criminal behavior are argued to increase the probability that such behavioral acts will be repeated again in the future. Paternoster and Brame (1997) point out that Moffitt allows for a possible small state dependence effect for the LCP group due to the potential continuing ensnarement (cumulative continuity) processes during adolescence. They also note, however, that most of the correlation should be almost entirely due to the time-invariant high level of criminal propensity in this group and that any observed state dependence effect for the LCP group should pale in comparison to the observed effect in the AL group.

Theoretical Summary

In this section we provide a brief summary of the main theoretical points of the discussions above. In a nutshell, the theoretical controversy between these three theories boils down to a single question (Cohen and Vila 1996): how stable or inflexible are individual differences in the propensity to engage in criminal/antisocial activities across the life course? Because each theory envisions the stability (or instability) of criminal propensity very differently, each makes different predictions regarding both the relationship between age and crime and the relationship between past and subsequent criminal acts, the questions central to this study.

To Gottfredson and Hirschi, between-individual variation in criminal propensity (i.e. amount of self-control) is sufficient to explain both the relationship between age and crime and the relationship between past and subsequent criminal activity. All offenders decrease their offending over time, and the between-individual differences that exist at any one point in time (around age 8) continue to exist at all other points in time. The shape of the age–crime curve is hypothesized to be robust from person to person (i.e. the shape is invariant). According to Gottfredson and Hirschi (1990), the propensity to engage in criminal activities is stable over time; change is only 'apparent.' The age effect (which applies to all offenders equally) cannot be explained by 'impotent' sociological variables such as marriage, parenthood, jobs, or education. To be succinct, their viewpoint is that desistence 'just happens.' Further, controlling for stable criminal propensity (which naturally induces a correlation between offending at any two points in time), the correlation between past and subsequent criminal acts will disappear, as the correlation is spuriously due to population heterogeneity in the distribution of criminal propensity.

To Sampson and Laub, the relationship between age and crime is due to the varying levels of informal social control across the life course. Adolescence is a period of time when these forces are the weakest (the social bond undergoes strain and is weakened during this segment of the life course), but in late adolescence and early adulthood the bond is re-established and the increasing forces of social control that come with the salient life events of adulthood serve to reduce criminal activity throughout adulthood. It is important to note that Sampson and Laub foresee change as a possibility for all offenders, whether of high or low criminal propensity. The opportunity for change is available for all individuals even though some individuals may not experience change at all, and it may come at later ages compared to others. Sampson and Laub's theory posits that there will be a causal relationship between past and subsequent criminal activity, even after controlling for persistent differences in the propensity to offend, because criminal activity serves to reduce opportunities for pro-social activities and makes continuing in a lifestyle of crime more likely.

Moffitt's dual taxonomy theory predicts separate patterns of both continuity and change, but each is applicable to only one of the offender types. Change is open to and required from the adolescent-limited offender group, whereas continuity defines the life-course-persistent offenders. After all, they would not be labeled as 'life-course-persistent' if they were expected to desist from criminal activities during their life course. Moffitt also proposes that it is the consequence of mixing the dual offender categories together in the aggregate age–crime curve that is responsible for the observed shape of the aggregate age–crime curve. If one were to separate out the two *hypothetical* groups, one should find two types (and two types only) with radically different offending trajectories. One trajectory should have relatively stable crime rates across time, while the other group's trajectory should have a rapid surge in early adolescence and a similar decline at the end of adolescence. With respect to the relationship between past and subsequent criminal activity, Moffitt implies that the effect should be nonexistent in the LCP group (their offending patterns are largely driven by a failed socialization process during childhood), whereas there should be a strong, *causal* state dependence effect in the AL group (whose reduced offending patterns are largely the result of the 'mature status' benefits of criminal activity).

To make the implications of each theory for the relationship between age and crime more concrete, consider the graphical representations of each theory's age–crime explanation as displayed in Figures 2.1–2.3. The 'invariance argument' of Gottfredson and Hirschi is presented in Figure 2.1, by three longitudinal offending trajectories—one for high-, medium-, and low-rate offenders—using hypothetical data generated to represent their argument. Each one of the curves follows the inverted-J pattern, and, further, the relative differences between each of the curves are proportional across the age span. The offending rate for the medium-rate group is always one-half the offending rate of the high-rate group, whereas the low-rate group's offending rate is one-tenth of the high-rate group's rate. What causes the differences between the groups is varying levels of self-control, but the actual shape of

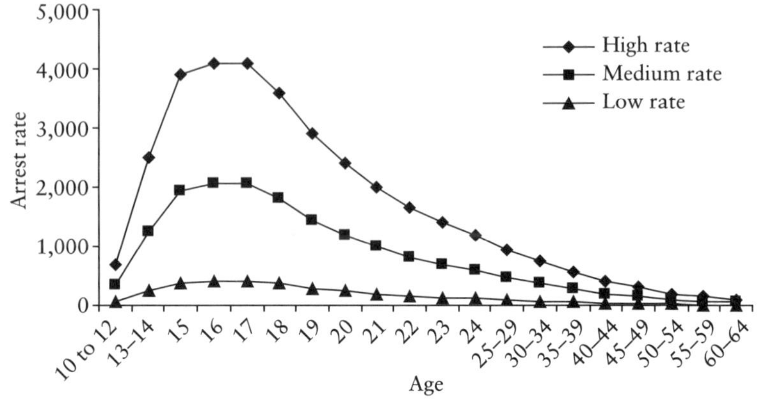

FIGURE 2.1. Graphical representation of the Gottfredson and Hirschi argument concerning the age–crime relationship, by offender type.

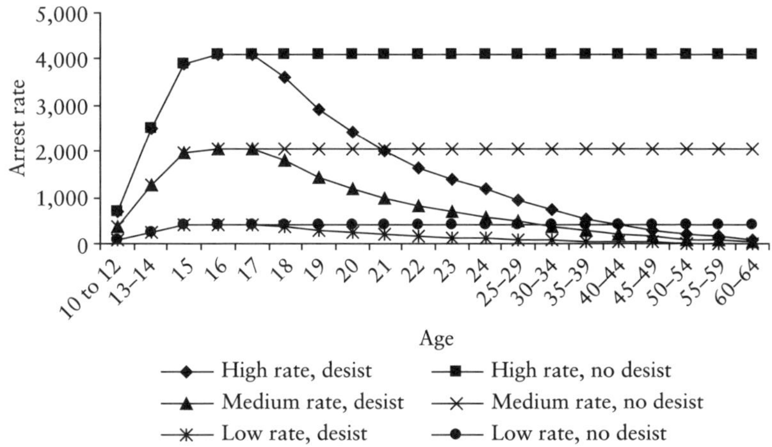

FIGURE 2.2. Graphical representation of the Sampson and Laub argument concerning the age–crime relationship, by offender type.

the curves is identical. The low self-control (high-rate) offenders will start their offending earlier, indefinitely commit offenses at higher rates than the two other groups, and will persist in offending further into adulthood. Thus, varying ages of onset and varying ages at termination from criminal activity merely reflect differences in the distribution of self-control across the population.

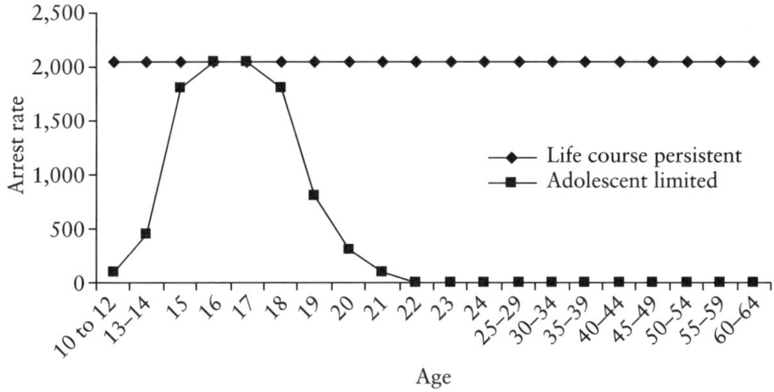

FIGURE 2.3. Graphical representation of the Moffitt argument concerning the age–crime relationship, by offender type.

Figure 2.2 portrays the pattern suggested by Sampson and Laub, only instead of three trajectories as in Figure 2.1, this figure contains six longitudinal trajectories. All three trajectories that appear in Figure 2.1 also appear in Figure 2.2, only now three trajectories that do not display the 'decline in crime' with age pattern (i.e. desistence) are also included. For illustrative purposes, consider just the two high-rate trajectories. The trajectory that displays a pattern of desistence ('high rate, desist') would correspond to a group of high-rate offenders that experienced the salient life events or 'turning points' (e.g. cohesive marriages and stable jobs) during their adulthood. This group of offenders would be theorized to have come under increasing informal social control during adulthood as a consequence of the transitions, and thus their trajectory exhibits a downward pattern during this time (as a consequence of their growing social capital 'investment'). The other group, however, would be thought to have missed out on experiencing the key transitional events of adulthood (for a variety of reasons, including just pure bad luck), and thus they have not experienced the benefits of increasing informal social control during this time; their trajectory simply maintains itself. Two final points concerning Figure 2.2 are in order. First, the trajectories in this figure were generated to explicitly illustrate Sampson and Laub's notion that change is possible for any offender type, regardless of their prior offending behavior. Even high-rate offenders can experience change. Second, Sampson and Laub posit that adulthood is the precise period of time when pre-existing differences become less important than whether they experience the salient life events that lead to increasing levels of informal social control. Some offenders will experience the sources of informal social control (i.e. have cohesive marriages and stable jobs), but others will not experience such benefits (in terms of reduced crime) of those sources of social control. In other words, Sampson and Laub would expect significant amounts of change during adulthood that cannot be simply explained away as the mere unfolding of pre-existing differences carrying over from the childhood years (Sampson 2000).

Finally, Figure 2.3 graphically represents Moffitt's argument with respect to the age–crime relationship. The life-course-persistent group maintains a persistent offending rate across time, whereas the adolescent-limited group confine their high rates of offending to the adolescent years. It is important to note that, as argued by Moffitt, the two groups are indistinguishable during the adolescent years, and any cross-sectional data gathered during this time period will not be able to separate out the two groups (nor their unique etiological explanation of crime). Similar to the implications of the Sampson and Laub explanation, longitudinal data is viewed as absolutely critical for understanding criminal behavior.

Having now completed the presentation of the theoretical framework that informs this study, attention in the next chapter is focused on reviewing the previous research on the age–crime and continuity–discontinuity issues.

3

Empirical Research Review and Hypotheses

The theoretical review in the previous chapter sets the stage for a thorough summary of the extant empirical literature concerning the key issues of this study: (1) the relationship between age and crime (and how such a relationship supports or refutes the existence of two discrete groups of offenders and the stability of differences in criminal propensity over time within identifiable groups) and (2) the relationship between past and subsequent criminal activity among individuals in our samples. The two main sections of this chapter review previous studies that have addressed these issues. Included at the end of both sections is a discussion of the general findings, the limitations of the prior research, and the hypotheses that guide this study. This chapter concludes with a discussion of the possible contributions this study can make to the extant literature.

Studies of the Age–Crime Curve

Given the concerns of Blumstein and colleagues (1986, 1988*a*, 1988*b*) and Moffitt (1993, 1997) that age–crime curves aggregated over individuals (i.e. calculated for samples as a whole) may conceal considerable heterogeneity in the offending trajectories of individuals, this review is limited to studies in which the authors have disaggregated their samples into 'latent classes' or 'latent groups' on the basis of the similarity of their longitudinal offending trajectories. Land (1992) has noted that distinguishing between the various age–crime relationship arguments requires the use of models specified at the individual level that specifically allow for incorporating controls for heterogeneity in the propensity to offend. The statistical methods available for modeling the presence of separate trajectories have only become available since Nagin and Land (1993) formulated a statistical model consistent with Land's (1992) recommendations.

Nagin and Land (1993) introduced the use of semiparametric mixture models to the discipline of criminology as a statistical method able to identify distinct trajectories of criminal offending. Accordingly, all of the studies reviewed below employ the use of the finite mixture methods of Nagin and Land. These finite mixture methods assign each individual to the latent class with the trajectory that most closely resembles the individual's actual observed crime trajectory. Briefly, the mixture methods of Nagin and Land explicitly assume that the sample (population) is composed of a 'mixture' of internally homogenous groups, each with their own distinct trajectory, and this modeling strategy both extracts the underlying trajectories present in the data and assigns each individual to the group to which he/she has the highest posterior probability of belonging (Nagin 1999).[1] Table 3.1 summarizes the key information contained in the individual studies reviewed here.[2] The interested reader is encouraged to examine the original articles for their graphical depictions of the trajectories.

As previously mentioned, Nagin and Land (1993) were the first to present evidence concerning both the number of distinct latent classes or offender groups and to discuss the relationship between age and crime for each specific group. In this influential article, they presented their semiparametric finite mixture Poisson model and applied it to the data from the Cambridge Study in Delinquent Development of West and Farrington (1973, 1977), which is a prospective study of 411 males from a working-class section of London that began in 1961 when the boys were 8 years old.

[1] In essence, the model fits separate constants and age parameters for each latent class, which allows the shape of each latent class's trajectory to be distinct.

[2] Two studies (Fergusson, Horwood, and Nagin 2000; and Chung *et al.* 2002) that employ the use of finite mixture models are not reviewed here. Fergusson, Horwood, and Nagin (2000) studied the age–crime curve for a sample of adolescents born in Christchurch, New Zealand, in 1977. Criminal offending data were only available from ages 12 to 18, and the authors note that their study thus presents a very limited view of the age–crime curve because both the childhood and adulthood years were truncated within the analysis. The other study, by Chung *et al.* (2002), used data from the Seattle Social Development Project (SSDP), a longitudinal study of male and female youths originally drawn from 18 Seattle public elementary schools. The dependent variable in the study consisted of self-report *offense seriousness* scores (measured at five time points between ages 13 and 21). Since their results do not speak to the issue of trajectories of criminal offending, but rather to trajectories of offense seriousness, the reported results provide ambiguous evidence concerning the relationship between age and crime as used herein.

TABLE 3.1. Summary information of prior studies of the age–crime relationship

Authors	*Data source*	*Sample size*	*Gender*	*Ages studied*	*Risk level*[a]	*Dependent variable*	*Classes found*
Nagin and Land (1993)	1961 Cambridge Study	403	Males	10–32	Low	11 two-year conviction counts	4
D'Unger *et al.* (1998)	1958 Philadelphia Birth Cohort	1,000	Males	8–26	Low	Police contact counts	5
	1942 Racine Birth Cohort	353	Males	8–30	Low	Police contact counts	5
	1949 Racine Birth Cohort	721	Males	8–25	Low	Police contact counts	4
	1955 Racine Birth Cohort	1,067	Males	8–22	Low	Police contact counts	5
Laub, Nagin, and Sampson (1998)	1950 Glueck Study	480	Males	7–32	High	Arrest counts	4
McDermott and Nagin (2001)	1977 National Youth Survey	835	Males	11–24	Low	8 years of self-reported serious offenses	3
Piquero *et al.* (2001)	California Youth Authority Parolees	272	Males	18–33	High	Arrest counts	6

[a] *Risk* level is defined here as 'Low' and 'High'. Low-risk samples correspond to general population samples that are likely to include a majority of low-risk cases in the data. High-risk samples, on the other hand, refers to samples where high-risk cases will constitute the majority of cases (e.g. samples of parolees).

The Nagin and Land study used criminal conviction data gathered between the ages of 10 and 32, with eleven time 'periods' of conviction counts comprising the dependent variables used in the analyses (e.g. convictions at ages 10 and 11 constituted one 'period' of data, 12 and 13 another period, and so on).

Applying the semiparametric mixed Poisson model to these data, Nagin and Land uncovered four distinct groups of offenders. The groups were named according to their offending 'style': 'non-offenders' (64% of the sample), 'adolescent-limited' (12.7%), 'low-rate chronics' (9.9%), and 'high-rate chronics' (13.4%). The non-offenders group was comprised of the sample members who had no convictions during the follow-up period. Obviously, the use of convictions (rather than police contacts or arrests) made it likely that this category would constitute the largest group in the data set.

Importantly, Nagin and Land uncovered three different groups of offenders within these data, each with their own distinct offending trajectory. They noted that there was considerable heterogeneity in the peak age of offending among the various groups. The peak age of offending for the 'adolescent-limited' group was 14, whereas it was 18 and 22, respectively, in the 'high-rate chronics' and 'low-rate chronics' groups. The rate of offending at the peak age (as measured though conviction counts) also varied dramatically among the three groups: with 0.63 convictions for the 'adolescent-limited,' 1.22 convictions for the 'high-rate chronics,' and 0.27 for the 'low-rate chronics.'

Interestingly, their analyses contradicted the assertions of Gottfredson and Hirschi (1990), by finding that between-group age differences in convictions were *not* stable over time. Although the 'low-rate chronics' group did have a peak offending age, their overall trajectory was amazingly flat between the ages of 16 and 30, and the difference in offending rates between the low- and high-rate chronics groups was only 0.15 by age 30, whereas the difference was about 1.0 at age 16. The 'high-rate chronics' group was already highly active in crime at age 10, with this group already having an average conviction rate of roughly 0.8 convictions at that precocious age. This group did, however, show a significant decrease in their conviction patterns (after their peak rate at age 18) as they progressed through adulthood, a finding that is consistent with the assumptions of both Sampson and Laub (1993) and Gottfredson and Hirschi (1990). By finding a 'low-rate chronics' group, Nagin and Land were the first researchers to offer empirical evidence of considerably more heterogeneity than the two subgroups posited by Moffitt's dual taxonomy theory (1993, 1997).

D'Unger and colleagues (D'Unger *et al.* 1998) conducted the most extensive examination of the age–crime curve to date when they analysed five separate data sets. One set of data pertained to the same set employed in the Nagin and Land (1993) study, and since the results obtained in these two studies are identical, they are not discussed here. The four new sets of results presented by D'Unger and her colleagues include analyses of data from the 1958 Philadelphia Birth Cohort study (Tracy, Wolfgang, and Figlio 1990), and the 1942, 1949, and 1955 Racine Birth Cohort studies (Shannon 1988, 1991).

The 1958 Philadelphia Birth Cohort study longitudinally tracked all 13,160 males and 14,000 females born in Philadelphia in 1958 and who resided in the city from their 10th through their 18th birthday. The frequency of 'police contact' for felony and/or misdemeanor criminal offenses was collected through age 26 from Philadelphia Police Department records. Police contacts included both actual arrests by law enforcement personnel as well as law enforcement 'contacts' that were handled 'remedially' or 'informally' (e.g. released at the scene or released to parents) and did not involve a formal arrest where the individual is taken into custody (Tracy and Kempf-Leonard 1996). For computational reasons, D'Unger *et al.* (1998) estimated their models on a random sample of 1,000 males.[3]

D'Unger *et al.* (1998) found a five-class or group model to be the best fit to these data, and named their classes by the nature of the respective offending trajectories of the groups. The largest group was labeled 'non-offenders' (comprising 61% of the sample), and the other groups included a 'high-rate adolescence peaked' group (1%), a 'low-rate adolescence peaked' group (9%), a 'low-rate chronics' group (21%), and a 'high-rate chronics' group (8%).[4] Interestingly, the four groups who engaged in some level of offending bifurcated into high- and low-rate versions of 'adolescence peaked' and 'chronic' types that tracked each other fairly well over time.

[3] Estimation times of finite mixture models tend to increase greatly with sample size (Vermunt and Magidson 2000). Also, to keep the results comparable to those obtained by Nagin and Land (1993), only males were included in these analyses.

[4] D'Unger *et al.* (1998) refer to the group as 'adolescence peaked' rather than 'adolescent-limited' because their offending patterns included ages outside the adolescent years of 13–17.

Although changes in the rates of offending varied both within and among the 'adolescence peaked' and the 'chronics' offender groups, each group showed a decrease in offending throughout adulthood. The peak ages of offending were 16 for the 'adolescence peaked' groups, and 18 for the chronic groups. The offense rates peaked at 1.0 (for the 'low-rate adolescence peaked' group), 3.3 (for the 'high-rate adolescence peaked' group), 0.21 (for the 'low-rate chronics' group), and 0.95 (for the 'high-rate chronics' group). By age 26, however, only the 'high-rate chronics group' still had a non-zero offending rate, and their rate at that age was roughly one-quarter of its peak rate at age 18.

The Racine Birth Cohorts longitudinally tracked the offense histories of all individuals born in Racine, Wisconsin, in 1942, 1949, and 1955. For research with these data sets, the dependent variables were the number of police contacts for felony and misdemeanor criminal offenses between the ages 8 and 30 (1942 cohort), ages 8 and 25 (1949 cohort), and ages 8 and 22 (1955 cohort). To make these findings comparable with the previous studies discussed above, the authors limited their analyses to the white and black male members of the samples. This resulted in final sample sizes of 353 (for 1942), 721 (for 1949), and 1,067 (for 1955) individuals, respectively.

For the 1942 birth cohort, D'Unger *et al.* found the best-fitting model to have five distinct offender groups. These groups included a 'non-offenders' group (34.6%), an 'adolescence peaked' (20%) group, a 'low-rate chronics' (31.4%) group, a 'high-rate chronics' group (8.8%), and a 'late-onset chronics' group (5.1%). Unlike the findings of previously reviewed studies, one offender group was located in this data set that actually increased their offending with age (the 'late-onset chronics' group), with the peak rate of offending for this group occurring at age 28, where it then stabilized through the end of the follow-up period. At age 16, this group had an offending pattern that virtually tracked the 'adolescence peaked' group. At that point, however, the two trajectories diverged, with the 'late-onset chronics' group continuing to escalate their offending behavior, while the 'adolescence peaked' group began to desist from offending. Interestingly, the high- and low-rate chronics groups differed substantially in their offending rates between ages 16 and 22 (with their offending rates differing by about 1.0 police contacts per year). By the end of the follow-up period, however, the offending rates of these two groups were nearly identical.

The 'high-rate chronics' group experienced a significant decline in offending in early adulthood, whereas the 'low-rate chronics' group was observed to have exhibited a much slower rate of decrease in their offending rate.

A four-class (or group) model for the 1949 sample provided the best fit to this data set. The group trajectories found by D'Unger *et al.* for this sample included a 'non-offenders' group (35%), 'high-rate chronics' group (peak age = 18; peak rate = 2.1; 5% of sample), a 'low-rate adolescence peaked' group (peak age = 18, peak rate = 0.25; 40% of sample), and a 'high-rate adolescence peaked' group (peak age = 18; peak rate = 0.75; 19% of sample). By age 25, both the low-rate and high-rate adolescence peaked groups had virtually desisted from offending (as measured by police contacts), whereas the 'high-rate chronics' group was still experiencing roughly 1.5 police contacts per year at this period in their lives. It is interesting to note that this is the only data set for which the trajectories generally followed the proportional changes across time argument proposed by Gottfredson and Hirschi (1990).

For the 1955 cohort, a five-group model was found to provide the most accurate fit to the data. The five groups included a 'non-offenders' group (44.5%), an 'early-onset adolescence peaked' group (2.2%), a 'late-onset adolescence peaked' group (15.4%), 'low-rate chronics' group (30.1%), and 'high-rate chronics' group (7.8%). Unlike the results from the Philadelphia Birth Cohort data, however, the 'adolescence peaked' trajectories did not neatly bifurcate into simply high- and low-rate versions; they differed greatly on their age of onset as well as their rates of offending. Also, the crime trajectories of the various groups did not remain proportional; rather the rate of change of the trajectories varied considerably between groups. For example, at age 8 the 'early-onset adolescence peaked' group and the 'high-rate chronics' were very similar in offending rates. At age 16 their trajectories differed by about 2 arrests per year, and then by age 22 they were nearly identical again. Similarly, the trajectories of the 'low-rate chronics' and the 'late-onset adolescence peaked' groups were identical until age 15, at which point the 'adolescence peaked group' had a surge in offending, while the offending by the 'low-rate chronics' held fairly constant thereafter. By age 22, the 'late-onset adolescence peaked group' had decreased their offending back to a level near that of the 'low-rate chronics' group.

The results of the studies reviewed here so far have shed doubt on the assertion of Gottfredson and Hirschi that there is a relative stability of between-group differences in offending across time as well as the contention by Moffitt that there are only two discrete groups of offenders in the population. Next, we turn our attention to the first analysis of the longitudinal offending patterns among discrete offender groups within a 'high-risk' sample.

Laub, Nagin, and Sampson (1998) conducted an analysis of the longitudinal offending patterns of the 480 delinquent boys from the original Glueck study of the criminal careers of delinquent boys in Boston (Glueck and Glueck 1950, 1968).[5] All 480 boys were white and all had appeared in the Boston Juvenile Court in the late 1930s. The Gluecks followed the boys into adulthood until the age of 32. Sampson and Laub (1990, 1993; Laub and Sampson 1988) subsequently reconstructed these data and put them into machine-readable form, and then used these data to develop and test their theory of informal social control. In their 1998 study, Laub, Nagin, and Sampson used the finite mixture methods of Nagin and Land to ascertain if there were distinct groups of offenders even within this select group of chronically delinquent boys.[6]

For this study, the dependent variable was the count number of arrests in each year between the ages of 7 and 32. The authors found that allowing for four distinct groups (or trajectories) provided the best fit to these data. Since all of the members of this sample were official delinquents, there was obviously no 'non-offenders' group in this data set. There was, however, a significant amount of heterogeneity even within this select sample of chronic juvenile delinquents. Further, even though all four of the offender trajectories were very similar in their offending rates up through

[5] Laub and Sampson (2003; Sampson and Laub 2003) have recently updated the Glueck data to age 70. In the final chapter of this book, we connect our results to their most recent work. Here we briefly note that their most recent analyses resulted in six latent classes and that 'crime declines with age sooner or later for all offender groups' (Sampson and Laub 2003: 555).

[6] In further analyses, Laub, Nagin, and Sampson (1998) also used the resulting latent class indicators as a method of controlling for persistent individual differences in models testing the crime-preventive benefits of a cohesive marriage. The results of their analyses indicated that, even after controlling for unobserved heterogeneity in criminal propensity, a cohesive marriage was a critical factor in the desistence process. Consistent with their age-graded theory, the benefits of a cohesive marriage accrued gradually over time.

age 13, from that point on there was significant variability in the shape of each group's crime trajectory.

'Group 1' consisted of a high-rate chronic group that had an observed peak offending age of 18 (at about 3 arrests per year), and thereafter their trajectory was relatively constant until they reached their late twenties, when their offending rates began to decline. Only 11 individuals in the sample were assigned to this group. 'Group 2' was a more moderate chronic offender group, with a peak offending rate of about 1.2 arrests per year at around age 18. This group comprised about 19 per cent of the sample. The offending rate of 'Group 2' was relatively constant during their twenties, and began to decline by the end of the follow-up period (ages 30–32). 'Group 3' exhibited an offending pattern very similar to 'Group 2' through age 16, but then experienced a significant decline in their offending rate over the remaining age distribution curve. By age 32, this group had a negligible offending rate, whereas 'Group 2' was still offending at about 0.8 arrests per year at this age. 'Group 4' was the group with the lowest offending rate (peak offending rate was 0.7 at age 16). This group, which comprised about 31 per cent of the sample, also had a rather negligible offending rate (of about 0.1) by age 26, where the rate continued to hover for the remaining six years of the follow-up period. The results of this study should be viewed with caution, however, because the subjects in the Glueck data set were not randomly selected from the population, nor randomly selected from juvenile court cases (see Cohen and Vila 1996). Because the results of this study are based on a matching sample that was drawn by convenience from Boston juvenile court records, the generalizability of the results beyond their obtained sample are uncertain.

Using a national probability sample to avoid possible sampling bias, McDermott and Nagin (2001) studied the self-reported offending patterns of the 835 male respondents in the National Youth Survey. The segment of the age distribution studied ranged from 11 through 24, but fewer than half of the respondents were available for sampling at ages 11–13 and 20–24.[7] Therefore, the lack of available data for estimating these segments of the

[7] Their analyses covered a period of eight 'age years', with the actual ages studied varying between the respondents depending on the age of the respondent at the first wave of the interviews. There were actually only six measurement periods used in the analyses due to unequal spacing of the last interview.

age–crime curve demands caution when interpreting the reported results. The dependent variable for this study was a count of self-reported involvement in rape, auto theft, theft of goods worth more than $50, purchasing stolen property worth more than $50, and breaking and entering.

McDermott and Nagin (2001) found that a three-class model provided the best fit to these data. 'Group 1' was engaged in offending from ages 11 through 20 at a relatively constant rate (between 1.0 and 1.3 offenses), at which point their offending patterns were found to decline. The offending rate of 'Group 1' peaked at age 15. It should be noted that 748 individuals (or 89% of the sample) in this analysis were assigned to 'Group 1', and that most of these individuals reported no criminal activity at each age measured. 'Group 2,' comprising about 6 per cent of the sample, had a peak of offending at age 11, with 20 offenses per year. Thereafter, this group showed a significant decline in the offending rate through age 19, at which point the rate leveled off at around 5 offenses per year, which continued through age 24. The offending pattern by 'Group 3' was nearly antithetical to the pattern observed for 'Group 2.' 'Group 3,' which contained 5 per cent of the sample, showed a precipitous increase in their offending from ages 11 through 21, where the offense rate peaked at a rate of 30 offenses per year. The offense rate then declined to 23 offenses per year by age 24.

In still another study, Piquero *et al.* (2001) present an analysis of the age–crime curve for a sample of high-risk cases. This study involved an analysis of the adult offending patterns of a sample of 272 parolees released from the California Youth Authority (CYA) between 1960 and 1970. This is the same youthful offender correctional system from which we analyzed data in this study, although the data gathered by Piquero *et al.* pre-date the large increase in violent offending that occurred in the state of California in the 1980s and it did not constitute a random sample of CYA wards. The 272 parolees in the Piquero *et al.* study were 'older, had more serious commitment offenses, and/or were more uncooperative in other CYA institutions' (2001: 57) compared to most of the youths housed in this correctional system. These youthful offenders were paroled at age 18 from the CYA and were then followed for sixteen years until age 33. The dependent variable was a count of arrest events between the ages of 18 and 33. Thus, while their study concerns a limited segment of the age–crime curve (i.e. adulthood only), it is important for inclusion in our review because the authors found considerable heterogeneity in the adult offending trajectories of this select sample of offenders.

In fact, Piquero *et al.* (2001) report that a model allowing for six distinct trajectories provided the best fit to these data. Importantly, this study found a six-class model to fit the data with and without controls for 'exposure time' (i.e. time not incarcerated), although the authors noted that the scale of the arrests trajectories, especially during their early twenties, was affected by controlling for exposure time. In the nomenclature of criminological research, exposure time is referred to as 'time on the street' and is used often to control for the amount of time spent incarcerated during the sample period. When a person is incarcerated, they are denied the opportunity to victimize the general non-institutionalized population simply as a consequence of their isolation or 'incapacitation' and not because of any change in their motivation to commit criminal behavior in general.[8]

For the models without a control for exposure time, 'Latent Class 1' (18% of the sample) was a group that increased their offending through age 21, which was their peak age of offending (at two offenses per year). This group then decreased their rate of offending through age 33; their offending rate was negligible from age 29 onward. 'Latent Class 2' (21% of the sample) displayed a trajectory very similar to 'Latent Class 1,' only their offending rate was roughly twice the rate of 'Latent Class 1.' Their rate peaked at age 21 and then decreased thereafter, but they still had a positive offending rate at age 33 (at about 0.75 arrests per year). 'Latent Class 3' (7% of the sample) peaked their offending during the first year after release (age 18), had a small decrease in their offending rate during the early twenties, and then had a relatively constant rate (at about 3 offenses per year) through the remaining ages in the distribution. 'Latent Class 4' displayed a trajectory very similar to 'Latent Class 3,' albeit at a lower rate of offending than 'Latent Class 3,' from ages 18 though 28. 'Class 4s' (18% of the sample) arrest rate also peaked at age 18, then held at a relatively constant

[8] The logic of 'street time' is that someone who spends twelve months 'on the street' and is arrested one time is very different from an individual who spends one month on the street and is arrested one time.

rate through age 28 at about one offense per year, and then displayed a decreasing offense rate through age 33. The fifth latent class (24% of the sample) also had a peak rate of arrest at age 18 (at two offenses per year), then displayed a decreasing arrest rate through age 25, at which point this rate became stable at about 0.5 arrests per year. Interestingly, the sixth latent class (10%) had a very small offense rate at age 18 (about 0.25 arrests per year), but then essentially desisted entirely over the remaining ages. In other words, this group was able to essentially remain arrest-free after parole. It is interesting to ponder whether this group was comprised of an 'adolescent-limited' group who displayed a high offending rate during their adolescent years but then was able to remain arrest-free during adulthood.

Two important differences arose after allowing for an 'offset' or control for crime exposure time in the Piquero *et al.* study. First, the predicted arrest count was of greater magnitude for both 'Latent Class 2' and 'Latent Class 3.' 'Latent Class 2' peaked two years earlier than did 'Class 3' at a rate of 7 arrests per year, but then exhibited a pronounced declining arrest rate through age 25, at which point the trajectory assumed the same shape it did in models without controls for 'time on the street.' 'Latent Class 3' also did not experience its decline in the early twenties, but rather this group's arrest trajectory held rather constant over most of the remaining age distribution (at a rate of about 7 arrests). While in their early thirties, the group had a decrease in offending of about one arrest per year, for the most part, the overall shape of those two curves did not vary dramatically between the two models. A second difference among the groups noted by Piquero *et al.* (2001) was that 'Latent Class 4' also did not experience a decline in offending in the early twenties or a further decline in the thirties, but rather this group had a constant arrest rate over the entire age distribution (at about three arrests per year). The remaining three classes had trajectories that were essentially identical in both models. Piquero *et al.* (2001: 68) concluded that 'the general shape of the arrest trend appears to be robust to controls for exposure time.' The percentage of cases assigned to each latent class was virtually identical across the two models as well. Piquero and his colleagues report that more than anything else, it was the magnitude of the arrests scale that was affected the most by controlling for street or exposure time. Nonetheless, the results from both of their models indicate that there is significant heterogeneity in the adult arrest patterns of these serious offenders, but how that adulthood heterogeneity related to prior existing differences could not be determined with these data. Indeed, the results of this study also leave one wondering if the findings would have changed had they access to either the juvenile arrest histories of their sample members or to a much larger, random sample of youthful offenders. Our point is that with an overall sample size of only 272 cases that were not randomly drawn, the generalizability of the findings from this study must be viewed cautiously.

We have now completed our review of the prior studies that have addressed the age–crime relationship within discrete offender groups (that are internally homogeneous with respect to their offending patterns across time). In the next section, we place the results of these studies into perspective with a discussion that focuses on both the significant themes that have emerged and the methodological limitations of these prior studies. We then specify four of the eight hypotheses to be tested in our study.

Discussion and Hypotheses Related to the Age–Crime Relationship

A general summary of many of the studies we have reviewed here can be found in the first, and arguably definitive, study concerning the relationship between age and crime within distinct offender groups by Nagin and Land. In this study, Nagin and Land (1993: 358) noted, 'our findings point to large variation across the population not only in offending levels by age but also in the trajectory of offending over age.' The results of their study are illustrative of several themes in the literature particularly relevant to the study we will conduct herein.

First, there appears to be a considerable amount of individual variation in the offending rates of individuals. This heterogeneity in offending propensity has been documented across a variety of different settings, including birth cohorts from a small Midwestern town such as Racine, to a large urban city such as Philadelphia (D'Unger *et al.* 1998), in a random sample of the general population (McDermott and Nagin 2001) to samples of the serious youthful offender population from Boston and California (Laub, Nagin, and Sampson 1998; Piquero *et al.* 2001), in a nationwide sample that uses self-report data (McDermott and Nagin 2001) to samples that use official data (Nagin and Land 1993; Piquero *et al.* 2001), and across varying cultural settings such as England (Nagin and Land 1993) and New Zealand (Fergusson, Horwood, and Nagin 2000). The generalizability of the finding of heterogeneity in individual offending is extremely important because samples are often treated as if one trajectory or group is present in the data and as if the effects of persistent heterogeneity are trivial. Such short-sightedness by researchers can lead to misleading and erroneous conclusions (D'Unger *et al.* 1998; Land, Nagin, and McCall 2001; Maltz 1994; Moffitt 1993, 1997).

A second theme in this literature concerns the significant amount of between-group heterogeneity displayed with respect to the direction and nature of change in the shape of individual's crime trajectories across the age distribution. Given that the theories of Gottfredson and Hirschi (1990) and Moffitt (1993, 1997) predict neat, clearly defined changes in offending trajectories over time, while Sampson and Laub (1993) predict more heterogeneity in crime trajectories over time (especially in the adult years), the evidence at this point would appear to lend more support for the theoretical position of Sampson and Laub. For example, the McDermott and Nagin (2001) study found a crime trajectory that continued to increase across age, while D'Unger *et al.* (1998) discovered high- and low-rate 'chronics' display markedly slower change in their crime trajectories in comparison to the adolescence peaked groups in their data. Laub, Nagin, and Sampson (1998) report crime trajectories in their sample that were quite similar at early ages to show markedly differential growth patterns during adulthood.

Still a third theme contained in this literature involves two trajectory 'regularities' in many of the studies reviewed here. The first regularity is that two distinct primary groups have been uncovered across many of the studies: (1) the 'chronic offender' group where crime peaks between ages 17–21 and then drops slowly in the remaining years that they are in their twenties and (2) the 'adolescent peaked' group where crime peaks between ages 15–18 and then drops rapidly to near zero by age 22 (D'Unger *et al.* 1998). The second common pattern or regularity within these studies is a common crime trajectory shape that often bifurcates into high- and low-rate groups that track each other over the age distribution (D'Unger *et al.* 1998).

Yet, even in the face of these regularities, it should be noted that neither the longitudinal shapes nor the number of distinct trajectories were entirely consistent across the various studies discussed above. For example, several crime trajectory patterns have only been identified in one or two of these studies, most notably the 'late-onset chronic' offender found in D'Unger *et al.*'s (1998) analysis of the 1942 Racine Birth Cohort. While all of the aforementioned studies uncovered more than two discrete groups, the exact number of classes has ranged from three in the McDermott and Nagin (2001) study to six in the Piquero *et al.* (2001) study. Most studies report the identification of four or five distinct crime trajectories among their data. Notably this finding directly contradicts Moffitt's hypothesis of two distinct offender trajectories and suggests that more than two trajectories are needed to capture the variation of offending trajectories in the population. If there are not just two distinct offender trajectories, then how many are sufficient to accurately reflect existing crime patterns over the age distribution? Does the number of crime trajectories identified depend on the sample composition? How stable are the identified latent classes within a given population over time? While definitive answers to these questions will require much future research, results such as those we present in Chapter 7 can expand our understanding of these issues.

The current literature of the age–crime curve for distinct groups of offenders has several limitations that highlight the need for further study. First, some of the previous studies have focused on rather limited segments of the age distribution (due to limitations of the data sets), with several studies not beginning their measurement of offending behaviors until the onset of adolescence or later, and most of the studies ending their follow-up periods prior to or around the age of 25. The study of Laub, Nagin, and Sampson (1998) has the longest follow-up period to date, examining the nature of the offending trajectories of 480 delinquents from age 7 through age 32. The nature and shape of offending patterns beyond the early thirties are currently not well understood. Second, the study of D'Unger *et al.* (1998) is the only study to compare the results from data sets generalizable to the same population over time. This makes it very difficult to replicate not only the existence of a crime trajectory group over time, but also whether there are any changes in the precise number or nature of the offending trajectories over time. As such, D'Unger *et al.* (1998) argue that replication of offending trajectories is a critical research need that is necessary to prevent reifying any particular identified offending trajectory as a stable element in a population. As D'Unger *et al.* note (1998: 1624–5):

> The effects of age, cohort or sample composition, and historical setting all play important roles in influencing individual development, hence the variation in trajectories over time. Social context must be viewed as a 'force in development' (Elder and O'Rand 1995), which has the power to alter trajectories of myriad types of behaviour.

A final limitation of the previous research reviewed here concerns the analyses of the 'high-risk' samples; only two studies have focused on select samples of 'high-risk' offenders. Both of those studies, however, have limitations that require additional research on this critical segment of the offending population. The Laub, Nagin, and Sampson (1998) study was based on the offending patterns of a non-random sample of white, male delinquents from Boston measured from the 1930s to the 1960s, and thus a key question is whether trajectories similar to the ones they describe can be found in more contemporary samples of the population. This is especially significant given that the nature of criminal offending appears to have changed dramatically (i.e. became more violent) after the point in time when Laub, Nagin, and Sampson's data were gathered. Piquero *et al.* (2001), on the other hand, only had access to data regarding offending patterns of a sample of serious youthful offenders during their adult years (age 18–33). Data from these subject's juvenile years were entirely absent from the analyses. This limitation raises several interesting questions with respect to this age segment of the population: (1) how do differences in offending trajectories during the juvenile years relate to the nature of offending during the adult years; and (2) is there an adolescent-peaked group within this population?[9] Furthermore, both of these studies were based on comparably 'small samples,' and thus we wonder to what degree their identification (of a particular latent class) is a consequence of sampling variation? Again, this question becomes more interesting once we consider that neither of the samples used in these two studies was randomly drawn. Thus, it is our contention that there is a critical need for subsequent empirical

[9] Recall that Piquero *et al.* (2001) found a group with an offending trajectory that by age 20 had terminated their criminal activity (as measured by arrests).

investigations of the nature of offending trajectories with random samples from the population of serious youthful offenders, a contention that has been echoed by Laub and Sampson (2001), Scholte (1999), and Tolan and Gorman-Smith (1998).

Given the findings and limitations of the literature discussed above, our study will investigate four hypotheses related to the age–crime curve using three relatively large, random samples of serious youthful offenders (to be described in greater detail in Chapter 5):

H_1: There are multiple groups or latent classes of offenders with distinct arrest trajectories even on the high end of the criminal propensity continuum where the serious youthful offenders are located.
H_2: There are more than two groups of offenders with distinctly different arrest trajectories even on the high end of the criminal propensity continuum.
H_3: There is an adolescence-peaked group even in samples of serious youthful offenders.
H_4: The age–crime curve is invariant among the latent classes of serious youthful offenders. Between-group differences will not vary across time.

These hypotheses are largely based on both the prior empirical results from the Laub, Nagin, and Sampson (1998) and Piquero *et al.* (2001) studies that indicate there is a significant level of heterogeneity in the offending patterns of serious youthful offenders, as well as the theoretical arguments of Cohen and Vila (1996) and D'Unger *et al.* (1998) that hypothesize the possibility of greater heterogeneity on the far right tail of the crime continuum than previously suggested. H_2 and H_3 are central to Moffitt's (1993, 1997) theoretical perspective, while H_4 is central to the theories of Gottfredson and Hirschi (1990) and Sampson and Laub (1993). Evidence supporting H_2 would cast doubt on the adequacy of Moffitt's theory that there are *only* two offender groups in the population. Evidence supporting H_4 would support Gottfredson and Hirschi (1990), while evidence refuting it would support the theoretical position of Sampson and Laub (1993).

Findings in support of these hypotheses are important for the crime literature because serious youthful offenders are often referred to as being 'relatively homogeneous' (Ge, Donnellan, and Wenk 2001: 750). As a whole, serious youthful offenders are an elusive class of offenders because they are (fortunately) relatively rare in the population of offenders (Cernkovich, Giordano, and Pugh 1985). Researchers thus are often forced to empirically 'lump' together offenders who have met some minimum definitional criteria that usually involve a measure of either seriousness and/or chronicity of offending (McDermott 1983). After 'making the cut,' this group of offenders is usually isolated and treated as a homogeneous group (often labeled as the 'chronic offender' group).[10] If there is significant heterogeneity in the propensity to offend within this group of offenders, recognition of that fact is important to the crime literature for both its theoretical and public policy implications.[11]

The results supporting or disconfirming these four hypotheses will be presented in Chapter 7. In that chapter, we will apply Nagin and Land's (1993) semiparametric mixed Poisson model to each of the three samples employed in our study. After determining the optimal number of latent classes of serious offenders present in each sample, the arrest trajectories will be graphed over the age distribution. Comparisons of the trajectories will be made concerning the patterns of offending displayed over time within and between the latent classes.

Studies of the Relationship of Past to Subsequent Criminal Activity

We now turn our attention to reviewing previous studies of the second critical issue addressed in this study—the relationship between past and subsequent criminal activity. Since investigating

[10] Loeber, Farrington, and Waschbusch (1998) provide an extensive discussion of the variable cut-off points that have been used in an attempt to isolate the type of offenders described in our study.

[11] For example, Ge, Donnellan, and Wenk (2001) analyse the arrest patterns of a sample of 2,263 males committed to the CYA in 1964 and 1965. The authors analyze the arrest patterns of the CYA wards at ages 18–20, 21–25, 26–30, and over 31 using a series of ordinary least squares regression models. The authors conclude (from a state dependence position) that 'early problem behaviors exert a significant influence on persistent offending. Early involvement with alcohol and drug use was a significant predictor of adult arrest frequency. This suggests that early substance use and abuse can influence criminal behavior throughout the life span.' Their analyses did not control for unobserved heterogeneity, however, and thus it could simply be that early drug use and abuse is correlated with the unmeasured (or at least the poorly measured) heterogeneity in the propensity to offend. Lacking controls for unmeasured heterogeneity, this finding is subject to criticism as a methodological artifact that would disappear if one were to use a more appropriate statistical model. See the section below describing studies of the relationship between past and subsequent criminal activity for a further discussion of the importance of unmeasured heterogeneity.

the relationship between past and subsequent criminal activity requires longitudinal (panel) data on a set of individuals, the studies reviewed here are limited to those studies following a panel of individuals over time. Furthermore, given the differential explanations of the population heterogeneity and state dependence positions for the underlying causes of the correlation between criminal activity at two different points in time, all of the studies reviewed here also control for individual differences in the propensity to commit criminal acts.

Historically, controlling for differences in criminal propensity has been most often attempted by including control variables measuring individual characteristics or other factors considered relevant in a regression model. However, multiple studies (Bushway, Brame, and Paternoster 1999; Nagin and Paternoster 2000; Paternoster and Brame 1997; Paternoster, Brame, and Farrington 2001) argue that there are two principal problems with this method of controlling for individual differences. First, criminologists cannot agree on the precise and most appropriate measures or variables that reasonably capture individual differences in criminal propensity. Second, even if there was such a consensus on relevant variables, most data sets probably would not have some, most, or perhaps any of those key measures.

The end result of such problems, as noted by Nagin and Paternoster (2000: 131), is that 'researchers would have no way of knowing if they have captured a sizeable share of the between-individual variation in criminal propensity with the measures they have available to them. Consequently, perhaps the lion's share of criminal propensity would be unmeasured or unobserved.' Simulations by Bushway, Brame, and Paternoster (1999) show that failing to account for unobserved heterogeneity leads to seriously biased estimates that favor the state dependence argument (see also Heckman 1981*c*; Hsiao 1986). Unobserved heterogeneity is, in essence, akin to omitting a key variable from the model specification, resulting in biased estimates of the other included covariates that are correlated with the omitted variable (Bushway, Brame, and Paternoster 1999; Nagin and Paternoster 2000). Since prior criminal activity will be positively correlated with criminal propensity, failure to adequately control for persistent unobserved heterogeneity (in criminal propensity among individuals) will lead to positively biased coefficients for the variable representing prior criminal activity. In other words, without statistically controlling for persistent individual differences, the coefficient for the prior criminal activity variable will absorb the effect of the omitted variable (individual differences in criminal propensity), resulting in an overestimate of the effect of prior criminal activity on present criminal activity. As Nagin and Paternoster (2000: 131) explicate, 'if there is unobserved heterogenity that accounts for offending over time, the failure to explicitly consider this will lead to biased estimates of observed time-varying factors.'

Thus, all of the studies to be reviewed below make use of statistical techniques controlling for unobserved or 'hidden' heterogeneity. These studies have used one of two statistical methods (and in one case both methods) to account for unobserved heterogeneity: (1) parametric random effects statistical models or (2) semiparametric random effects statistical models.[12] The primary difference between the two methods concerns the distribution of the unobserved heterogeneity. The parametric random effects models assume that the unobserved heterogeneity is *continuously distributed* in the population according to some known (mathematically tractable) parametric distributional form (e.g. it is normally distributed). The semiparametric form of the models *nonparametrically approximate* the form of the unobserved heterogeneity, assuming only that an approximation can be accomplished using a discrete, multinomial distribution (Heckman and Singer 1984; Land, McCall, and Nagin 1996; Nagin and Land 1993). This semiparametric random effects model is, in fact, the finite mixture model of Nagin and Land (1993) previously discussed. Each 'latent

[12] For readers desiring more information on these models at this point in their reading, the models are described in Chapter 5. Briefly, the parametric random effects model assumes that the error term for an individual at any point in time is composed of two components: a time-invariant, individual-specific term and a pure random disturbance term (that is distributed according to some parametric assumption, usually the normal distribution). The individual-specific component, which is invariant over time, is presumed to capture persistent, unmeasured individual differences in the propensity to offend. The correlation of an individual's error term over time (referred to as rho or ρ) is calculated as the variance of the individual-specific terms divided by the variance of the total error term (Hsiao 1986; Nagin and Paternoster 1991). Rho (ρ) is an estimate of the proportion of the variance of the error term that is due to persistent (time-stable) heterogeneity. If $\rho = 1$, the variance of the error term is entirely due to heterogeneity, whereas if $\rho = 0$, then persistent heterogeneity is negligible (Nagin and Paternoster 1991).

class' is assumed to be a single 'point-of-support' or 'segment' of the multinomial distribution, and the distribution of unobserved heterogeneity (known as the mixing distribution in statistics jargon) is approximated using a finite number of points-of-support. Within each 'segment' of the sample, individuals are internally homogeneous with respect to criminal propensity, but individuals from different segments have varying propensities to engage in criminal activities.

As Bushway, Brame, and Paternoster (1999) note, both of these models make assumptions, and the degree to which the assumptions are tenable is key to the robustness of any observed results. The parametric form of the models is more restrictive and more efficient than is the semiparametric form, which is less restrictive and hence also less efficient. Violations of the assumptions of each model, including the assumption of the distribution of unobserved heterogeneity, can have a significant impact on the conclusions based upon the results obtained from each model. We will return to this significant issue of 'violating assumptions' later in our discussion of the studies that address the relationship between past and subsequent criminal activity.

First, however, the results of several studies will be reviewed as they were reported in the original articles. In the following discussion, we try to stay substantively focused, but will include methodologically technical comments and footnotes when necessary. It should be stated that modeling the relationship between past and subsequent criminal activity is methodologically complicated, a point that should not be underemphasized (Nagin and Paternoster 2000). The old adage, 'the devil is in the details,' is quite appropriate for this issue. Table 3.2 presents key information from the different studies to be reviewed below that examine the relationship between past and subsequent criminal activity.

One of the key studies regarding the relationship between past and subsequent criminal activity was that of Nagin and Paternoster (1991). It is a study of 1,163 respondents in a convenience sample of students from nine high schools in South Carolina. This panel began in 1981 and had subsequent 'follow-up waves' in 1982 and 1983. Although there were initially 2,700 sophomore respondents, at the final wave only 1,250 senior respondents remained in the panel, and of these, only 1,163 filled out the information on relevant covariates deemed necessary for inclusion in the study by the authors. The dependent variable was constructed as a binary variable representing self-reported participation in three types of

TABLE 3.2. Summary information of prior studies of the relationship between past and future criminal activity

Authors	*Data source*	*Sample size*	*Gender*	*Periods studied*	*Risk level*[a]	*Dependent variable*	*Finding*[b]
Nagin and Paternoster (1991)	1981 South Carolina High School Survey	1,163	Males/ Females	2	Low	Binary indicator of self-reported property crimes	SD
Nagin and Farrington (1992)	1961 Cambridge Study	403	Males	11	Low	Two-year binary indicator of convictions	Mixed
Sampson and Laub (1993)	1950 Glueck Study	690	Males	2	High	Arrest counts between ages 25–32 and 32–45	Mixed
Land and Nagin (1996)	1961 Cambridge Study	403	Males	11	Low	Two-year binary indicator of convictions	Mixed
Paternoster *et al.* (1997)	1988–1989 NC Div. of Youth Services Releases	838	Males	4–6	High	Yearly arrest counts	Mixed
Paternoster and Brame (1997)	1977 National Youth Survey	479	Males/ Females	5	Low	Binary and count indicators of self-reported delinquency	Mixed
Bushway, Brame, and Paternoster (1999)	1958 Philadelphia Birth Cohort	13,160	Males	7	Low	3-year binary indicator of police contact	Mixed

[a] *Risk* level is defined here as 'Low' and 'High'. Low-risk samples correspond to general population samples that are likely to include a majority of low-risk cases in the data. High-risk samples, on the other hand, refer to samples where high-risk cases will constitute the majority of cases (e.g. samples of parolees).
[b] *Finding:* SD = state dependence; PH = population heterogeneity; Mixed = both state dependence and population heterogeneity.

property crimes: stealing something valued less than \$10, stealing something valued between \$10 and \$50, and breaking into a building and stealing something. Most respondents who indicated they had participated in one of these crimes had only stolen something valued at less than \$10. The panel assessed the dependent variable at two different points in time: participation between waves 1 and 2, and participation between waves 2 and 3. As the authors point out, the length of this panel (2 points in time) is the absolute minimum number of periods needed to estimate a panel model. In their model, the lagged dependent variable (participation in crime during the prior measured period) is the parameter estimate providing evidence for or against a process of state dependence.

Using a (parametric) random effects probit model, Nagin and Paternoster found a significant correlation between participation in the property crimes at the two points in time, even after accounting for unobserved heterogeneity through the use of the random effects model. Participating in the property crime between waves 1 and 2 significantly increased the odds of participating in crime between waves 2 and 3, net of persistent heterogeneity (rho was estimated to be equal to 0, indicating that persistent heterogeneity was negligible). According to Nagin and Paternoster (1991: 183), 'the results revealed that prior participation in crime had a positive and significant association with subsequent participation, controlling for the possibility of unobserved heterogeneity.' This finding is consistent with the hypothesis that prior participation reduces the barrier against subsequent participation in crime. The authors were notably cautious in their conclusions, noting that it was an 'exploratory' study with 'suggestive results', because of several methodological limitations including the use of a non-random convenience sample, the built-in assumptions of the random effects model concerning the distribution of the heterogeneity (i.e. that it was normally distributed), and because the 'initial conditions' assumption of the model was clearly violated.[13] Furthermore, due

[13] The initial conditions assumption refers to the assumption that, at the first wave of the study, none of the respondents had already initiated the process (i.e. been involved in property crime activity). This assumption is required so that the model is able to obtain an unbiased estimate of the individual-specific component of the error term. It turns out that this assumption is fundamentally critical to calculating unbiased estimates concerning the relationship between past and subsequent criminal activity (Brame, Bushway, and Paternoster 1999).

to heavy sample attrition (57% dropped out of the panel before the final wave), the potential 'homogenization' of the sample with respect to criminal propensity could not be ruled out.

In addition to presenting some initial findings on the relationship of past to subsequent criminal activity, the study by Nagin and Paternoster (1991) was also noteworthy because (1) it was the first study to explicitly address and elaborate the state dependence versus population heterogeneity arguments for crime, (2) they proposed the use of the random effects models as a viable method for addressing the issues surrounding the continuity in offending patterns, and, perhaps more importantly, because (3) their findings were so provocative as to stimulate continued research on these issues.

Soon after the publication of the Nagin and Paternoster (1991) study, Nagin and Farrington (1992*a*) presented results bearing on the issue of the relationship between prior and subsequent crime by using the data from the Cambridge Study in Delinquent Development previously described. Recall that this study employs twenty-two years' worth of conviction data covering the ages of 10–32 for 403 London-born males. The dependent variable for each period was a binary indicator of conviction during consecutive two-year periods (e.g. any conviction during ages 10 and 11 constituted the offense or dependent variable for the first period). Following the lead of Nagin and Paternoster (1991), Nagin and Farrington (1992*a*) also used the random effects probit model that assumes unobserved heterogeneity to be normally distributed. Interest focused on the parameter estimate for the binary variable that indicated whether or not the individual had been convicted in the prior period (i.e. this is the lagged dependent variable). The coefficient for that variable represents the estimate of the state dependence effect for these data.

In contrast to the findings of Nagin and Paternoster (1991), this study found a highly significant, strong effect of persistent unobserved heterogeneity that served to significantly reduce the association between past and subsequent criminal activity. In the model ignoring persistent heterogeneity (i.e. a standard probit model), the parameter estimate relating conviction in the prior period to conviction in the subsequent measured period was 1.16. In the model controlling for persistent heterogeneity, the estimate was reduced in magnitude to 0.446, roughly a 62 per cent reduction in the magnitude of the effect. Rho (the within-individual correlation of the error term across time) was estimated to be 0.4, indicating that 40 per cent of the unexplained error variance was estimated to be due to persistent hidden heterogeneity. Nagin and Farrington (1992*a*: 253) focused their attention on the reduction of the magnitude of the state dependence parameter after controlling for unobserved heterogeneity and the large magnitude of the rho estimate. They concluded that the results were most consistent with the population heterogeneity position and that 'evidence of true state dependence is limited. After controlling for persistent unobserved heterogeneity, the association between past and subsequent participation is greatly diminished.' However, closer examination of their results more clearly supports a 'mixed' model where both population heterogeneity and state dependence processes are at work (Paternoster *et al.* 1997). Nonetheless, this study is important because it demonstrates that population heterogeneity, if left uncontrolled, could have serious effects on the estimates of variables indicating evidence in support of the state dependence process.

Although not explicitly addressing the relationship between past and subsequent criminal activity, further analyses of the Cambridge data by Nagin and Farrington (1992*b*) also revealed strong effects of persistent unobserved heterogeneity. Employing the same data and statistical models from the previous study, Nagin and Farrington (1992*b*) investigated whether age of onset had a significant effect on the probability of conviction in the eleven-period panel, net of the effects of persistent unobserved heterogeneity. The state dependence interpretation of the age of onset variable is that early conviction has a significant causal impact on the probability of subsequent criminal activity (i.e. conviction causes changes in their life circumstances, such as increasing the likelihood of association with delinquent peers or reducing the social bond, that makes continuing in a life of crime more likely), whereas the population heterogeneity interpretation is that the age of onset variable is merely a proxy measure indicating the level of criminal propensity (i.e. individuals with an earlier age of onset have the highest criminal propensity levels). In the model without controls for persistent unobserved heterogeneity, the age of onset variable was found to have a large and highly significant negative effect, indicating that as the age at first conviction increased, the odds of a subsequent conviction decreased.[14] However, in the model controlling for unobserved heterogeneity (i.e. in the random effects probit model), the inverse association between age at first conviction and the odds of a subsequent conviction was reduced to insignificance and near zero in absolute magnitude. In other words, the inverse association between prior and subsequent criminal activity was entirely attributable to the effects of persistent unobserved heterogeneity (i.e. due to time-stable differences).

In an empirical test of their age-graded social control theory, Sampson and Laub (1993) presented a two-period panel analysis of arrest counts between ages 25–32 (period 1) and ages 32–45 (period 2). These analyses employed the use of the Glueck data described earlier, plus results from the matched 'control group.' Here 'non-delinquent' cases were matched (case by case) to their 'delinquent' pairs on the basis of age, ethnicity (e.g. Irish, Italian, German, Jewish), and neighbourhood (n = 289 for the delinquents; n = 401 for the matched control group).[15] Sampson and Laub utilized a generalized least squares (GLS) random effects model (which is in essence a random effects OLS model) and they found results consistent with those of Nagin and Farrington (1992*a*).

In the models estimated on both the delinquents and the control group, Sampson and Laub found significant levels of persistent unobserved heterogeneity (rho = 0.22 and 0.29 for the delinquents and control groups, respectively). Furthermore, they found that even after controlling for persistent unobserved heterogeneity, both the unofficial and official juvenile delinquency behavioral variables were positively and significantly related to observed crime frequencies between ages 25 and 45. These results were found in the models for both the delinquent group and the control group. Similarly, the results of their analyses also indicated that several other variables representing the state dependence position were

[14] The actual specification employed the use of two variables to capture the effect of age of onset. One variable indicated if the individual had ever been convicted in a prior period, while the other variable indicated the actual age of onset. The use of two variables allowed the state dependence effect to decrease as the age of onset increased (i.e. it allowed the positive impact of the first variable to be magnified by an early age of onset).

[15] Sampson and Laub (1993) present sample sizes for the 'pooled' data sets. Since their analyses are based on a two-period panel model, we have divided the pooled sample sizes by two to arrive at the sample size.

significantly related to engaging in crime during adulthood, even after controlling for persistent individual differences. For example, the models for both the 'experimental and control' groups indicated that job stability had significant negative effects on adult crime frequency. This suggested that individuals with less stable job histories were more likely to engage in crime during adulthood, net of the effects of persistent individual differences and measures of juvenile offending frequency. According to Sampson and Laub (1993: 198–9), 'these findings support the idea that state dependence underlies the effects of both prior crime and weak social bonds.' When all the evidence presented by Sampson and Laub (1993) is considered together, however, their data clearly support the 'mixed' position—both population heterogeneity and state dependence processes were found to be present within the Glueck data.[16]

In a re-analysis of the Cambridge data used in their initial (1993) article, Land and Nagin (1996) present further evidence concerning the link between having a prior conviction (at any point in the individual's past) and the probability of a subsequent conviction at a given age. Employing their semiparametric finite (Poisson) mixture model, Land and Nagin (1996) find evidence to support the mixed position that dovetails squarely with the conclusions of Nagin and Farrington (1992*a*), who had analyzed the same data with the parametric random effects probit model.[17] The analyses by

[16] Sampson and Laub (1996) analyzed the military arrest history of the samples and also found that early entry into the military significantly improved the lives of the structurally disadvantaged and delinquent men. Thus, military service appeared to be a 'turning point' in the lives of these men, allowing them to enrich their lives, including their occupational status, job stability, and socio-economic achievement in adulthood. This effect was especially pronounced among the veterans previously stigmatized as official delinquents. In other words, events during adulthood have important consequences for subsequent outcomes. It should be noted, however, that Laub and Sampson (1998) also present evidence in support of the population heterogeneity argument. In these analyses, Laub and Sampson (1998) found that the delinquent group was significantly less likely to take advantage of educational opportunities available both while in the military and through the G.I. educational bill, and that the chronic offenders were significantly less likely to achieve good marriages.

[17] Technically speaking, Land and Nagin (1996) estimated a multiple-spell discrete-time hazard model of the time until conviction (i.e. years until or years between convictions). Land and Nagin (1996) show that under regular conditions, the micro-level Poisson model is equivalent to a discrete-time hazard model. See Land, Nagin, and McCall (2001) for further information regarding this event history formulation of the finite mixture model.

Land and Nagin (1996) were the first to use the finite mixture models (allowing for a nonparametric specification of the distribution of unobserved heterogeneity) to address the question of whether past evidence of engaging in criminal activity has a significant effect on subsequent criminality after controlling for unobserved heterogeneity. Consistent with the conclusions of their initial (1993) article, Land and Nagin (1996) found significant differences in the propensity to offend within the sample. They uncovered the same four distinct trajectory patterns reported in their earlier article. Land and Nagin again uncovered four distinct trajectory patterns as in their earlier article, and the probability of surviving without a conviction varied dramatically across the groups.

Land and Nagin also included a variable in their models to assess whether or not the individual had ever been previously convicted. The parameter estimate for the prior conviction variable indicated that individuals with a prior conviction had a higher 'hazard' of being convicted at a given age. Notably, this parameter estimate was calculated net of the effects of unobserved individual differences that were captured through the use of the points-of-support approach to estimate unmeasured heterogeneity in the offending population. Stated differently, if you compared an 'unconvicted' individual with an already 'convicted' individual within the same 'segment' or 'point-of-support' of the unmeasured heterogeneity distribution and at the same age, the individual who had been convicted at a prior age had a much greater chance of being convicted at that age. For example, at age 16 the probability of 'onset' (or first conviction) within the 'high-level chronics' group was 0.321, whereas the 'post-onset' probability of conviction within this group was 0.695.

It is worth noting that in their initial article, Nagin and Land (1993) also modeled a state dependence variable (lagged indicator of conviction in the prior period), but they did so within the 'intermittency' portion of their model that only included controls for observed heterogeneity (through the inclusion of observed variables) rather than unobserved heterogeneity.[18] The intermittency concept allows for the possibility that periods of criminal activity

[18] The technical aspect of the intermittency component of their model is that it permits their semiparametric mixed Poisson model to be generalized as a 'zero inflated Poisson' model, which allows for more zeroes than would be expected by the standard Poisson distribution (Lambert 1992; Mullahy 1986; Zorn 1998).

may be interspersed with periods of inactivity, yet this inactivity does not signal the end of an individual's 'criminal career.' This portion of the model substantively investigates the factors that predict the probability of being an 'active' offender at a given age. Nagin and Land specified this component of the model to be predicted by age, age squared, a lagged indicator of conviction in the prior period, and a composite, time-stable measure called TOT (that was composed of measures of risk-taking attitude, parental criminality, a poor parenting indictor, and IQ). The parameter estimate for the lagged conviction indicator was significantly and positively related to the probability of being an active offender at a given age. It is interesting to note that the parameter estimate (1.09) for the lagged conviction indicator was nearly identical to the parameter estimate that Nagin and Farrington (1992*a*) found (1.16) in their standard probit model that did not account for unobserved heterogeneity. The intermittency component of the Nagin and Land (1993) analyses was important, since it explicitly demonstrated the presence of within-individual variation in criminal offending, but the authors noted that the theoretical importance of the concept of intermittency was problematic.

Subsequently, however, Horney, Osgood, and Marshall (1995) proposed an explanation for the periods of intermittent offending noted in the Nagin and Land study. These authors connected the possibility of periods of activity as being interspersed with periods of inactivity by drawing on the theory of Sampson and Laub. They argued that the 'intermittency' effect could be explained by short-term changes in 'local life circumstances.' Adopting a clear 'mixed' position, they noted (Horney, Osgood, and Marshall 1995: 658–9):

> Although a persistent underlying trait like self-control can influence both an individual's overall level of offending and his or her stability of marriage and employment, that shared influence does not mean that a relationship between offending and the life circumstances is necessarily spurious. It is still possible that involvement in those social institutions influences the likelihood of offending *during the time of involvement*. The high crime rate of the most persistent offender, rather than indicating a total lack of investment in social institutions, may instead reflect alternating periods of criminal activity and inactivity.

Using data on short-term variations in both 'social bonding' variables (such as going to school, working, living with a wife, drinking heavily, using drugs) and short-term variations of offending behaviors among a sample of incarcerated prisoners, the results of Horney, Osgood, and Marshall's (1995) hierarchical linear models analysis showed that short-term, within-individual changes in offending behavior were strongly related to changes in the local life circumstances of the offenders, net of controls for unmeasured heterogeneity in the propensity to offend. The men in this sample (600 serious adult offenders) were significantly less likely to be involved in criminal activity when they were working, were not using drugs or alcohol, and were living with their wives. This finding is entirely consistent with a 'state dependence' position and clearly highlights that short-term change in the offenders' criminal activity is intrinsically related to short-term improvement (or worsening) of their local life circumstances. The implication here is that if criminal arrest/conviction 'worsens' the local life circumstances of offenders through its 'negative effects' on the odds of obtaining a job, going to school, or living with a wife, then (even after controlling for individual criminal propensity) a strong association between previous and current offending is to be expected.

A more recent study concerning unobserved heterogeneity by Paternoster *et al.* (1997) followed the example of Sampson and Laub (1993) by examining the offending patterns of a sample of high-risk youthful offenders. Using a sample of 838 young, male offenders released from the training schools of the North Carolina Division of Youth Services in 1988–9, Paternoster *et al.* (1997) examined the yearly arrest counts of the offenders between the date of release and November 1994, when the follow-up period ended. Using the random effects negative binomial panel model, the results of their analyses are based on four to six years of arrest counts (i.e. an unbalanced panel) in the post-release period. Here the unobserved heterogeneity was assumed to be distributed according to the beta distribution.

Similar to Nagin and Farrington's study (1992*a*), Paternoster and his colleagues (1997) presented results in their study from both the standard negative binomial model with and without random effects for unobserved heterogeneity. A comparison of the log-likelihoods from the two models was used to test for the presence of significant persistent unobserved heterogeneity in the data, and a comparison of the results led the authors to conclude that there was a highly significant level of unobserved heterogeneity present in the data. The link between past and subsequent criminal activity was ascertained through the parameter estimate for the variable indicating whether the individual had been arrested in the previous year. The parameter estimate for the 'state dependence' variable was 0.631 and highly significant (t-value = 8.82) in the negative binomial model that only controlled for heterogeneity through the inclusion of observed (measured) covariates such as previous juvenile adjudications, race, gender, child abuse, family structure variables, and parental criminality. The parameter estimate was reduced to 0.228 in the random effects model, allowing for both measured and unmeasured heterogeneity, thus indicating a substantial reduction in the magnitude of this effect (64% reduction in absolute size) after controlling for persistent individual differences. However, it should be noted that there was still a significant and positive effect even after allowing for persistent individual differences in the proclivity to offend. Thus, these results also indicate support for the mixed position that allows for both population heterogeneity and state dependence processes as causes of criminal offending.

In the aforementioned study, Paternoster *et al.* (1997) further tested for differential effects of the state dependence process between the 'life-course-persistent' and the 'adolescent-limited' offenders as hypothesized by Moffitt (and by Patterson). Recall that the arguments of Moffitt (1993, 1997) led to the conclusion that the offending patterns of the life-course-persistent group should be dominated by a static, population heterogeneity process (that has run its full course by the end of childhood/beginning of adolescence), whereas the offending patterns of the adolescent-limited group should be dominated by the state dependence processes and should be relatively unaffected by variables representing individual differences.

Age at first adjudication was used here by Paternoster and his colleagues (1997) as a proxy variable representing whether the case is a life-course-persistent (high criminal propensity) or an adolescent-limited (low criminal propensity) offender. In a series of models (fourteen separate models to be exact), the authors use different cut-points for the age at which to divide the sample into the 'low' and 'high' criminal propensity groups, and then tested for differential state dependence effects on the basis of models run on the 'low' and 'high' criminal propensity groups separately.[19]

[19] Specifically, they tested whether the difference in the effect of the indicator of arrest in the prior period was statistically different from zero between the two groups.

The authors found age 15 to be a cut-point that generated different (arguably minor) state dependence effects between these two groups. The authors also found, however, that any estimated differential effects were highly sensitive to the age (at first adjudication) used to divide the sample into the two groups. As noted by Paternoster *et al.* (1997: 261), 'this result [the age 15 cut-point] strikes us as being consistent with the predictions offered by developmental theorists, but the lack of robustness in this result due to slight variations in the early/late onset sample division scheme leaves us with some question as to whether the result is artifactual.'

In a different study using the panel self-report data from the National Youth Survey, Paternoster and Brame (1997) investigated the relationship between past and subsequent criminal activity among a sample of more 'conventional' youths than those studied in the earlier Paternoster *et al.* (1997) study. This study used the 479 respondents who were aged 11 or 12 in the first wave of the NYS study and followed them over the next four waves of the study (to age 15 or 16). Paternoster and Brame estimated random effects probit and negative binomial models on the binary and count variables, respectively, reflecting self-reported delinquent activity. The delinquent acts used in constructing the measures were theft exceeding $5, motor vehicle theft, aggravated assault, sexual assault, gang fights, robbery, and breaking and entering (e.g. burglary). Paternoster and Brame were interested in the effects of two state dependence variables: a binary variable indicating delinquent behavior in the prior period (wave) and exposure to delinquent peers (proportion of friends who engage in delinquent acts).

The results of their analyses indicated that both prior delinquent activity and exposure to delinquent peers were positively and significantly related to current criminal activity. Controlling for persistent unobserved heterogeneity, which was found to be highly significant, the parameter estimate of the indicator of criminal activity in the prior wave was 0.86 in the probit model (participation model) and 0.984 in the negative binomial model (frequency model). The estimate from the logit model was very similar in magnitude to the estimate of Nagin and Paternoster (1991) in their analysis of the offending patterns of another 'conventional' sample. Similar to the Paternoster *et al.* (1997) study, Paternoster and Brame also test as to whether separate, distinct models (as hypothesized in Moffitt's theory) are necessary for describing the offending patterns of the life-course-persistent ('early starter') and adolescent-limited ('late starter') offenders. After dividing the sample into two groups on the basis of their 'offending propensity' at age 12, separate models were estimated on the two groups. The findings of these analyses also indicate (like the Paternoster *et al.* [1997] study) that there is no strong 'statistical evidence that these dynamic variables [prior offending and delinquent peers] exert different effects within groups of youngsters defined on the basis of their offending propensity at ages of 11 or 12 years and followed well into adolescence' (Paternoster and Brame 1997: 74).

More recently, in a discussion and comparison of three different methodological approaches to studying the relationship between past and subsequent criminal activity, Bushway, Brame, and Paternoster (1999) have presented an empirical application of the three different statistical approaches (random effects, semiparametric random effects, and fixed effects models) with the 1958 Philadelphia Birth Cohort data.[20] Using the 13,160 males in the birth cohort and seven periods of data covering ages 6–26 (each period covered three 'age years'), Bushway, Brame, and Paternoster (1999) apply a parametric random effects probit model, a semiparametric random effects probit model (like that used by Nagin and Land), and a conditional fixed effects logit model to a binary indicator of police contact during each period.[21] This was the first published presentation and application of the conditional fixed effects model as a potential methodological approach to study the

[20] Recall that Land, McCall, and Nagin (1996) also modeled the longitudinal offending patterns of the 1958 Philadelphia Birth Cohort. Land, McCall, and Nagin (1996) did include a state dependence variable (lagged indicator of conviction in the prior period) in their specification, but they did so within the 'intermittency' portion of their model that only included controls for observed heterogeneity (through the inclusion of observed variables) rather than unobserved heterogeneity. Nonetheless, the parameter estimate for the state dependence variable (in the intermittency part of their model) was 0.907 and highly significant.

[21] Conceptually, the conditional fixed effects logit model controls for persistent (time-stable) unobserved heterogeneity through the inclusion of a separate 'intercept' or constant for each individual, although for numerical reasons these 'intercepts' are 'conditioned' out of the likelihood function during estimation. In other words, this estimator makes no assumption about the mixing distribution. However, a significant limitation of the model is that it does not permit the use of exogenous variables including age or trend variables. As noted by Bushway, Brame, and Paternoster (1999), the strong age or 'trend' effects associated with criminal activity makes this is a serious limitation of this model (see also Maddala 1987; Hamerle and Ronning 1995).

processes of continuity and change in criminal offending over time. Similar to previous studies, the state dependence effect was modeled through the inclusion of a binary variable indicating police contact in the prior time period.

Results from two random effects probit models were presented first. The first model did not control for age ('trend') effects, and resulted in a parameter estimate for the state dependence variable (police contact in prior time period) of 1.052, which was highly significant (t-value = 48.13). The second model, which did control for time trend effects, produced a numerical estimate of 0.611 (t-value = 25.23) for the lagged police contact variable, indicating that a portion of the state dependence effect was partially the result of general temporal shifts in the probability of police contact. Both of these random effect models produced highly significant estimates of persistent unobserved heterogeneity (rho = 0.120 and 0.331 in the first and second model, respectively).

Next, semiparametric probit models with two (no time trend controls) and three (time trend controls) points-of-support were applied to the data. In the model with no time trend controls, the state dependence effect estimate was 1.035 (t-value = 49.25), while in the model with time trend controls the estimate was 0.608 (t-value = 23.72). It is interesting to note the nearly identical estimates of the state dependence effects from both the parametric and the semiparametric formulations of the probit model.

The results of the conditional fixed effects logit model, which specifically limits the independent variables in the model to the lagged dependent variable only, estimated the state dependence effect to be 1.591. Finally, after translating the 'logit' coefficient into 'probit units' by dividing the estimate by 1.6, the estimate was essentially identical (0.994) to the estimates obtained from the parametric and semiparametric models with no trend controls.

Discussion and Hypotheses Related to the Past and Subsequent Crime Relationship

There are two clear themes in the past decade of research on the relationship between past and subsequent criminal activity. First, there is unquestionably strong evidence of a significant amount of population heterogeneity in the propensity to commit criminal acts. Population heterogeneity was found to be significant in the sample of 'conventional' respondents (Paternoster and Brame 1997), samples that over-represent individuals from an urban area (Bushway, Brame, and Paternoster 1999) and also in a predominantly working-class area (Land and Nagin 1996; Nagin and Farrington 1992*a*), as well as in samples consisting of 'high-risk' youthful offenders (Paternoster *et al.* 1997; Sampson and Laub 1993). Only one study (Nagin and Paternoster 1991) failed to uncover a statistically significant amount of unobserved heterogeneity in their sample. From the state dependence perspective, prior involvement in crime exerts a real (causal) effect on subsequent criminality, possibly through its attenuating effects on the social bond, and the constraints it places on future legitimate opportunities (Sampson and Laub 1993), and/or its disruptive effects on 'local life circumstances' (Horney, Osgood, and Marshall 1995). Despite the findings of significant population heterogeneity in offending patterns over time, Nagin and Paternoster (2000) have noted that the challenging assertions of Gottfredson and Hirschi (1990) are critical to the field of criminology (both theoretically and empirically) because they have forced the discipline to acknowledge the importance of early life events, especially those within the family, and to consider how those events may have enduring consequences for individual criminal behavior over time.[22] In other words, the controversial and provocative theoretical arguments of Gottfredson and Hirschi (1990) have helped move the theoretical and empirical 'lenses' of criminologists away from being obstinately fixated on the adolescent years only.

A second theme in the literature of the relationship between past and subsequent criminal activity stresses the importance of state dependence processes in the lives of offenders. All of the studies reviewed above report statistically significant evidence in support of the state dependence position. That is, controlling for unobserved heterogeneity in the propensity to offend, previous criminal activity was still positively and significantly related to the probability or frequency of current offending. Thus, despite individual differences in the propensity to offend, changes in the lives of offenders appear to have important influences on subsequent criminal activity. Furthermore, these changes appear to be beyond the explanation of

[22] Cohen (1987) has made similar arguments about the theoretical importance of the Wilson and Herrnstein (1985) population heterogeneity theory.

a pure population heterogeneity argument. From the state dependence perspective, prior involvement in crime exerts a real (causal) effect on subsequent criminality though its attenuating effects on the social bond, and the constraints it places on future legitimate opportunities (Sampson and Laub 1993), and/or its disruptive effects on 'local life circumstances' (Horney, Osgood, and Marshall 1995). The empirical evidence thus indicates that whatever one's initial risk of crime, 'things can get better and they can get worse' (Nagin and Paternoster 2000: 137). Nagin and Paternoster note that Sampson and Laub's theory has been important to the field of criminology because it brought the relevance of state dependence processes back into the view of criminologists after a period of time when the trend in criminology was to 'push the causes of crime further back in the life course' (Grasmick *et al.* 1993: 5). Sampson and Laub thus reminded the discipline that events transpiring after adolescence have potentially serious and important consequences for maintaining or changing previous behavior patterns.

Clearly, however, a summary that perhaps best characterizes the current research to date on this topic is that both causal processes appear to be influencing participation in criminal activity; that is, the evidence supports the 'mixed' model where state dependence and population heterogeneity processes are both seen as necessary to explain both continuity and change in criminal behavioral patterns over time. In our judgement, the best example of the 'mixed' position is found in the two studies that compare the magnitude of the state dependence effects both prior to and after controlling for individual differences in the propensity to offend. The studies we speak of are the ones conducted by Nagin and Farrington (1992*a*) and Paternoster *et al.* (1997). In the standard probit models (without a correction for unobserved individual differences), the magnitude of the estimates prior to and after controlling for individual differences in the propensity to offend are 1.16 and 0.631 for the Nagin and Farrington (1992*a*) and Paternoster *et al.* (1997) studies, respectively; whereas in the parametric random effects models, the corresponding parameter estimates are 0.446 and 0.228. Yet, even in the face of a roughly 63 per cent reduction in the size of the parameter estimates (after controlling for unmeasured individual differences), the state dependence variables in both studies still remained positive, significant, and substantively meaningful. Thus, it appears that just as the pure state dependence perspective must concede that a significant amount of the link between past and subsequent criminal behavior is due to persistent individual differences in the proclivity to offend, the pure population heterogeneity perspective must concede that prior individual differences cannot explain all of the association between criminal activity at different points in time.

Recently, however, studies by Brame, Bushway, and Paternoster (1999) and Bushway, Brame, and Paternoster (1999) have each raised concerns about the validity of these important substantive conclusions due to possible artifactual flaws in prior research designs. These potential flaws concern the two main assumptions of the parametric random effects models regarding: (1) the distribution of the unobserved heterogeneity (i.e. the mixing distribution) and (2) the initial conditions assumption.

First, the possible problem with the assumption concerning the mixing distribution is that the correct statistical inferences concerning (dynamic) state dependence variables require that the mixing distribution be correctly specified (Bushway, Brame, and Paternoster 1999). As it now stands, currently, there is no agreed upon distribution assumed to correctly capture the distribution of criminal propensity in the population (Land and Nagin 1996; Nagin 2004), and, further, the nature of the distribution may be very different in 'low-risk' samples compared to that in 'high-risk' samples. It was such uncertainty regarding the actual mixing distribution in the population that led to Heckman and Singer's (1984) 'point-of-support' approximation (subsequently generalized by Nagin and Land to mixtures of Poisson models for event count data) whereby the continuous distribution, *whatever its shape*, is approximated by a discrete, multinomial distribution. The failure to correctly specify the unobserved heterogeneity distribution may result in both biased estimates and/or inflated significance tests (Bushway, Brame, and Paternoster 1999; Heckman and Singer 1984; Land, McCall, and Nagin 1996). For example, simulations by Bushway, Brame, and Paternoster (1999) showed that, when the actual distribution of unobserved heterogeneity becomes more skewed relative to the assumed normal distribution, the bias in the state dependence parameters becomes larger, thereby unjustly favoring the state dependence explanation.

Second, the initial conditions assumption requires that the behavioral process under study (e.g. criminal offending here) be observed at the initial start of the process (Hsiao 1986). Under this assumption, the lagged value will be zero for all cases during the first period under study (precisely because the process has not started). This condition ensures the lack of correlation between the lagged value in the first period and the time-stable (individual-specific) component of the error term in the model. Hsiao (1986) shows that it is this initial conditions process that allows the error term to fully incorporate heterogeneity in individual differences, and if one can meet this assumption, then the effect of the lagged value on the current value will be consistent, even if the lagged outcome value in subsequent periods is correlated with the persistent unobserved heterogeneity (Brame, Bushway, and Paternoster 1999).

As shown by Heckman (1981*c*) and Hsiao (1986), then, the main problem with violating the initial conditions assumption is that the parameter estimate for the lagged values of the outcome variable will be upwardly biased (i.e. favoring the state dependence perspective). The simulations of Brame, Bushway, and Paternoster (1999) provide further evidence that a failure to meet the initial conditions assumption upwardly biases the estimate of the lagged value (i.e. the state dependence effect). As Brame, Bushway, and Paternoster (1999: 612) note, 'the failure to observe initial conditions guarantees that the parameter estimates from the random-effects model will be biased and inconsistent.' The upwardly biased estimate is a direct consequence of the confounding of prior offending with the unobserved heterogeneity, whereby the parameter estimate for the lagged value absorbs some of the variation that should be rightly attributed to the time-invariant (individual-specific) component of the error term that represents population heterogeneity (Heckman 1981*c*).

Brame, Bushway, and Paternoster (1999) re-analyzed the data from the Paternoster and Brame (1997) study to see if the violation of the initial conditions in the data led to any erroneous conclusions regarding the impact of the state dependence variables. Using Heckman's (1981*c*) approximation method, developed to correct for violations of the initial conditions assumption, they found a further reduction in the importance of the state dependence variables (lessening the impact of the delinquent peer exposure variable and a complete reduction to non-significance of the prior offending variable) after the application of this correction. The authors thus concluded that 'reported coefficient estimates for dynamic factors could be biased because of problems with initial conditions' (Brame, Bushway, and Paternoster 1999: 636).

As a result of such analyses, a general doubt lingers in the field regarding the robustness and validity of the findings of previous studies: 'in the absence of clear knowledge about fidelity to model assumptions, researchers should adopt a healthy amount of skepticism in their observed findings' (Nagin and Paternoster 2000: 140). Supporting this notion (in a critical essay on the superfluous treatment of the assumptions of statistical models), Maltz (1994) has persuasively warned that criminologists must devote more attention to checking the assumptions of the statistical models they apply to crime data or risk possibly generating publishable yet erroneous/invalid results. Consider, for example, the two following points regarding the seven primary studies reviewed above. First, five of these studies rely entirely on the parametric random effects model and make no attempt (for obvious reasons of both data and software limitations) to check the robustness of their findings to the assumed distribution of the unobserved heterogeneity in their data. The two notable exceptions that do take advantage of the semiparametric formulation of the random effects model are the studies of Land and Nagin (1996) and Bushway, Brame, and Paternoster (1999). While the Nagin and Farrington (1992*a*) study did make use of the same data set as did Land and Nagin (1996), the state dependence variable relating past to current participation in criminal activity was specified differently between the two studies. The results of the analyses presented by Bushway, Brame, and Paternoster (1999) yielded virtually identical numerical and substantive results in both the parametric and semiparametric formulations of their statistical models. To date, then, the only study that has calculated the state dependence effect (with the same data and the same exact model specification) with both the parametric and semiparametric random effects models yielded identical substantive results for both models. As Bushway, Brame, and Paternoster (1999: 53) state, however, 'since there is no reason to believe, a priori, that the results of our substantive analyses are generalizable beyond the specific data set that we used, we think that multiple-method strategies for investigating questions such as the one addressed here . . . are necessary.' Thus, the degree to which the assumptions of the statistical models yield any substantive differences in the conclusions requires testing with other data sets such as those to be used in this study.

Second, only two of the six studies that employ the parametric random effects model use data that unquestionably do not violate the initial conditions assumption. These two studies are those of Nagin and Farrington (1992*a*) and Bushway, Brame, and Paternoster (1999). In the other four studies, the offending process had already been initiated at the point in time that each study began their panel, and thus there is a possibility that the estimates of the variables representing the association between past and subsequent criminal activity would be upwardly biased.

Indeed, the two studies using samples of high-risk respondents (Paternoster *et al.* 1997; Sampson and Laub 1993) relied entirely on the parametric random effects model and began their panel studies at a point in time when all of the respondents had already begun their criminal offending. Given the findings of Brame, Bushway, and Paternoster (1999) and Bushway, Brame, and Paternoster (1999) regarding the consequences of violating, these two aforementioned studies are suspect. This point is fundamentally critical because as Nagin and Farrington (1992*a*), Paternoster and Brame (1997), and Nagin and Paternoster (2000) have all hypothesized, the importance of state dependence variables may depend on the nature of the sample employed in one's study. Again, this assertion is based on the fact that studies showing stronger support for the state dependence perspective tend to employ 'low-risk' samples (and self-report data), whereas studies showing stronger support for the population heterogeneity perspective tend to employ 'higher-risk' samples and to use official statistics such as arrest or conviction data.[23] Paternoster and Brame (1997) speculated that such findings are consistent with the theoretical propositions of Moffitt's (1993) dual taxonomy theory because samples consisting of 'higher-risk' cases should contain a larger percentage of 'life-course-persistent' offenders (whose behavior is governed by static processes), whereas 'adolescent-limited' offenders (whose behavior is governed by dynamic processes) should constitute the majority of the respondents in 'low-risk' samples (see also Cernkovich and Giordano 2001).

In sum, there currently is some ambiguity about the state of the extant empirical evidence regarding the relationship between

[23] Again, it is important to bear in mind that while nearly all studies find evidence in support of both positions; it is the degree of support for each position that this issue concerns.

past and subsequent criminal activity, especially with respect to how robust the findings are with respect to assumptions of the statistical models employed and how important state dependence processes are in the population of 'high-risk' offenders. We concur with Nagin and Paternoster (2000: 131) that 'only by examining the sensitivity or robustness of research findings with different statistical models and different data can the field hope to come to an understanding about the tenability of population heterogeneity and state dependence.' Cernkovich and Giordano (2001) also have recently commented that there simply is 'scant evidence' regarding the empirical importance of these two explanations (state dependence and population heterogeneity) for continuity and discontinuity of criminal offending patterns across the life course, especially in both the serious offender population and in data sets that include ages beyond adolescence (see also Farrington 2003).

In direct response to these calls for further investigations of this key theoretical issue, our study will test the following four hypotheses concerning the relationship between past and subsequent criminal offending behavior:

H_5: There will be a statistically significant positive association between past and subsequent offending behavior.
H_6: After controlling for persistent individual differences in criminal propensity, the association between past and subsequent offending will be reduced to a non-significant level.
H_7: After controlling for persistent individual differences in criminal propensity, the association between past and subsequent offending behavior will be reduced in magnitude but will still be positive and statistically significant.
H_8: The association between past and subsequent offending behavior will be non-significant for the 'life-course-persistent' (high criminal propensity) group(s), while the effect should be substantial and significant for the 'adolescent-peaked' group.

The key hypotheses for the three theories discussed in this study are H_6, H_7, and H_8. Evidence supporting H_6 would lend credence to the theory of Gottfredson and Hirschi's self-control theory. Evidence supporting H_7 would be consistent with the predictions of Sampson and Laub's age-graded social control theory, and evidence supporting H_8 would appear to validate Moffitt's dual taxonomy theory.

Results concerning these four hypotheses are presented in Chapter 8 of this study. Here we will draw and build on the multi-method approach of Bushway, Brame, and Paternoster (1999) to test $\mathbf{H}_6$ and $\mathbf{H}_7$. More specifically, we will use both the parametric negative binomial random effects model and the semi-parametric mixed Poisson model of Nagin and Land to test these hypotheses. In addition, we will also employ standard negative binomial models with a set of binary variables that indicate latent class membership (from the latent class results presented in Chapter 7) to more definitively test the robustness of the presence (or absence) of state dependence effects in a longitudinal panel analysis of the offending patterns for three samples of California Youth Authority parolees.

To test the last hypothesis ($\mathbf{H}_{8,}$) separate models will be estimated on offenders assigned to a given latent class. It should be noted that $\mathbf{H}_8$ is a conditional hypothesis that requires the identification of an 'adolescent-peaked' group in the data sets. To date, tests concerning $\mathbf{H}_8$ have been accomplished after dividing the samples into two groups on more arbitrary grounds (e.g. age of onset) rather than by calculating the effects within a group shown to actually offend in an 'adolescent-limited' fashion. Before concluding the present chapter and moving on to Chapter 4, where we briefly describe the California Youth Authority, we discuss the potential contributions this study can make to the discipline of criminology.

Contributions to the Discipline

The proposed research conducted herein will attempt to make several contributions to the discipline of criminology. These contributions include a general accretion of knowledge to the study of the continuity and discontinuity of criminal offending patterns over the life course of chronic serious youthful offenders, as well as specific contributions that advance our current knowledge concerning both the relationships between age and crime and between past and subsequent criminal activity. A major potential contribution of this study centers on the nature of the samples employed in our analyses: the fact that we have acquired three separate samples from three different time periods, that the subjects in our study are followed over a longer period of time than most of the previous studies, and that the sample sizes employed here are larger than those used in previous studies makes our study unique.[24] Youthful offenders who commit the most serious crimes at a disproportionately high rate have to date been largely unavailable to social scientists (see, e.g., Cernkovich, Giordano, and Pugh 1985; Cernkovich and Giordano 2001; Laub and Sampson 2001), and therefore a detailed empirical analysis of their longitudinal criminal offending patterns will provide social scientists and policy makers with a more accurate characterization and deeper understanding of the longitudinal patterns of criminal activity across the life course of this select group of offenders.

To be more specific, we note that to date much of our knowledge concerning the serious, persistent young offender has been derived through analyses of the most frequent offenders (usually referred to as the chronic offenders) in birth cohort studies such as the 1945 and 1958 Philadelphia birth cohorts and with general population samples. The major finding of these Philadelphia birth cohort studies was that roughly 6 to 7 per cent of the individuals in the cohorts were responsible for more than half of all of the officially recorded police contacts reported for these cohorts (see, e.g., Tracy, Wolfgang, and Figlio 1985; Wolfgang, Figlio, and Sellin 1972). For example, Wolfgang and his colleagues report in the 1972 study that these young 'chronic criminals' were responsible for committing 63 per cent of all known Index crimes committed by the birth cohort members (as measured through police contacts)—including 82 per cent of all robberies, 73 per cent of all rapes, 69 per cent of all aggravated assaults, and 71 per cent of the murders.[25]

However, several re-analyses of the 1945 birth cohort data question exactly how chronic or serious most of the chronic offenders in these types of samples (e.g. birth cohort studies and/or national probability samples) really are. For example, analyses by Bernard and Ritti (1991) indicated that only 35 per cent of all police contacts in the Philadelphia birth cohort ever resulted in an actual

[24] The bulk of the analyses in this study involve the longitudinal offending patterns of 4,866 sample subjects (n = 1,989 in the 1981–2 sample, n = 1,443 in the 1986–7 sample, and n = 1,434 in the 1991–2 sample).

[25] It was findings such as these that initially aroused interest in the application of selective incapacitation policies. Of course, selective incapacitation policies will only produce their desired effect if the high-rate offenders commit crimes at a relatively constant, stable rate across the age distribution (see Ezell and Cohen 1997; Gottfredson and Hirschi 1986; Haapanen 1990).

formal arrest, and that an astounding 31 per cent of the 627 'chronic' offenders (those with five or more police contacts) identified in the 1972 study were either never arrested (n = 48) or arrested only one time (n = 145) in their entire juvenile criminal career. Similarly, analyses by Weitekamp *et al.* (1995) showed that 73 per cent of the aggravated assaults in the 1945 Philadelphia birth cohort were committed by 32 of the 627 chronic offenders and 71 per cent of the homicides were committed by only 10 of the chronic offenders. In addition, studies of criminal offending that employ the use of general population samples generally contain too few serious youthful offenders (because of their low base rate in the population) to allow for reliable descriptions and investigations of their offending behaviors over time (see, e.g., Cernkovich, Giordano, and Pugh 1985; Loeber and Farrington 1998). For comparative purposes, we inform our readers that it has been estimated that only 1 out of every 1,000 police contacts will result in a single case being committed to the California Youth Authority (Legislative Analysts Office 1995).

Second, the length of time that the cases in our three samples will be longitudinally tracked allows for rigorous testing of the extent and nature of the patterns of continuity among this population. Standard (between-individual) empirical assessments of continuity in offending behavior often use cross-sectional data and/or short-term panel data that preclude most studies from addressing the main questions to be investigated in our study (as they generally require the use of extensive longitudinal data):

> Most criminological research consists of cross-sectional 'snap-shots' or short-term panel studies of crime over the full life span. As a consequence, relatively little is known about desistence and, for that matter, the processes of persistent criminal behavior through the life course. Indeed, the characteristics that distinguish persistence in a life of crime from desistence within any group of high-risk offenders are generally unknown.
>
> (Laub and Sampson 2001: 1)

Our study will attempt to addresses this limitation in the empirical literature by following three samples of chronic serious offenders from the date of their first recorded arrest up until 30 June 2000.[26]

[26] For the three release samples combined, the earliest year of birth was 1956 and the latest was 1978. The 25th percentile for the year of birth was 1963, the median was 1967, and the 75th percentile was 1971.

As we demonstrate latter, the follow-up period for our data is considerably longer than the previous studies reviewed above.

Laub and Sampson (2001) also point out that our knowledge of the long-term offending patterns among serious offenders has been hampered, not only by a lack of studies that longitudinally follow this group for extended periods of time, but also because of the disjunction between the juvenile and adult record systems. Crime data often suffer from the division of juvenile and adult criminal record-keeping systems, meaning that there is often a dearth of data bridging the juvenile and adult years in longitudinal studies and that many data sets are often blind to criminal activity on the other side of the juvenile–adult age boundary (Blumstein *et al.* 1986; Cernkovich and Giordano 2001; Laub and Sampson 2001). The research undertaken in our study is unique because it entails following three samples of youthful offenders from the date of their initial arrest, through the year(s) they were incarcerated in the California Youth Authority, and then into adulthood, and well into adulthood for some individuals (age 43 was the oldest age). The first sample in our study was released on parole in fiscal year 1981–2 and was followed up through their late thirties to early forties (depending on age at time of release from the CYA). The second sample was released in fiscal year 1986–7 and followed up through their early to mid-thirties. Finally, the third sample was released in fiscal year 1991–2 and followed up through their mid- to late twenties.[27] We believe that these data sets comprise one of the most comprehensive sets of longitudinal data on the serious youthful offender population that has yet been gathered. In sum, the frequency and seriousness of criminal activity displayed among our samples, the length of the follow-up period employed here, and the sophistication of the statistical models employed in our study should allow for a rigorous examination of criminal offending patterns over the life course with respect to the critical substantive and methodological issues identified in this chapter.

The empirical fact is that we currently know very little about the offending patterns of very serious youthful offenders; we simply lack evidence regarding fundamental questions concerning the criminal offending patterns of these individuals. In a recent book

[27] For the 1981–2, 1986–7, and 1991–2 samples, the average ages at the end of follow-up period (30 June 2000) were 37, 33, and 27, respectively.

surveying the current state of empirical knowledge on serious and violent juvenile offenders, the editors concluded with a section entitled, 'Developing a Research Agenda.' Here, they noted that there are currently many 'gaps' in the knowledge concerning the nature and development of the longitudinal criminal offending patterns of serious and violent juvenile offenders, including the validity of offender typologies (e.g. 'life-course-persistent' and 'adolescent-limited' offenders) in this population, the nature and extent of the adult criminal offending patterns and adult life experiences of this group of offenders, and which covariates predict a continued persistence in offending within this group (Loeber and Farrington 1998). Similarly, Laub and Sampson (2001: 10) call for a theoretical and empirical focus on the patterns of continuity (persistence) and discontinuity (desistence) among samples of persistent and serious offenders, noting that 'criminologists should not spend much time or energy studying termination and desistence for low-rate offenders' because such offending is normative during adolescence. The analyses in this study hence should provide needed evidence concerning the nature and extent of criminal offending across the life courses of the most serious youthful offenders.

In sum, we currently have very limited information concerning the actual shape of the aggregate age–crime curve within the serious offender population, on what 'latent classes' of offenders are present in such a population, and if the identified latent classes are resilient across time. As Cernkovich and Giordano (2001: 405–6) note:

> if we accept the premise that there is a small group of offenders who do not begin and age out of crime in the same fashion as most offenders, then it is important that researchers examine in detail the extent to which the stability–change paradox is a function of the existence of two distinct populations of offenders . . . however this issue has not been systematically examined, in part because of the relatively scant (though increasing) research focusing on serious chronic offenders . . . it is essential that the research agenda be expanded to include an even greater focus on this group and . . . that it include attention to patterns of antisocial activity prior to and beyond the adolescent years.

Furthermore, even though there is a group of offenders who have been semantically labeled 'life-course-persistent', to date there is no convincing empirical evidence to prove that this group of offenders is deserving of such a demonstrative label. A key question yet to be answered is: how persistent are the 'life-course-persistent' offenders? Due to the highly selective nature of who gets committed to the California Youth Authority, samples of offenders released from the CYA have a unique potential to address this question. The data we describe in Chapter 6 aim to address these specific limitations by applying Nagin and Land's finite mixture model to the three large samples of serious youthful offenders that are followed for an extensive period of time.

Our review of the prior studies of the relationship between past and subsequent criminal activity also made it clear that there is a critical need for the continued examination of this topic. As indicated above, previous studies have consistently found evidence in support of the mixed-model position; however, questions remain regarding the authenticity of the state dependence effects uncovered in the prior research, especially within high-risk samples, due to the possible methodological consequences of violating the assumptions of the parametric random effects models. The results to be presented in Chapter 8 of this study should contribute to the extant literature on this topic by examining the relationship between past and subsequent criminal offending.

Before getting to the methods and the data analysis chapters in this study, however, our attention in the next chapter is first focused on the California Youth Authority, the institution from which our samples have been released on parole.

4

The California Youth Authority

As argued in Chapter 3, one of the contributions of this study is derived from the nature of the data to be used in the analyses. No other published research to date analyzes such a large, contemporary sample of America's most serious youthful offenders over such a long period of time. To successfully argue that our samples represent California's most serious youthful offenders, readers must first understand the California Youth Authority's (CYA) role in the state's judicial system and how offenders end up as 'wards' in their institutions. Thus, in this chapter, we briefly describe the CYA in order to contextualize the nature of the data in this study.

The California Youth Authority

Stated succinctly, the CYA is:

> the state-level placement option for juvenile offenders in California and is intended for young offenders who require treatment or control that cannot be provided locally. The CYA gets the most serious young offenders in the state, both by virtue of the seriousness of their current criminal behaviors and by having failed at numerous attempts to change their behavior at the local and county levels.
>
> (Haapanen and Britton 2002: 220)

The CYA is the sole statewide agency in California with control over youthful offenders.[1] The CYA was originally established (in 1941) to serve two purposes. First, it was to be a sentencing alternative (instead of the adult Department of Corrections) for young adult criminals between the ages of 18 and 21, and second, it was to be a dispositional alternative for juveniles adjudicated

[1] The juvenile justice system in California is largely structured at the county level. The majority of all offenders are handled at the county level.

in juvenile court for both criminal and status offences (State of California 1993).[2] The original paradigm under which the CYA was founded and operated was known as the 'medical model' or 'rehabilitative ideal,' and legislators originally conceived of the CYA as an alternative way to treat young offenders outside of the criminal justice system, hopefully preventing these young offenders from becoming 'career criminals' (Bolen 1972).

From the 1940s through the early 1970s, the California Youth Authority was renowned as a pioneer in the development of experimental and innovative programs that tested the key tenets of the rehabilitative ideal. During this time, the CYA (largely in response to overwhelming demand for its institutional services) established innovative treatment projects, diversion programs, and probation subsidy services, as well as establishing youth services bureaux designed to prevent crime and delinquency (Bolen 1972).

Through the mid-1970s, the CYA effectively maintained its reputation as a progressive and innovative treatment system for youthful offenders. However, a noticeable shift occurred in the CYA by the mid-1970s. A myriad of forces were responsible for the changes, including administrative, legislative, and case law adjustments, changes in the nature of the youthful offender population itself, and a developing general negative public opinion regarding the appropriateness and effectiveness of the rehabilitative ideal (Bolen 1972; DeMuro, DeMuro, and Lerner 1988; State of California 1993, 1996). The result was that by the early 1980s there had been a shift in policy to one that emphasized a 'get tough on crime' orientation favoring punishment, just deserts, and incapacitation (see, e.g., DeMuro, DeMuro, and Lerner 1988; Little Hoover Commission 1994; State of California 1996). For example, in 1970 the average time served in the CYA for first commitments was 10.5 months, in 1980 it was 13 months, and in 1990 it was 25.4 months (CYA 1971, 1981, 1991). By 1998 the mean time served had increased all the way to 32 months (CYA 1999). Symbolic of all these changes, the CYA Director Francisco Alarcon removed the words 'Training Schools' from the names of CYA facilities in 1997, replacing this with 'Correctional Facilities,' which was argued to be more descriptively appropriate (Gladstone and Rainey 1999).

[2] The age demarcating the end of the juvenile years in the state of California is age 18. The term 'youthful' is generally used to represent ages under 21.

By the early 1980s, the final result of these developments was a new reputation of the CYA as the 'placement of last resort' for the youthful offender population in the nation's most populated state (Little Hoover Commission 1994). The CYA increasingly came to be viewed as a 'post graduate school requiring an undergraduate degree in unsuccessful disposition for admittance' (State of California 1993: 8).

The core of the treatment program in the CYA institutions is theoretically designed to help the wards overcome deficits in education, employment skills, and basic social skills, and the CYA offers several specialized and supplementary programs (e.g. counseling for substance abuse and sex offenders, victims awareness programs) in its efforts to rehabilitate wards into productive, law-abiding citizens. However, it should be noted that the CYA has been subject to severe criticism over the last twenty or so years with respect to the size and design of its institutions, the availability and actual delivery of its programs in practice, the methods and delivery of security inside the institutions, abuse of the wards by staff, and the phenomenal rate of violence inside the institutions (see, e.g., DeMuro, DeMuro, and Lerner 1988; Gladstone and Rainey 1999; Krisberg 2003; Lerner 1982, 1986, 1989; Little Hoover Commission 1994; Rainey and Gladstone 1999).[3]

Becoming a Ward of the California Youth Authority

According to California law, an offender can only be committed to the CYA after a judge finds it probable that the offender will benefit from treatment at the CYA (Cal. Welf. & Inst. Code: 707.2).[4] County probation officers first make a placement recommendation to the judge after examining local treatment options, the youth's prior record, the current commitment offense, and other relevant factors. After considering the recommendation of the probation

[3] We have made several other resources regarding the CYA (including more on its history and the criticisms of it) available via the web; see Appendix C).

[4] Becoming a ward of the CYA is an extremely complex process not easily reducible to blanket statements, and the legislation regarding eligibility has changed considerably over the last twenty years. Here we intend to present a description of this process so that the reader understands the nature of individuals that end up in the CYA especially for the time period studied here (1980–91), but we do not claim that this is an exhaustive treatment of the process of becoming a CYA ward. This is but an informative description of the process.

department, a CYA placement for the offender can be recommended if the judge believes that no suitable local treatment is available, although the judge's recommendation can be challenged by the youth's attorney and is subject to further appellate review (State of California 1993; Little Hoover Commission 1994). At this point, the youth's probation report and the judge's order are sent to the CYA intake unit, and the intake unit decides (based on this material) whether it is likely that the youth would benefit from treatment at the CYA. The notion of whether a potential commitment will benefit from treatment involves (State of California 1993): (1) determining the possibility the youth will '*materially benefit*' from treatment such that either the offender's criminal propensity can be reduced or eliminated within the available confinement/jurisdiction time (and 'adequate facilities' exist) or incapacitation is necessary for the protection of the public; and (2) determining if there is a reasonable possibility that incarcerating the youth in the adult Department of Corrections would *exacerbate* the offender's criminal propensity in comparison with confinement in the CYA.[5] The first standard is applied to possible commitments from both juvenile court and adult court, while the second standard is applied only to possible commitments from adult court (State of California 1993). The CYA has the right to refuse admittance to any youth it believes might not benefit from its care and treatment, but the CYA rarely refuses admission to commitments from the juvenile court (State of California 1993; Little Hoover Commission 1994).

Once an offender is committed and accepted for treatment in the CYA (i.e. found amenable to treatment), he or she makes an initial appearance before the Youthful Offender Parole Board (YOPB). The YOPB is staffed by seven members appointed by the governor who have the formal responsibility for making treatment decisions of all offenders committed to the CYA. The decisions made by YOPB include: establishing dates of parole consideration hearings, dates of actual parole release, determining the conditions of parole, deciding when violations of the terms of parole occur, and deciding whether to 'revoke' an offender's parole (Little Hoover Commission 1994). The YOPB also determines the various treatment

[5] See State of California (1993) for a complete discussion of determining whether a ward will 'materially benefit' from treatment in the CYA.

programmes that would presumably benefit each ward and that must be completed before he or she becomes eligible for parole.

The YOPB uses several criteria in determining the length of time a ward will serve prior to their earliest parole consideration date. For most offenders, their initial sentence length has historically varied from approximately 1–7 years, depending on the severity of the commitment offense. The base commitment offenses for which youthful offenders are committed to the CYA are divided into seven categories. Category 1 contains the most serious offenses including murder and kidnapping with serious injury, whereas Category 7 contains minor crimes such as petty theft and vandalism. The YOPB can, however, deviate from the recommended sentence length by considering the youth's prior record and any mitigating or aggravating circumstances surrounding the commitment offense (Little Hoover Commission 1994: 106). However, no ward can serve time exceeding either (1) the amount of time that an adult could serve for the same offense (Cal. Welf. & Inst. Code: 1766) or (2) beyond the set age (of 21, 23, or 25), at which point the CYA loses its jurisdiction (Cal. Welf. & Inst. Code: 1766).

Types of CYA Commitments

Historically speaking, youthful offenders have been committed to the CYA as one of three broad commitment types: juvenile court, adult court, and state prison 'housing cases' (State of California 1993). A *juvenile court commitment* has historically referred to a juvenile who was (1) between the ages of 11 and 17 at the time of their criminal offense, (2) adjudicated in juvenile court, and then (3) committed directly to the CYA from the juvenile courts. An *adult court commitment* refers to two different types of offenders committed to the CYA. The first group refers to juveniles remanded to and convicted in adult criminal court (not sentenced for a life term) and then subsequently found amenable for treatment in the CYA.[6] The second group refers to young adults between the ages of 18 and 21 who were convicted in adult court and were found amenable for treatment in the CYA. Adult court commitments were

[6] To clarify consider this point, 'a central premise of the YA's application of the Welf. & Inst. Code 707.2 is that remanded wards will be accepted as direct YA commitments if they meet one of the two amenability criteria, i.e. material benefit and exacerbation' (State of California 1993: 6).

still considered 'regular YA' cases, were assigned a normal 5-digit CYA number, and were subject to the jurisdiction of YOPB. In 1982, however, California voters passed Proposition 8 that prevented direct commitments from the adult criminal court for offenders aged 18–21 convicted of a 'serious felony' (State of California 1993). Before the passage of this proposition, about 50 per cent of the commitments to the CYA were adult referrals, and the passage of Proposition 8 served to appreciably reduce the percentage of adult court commitments (State of California 1993).[7]

Finally, a *state prison commitment* (often known as a *housing case* or *M Case*) refers to an offender who was under the age of 21 (including both adults and remanded juveniles) at the time he/she was *sentenced to* the California Department of Corrections (CDC). These offenders from adult criminal court were 'housed' in the CYA if they met a number of conditions, including (but not limited to) space availability, treatment availability, not currently on parole from the CYA, not previously determined to be non-amenable to CYA treatment, and not previously discharged as a ward of the CYA (State of California 1993). M Cases, unlike direct adult court commitments, could be transferred to the CDC if they presented either a 'threat to institutional security' or were found to be 'intractable'. M Cases were not 'regular YA' cases, were not assigned a normal 5-digit CYA number (instead receiving a number such as M0001), and were not subject to the YOPB (and thus these offenders did not make formal appearances before it). This M Case pathway to the CYA began in 1983 as a response to Proposition 8, which explicitly prohibited commitment to the CYA for offenders sentenced in adult court for the commission of a serious felony (e.g. felony Index crimes).

To clarify, Figure 4.1 depicts six possible routes into the CYA for both juvenile and young adult offenders. The far left path in Figure 4.1 (Route 1) depicts the pathway for the juvenile offenders found 'fit' for juvenile court and committed directly to the CYA.

[7] For example, in 1980 the CYA population was composed of 55.2 per cent juvenile court commitments and 44.8 per cent adult court commitments. In 1995 the corresponding figures were 81 per cent and 19 per cent (adult court commitments here include both direct commitments and M Cases) (State of California 1993; Legislative Analysts Office 1996). Finally, by 31 December 2000, 95.4 per cent of the population was made up of juvenile court commitments (Legislative Analysts Office 2001).

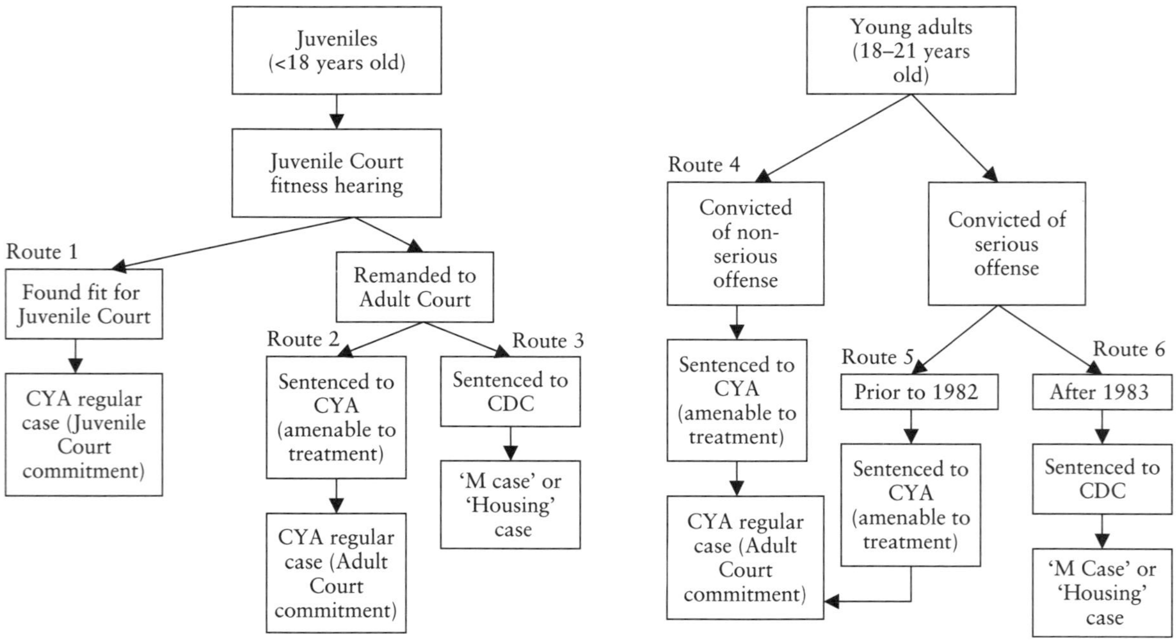

FIGURE 4.1. Graphical depiction of routes of entrance into the California Youth Authority.

The other two pathways reflect how juveniles (under the age of 18) found to be 'unfit' for regular juvenile court and 'waived/remanded' to adult court ended up in the CYA. Recall, juveniles remanded to adult court could have subsequently been committed to the CYA as a direct adult court commitment as long as they were perceived to be 'amenable to treatment' in the CYA; this is Route 2 depicted in Figure 4.1. Route 3 depicts a pathway that opened up in 1983 as a response to Proposition 8, a juvenile M Case. Thus, one segment of the 'M Case' population refers to juvenile offenders (less than age 18 at the time of the offense) who were then remanded to and convicted in adult court, subsequently sentenced to the CDC, and then finally ordered housed in the CYA.[8]

The right-hand side of Figure 4.1 depicts three routes to the CYA for young adult offenders. First, young adult offenders convicted of a relatively non-serious offense in adult court could have been directly committed to the CYA as an adult court commitment (Route 4). Otherwise, if one were sentenced before or after Proposition 8, young adult offenders could have been committed directly to the CYA if they were deemed amenable to treatment (Route 5), or they could have been 'housed' in the CYA if they met strict regulations and qualified as an M Case (Route 6). Incidentally, legislation passed in 1996 nearly removed this route into the CYA, while legislation in 1998 served to entirely remove this route.[9]

In addition to being classified according to whether a ward is committed from the juvenile court, adult court, or as an M Case, wards in custody of the CYA are also classified on the basis of three broad additional categories: (1) *first commitments*, (2) *parole violators*, and (3) *recommitments*. First commitments are wards committed to the CYA for the first time. Parole violators are wards previously incarcerated in the CYA, released on parole, and who then have had their parole revoked for violation(s) of the terms of parole (e.g. arrest for a criminal offense, gang activity, positive drug

[8] In 2000, legislation was passed that prohibited the sentencing of remanded juveniles ages 16 or older that were convicted in adult court to the CYA (CYA 2001).

[9] The 1996 legislation limits M Cases housed in the CYA to those under age 18 at the time of sentencing or those who have a potential release date set by the CDC to be prior to age 21. Prior to this legislation, M Cases could have been housed at the CYA until the age of 25. M Cases that will not be released before age 21 are now automatically transferred to the CDC at age 18 (Legislative Analysts Office 2001). The 1998 legislation prohibited the commitment of individuals over the age of 18.

TABLE 4.1. Characteristics of the California Youth Authority and first commitments, by year

Characteristic	*Year*												
	1980	*1981*	*1982*	*1983*	*1984*	*1985*	*1986*	*1987*	*1988*	*1989*	*1990*	*1991*	*1992*
CYA													
Total admissions	3,968	4,083	3,316	2,891	3,216	3,756	3,835	3,643	3,776	3,631	3,615	3,474	3,837
Average daily population	5,179	5,699	5,810	5,869	6,081	6,638	7,680	8,448	8,812	8,394	8,096	8,098	8,310
% capacity	92	102	102	103	103	114	131	146	154	141	132	129	126
First commitments													
Length of stay (in months)	12.9	13.1	14.2	15	16.1	17.1	17.8	18.8	21.9	21.6	22.1	21.8	24.9
Court													
Juvenile %	55.2	53.1	67.3	77.2	66.2	58.9	60.7	66.9	68.9	66.7	67.3	70.9	69.4
Criminal (adult) %	44.8	46.9	32.7	22.8	33.8	41.1	39.3	33.1	31.1	33.3	32.7	29.1	30.6
Commitment Offense													
Violent %	49.9	49.1	45.0	42.1	41.2	39.8	38.3	35.2	37.4	41.0	47.6	51.3	57.2
Property %	43.5	44.9	47.5	47.7	46.5	47.3	44.2	42.7	38.2	34.9	32.5	31.8	28.4
Drug %	2.3	2.1	2.7	5.6	5.6	7.0	12.0	15.9	18.4	18.6	15.0	11.0	9.1
Other %	4.3	3.9	4.8	4.6	6.7	5.9	5.5	6.2	6.0	5.5	4.9	5.9	5.3
Ethnicity:													
White %	33.7	31.9	32.5	31.1	31.1	34.4	30.5	27.7	25.8	22.9	20.4	18.4	17.2
Hispanic %	28.6	27.5	28.2	30.8	29.8	29.9	30.7	32.4	30.5	33.6	38.6	40.9	46.2
African-American %	35.4	38.0	36.7	35.2	36.0	32.6	34.2	36.0	39.0	37.5	34.3	31.7	29.0
Other %	2.3	2.6	2.6	2.9	3.1	3.1	4.6	3.9	4.7	6.0	6.7	9.0	7.6

Note: Adapted from 'California Youth Authority Committee Report: A Study of the Departmental Ward Intake Policy' (State of California 1993), and also incorporating information provided by the Ward Information and Parole Research Bureau of the CYA. With the exception of the 'Length of stay' calculation (which is based on first commitments *released* during that year), the characteristics listed in this table refer to first commitments *admitted* to the CYA during the specified year.

test, failure to be employed, and AWOL). Finally, recommitments are wards previously committed to the CYA, released from the CYA, and then subsequently recommitted to the CYA again for a new criminal offense.

A basic description of the CYA during the time period covering our sampling frames can be found in Table 4.1, which shows the average daily population, the average length of stay for wards paroled during each year depicted, and some characteristics of first commitments to the CYA from 1980 to 1992. The policy changes noted earlier reflect the CYA as increasingly becoming an institution focused on housing offenders for longer periods of time. Table 4.1 indicates that there was a general linear upward trend over this period in both the average daily population at CYA facilities, and in the average length of time served by wards. Comparing 1981 to 1992, for instance, the data show that the average daily CYA population increased from 5,699 to 8,310 persons (a 46% increase), while the average length of stay at a CYA facility went from 13.1 months to 24.9 months (a 90% increase).

Given the dramatic increase in the average length of stay seen in Table 4.1, an interesting question arises. The question concerns whether that increase in time served was due to changes in the types

TABLE 4.2. Average length of stay (in months), by commitment offense and year of release

Year of release	*First degree murder*	*Aggravated assault*	*Enhanced robbery*	*First degree burglary*	*Narcotic sales*	*Narcotic possession*
1980	32.1	NA	18.7	12.6	14.6	12.7
1981	38.1	17.2	19.0	12.9	10.2	10.8
1982	41.1	19.3	19.9	12.8	15.1	11.4
1983	53.5	20.3	21.4	15.2	14.9	12.4
1984	49.5	21.3	24.6	13.1	17.1	11.6
1985	51.7	23.7	25.0	14.7	20.9	13.7
1986	55.2	25.6	28.2	17.1	14.2	15.8
1987	62.8	27.2	28.3	19.9	18.3	19.0
1988	63.8	30.7	36.9	23.7	23.7	21.0
1989	72.0	32.1	35.3	23.3	25.8	21.7
1990	74.5	29.0	34.3	23.2	25.5	23.4
1991	76.9	28.8	32.7	22.6	25.1	22.6
1992	74.5	28.2	31.5	21.8	25.9	21.7

Note: Information was obtained from the summary reports entitled 'Length of Stay of Youth Authority Wards' that are produced each year by the Ward Information and Parole Research Bureau of the CYA. First degree murder in 1980 was for all types of murder.

of offenses that offenders were sentenced to the CYA for committing (e.g. an increasing number of cases sentenced for violent offenses) or whether that increase was occurring 'across the board' for most offense types. Table 4.2 shows the actual average length of time (in months) served prior to release on parole for six different commitment offense types. The general trend in this table clearly indicates an overall tendency to keep wards incarcerated for longer periods over time for all offenses. For example, wards committed for aggravated assault that were released in 1981 spent 17.2 months in the CYA on average, whereas the individuals released in 1992 for committing the same offense 28.2 months in the CYA. For robbery, the comparable numbers for those two time points were 19 and 31.5 months, respectively.

Having described the CYA and thus the nature of the offenders in our sample, we next turn our attention to describing the specific data we used to conduct the subsequent analyses of this study.

5

Data and Methods

This chapter details the data and methods to be used in the analyses to be presented in Chapters 6, 7, and 8. The first section of this chapter describes the data sources, the specific variables to be used in the data sets, and the limitations of these data. This section also contains a description of how the final analytic samples were constructed. We conclude this chapter with a brief discussion of the statistical methods to be employed in our study. Readers interested in a thorough discussion of these methods are directed to Appendix A, which contains a technical description and comparison of the Poisson model, the standard negative binomial model, the finite mixture or semiparametric random effects Poisson model of Nagin and Land (1993; Land and Nagin 1996; Land, McCall, and Nagin 1996), and the parametric random effects negative binomial model.

The Three Release Samples

As mentioned previously, the data used in this study consist of three samples of California Youth Authority wards. Norman Skonovd and Rudy Haapanen of the CYA's Research Bureau had previously collected the data for the two earliest samples (1981–2, 1986–7) (Skonovd and Haapanen 2000); the data for the 1991–2 sample were collected by the authors (with funding for the data collection provided by a grant from the National Institute of Justice).[1] To maintain consistency across the three samples, the 1991–2 sample was coded according to the same rules and procedures used in collecting the two prior samples. The only differences in the coding rules pertained to the data on prior criminal history (as described below).

[1] NIJ Grant Number #98—CE—VX—0026.

The two earliest samples are based on data collected on 2,086 wards released from the California Department of the Youth Authority institutions in fiscal year 1981–2 (1 July 1981 to 30 June 1982) and 2,078 wards released in fiscal year 1986–7 (1 July 1986 to 30 June 1987).[2] Initially, a random sample of 2,200 wards was drawn from the 4,425 wards released from Youth Authority institutions in fiscal year 1981–2 and another random sample was obtained for 2,200 wards from the 3,048 wards released in fiscal year 1986–7 (Skonovd and Haapanen 2000). Of the 2,200 wards in the 1981–2 sample, 114 cases were removed from the study because their records were 'court-ordered seals,' which prevents any access to their files.[3] This resulted in a 2,086 ward data file for this baseline data set. Of the 2,200 wards in the 1986–7 sample, 122 cases were removed for the same reason. This resulted in a 2,078 ward data file for the second data set. Together, these two samples provide records on 4,164 individual wards.

The arrest data for these two samples originally were only available through 31 December 1991 for the 1981–2 sample and through 31 December 1990 for the 1986–7 sample. We have, however, updated the arrest data for these two samples through 30 June 2000. The fact that the coded cases did not appear to be significantly different from the initial sample on any critical variables is not surprising given that 70 per cent of the initial sample was coded and that the cases were strictly coded according to their random numbers.

The 1991–2 sample is based on data collected on 1,527 wards released from the California Department of the Youth Authority institutions in fiscal year 1991–2 (1 July 1991 to 30 June 1992). Initially, a random sample of 2,198 wards was drawn from the total of 4,030 wards released from Youth Authority institutions in that fiscal year.[4] Of the 2,198 cases, 13 of the sample members were

[2] Throughout this study, the term '*sample stay*' is used to refer to the incarceration period in the CYA that resulted in the ward being released during the sampling time frame. The date of release for the sample stay was the key defining element that resulted in the ward having been included in one of the samples.

[3] When a CYA ward's records are ordered 'sealed' by the court, the ward's CYA Master Files are sealed and the ward's 5-digit 'YA number' is replaced with an S and 4 digits (e.g. S0001). Law then prohibits access to the ward's juvenile offending history and CYA Master File.

[4] The sample initially consisted of 2,200 cases, but two individuals were sampled twice because they had been released twice during the sampling time frame. We only

subsequently removed because their records were 'court-ordered seals' (resulting in an initial file of 2,185 cases).

Importantly, prior to beginning the formal coding on the 1991–2 sample, concerns arose over possible time and budget limitations given that cases were taking longer to code by coders at the culmination of the training sessions than previously estimated. The decision was made that guaranteeing accuracy of the coded cases would be of greater value compared to the speedy collection of data for the entire 2,198 cases. Accordingly, a random number was assigned to each case in the sample at the outset of the formal coding process, and cases were then coded according to their random number (rank ordered from lowest to highest). This ensured that at the end of the available time allotted and available financial resources, the resulting sample would still be a random subset of the initial sample. At the point in time when both the time and financial resources had been exhausted, 1,527 of the original 2,198 (70%) cases had been coded. Thus, the final file for the 1991–2 sample consisted of a total of 1,527 wards. Comparisons of the wards coded with the original entire sample indicated no significant differences in terms of ethnicity, county of commitment, commitment offense, court of commitment, and the probability of arrest after release from the CYA.[5] The fact that the coded cases did not appear to be significantly different from the remainder of the initial sample on any critical variables is not surprising given that 70 per cent of the initial sample was coded and that the cases were strictly coded according to their random numbers; thus, the 'randomness' of the file was maintained even though the entire sample initially drawn could not be coded.

We have also updated mortality data for the two earliest samples and collected original mortality data on the 1991–2 sample though

allowed each of these individual's one record in the data file, and we selected the later release date for these two individuals. The later release data was selected so as to not artificially create a very rapid failure time, which would have been assured if we had chosen the earlier release date.

[5] The comparisons were made based on the fact that some variables were available regardless of whether the case was coded. Certain information is available on all wards committed to the CYA through the OBITS (Offender Based Institutional Tracking System) computer system. Further, since the arrest data after the sample release was obtained electronically, we obtained the post-release criminal history data on all available cases.

31 December 1999. The possible mortality of the subjects in this study is important for two reasons. First, we did not want a ward to appear as 'arrest-free' simply as a function of his death. Thus, wards who had died were removed from the risk of arrest after the point in time at which they were found to have been deceased. Second, as argued by Gottfredson and Hirschi (1990: 94), serious chronic offenders should experience 'death at higher rates than the general population.' Analyses by Dobrin (2001) showed that individuals with criminal arrests in their backgrounds have a greater chance of dying by homicide compared to individuals with no criminal arrests in their backgrounds. Preliminary analyses of the previously collected mortality data on the two earliest data sets analyzed herein lend some credibility to this assertion as well (see Lattimore, Linster, and MacDonald 1997).

Data Sources and Variables

The sources of information that were used to collect the data varied according to both the type of data element and whether the data element was referring to a characteristic or behavior prior to or after the date of release from the CYA that resulted in the ward being included in the sample. We will refer to these two different segments of the data collection process as the 'pre-release' and the 'post-release' periods. The key division point is the date of release for the 'sample stay,' which refers to the specific incarceration or 'stay' at the CYA that resulted in the ward's inclusion in one of the three samples employed in our analyses. The 'pre-release' period refers to time prior to the sample release, while the 'post-release' period refers to time after the date of parole release.

Pre-release Data: Case Characteristics Information

Data for the pre-release period on the characteristics of the cases were collected from two sources: (1) Youth Authority's electronically stored information on the ward and (2) Youth Authority's 'hard copy' ward Master Files. From various computer files within the CYA and the CYA's Offender Based Institutional Tracking System (OBITS), data were obtained for the following variables:

- *Dates of admission and release for sample stay*
- *Base commitment offense* (e.g. adjudication for murder, forcible rape, burglary, robbery)

- *Admission status* (first commitment, parole violator, recommitment)
- *Date of birth*
- *Gender*
- *Ethnicity* (White, African-American, Hispanic, Asian, Native American, Filipino, Pacific Islander, Other)
- *Court of commitment* (juvenile court or adult criminal court)
- *M Case* (CDC 'Housing' Case)
- *County of commitment* (e.g. Los Angeles, Sacramento, San Diego, San Francisco)
- *Major* CYA *infractions* (DDMS violations) for such things as fighting and gang behavior.

The second data source is the individual, hard copy Master File completed for each ward. The Master File contains all available prescribed program and parole data, as well as data pertaining to the ward's entire medical, educational, psychosocial, and criminal history up through the date of discharge from Youth Authority's jurisdiction.

Trained coders reviewed and coded relevant data from the following types of documents: police, probation, and court reports, Youth Authority staff reports and documents, consultant reports and evaluations, and letters and appeals. Information from these sources was coded according to uniform guidelines. The Master File was the major source of information regarding the prior behavior and characteristics of the cases. Information regarding prior criminal record, as well as family background, substance abuse, gang activity, and prior placement information is either not available in OBITS, or it is not as complete or accurate as that contained in the Master File. The following variables were coded from the detailed information contained in the Master Files:[6]

- *Family violence*: Evidence of violence among the family members (not including the ward).
- *Parental alcohol or drug dependence*: Evidence that the ward's parents or guardians had an alcohol or drug dependence problem (e.g. arrests for drug offenses, been in treatment for

[6] In the following descriptions, 'parental' indicates the ward's parents unless the parents are no longer the guardians of the ward. In that case, parental refers to the ward's guardians.

drug/alcohol problems). Social drinking or occasional marijuana use was not recorded as evidence.

- *Parental criminality*: Evidence the ward's parents had been involved in criminal activity (e.g. prior arrests or incarcerations). A single arrest for drunk driving was not recorded as such evidence.
- *Sibling criminality/delinquency*: Evidence the ward's siblings had been previously involved in criminal or delinquent activity (e.g. prior arrests or incarcerations). One arrest for drunk driving was not recorded as evidence.
- *Parental lack of supervision/neglect*: Evidence that the ward was not adequately supervised or ward was neglected by his or her parents (e.g. ward was removed from custody of parents due to the behavior of the parents; parents do not know where the ward is usually).
- *Ineffective parental control*: Evidence that the parents had ineffective or inconsistent control over the ward (e.g. ward arrested for being 'out of control' or noted in probation records as being 'out of control'). Naturally, arrests for criminal offenses were not recorded as evidence of being beyond the control of the parents.
- *Physical abuse*: Evidence that the ward was subject to either extreme punitiveness or physical abuse (e.g. parent arrested for abuse of the ward; severe whippings; spankings that cause injury). Spanking alone (without injury) was not recorded as evidence.
- *Sexual abuse*: Evidence that the ward was subjected to sexual abuse by others (e.g. molestation).
- *Drug abuse*: Evidence that the ward abused drugs (not including alcohol). Experimental drug or chemical use was not recorded as evidence of drug abuse. Frequent use of hard drugs such as cocaine, PCP, and heroin, and 'sniffing' were recorded as such evidence.
- *Gang member/association*: Evidence that ward associated with gang members, participated in gang activities for self-protection, or was a fully participating 'gang member' who engaged in 'gang banging.' Often association could be identified by the presence or nature of a 'moniker' (e.g. 'Little OG'), previous arrests for gang-related activities, or the presence of gang tattoos that denote affiliation.

- *Previous violent behavior*: Evidence that ward had previously been violent, including a record of assaultive behavior and/or arrests for violent offenses.
- *School dropout*: Evidence the ward had dropped out of school. Evidence for this variable included the ward not being enrolled in school, ward had not attended school for six months while free on the street, ward had been expelled, or the ward was absent without excuse more than they were present.

Pre-release Data: Arrest History Information

The arrest history of each ward prior to the sample stay was compiled using the information contained in the Master Files. The Master File contains all of the previous probation reports and court records of wards because that information is required to be submitted with the court order of commitment to the CYA. Using all of the available police reports and records, probation reports, court records, and CYA parole performance summary information (for the wards previously released from the CYA prior to the sample stay), the following variables were coded and checked for accuracy for each arrest event:

- *Date of arrest event*: The date the ward was arrested by law enforcement personnel. In the rare situation (<1% of the time) when that arrest date was not known, the date of the offense was coded.
- *Arrest charges*: Up to 3 arrest charges per arrest event were coded (i.e. some arrest events involved multiple charges against the offender). Only behaviors that reflect distinct law violations were coded as separate charges and only the most serious charge per behavior was coded; 'lesser-included' offenses were never coded. For example, if a ward was arrested for evading the police in a stolen car after a robbery, the three arrest charges would reflect each behavior (robbery, auto theft, evading the police). In the cases where a ward is arrested for grand theft auto, occasionally the 'lesser-included' offenses of possession of stolen property, and unlawful taking of a motor vehicle were also filed. We only coded the most serious arrest charge per behavior, and thus this arrest would reflect a single arrest charge (grand theft auto). Similarly, if a ward was arrested for attempted murder, as well as assault with a deadly weapon,

> and assault and battery, we only coded the attempted murder arrest charge (e.g. you cannot attempt to kill someone with a firearm without committing both assault with a deadly weapon and assault and battery). Allowing multiple arrest charges per arrest date is a more accurate way of cataloguing an individual's prior record (Geerken 1994).

As noted above, the only difference in coding procedures and rules between the two earlier samples and the most recent sample was in the coding of the criminal history data. In actuality, all distinct arrest charges for a given arrest event were coded for the 1991–2 sample, not just the three most serious charges. This allowed us to ascertain if there were any biases associated with using only the three most serious charges rather than all arrest charges. First, 93 per cent of the arrest events had three or fewer arrest charges; 98 per cent of the arrests only involved four or fewer arrest charges. Second, of the charges that were dropped as a result of our three-charge limit, over 70 per cent involved only charges for being drunk in public, possession of alcohol, giving false information to a police officer, being under the influence of a controlled substance, and other 'miscellaneous' minor charges. There was a precipitous drop-off in the seriousness of the arrest charges after the third arrest charge, and in no case did dropping these records result in a ward being misclassified as a non-violent or non-serious offender. Third, among the 1,460 males that were coded in the 1991–2 sample, the mean number of charges was 9.62 using only the three most serious charges, whereas it was only 9.8 if we allowed for the inclusion of all of the arrest charges. Thus, using only the three most serious charges seems to accurately depict the arrest histories of this sample with little possibility of bias.

To make the prior arrest data of the 1991–2 sample equivalent to the two prior samples, we employed the same process used in coding the earlier two samples to arrive at the three most serious charges per arrest event. Although that data were coded manually and then entered into a computer database, we automated the selecting of the three most serious charges using a computer program that pulled out the three most serious charges. First, all offenses were classified according their corresponding OBITS offense category (which ranges from 1 to 100), as was performed in the two prior samples. Then, the computer program pulled out the three most serious charges according to the seriousness hierarchy that was programmed into an algorithm. Any charges that were ranked fourth or lower according to the algorithm were then dropped. In all of the analyses in this study, only the three most serious charges per arrest event were employed for the 1991–2 sample.

Briefly, the algorithm always considers violent offenses the most serious charges, then serious property offenses (e.g. burglary, auto theft), followed by major drug offenses (e.g. sales and trafficking), and, finally, the least serious miscellaneous charges (e.g. petty theft, drunk in public, trespassing). A table listing the seriousness hierarchy of the offenses is available via the web (see Appendix C).

Post-release Data: Arrest History Information

The source of data for arrests that occur after release from the CYA for the 'sample stay' is the Automated Criminal History System maintained by California Bureau of Criminal Statistics and Criminal Identification of the California Department of Justice (CDOJ). This data source was used to obtain the post-release criminal history data because neither OBITS nor the Master Files contain any relevant arrest data subsequent to each ward's discharge from the Youth Authority (usually after a period of parole). The data from this third source are known as the California Information and Identification 'CII rap sheet' information. A list of CII identification numbers for the wards was submitted to the CDOJ, who then compiled a data file containing all of the information in the CII rap sheets (including arrest records) of the wards in our samples.

Whenever an individual is committed to the CYA, the ward is assigned a CII identification number and a computerized (automated) CII rap sheet file is initiated and maintained by the CDOJ. When an adult is arrested in California, the arrest is reported by the arresting law enforcement agency to the California Department of Justice (which houses the state repository for arrest data). If a ward is released while still a minor (under age 18), the CYA reports any criminal arrests of the ward while he or she is a minor to the CDOJ.

The files of the California Department of Justice were searched in late November of 2000. We permitted five months of 'lag time' to allow sufficient time for any arrests to be entered by the Department of Justice into the case's 'rap sheet' file. Thus, the arrests were considered censored on 30 June 2000 and any arrests occurring from that date forward were not included in the analyses for this study. The post-release exposure periods for the samples were between 18–19 years (depending on the date of release) for the 1981–2 sample, 13–14 years for the 1986–7 sample, and 8–9 years for the 1991–2 sample. The average ages at the end of follow-up period were 37, 33, and 27 for each of the release samples, respectively.

To make the post-release data equivalent to the prior arrest data, we included only the three most serious charges per arrest event. We extracted the three most serious charges using the same process described above for the 1991–2 prior arrest data. The following variables were obtained from the CII rap sheet data files:

- *Date of arrest event*: The date the ward was arrested by law enforcement personnel.
- *Arrest charges*: The three most serious arrest charges per arrest event.

Post-release Data: Mortality Information

Mortality data on the cases in the release samples were extracted from the Death Statistical Master Files (DSMF) of the California Department of Health and Human Services (DHS). The DSMF files are based on the death certificates completed by either the presiding physician at the time of death, or in the case of sudden or unexpected deaths such as homicide, suicide, or drug overdose, by the coroner or medical examiner investigating the deaths. The DSMF files for 1989–99 were used to obtain the mortality data, and thus the last known possible date of death for our data would be 31 December 1999. Death dates prior to 1 January 1989 for the 1981–2 and 1986–7 samples were obtained from data previously compiled by Skonovd and Haapanen (2000). Mortality data are crucial for the topics of this study, since they allow us to remove an individual from being 'at risk' of arrest when he is no longer alive. Thus, any cases that died after release will not be counted as individuals who were 'arrest-free' at any age purely as a result of their mortality. As will be shown in Chapter 6 of this study, a sizeable number of cases died (usually of homicide) after release from the CYA.

From the information contained in the DSMF files, we retrieved the following two variables:

- *Date of death*
- *Cause of death*: International Classification of Death (ICD) codes were used to identify the major cause of death (e.g. homicide, suicide, drug overdose, auto accident, and AIDS).

Post-release Data: Adult Incarceration Information

Due to the fact that the CII 'rap sheet' files only contains accurate reports of the dates of *intake* into the state penal system (California Department of Correction—CDC), we also obtained the adult incarceration records related to all of the stays in the CDC subsequent to release from the CYA for all of our sample members. Information on the following variables was made available to us:

- *Date of intake*
- *Date of release*
- *Commitment offense*: Criminal offense that resulted in the incarceration in the CDC.
- *Second strike*: Whether sentenced as a 'Second Strike' case.
- *Third strike*: Whether sentenced as a 'Third Strike' case.

Deriving the Analytical Samples

In order to be included in the analyses in this study, there were several conditions a case had to satisfy. Table 5.1 details the effects that adhering to the conditions for inclusion in the final analytical sample had on the final sample size.

The first constraint used in deriving the analytical sample was the gender of the ward; the analytical sample was limited to only male wards. This constraint was imposed for two primary reasons. The major reason the female wards were excluded was that there were simply too few females in each of the data sets to allow for separate models or reliable estimation of model parameters. Table 5.1 indicates that females constituted only about 4 per cent of each sample (n = 88, 81, and 87, for the 1981–2, 1986–7, and 1991–2 samples, respectively).[7]

[7] Removing the females with missing arrest data further reduced the small sample size. Further, recall that only 1,527 cases were actually coded in the 1991–2 sample. Of these 1,527 cases, only 67 of them (4%) were females.

TABLE 5.1. Constructing the analytical samples: Limiting the release samples by sex, M-Case status, and missing arrest data, by release sample

Limit imposed	*Release sample*								
	1981–2			*1986–7*			*1991–2*		
	Original	*Starting*	*Removed*	*Original*	*Starting*	*Removed*	*Original*	*Starting*	*Removed*
Step 1: Sex									
Female	88 (4%)	88 (4%)	88	81 (4%)	81 (4%)	81	87 (4%)	67 (4%)	67
Male	1,998 (96%)	**1,998 (96%)**	0	1,997 (96%)	**1,997 (96%)**	0	2,098 (96%)	**1,460 (96%)**	0
Total	2,086	2,086	88	2,078	2,078	81	2,185	1,527	67
Step 2: M Case status									
Yes	0 (0%)	0 (0%)	0	208 (10%)	203 (10%)	203	220 (10%)	0 (0%)	0
No	2,086 (100%)	**1,998 (100%)**	0	1,870 (90%)	**1,794 (90%)**	0	1,965 (90%)	**1,460 (100%)**	0
Total	2,086	1,998	0	2,078	1,997	203	2,185	1,460	0
Step 3: Missing pre-arrest data									
Yes	0 (0%)	0 (0%)	0	206 (10%)	151 (8%)	151	—	0 (0%)	0
No	2,086 (100%)	**1,998 (100%)**	0	1,872 (90%)	**1,643 (92%)**	0	—	**1,460 (100%)**	0
Total	2,086	1,998	0	2,078	1,794	151	—	1,460	0
Step 4: Missing post-arrest data									
Yes	8 (0.4%)	7 (0.4%)	7	18 (12%)	200 (12%)	200	71 (3%)	26 (2%)	26
No	2,078 (99.6%)	**1,991 (99.6%)**	0	1,830 (88%)	**1,443 (88%)**	0	2,114 (97%)	**1,434 (98%)**	0
Total	2,086	1,998	7	2,078	1,643	200	2,185	1,460	26
Step 5: Missing death date									
Yes	3 (0.001%)	2 (0.001)	2	0 (0%)	0 (0%)	0	0 (0%)	0 (0%)	0
No	2,083 (99.9%)	**1,989 (99.9%)**	0	2,078 (100%)	**1,443 (100%)**	0	2,185 (100%)	**1,434 (100%)**	0
Total	2,086	1,991	2	2,078	1,443	200	2,185	1,434	26
Final analytical sample		**1,989**			**1,443**		**1,434**		

Note: The numbers in **bold** indicate the frequency (percentage) of cases that are available at the 'start' of the next limiting step.

A second reason why the females were excluded is that there is much empirical evidence that shows that male and female offending patterns are not equivalent (see, e.g., D'Unger, Land, and McCall 2002). Thus, we preferred to exclude the female cases entirely. It was clear during the coding of the 1991–2 sample that there was a marked division between the offending patterns of the males and females, with the offending patterns of the male wards exhibiting significantly more frequent, more serious, and more violent behavior. This is not to say that the females in the original samples were not serious and/or violent offenders, but just that compared to the males in the sample they were not as violent. Comparing all of the males in the samples to all of the females, the mean number of prior criminal arrest charges was 9.80 for the males, and it was 6.8 for the females. Similarly, 90 per cent of the males in these three samples were rearrested in the post-period, whereas 76 per cent of the females were rearrested. However, the offending patterns of the females in these samples compared to typical females in the general population are certainly both much more frequent, more serious, and more violent; this was especially true for the female wards who were gang members. Nonetheless, the female cases were removed at this point, and the sample sizes at the end of this step were 1,998 (1981–2), 1,997 (1986–7), and 1,460 (1991–2), respectively.

The second constraint imposed for inclusion in our study was that only the cases that were 'regular' CYA cases (i.e. directly committed to the CYA) would be included in the final analytical samples. Thus, M Cases were not included in the final analytical samples. Recall that M Cases are the California Department of Corrections commitments 'housed' in Youth Authority facilities (i.e. juveniles who have been 'waived' to the adult criminal justice system or select young adult offenders). Due to the fact that M Cases are not subject to the YOPB control, they do not have extensive clinical summaries and Youthful Offender Parole Board-related records in their Master Files. Since they were not subject to overview by the YOPB, their Master Files are generally missing the reports and documentation that contain the necessary information for many of the variables previously described. Especially problematic was the fact that their previous offending patterns were not described in detail like those of the regular CYA cases. In sum, it was impossible to code these cases with the same detail and attention that was given to the CYA regular cases.[8]

As shown in Table 5.1, roughly 10 per cent of the initial 1986–7 and 1991–2 samples were M Cases released from the CYA institutions during the respective fiscal years. As noted above, both budget and time constraints were a problem with the coding of the 1991–2 sample, and as a result the decision was made that the M Cases would only be coded pending available time and budget resources after coding of all regular CYA cases. This decision was made after discussions with CYA Research Bureau personnel with considerable experience with CYA Master Files and after the review of the CYA Master Files of 10 randomly selected M Cases. The review of those 10 cases indicated that it was impossible to code the M Cases with the same accuracy and detail as the regular CYA cases. Thus, none of the 220 M Cases in the original 1991–2 sample was coded. As shown in Table 5.1, after removing the M Cases (that were coded) from the 1986–7 sample that entered this step, the resulting sample size of the 1986–7 sample was now 1,794 (1986–7); the samples for the 1981–2 and 1991–2 samples were unaffected by this step either because there were no M Cases in the CYA population (1981–2) or because the M Cases were not initially coded (1991–2).

The next two constraints required for inclusion in the final analytical sample concerned whether any of the 'pre-release' and 'post-release' arrest data were missing. Cases were not included if they were missing the prior criminal arrest history. This turned out to be a major problem only for the 1986–7 sample. Of the 1,794 male, regular CYA cases that entered this step for that sample, 151 (8%) were found to be entirely missing their arrest histories. Since we did not code those data, it is beyond our speculative powers to assess why those cases are missing their arrest data. Our analysis of the probability of arrest in the post-release period

[8] It bears noting that there are not only selection effects that determine which cases end up in the CYA as M Cases, but since all M Cases are subject to transfer to the CDC if they misbehave and threaten institutional security, it is likely that there are even heavier selection effects determining which M Cases are available to be released from the CYA in any given year. Comparatively, for the male regular CYA cases released in 1986–7, 91 per cent of them had been arrested once by the end of the follow-up, whereas 85 per cent of the male M Cases in that sample had been arrested at this time point. For the 1991–2 cases, the corresponding arrest percentages as of 30 June 2000 were 89 per cent (male regular CYA cases) and 80 per cent (male M Cases).

indicated that the cases missing their prior arrest histories were more likely to remain arrest-free in the post-release period than were those cases with available prior arrest data. Eighty-six per cent of the cases missing their prior arrest data were arrested after release, whereas 92 per cent of the cases not missing their data were arrested. Thus, both of these groups experienced what might be called 'excessive failure rates', but one group was marginally more excessive than the other.

Cases also were not included in the final analytic samples if we did not have access to their CII 'rap sheet' arrest data for the post-release period. There are a variety of reasons why an individual's CII identification number would not be available at a point in time after their release. Sometimes a ward's CII Identification Number is not entered into the OBITS system because it is not known or not available, and occasionally records are purged from OBITS (as a result of discharge from the jurisdiction of the CYA) prior to retrieving their CII number. The OBITS system was used to obtain the CII identification numbers that were submitted to the CDOJ, and thus if the CII identification numbers were missing in the OBITS system, the CII rap sheets for those wards could not be obtained. Missing CII identification numbers were only a problem in the 1986–7 sample, with 200 cases (out of the 1,643 that entered this step of the construction of the analytical sample) dropped because we had no access to their post-release arrest information. The number of cases dropped for the 1981–2 and 1991–2 samples was 7 and 26, respectively.

It appears that CII numbers were unavailable for some wards in the 1986–7 sample because their OBITS records had already been purged when the CII identification numbers for this sample were obtained. This occurred when the sample was initially drawn (Skonovd and Haapanen 2000). We compared the prior arrest histories of those missing arrest data and those not missing this information and found that the cases missing their CII numbers (and thus missing their post-release arrest data) had a higher mean number of prior arrest charges. The cases missing (n = 200) their post-release data had an average of 11.79 prior arrest charges for criminal offenses, whereas the group (n = 1443) with known CII numbers averaged 10.22 prior arrest charges. Further, a comparison of parole performance between the two groups indicated a similar finding: 90 per cent of those missing their CII numbers were given a 'Dishonorable Discharge' (and only 1 earned an 'Honorable Discharge'), whereas 78 per cent of those with valid CII data were 'Dishonorably Discharged' (9% of them earned an 'Honorable Discharge').

Since it is impossible to reliably impute a longitudinal pattern of arrest charges (over an extended segment of the age distribution), cases missing either of these portions of their criminal arrest histories were excluded from the final analytic samples. Missing arrest data proved not to be a problem for either the earliest (1981–2) or the latest (1991–2) release samples. For the 1986–7 sample, however, we suspect that, on average, there is little bias that results from missing data because an examination of those in the sample with and without missing arrest data were equally distributed among the highest and lowest parole failure risk offenders. Perhaps more importantly, it bears noting that even the lowest risk cases in these samples still have incredibly high failure rates. Complete arrest information was available in both the pre- and post-arrest periods for over 80 per cent of the male CYA regular cases. After removing the cases missing arrest data in either the pre- and/or post-release periods, the resulting sample sizes were 1,991 (1981–2), 1,443 (1986–7), and 1,434 (1991–2), respectively.

Two of the males in the 1981–2 sample were reported to have died, but the dates of their deaths were not recorded. Neither of these individuals had any arrests in the post period; these two cases were dropped, since it was unknown how long they were on the street before their deaths.

After removing the cases that failed one of the five steps in the hierarchical process, we obtained the final analytic samples that are used in the analyses presented herein.

Data Limitations

Before concluding this section on the nature of the data used in this study, a discussion of the possible limitations of the data is necessary. The first limitation of this study is that both the arrest and mortality data only use records from the state of California. To the degree the wards migrated outside of California and either died and/or were arrested elsewhere, the data will undercount the extent of these outcomes. We do not feel, however, that this is a fatal limitation within the serious youthful offender population studied here. Most of these wards (over 95%) show up in one of the sources of data in the post-release period (i.e. they died, were arrested, and/or were incarcerated in California at some point during the post-release period). Nonetheless, it is necessary to keep in mind that these data refer only to records from the state of California and thus may underestimate arrest (and mortality), particularly if they occurred outside California.

A second limitation of this study is that in the analyses that follow, we are unable to control for time spent in secure custody (time incapacitated), or stated differently, we are unable to adjust for differential rates of 'time on the street.' Although, as noted above, we did obtain adult incarceration records related to all of the stays in the CDC for all of our sample members, we did not have access to complete secure custody movements over the entire age distribution studied here. More specifically, recording time spent in secure custody during the juvenile years was extremely difficult based on the records available in the ward's Master File. While wards from certain select counties had detailed records allowing for an easy determination of street time, for wards from other counties it was extremely difficult to figure out when the ward was in and out of secure custody.[9] Also, we did not have access to subsequent movements in and out of the CYA after the ward was released for the 'sample stay.' Finally, during the adult years, we only had access to the state-level CDC movements, but we did not have any access to local-level movements in and out of jail. As such, in the analyses that follow, we are unable to enter a street time 'offset term' in the equations we estimate. We will complete, to the best of our ability, a descriptive analysis of the time spent in the CDC in an effort to ascertain whether that incarceration time could be responsible for the results we will report.[10]

[9] For the offense the ward was committed to the CYA for committing, the calculation of time spent incarcerated (even at the local level) was not problematic due to the required calculation of time spent incarcerated for the offense.

[10] The limited set of studies using finite mixture models that compare models with and without controls for time incarcerated indicate to us that the primary consequences of controlling for time incarcerated seems to be its effects on the scale of the dependent variable, the peak absolute age of offending, and determining the percentage of 'desistors,' rather than generating completely distinct trajectory shapes (Eggleston, Laub, and Sampson 2004; Laub and Sampson 2003; Piquero *et al.* 2001; Sampson and Laub 2003). Eggleston *et al.*'s (2004) comprehensive results do indicate that some of the trajectory attributes (e.g. peak age, peak rate) can be affected by controls for incarceration time. Nagin's (2004: 30) discussion of Eggleston *et al.*'s

A third limitation of this study is that the analyses are based entirely on official criminal justice data (i.e. arrest records). There are no self-report data available for these samples. The strength of self-report data is that it may allow for the investigation of hidden criminal activity patterns that do not depend on the offender being apprehended by law enforcement officials. Official arrest data, on the other hand, are entirely dependent on apprehension, and thus offenders who are actively offending but never get arrested do not appear in the official data records as an offender. To the degree that the wards in this sample were committing criminal acts and were not being arrested for them, the analyses here would understate the extent of their criminal activity. There is little doubt that the individuals in our samples committed many crimes for which they were not arrested, but there are three points that counter the argument that this limitation is a serious impediment to our analyses. First, the majority of studies comparing self-report data to official arrest data find that those offenders who report the most frequent and serious offenses are also consistently the most frequent and serious offenders in the official data (see, e.g., Farrington 1989; Hindelang, Hirschi, and Weis 1979, 1981; Huizinga and Elliott 1986). As Farrington (1989: 418) notes, self-report and official data generate 'comparable and complementary results on such important topics as prevalence, continuity, versatility, and specialization in different types of offenses.' Second, self-report data are not without criticism, especially with respect to the topics of interest in this study. Recent criticisms of self-report data include issues surrounding both the validity of these data (Piquero, MacIntosh, and Hickman 2002), the reliability of using self-report data to examine within-individual changes in the relationship between age and crime (Lauritsen 1998,

analyses (which also examined the effects of length of follow-up and controlling for mortality patterns) commented on the 'essential similarities of the trajectories.' The questions we focus on in this study are more contingent on the comparative shape of the different trajectories rather than the specific attributes of the trajectories that seem to be most affected by controls for incarceration. Consider the following quotes: 'the general shape of the arrest trend appears to be robust to controls for exposure time' (Piquero *et al.* 2001: 68) and 'when death and incarceration were accounted for, the patterns remained remarkably similar' (Sampson and Laub 2003: 586). If the results of those studies are generalizable to our data, controlling for time on the street would not have generated substantively different conclusions from those we present in Chapter 7. That said, we would have preferred to have been able to control for time on the street, and our inability to do so is a limitation of this study.

1999), and about how conclusions regarding the nature of the age–crime curve are likely to be 'compromised' when using longitudinal self-report data as a result of the selective attrition (when not properly accounted for) of the high-rate offenders (Brame and Piquero 2003).

Third, collecting self-report data that would allow one to examine the issues addressed in this study and to make reliable generalizations concerning the population of serious youthful offenders would be both economically and practically infeasible. Recall that the wards of the CYA represent less than 5 per cent of the known (arrested and processed) delinquents in the entire state of California. If one only wanted to study issues related to the development of criminal offending patterns of these serious offenders as they age, the initial sample size that would be required to encapsulate a considerable number of serious offenders (that are comparable to the CYA wards) in a sample would have to be so large that the research would be economically infeasible. This is especially true when you take into account that in order to reliably record the self-reported offense patterns at any given age, the interviews, beginning in early childhood, would have to be conducted across the entire state of California.

Certainly, some researchers would not agree with this conclusion and hold the belief that serious violent offenders can be accurately studied through self-report data found in samples of the general population. For example, Elliott (1994: 17) has argued that 'truly serious violent offenders are included and retained in longitudinal general population studies. In fact, persons with arrest histories and incarceration experience are among the most easily tracked, and seldom are lost in longitudinal studies.'[11] Our experience with the CYA data used in the present study does not lead us to the same

[11] There no doubt is a qualitative divide between what Elliott (1994) calls serious violent offenders in his sample and the youthful offenders in our CYA samples. To make this point clear, consider the following. Elliott (1994: 18) noted that by age 27 there was a 30 per cent cumulative prevalence rate of serious violent offending (i.e. admitting that they had done something seriously violent such as 'attacking someone with the idea of seriously hurting them') in the National Youth Survey data. In the samples used in our study, by the end of the follow-up period, 82 per cent of the cases had been arrested for a serious violent offense (and averaged three serious violent arrest charges such as homicide, aggravated assault, armed robbery, rape, and sodomy); further, an almost astounding 10 per cent of each sample had at least one homicide arrest charge in their records.

conclusion. The serious youthful offenders in our samples are the hardest of all offenders to track for interviewing because they are often literally and figuratively 'under the gun' of law enforcement officials, and thus often cannot be found at home. They are not hard to track in the sense that they have high migration rates across state lines, but this does not mean they are easily tracked within their neighborhoods. Let us suppose that you could easily locate them. These individuals both by their nature and legal status would probably not be open to the intrusive questioning by researchers about the patterns of their criminal activity, even after assurances of anonymity. Some of these individuals are the very people that were contained in metal cages in order to be taught by a CYA teacher (wearing a flak jacket). These individuals often have problems maintaining scheduled appointments with their parole officers under the threat of a loss of their freedom (and they are often AWOL for periods of time while on parole). Thus, the idea of scheduling a self-report interview and actually obtaining accurate data (that deals with very sensitive information regarding the offending behavior of individuals often under some form of supervision) seems an unrealistic expectation in our opinion. In our judgement, there simply is no better (actually feasible) way to study this population than through the use of official data.

Methodology

This section briefly describes the analytical methods employed in this study. Readers interested in a thorough and technical discussion of the methods employed and the reasoning behind their selection are invited to turn to Appendix A. Appendix A covers the statistical methods used to model count variables and includes discussions of the Poisson model, the negative binomial model, the parametric random effects negative binomial model, and the semiparametric mixed Poisson model of Nagin and Land (1993). Our discussion in this chapter contains a summary description of the actual analytical strategies we undertake in Chapters 7 and 8.

The Dependent Variable

The dependent variable assessed in Chapters 7 and 8 is the *count number of criminal arrest charges at each age*, with each individual's panel data beginning at age 7. This count variable does not include arrest charges for probation violations (e.g. out of control), parole violations (e.g. positive drug test), or traffic offenses (e.g. speeding, driving without a license). Instead, the dependent variable only counts arrest charges regarding the more 'garden variety street crime offenses' (e.g. homicide, robbery, burglary, theft, possession of drugs).

In the statistics literature, data like that used herein are known as *unbalanced panel* data sets because the cases in the samples have varying numbers of records in the final analytic files. The longitudinal offending sequence for each of the wards included in our samples began at age 7, and the sequence ended with the final age at which the case was known to be 'at risk'.[12] For most of the cases, the final age at risk was determined by the end of the follow-up period, but for some cases the final age was determined by the age at death. Given that the wards were of varying ages at the time of release from the CYA for the 'sample stay' (i.e. the stay at the CYA that resulted in the ward's inclusion in the sample), the maximum age at which each ward's criminal arrest history was available also varied. Full ages during which the wards were incarcerated in the CYA for the sample stay were removed from consideration of the risk of arrest. Appendix B contains a table with a detailed description of the percentages of each sample that had available criminal arrest histories at each age; here we simply present a brief description of the number of 'periods' or 'age years' (hereafter referred to as 'data points') that were available for analysis in each sample.

For the 1981–2 sample, age 43 was the maximum age at which a respondent's criminal arrest history was available, and roughly 50 per cent of the sample was observed through the age of 37. The number of data points used in the panel analyses varied from a minimum of 9 to a maximum of 37, and the average number of data points was 30.

For the 1986–7 sample, the oldest age at risk by the end of the follow-up period was 38, and 50 per cent of the sample was available for study after the age of 33. The minimum number of data points available for analysis within this sample was 11, the maximum was 32, and the average number of data points was 26.

[12] About five cases in each sample experienced their first arrest event at age 6. To keep the absolute size of the data sets to a minimum, those arrests charges were included in the age 7 counts for these cases.

The oldest age at which a case's criminal arrest history was available for study in the 1991–2 sample was 33, and the arrest histories for 50 per cent of the sample were only followed through the age of 27. The minimum number of data points available for analysis in this sample was 10, the maximum was 27, while the average number was 21.

Analytical Approach Employed in Chapter 7

As discussed in Chapter 3, the focus of Chapter 7 concerns the relationship between age and crime among latent classes of serious youthful offenders. In Chapter 7, we first estimate the following semiparametric mixed Poisson model using the final analytic sample constructed for each of the three samples.

Models allowing up to eight latent classes will be tested, and the BIC statistic along with empirical testing regarding whether the solutions are global maximums will be used to select the optimal number of latent classes or components in the mixture distribution. Here we will also test the hypothesis of Gottfredson and Hirschi that there is uniformity in the shape of the age–crime distribution by testing the statistical significance of allowing the magnitude of the age parameters to vary across the latent classes. Following the arrival at the optimal number of latent classes, the sample members will then be assigned to the latent class to which they have the highest probability of belonging. At this point, the basic descriptive features of the offending patterns of the latent classes will be discussed (e.g. age at first arrest, mean number of arrest charges), and then the observed and predicted offending trajectories across age will be graphed and compared. Finally, a descriptive analysis will be undertaken to examine what role, if any, adult incarceration time may have had on the decline in criminal offending among these three groups of serious youthful offenders.

In brief, the latent class analysis models developed by Nagin and Land (1993) and Land, McCall, and Nagin (1996) allow researchers to group individuals according to the similarity in their trajectories of arrests (or some other specific event type) over time. Latent class models may be specified to include varying numbers of 'points of support', which divide the sample into multiple categories of offenders. In other words, a model with two points of support would divide the sample into two categories of offenders, a model with four points of support would divide the sample into four categories of offenders, and so on. Since age variables (age and age-squared) are included in the estimation process, the model generates age-specific offending patterns for each of the latent classes over time. The group-specific parameter estimates for the random effects, age, and age-squared terms determine the shape of the arrest trajectories.

Analytical Approaches Employed in Chapter 8

In Chapter 8, the relationship between past and subsequent criminal activity will be examined. In that chapter we will employ the use of the multi-method approach of Bushway, Brame, and Paternoster (1999), which is essentially the 'compare and contrast strategy' first described by Heckman and Singer (1984). More specifically, we test the robustness of any observed effect of past and subsequent criminal behavior by employing several different methods of analysis. The relationship between past and subsequent criminal activity will be investigated in four stages. These stages involve the use of the semiparametric random effects model, the parametric random effects model, and the negative binomial model. We present more details on the precise specification used when we introduce each of those four stages in Chapter 8.

Before moving on to the main results of this study to be presented in Chapters 7 and 8, in Chapter 6 we will present a descriptive summary of the data used in this study. This description is important for documenting the basic facts concerning the criminal offending patterns of the sample members, including the nature of their criminal offending behaviors (i.e. the types of offenses for which they were arrested, age at first arrest), certain behavioral characteristics of the subjects (e.g. gang membership, drug abuse), and specifics regarding incidents of mortality and adult incarceration. For background information purposes, we also present a description of the trends in the crime, arrest, and incarceration rates in California from 1960 to 2000.

6

Descriptive Summary of Data

In this chapter, we present a descriptive summary of the data employed in this study. This description is important for documenting basic information regarding characteristics of our samples, including the basic nature of the extent and breadth of their criminal offending (e.g. number of arrest charges) and other background factors (e.g. gang membership). We also describe the mortality and adult incarceration experiences among the three samples. It is important to note at the outset that the goal of this chapter is not to present an explanation of the significant differences in the distributions of the variables among the three samples because (1) it is irrelevant to the main interests of this study, (2) the exposure or 'time at risk' was different for each of the samples, (3) it would involve an excessive number of tests of significance, and (4) we estimate the models for each sample separately. Rather, this chapter focuses on describing the distribution of the variables for each of the samples on the critical variables identified in Chapter 5. Differences between the samples will be discussed where they are deemed to be important. Before we present a summary of the data for the wards in this study, we first describe the crime, arrest, and incarceration rates in California from 1960 through 2000 in order to provide a historical context from which to view the data discussed herein.

Crime, Arrest, and Incarceration Rates in California

Three Index crime rates in California from 1960 through 2000 are presented in Figure 6.1—the total, property, and violent Index crimes rates.[1] As can be seen in all three crime curves, there was

[1] The data displayed in Figures 6.1 through 6.3 were obtained from various data tables in *Crime and Delinquency in California, 1998, Crime and Delinquency in*

FIGURE 6.1. California Index crime rates from 1960 through 2000, by crime type.

a general linear increase in the crime rates between 1960 and 1980. In 1960, the total Index crime rate was 1,441 crimes per 100,000 California residents, but by 1980 this rate had increased all the way to 3,922 Index crimes per 100,000 persons. The Index crime rate in 1980 represented a 170 per cent increase in crime compared with this rate in 1970. After 1980, however, the property and violent Index crime rates show different trends. For property crimes, the crime rate decreased from 1981 through 1985, where it then leveled off for the next six years. Around 1991, the property crime rate began to decrease once again, a pattern that continued essentially until 2000, when this time series ends. The drop in the property crime rate from 1991 to 2000 was approximately 50 per cent.

For violent offenses, however, the crime rate continued to climb from 1980 through 1992, where it peaked. Thus, there was a general linear upward trend in the violent crime rate from the early 1960s through the early 1990s. The upward trend in the violent crime rate between 1984 and the early 1990s enabled the total crime index trend to continue to increase slightly during this time

California, 1999, and *Crime and Delinquency in California, 2000* (California Department of Justice 1999, 2000, 2001).

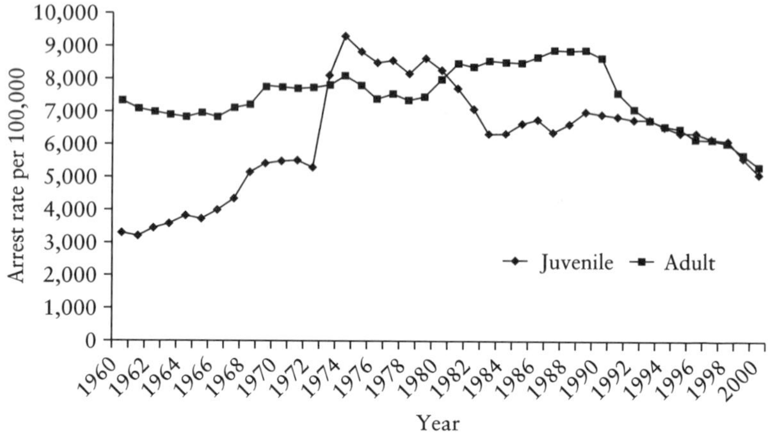

FIGURE 6.2. Juvenile and adult arrest rates from 1960 through 2000.

period. Yet, between 1992 and 1999, California's violent crime rate decreased by almost one-half from 1,103 violent crimes per 100,000 residents to 610 crimes per 100,000 persons. This rapidly decreasing crime trend during this time period was contrary to the expectations of several scholars who had predicted that waves of violent 'superpredators' or 'monsters' would be hitting and roaming the streets from the mid-1990s onward leading to a new crime wave (for more on this point, see Zimring 1998).

Consider next the reported arrest rates of both adults and juveniles in California (1960–2000) presented in Figure 6.2.[2] Compared to the juvenile arrest rate, the adult arrest rate from 1960 through the late 1980s displayed greater stability. The adult arrest rate slowly increased from 6,843 per 100,000 residents in 1966 to 8,900 per 100,000 residents in 1989, where it then began to descend until it reached 5,323 per 100,000 persons in 2000. In fact, between 1989 and 2000, the total adult arrest rate decreased by over 40 per cent. For juveniles, however, the arrest rate shows a somewhat different pattern. There was a general increase in the juvenile arrest rate between the early 1960s and the mid-1980s (especially around 1972–5). In fact,

[2] For comparative purposes, note that the earliest year of arrest in the 1981–2 sample was 1965. The interquartile range (IQR) of the year of first arrest for the 1981–2 sample was 1975 to 1978. For the 1986–7 sample, the earliest year of arrest was 1970, and the IQR was 1979 to 1982. For the 1991–2 sample, the comparable numbers were 1974 and {1984, 1987}.

the arrest rate increased from 3,300 per 100,000 residents (in 1960) to 9,300 per 100,000 persons in 1975; this increase in the rates amounts to a 180 per cent gain in the juvenile arrest rate. Between 1975 and 2000, the juvenile arrest rate would then decrease by nearly one-half.

Between the 1960s and the end of the twentieth century, both California and the United States itself went on what has been called an 'imprisonment binge' (Irwin and Austin 1997). During the decade between 1980 and 1990, for example, the number of persons incarcerated in California's prisons and jails quadrupled, increasing the state's inmate population by over 100,000 prisoners (Zimring and Hawkins 1994, 1997). Never before had 'a prison system grown so much in so short a time' (Zimring and Hawkins 1994: 83). Figure 6.3 contains a graph of California's adult incarceration rate (of CDC prisoners) between 1960 and 2000. As is clearly shown in this figure, there appears to have been a change in California's imprisonment rate around 1981 with respect to its increasing use of incarceration in the CDC as a major form of punishment. Between 1981 and 2000, the imprisonment rate in California increased by 250 per cent, with over 130,000 inmates having been added to the state's 'prison industrial complex' known as the CDC.

The descriptions of the arrest and incarceration rates presented in the aforementioned figures are important because they help

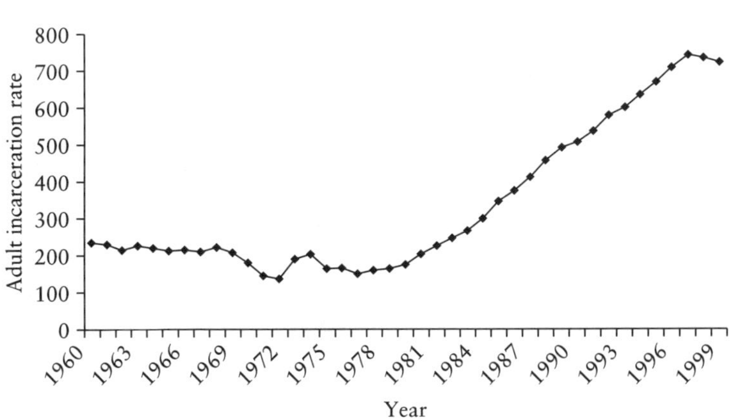

FIGURE 6.3. California's adult incarceration rate (CDC prisoners) from 1960 through 2000.

to convey the historical context in which a 'get tough on crime' atmosphere was to impact the lives of wards who were to come under the supervision of the California Youth Authority. The members of each of the samples employed in our study may have been released at different points in time, however, each was impacted by a 'get tough on crime' atmosphere that existed in the state and was directed at both adult and youthful offenders. In the next section, we show that not only were the members of our three samples deeply involved in serious crime, but that nearly all of these wards had been apprehended for engaging in some form of violent behavior at some point in their lives. In fact, the vast majority of these offenders had an arrest record for at least one serious violent offense.

Criminal Arrest Histories

Up to this point, we have merely verbally indicated that the wards of the CYA comprise a rather select group of very serious offenders in the state. In this section, we present empirical evidence to buttress this characterization. In the first part of this section, we describe the age of onset for first criminal arrest for members of our samples. The second part of this section contains a description of the overall offending patterns within the three samples, including arrest counts, and the means, and prevalence rates for specific crime types.

Age at First Arrest

Age of onset is a critically important variable in the discipline of criminology because not only is it one of the most significant predictors of the frequency and seriousness of subsequent offending, but it is also argued to be a highly significant predictor of the odds of becoming a persistent offender (see, e.g., Ayers *et al.* 1999; Elliott 1994; Farrington *et al.* 1991; Lahey *et al.* 1999; LeBlanc and Loeber 1998; Loeber 1982; Loeber, Farrington, and Waschbusch 1998; Tolan and Thomas 1995; Tracy and Kempf-Leonard 1996). Individuals with the earliest recorded ages of onset (whether measured through self-report or official data) tend to have the longest criminal careers and to be involved in the most serious and violent offenses. They also commit criminal acts at higher rates than do others. Indeed, age of onset is extremely important to the issues addressed in this study. Population heterogeneity theorists such as

Gottfredson and Hirschi argue that an early age of onset is but a proxy indicator of higher criminal propensity, and that is why individuals with earlier ages of onset have criminals careers that tend to be longer, more frequent, and more serious in nature (Dean, Brame, and Piquero 1996; Nagin and Farrington 1992*b*). State dependence theorists, on the other hand, argue that an early age of onset could *cause* an individual to have a longer, more frequent, and more serious criminal career as a result of the negative (state dependence) effects generated by the early arrest (Nagin and Farrington 1992*b*). To the dual taxonomy theorists such as Moffitt (and Patterson), age of onset is a marker variable that indicates whether the individual is in the life-course-persistent ('early onset') group or the adolescent-limited ('late onset') offender groups (Dean, Brame, and Piquero 1996; Nagin and Farrington 1992*b*; Thornberry and Krohn 2001).

Table 6.1 contains the means and the 25th, 50th, and 75th percentiles of the distributions of the age at first arrest for those in each sample and for all three samples combined. For comparative purposes, we also present the results on the basis of the court of commitment (juvenile court commitment and adult court commitments).

TABLE 6.1. Mean and percentiles of age at first criminal arrest distribution, by sample

	N	*Mean*	*Percentiles*		
			25th	*50th*	*75th*
All wards					
1981–2 sample	1,989	14.22	12.55	14.24	16.01
1986–7 sample	1,443	13.68	12.31	13.71	15.11
1991–2 sample	1,434	13.64	12.49	13.81	15.07
All 3 samples	4,866	13.89	12.45	13.93	15.40
Juvenile court commitments only					
1981–2 sample	1,068	12.98	11.70	13.29	14.51
1986–7 sample	1,089	13.21	12.01	13.39	14.55
1991–2 sample	1,308	13.50	12.42	13.74	14.92
All 3 samples	3,465	13.25	12.07	13.48	14.69
Adult criminal court commitments only					
1981–2 sample	921	15.67	13.91	15.84	18.07
1986–7 sample	354	15.14	13.67	15.09	16.93
1991–2 sample	126	15.05	13.61	15.20	16.77
All 3 samples	1,401	15.48	13.85	15.58	17.54

For all 4,866 cases in the three samples, the average age at first arrest was 13.89, and 75 per cent of the wards in each of the samples had been arrested prior to age 16. The median age at first arrest (13.81) was very similar to the mean age, although the distribution is (not surprisingly) slightly skewed right. In fact, a kernel density graph for the age at first arrest variable indicates that the distribution is fairly normally and symmetrically distributed around the mean, although it is slightly skewed right.

More importantly, though, there was not a large substantive difference in the mean (or median) age at first arrest among the three samples, although the 1981–2 sample cases were slightly older on average (14.2) than either the 1986–7 or 1991–2 samples (both averaged about 13.6 years). It is also very clear from these results that a sizeable percentage of each of the samples has a very precocious age at first arrest—roughly 25 per cent of the samples have been arrested before they turned 13 years old. Of those who were arrested before age 13, about 50 per cent were arrested before they turned 11 years old.

When the samples were further disaggregated on the basis of the court of commitment, we found that the average age at first arrest for the juvenile court wards (in all three samples combined) was 13.25, whereas it was 15.48 for the adult court commitments. More importantly, after disaggregating the samples by court of commitment, the small differences that existed between the samples virtually disappeared. The reason the 1981–2 sample had a slightly higher mean age at first arrest was purely a consequence of the fact that this sample had a higher percentage of adult court commitments, who 'on average' had older ages at first arrest than did the juvenile court wards. Nonetheless, the main point indicated in Table 6.1 is that on average, the age at first arrest occurred fairly early in the lives of the members of each of our samples and also that there was some variation around this average age even in this select group of offenders. A graph depicting the cumulative ages of first arrest for each of the samples and for the juvenile court commitments in each sample is available on the Internet (see Appendix C).

Criminal Arrest Patterns

Attention is now turned to the extent and nature of criminal activity in each of the samples. Table 6.2 contains information regarding the sum number of arrest charges, the mean number of arrest

TABLE 6.2. Sums, means, and participation rates of arrest charges, by sample

Charge type	1981–2 Sample (N=1,989)			1986–7 Sample (N=1,443)			1991–2 Sample (N=1,434)		
	Sum no. of charges	*Mean no. of charges*	*Participation rate*	*Sum no. of charges*	*Mean no. of charges*	*Participation rate*	*Sum no. of charges*	*Mean no. of charges*	*Participation rate*
Total	**45,312**	**22.78**	**100.00**	**30,776**	**21.33**	**100.00**	**23,742**	**16.56**	**100.00**
Total serious	**24,885**	**12.51**	**99.85**	**16,290**	**11.29**	**99.79**	**12,321**	**8.59**	**99.93**
Violent	**10,571**	**5.31**	**90.45**	**7,601**	**5.27**	**91.61**	**6,558**	**4.57**	**93.58**
Serious violent	6,198	3.12	83.01	4,313	2.99	81.57	3,544	2.47	81.73
Homicide	217	0.11	9.15	158	0.11	9.42	148	0.10	9.07
Forcible rape	356	0.18	11.97	222	0.15	10.53	161	0.11	8.37
Robbery	2,869	1.44	60.99	1,905	1.32	58.35	1,458	1.02	52.79
Aggravated assault	2,071	1.04	51.58	1,503	1.04	54.12	1,359	0.95	55.44
Kidnap/extortion	213	0.11	9.05	145	0.10	8.80	94	0.07	5.86
Child molestation	132	0.07	4.88	114	0.08	6.31	68	0.05	4.18
Sodomy/forced oral cop.	115	0.06	4.42	75	0.05	4.37	67	0.05	3.56
Weapon discharge	225	0.11	9.35	191	0.13	11.43	189	0.13	11.09
Simple assault	4,373	2.20	64.91	3,288	2.28	71.52	3,014	2.10	69.46
Property	**17,337**	**8.72**	**95.48**	**10,415**	**7.22**	**95.01**	**7,242**	**5.05**	**90.31**
Serious property	14,175	7.13	94.02	8,297	5.75	92.52	6,011	4.19	87.59
Burglary	6,922	3.48	84.82	3,722	2.58	79.63	2,059	1.44	62.62
Auto theft	3,169	1.59	58.97	1,977	1.37	55.79	2,103	1.47	62.97

Major theft	3,938	1.98	67.87	2,524	1.75	67.98	1,773	1.24	57.53
Arson	146	0.07	6.33	74	0.05	4.44	76	0.05	4.18
Petty theft	3,162	1.59	61.49	2,118	1.47	58.84	1,231	0.86	44.21
Drug	**9,362**	**4.71**	**77.33**	**7,115**	**4.93**	**80.39**	**4,221**	**2.94**	**72.45**
Serious drug	4,512	2.27	63.15	3,680	2.55	68.68	2,766	1.93	62.34
Sales/trafficking	739	0.37	20.71	660	0.46	24.88	571	0.40	24.13
Posess./poss. for sale	3,773	1.90	60.78	3,020	2.09	65.49	2,195	1.53	59.00
Other drug offenses	4,850	2.44	55.66	3,435	2.38	55.72	1,455	1.01	38.01
Other residual offenses	**8,042**	**4.04**	**86.22**	**5,645**	**3.91**	**90.02**	**5,721**	**3.99**	**90.66**
Felony Weapon poss.	1,379	0.69	37.91	989	0.69	38.46	836	0.58	37.80
Other sex offenses	337	0.17	10.06	193	0.13	8.18	158	0.11	7.88
Other felony offenses	540	0.27	19.26	410	0.28	21.83	522	0.36	26.71
Escape from secure fac.	785	0.39	24.38	551	0.38	25.02	512	0.36	22.80
Other misc misd.	5,001	2.51	76.77	3,502	2.43	79.90	3,693	2.58	81.31

Notes: Participation rate indicates the percentage of the cases in the samples with at least one arrest charge of that type. 'Serious violent' includes all violent charges excluding simple assault charges. 'Serious property' includes all property charges except for the 'Petty theft' category. 'Serious drug' includes all drug charges except the 'Other drug offenses' category. 'Total serious' includes the following: All 'Serious violent' charges, 'Serious property' charges, and 'Serious drug' charges.

charges per case, and the participation rate for each offence type for each of the samples. The offenses have been broadly categorized into six main categories (which are in bold type in the Table 6.2): (1) total; (2) total serious; (3) violent; (4) property; (5) drug; and (6) residual.[3] Attention here focuses on the results concerning the six main categories, but results are also presented in the table for twenty-five offense categories subordinate to the six main categories listed above. In total, the 4,866 cases in the three samples amassed 99,830 arrest charges by 30 June 2000. Because the total time 'at risk' varies greatly between the samples, we keep comparisons between the samples to a minimum.

The 1981–2 Sample

The 1,989 members of the 1981–2 sample accumulated 45,312 arrest charges. This averages out to just under 23 arrest charges per ward. Of the 23 average arrest charges, just over 50 per cent of them (12.51) were for serious crimes such as homicide, robbery, aggravated assault, grand theft, auto theft, burglary, and drug trafficking. Disaggregating the arrests into violent, property, drug, and residual offenses, we see that these offenders are quite versatile in their criminal behavior, engaging in a wide array of offenses. On average, each of these wards had 5.3 arrest charges for violent offenses, 8.72 arrest charges for property crimes, 4.7 charges for drug offenses, and about 4 charges for residual offenses.

Looking at a few of the subcategories, we see that our sample members averaged about three serious violent offenses (which includes all of the violent offenses except simple assault), and they were arrested for two simple assault charges on average. Most of the property charges for this sample were also serious in nature. For example, they were arrested, on average, for 3.5 burglary charges. They were also arrested on average for 2.5 'miscellaneous' arrest charges (e.g. disturbing the peace, vandalism, tampering with an auto, and giving false information to a police officer).

The participation rates of the various crime types also speak to the wide variety of criminal activities in which the majority of these cases were involved at some point in their lives. Consider that over 90 per cent of the sample members were arrested for at least one

[3] A complete description of the specific offenses used in generating these variables is available on the Internet (see Appendix C).

violent offense, and over 83 per cent had at least one serious violent offense such as homicide, forcible rape, robbery, or aggravated assault. The most prevalent violent offense types were robbery (61%), aggravated assault (52%), and simple assault (65%). Almost every case in the sample was arrested for at least one serious property offense (94%), and over 85 per cent of the cases had at least one arrest charge for burglary. Sixty per cent of the cases had been arrested for auto theft. Three-quarters of the sample had at least one drug arrest charge in their arrest histories, and about 60 per cent had been arrested at some point for either possessing illegal narcotics/marijuana or for possession these illegal commodities with the intent to sell; about 20 per cent had been arrested for a drug trafficking charge.

The 1986–7 Sample

The cases in this sample (N = 1,443) accrued 30,776 arrest charges by the end of the follow-up period, with an average of about 21 arrest charges per case. Similar to the 1981–2 sample, about half of their arrest charges were for serious offenses. These offenders were arrested on average for 5.27 violent offenses, 7.22 property offenses, about five drug offenses, and about four residual offenses. Looking at some of the specific offense categories in Table 6.2, we find that these individuals were arrested on average for three serious violent offenses, and just under 2.3 simple assault charges. With respect to their property offending, they were arrested on average for 5.75 serious property offenses, including an average of 2.6 burglary charges and 1.75 major theft charges (e.g. grand theft, forgery, possession of stolen property). This sample was also heavily involved in drug offenses, and indeed, even accrued more drug arrests (on average) than did the 1981–2 sample. On average, the 1986–7 sample was arrested for two possession/possession for drug sale charges and 2.4 'other' drug offenses (e.g. under the influence of drugs, possession of drug paraphernalia, possession of hypodermic needle/syringe).

Again, an examination of the participation rates of the specific crime types confirms the extensive nature of the criminal activity of the 1986–7 sample. Ninety-two per cent of the sample had been arrested at least once for a violent offense, and about 82 per cent of the sample was arrested for a serious violent offense. Roughly 60 per cent was arrested for a robbery charge, 54 per cent for aggravated assault, and 72 per cent for a simple assault offense. Like the previous sample, the members of the 1986–7 sample were extensively involved in both property and drug crimes as well. Ninety-five per cent of the sample was arrested for at least one property offense, 80 per cent had a burglary charge, and similarly, 80 per cent of the sample had been arrested for at least one drug charge; with 70 per cent having been arrested for at least one serious drug charge. This sample was also heavily involved in the residual offense category as well, with 90 per cent having at least one charge for offenses under this heading, with nearly 40 per cent having been arrested on a felony weapons charge (e.g. possession of a machine gun, possession of a 'sawed-off shotgun').

The 1991–2 Sample

Finally, Table 6.2 indicates that the 1991–2 sample was also heavily involved in criminal activities. The 1,434 members of this sample were arrested for 23,742 criminal charges. The 'average' case in this sample was arrested for 16.56 charges, and once again, we see that over one-half of their arrest charges were for serious offenses. On average, they were arrested for 4.6 violent offenses, 5.1 property offenses, 2.9 drug offenses, and 4 residual offenses. Some of the arrest charge totals for specific offenses include an average of 2.5 serious violent charges, 2.1 simple assault charges, 4.2 serious property charges, 1.9 serious drug charges, and 2.6 'miscellaneous' charges.

The participation rates also indicate that the members of this 1991–2 sample were involved in a wide assortment of offense types. Indeed, 94 per cent had at least one violent offense in their arrest history, 82 per cent had been arrested for a serious violent offense—53 per cent for robbery, 55 per cent for aggravated assault, and 70 per cent had an arrest for simple assault. Again, we find that 90 per cent of this sample had been arrested for a property offense, and that nearly an equal proportion of the cases (88%) also had at least one serious property charge in their arrest history. Over 70 per cent of the sample had been arrested on a drug charge, and 60 per cent had an arrest charge for either possession of drugs or possession of drugs with the intent to sell. Finally, about 90 per cent of the 1991–2 sample had been arrested for a residual offense, including 38 per cent for a felony, weapon possession charge and 23 per cent for an escape/attempted escape from a secure custody facility (e.g. jail, juvenile hall, CYA, CDC). Many of these escapes were rather dramatic. For example, one case was on his way to the county jail having already been arrested for burglary. While en route to the jail, the ward dove head first through the rear passenger's side window *while the window was rolled up and the police car was moving* at about 25 miles per hour. This case was arrested a couple months later, at which point he was charged with misdemeanor theft of county property (the handcuffs) and escape. Another case involved a ward who had been arrested by his parole agent on a burglary warrant charge. While the parole agent was talking to the ward's parents, the ward jumped through a second story window *while hand-cuffed* and then escaped through a field in the backyard.

In sum, the results in Table 6.2 speak to the great quantity of criminal offending among these 4,866 individuals (who amassed almost 100,000 arrest charges in total or about 20 charges each), but these data also speak to the seriousness of their offending patterns. Almost all of the sample members had at least one serious offense in their arrest histories, and about half of all of the total arrest charges were for serious criminal offenses.[4] Furthermore, and perhaps more importantly, over 80 per cent of the members of each sample had been arrested for at least one serious violent offense. Indeed, nearly 10 per cent of each sample had been arrested at least once for homicide, and over half of the members in each sample had been arrested at least once for both aggravated assault (e.g. assault with a deadly weapon, aggravated assault on a poilice officer) and robbery.

To conclude this section, we make a comparison to the Glueck's data utilized by Sampson and Laub (1993) to study crime among high-risk offenders. The Glueck's sample has been characterized as a group of serious and persistent offenders (Sampson and Laub 1993; Sampson 2000) and according to these authors (who also coded the three most serious charges per arrests), the 480 male juvenile delinquents had been arrested for 6,300 criminal charges by age 32. This resulted in an average arrest charge total of 13.13 charges through age 32. For the two samples in our study that had a significant proportion of the sample at risk through age 32 (the

[4] The handful of cases not arrested for a serious offense were chronically involved in either petty theft and/or simple assault.

1981–2 and 1986–7 samples), we calculated the arrest charge totals through age 32 for the proportion of each sample that was at risk to this age. For the data used here, the comparable arrest charge averages were 21 in the 1981–2 sample and 20.91 in the 1986–7 sample. Thus, the offenders in our study average around 7 more arrest charges by age 32 in comparison to the juvenile delinquents in the Glueck's data used by Sampson and Laub.

Post-release Recidivism Rates

In this section, we discuss the post-release recidivism rates for each of the parole release samples. Here, we use arrest for a new criminal charge as our measure of recidivism, whereas the CYA generally reports parole removal rates (which include parole revocations, CYA recommitments for law violators, and discharges due to jail and prison commitments for law violations) in the 24 months since release as its measure of recidivism. We note that on 5 May 1998, the Director of the CYA at that time (Francisco Alarcon) released the following press release: 'The recidivism rate for offenders released from the California Youth Authority (CYA) has reached its lowest level in nearly two decades, according to a parole performance report released by CYA Director Francisco J. Alarcon.' The report, which is based on findings from 3,212 offenders released to parole in 1995, shows that less than half (49.6%) violated their parole within 24 months—down from a 55.1 per cent recidivism rate for those offenders released in 1994. In addition, the report reflects the largest single year drop from 55.1 per cent last year to 49.6 per cent for the 1995 releases. The parole failure rate for females dropped to 24.8 per cent, its lowest since 1979, and the rate for males declined to 50.6 per cent, down from a high of 61.7 per cent in 1986. 'These numbers reflect an improved success rate for CYA parolees, and that translates into a positive impact on public safety and hundreds of fewer victims of crime,' said Alarcon. 'We incarcerate the most serious and violent young offenders in California, and the fact that we're effectively reaching over half of them speaks to the quality of our staff and our institutional programs' (http://www.cya.ca.gov/Library/news/recidvsm.html, 17 Sept. 2002).

These statistics, however, must be interpreted with caution because they rely on the CYA's basic measure of recidivism—the 24-month parole outcome. In our opinion, this 24-month parole performance measure is a flawed measure of recidivism. It includes data only for the period in which wards are under the supervision of CYA parole agents. Over the past two decades, an increasing proportion of CYA wards have been released with little or no jurisdiction time available for parole supervision (i.e. their period of parole supervision does not cover the full 24 months). Therefore, we believe that actual criminal arrests are a better indicator of the post-release performance of these wards because arrest data are not dependent on the length of parole supervision, and thus are a better indicator of post-release performance. Further, as Maltz (1984) argues, failure on parole can arise for many reasons, some of which are not even violations of the criminal law (e.g. failure to obtain a job).

Using subsequent arrests for a new criminal charge as our measure of recidivism, Table 6.3 contains the estimated and actual

TABLE 6.3. Estimated survival probability of remaining 'arrest-free' from a new criminal charge as a function of years since release

Years since release	*Estimated survival probability in each sample*		
	1981–2	*1986–7*	*1991–2*
1	0.502	0.458	0.482
2	0.342	0.299	0.306
3	0.255	0.217	0.225
4	0.210	0.162	0.171
5	0.180	0.128	0.136
6	0.160	0.117	0.114
7	0.147	0.106	0.107
8	0.135	0.095	0.098
9	0.128	0.089	—
10	0.122	0.084	—
11	0.119	0.081	—
12	0.113	0.080	—
13	0.111	0.077	—
14	0.107	—	—
15	0.105	—	—
16	0.103	—	—
17	0.096	—	—
18	0.094	—	—
Estimated median survival days	368	309	344
Observed survival rate	0.102	0.086	0.111

Note: The observed survival rate reflects the actual probability of remaining arrest-free (i.e. no new criminal arrest charge) through 30 June 2000. It does not account for the fact that some cases were not at risk of arrest over the entire follow-up period (i.e. some cases died before the end of the follow-up period). The estimated survival probability presented above properly accounts for the effects of this 'censoring' of at risk time.

probability of surviving or remaining 'arrest-free' for various periods of post-release time. The estimated survival probability columns represent the estimated probability of 'surviving arrest-free' up to at least the specified time period in each row (representing each year after release). This statistic was obtained using the Kaplan-Meier product-limit formula defined as:

$$\hat{S}(t) = \prod_{j:t_j \leq t} \left[1 - \frac{d_j}{n_j}\right], \qquad (1)$$

where n_j represents the number of individuals at risk at time t_j (i.e. those not arrested yet and still under observation) and d_j represents the number of individuals at risk who were arrested during time t_j (Allison 1995). The quantity in the brackets represents the conditional probability of remaining arrest-free during a given interval of time given that the individual has remained arrest-free up to that point in time (Allison 1995). The product-limit estimate represents the product of these conditional survival probabilities up to a specified period of time. This method of calculating the survival probability properly accounts for the effects of the 'right-censoring' in this data that results from the fact that not all individuals were at risk during the entire follow-up period because some of the subjects had died (as described in a subsequent section below) and therefore were not at risk of being arrested.

In Table 6.3, we see that there was a considerably high rate of arrest during the first year of parole release for all three samples. In fact, roughly 50 per cent or more of each sample was arrested for a new criminal arrest charge within the first 365 days after release on parole. More specifically, the estimated probability of surviving arrest-free past the first year of release was 0.502 in the 1981–2 sample, 0.458 in the 1986–7 sample, and 0.482 in the 1991–2 sample. The estimated median number of days until arrest ranged from 309 in the 1986–7 sample to 368 in the 1981–2 sample, with the 1991–2 sample having an estimated median time until arrest of 344 days. By the end of the third year, roughly 75 per cent or more of each sample had been arrested for a new criminal charge. By the end of the eighth year of the follow-up period (the last point in time at which members of all three samples were measured), the estimated survival probabilities were each at around 0.10 (about 10% had not been arrested yet), indicating approximately a 90 per cent failure rate. The 1981–2

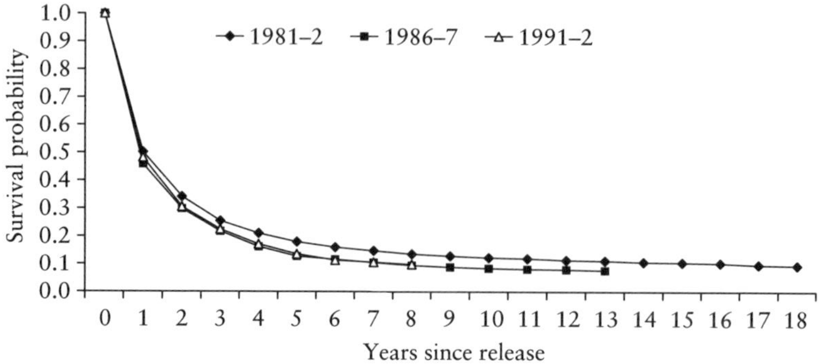

FIGURE 6.4. Estimated survival probabilities of remaining arrest-free as a function of years since release.

sample had the highest estimated probability of surviving arrest-free for at least eight years (13.5%), and the other two release samples were just under 0.10 (0.095 for the 1986–7 sample; 0.098 in the 1991–2 sample). Indeed, by the end of the follow-up period (30 June 2000), the estimated probability of surviving arrest-free was under 0.10 in all three samples.

In Figure 6.4, we depict a graphic portrayal of the survival probabilities presented in Table 6.3. There are several interesting, illustrative points concerning the recidivism rates of the three samples that can be gleaned from the survival curves presented in this figure. First, the survival curves presented in Figure 6.4 clearly indicate that the CYA wards in all three samples were at an exceptionally high risk of arrest for a new criminal charge during the first year of release (i.e. the drop in the curves is exceptionally steep in the first year). Second, it is also clear that there was a significant decline in the rate of a first arrest (for a new criminal offense) after the third year of release given that an individual was able to remain arrest-free for the first three years (i.e. the curves start to level off, although they are still dropping in each year). Third, the curves presented in Figure 6.4 also make it clear that relatively few individuals in the three release samples were able to remain arrest-free during the follow-up period. In fact, we believe that these results point to the inadequacy of the CYA's generally employed recidivism measure (parole removal within 24 months of release), and that the more adequate measure of recidivism rates of CYA ward's employed here indicate that the recidivism rates of individuals released from the CYA are considerably higher than those presented by the CYA.[5]

Finally, with respect to comparing the survival curves of the three samples, it is evident from these curves (which connect the survival probabilities at the various time points) presented in Figure 6.4 that the survival curves of the 1986–7 and 1991–2 samples were nearly identical, while the 1981–2 sample had a curve that was marginally elevated above the other two samples (indicating a *marginally* better chance of remaining arrest-free). However, we will show in Chapter 7 that there is a 'class' of offenders in the 1981–2 sample that was unique to this sample and was composed of a group of males who: (1) had a later age at first arrest, (2) had a very low rate of arrest over time, and (3) were largely sentenced from the adult criminal courts. This class or group of offenders was removed from the CYA population as a result of the legislative changes described in the Chapter 4. Removing this group of offenders from the sample used to calculate the survival probabilities presented in Table 6.3 and Figure 6.4 resulted in nearly identical survival curves for each of the three data sets. In fact, after removing this class of offenders from the 1981–2 sample, the survival curves across time for all three samples collapsed on one another to the point that they could have been represented by a single survival curve. In other words, the survival probabilities were essentially identical in all three samples—the marginal survival curves indicate that there were no significant differences in the recidivism rates between these three samples, especially after removing the one class of offenders unique to the 1981–2 sample (and who were removed from the CYA population purely as a result of legislative changes). Given the increase sentence lengths prescribed by the YOPB for some offenses at the end of 1982 and 1986, noted in Chapter 4, any specific deterrence effects designed to result from these policy changes appear to be notably absent in these data.

Background Characteristics Variables

The data displayed in Table 6.4 depict the background characteristics of the wards in our study at the time they were incarcerated in

[5] This point is supported to an even greater degree by the fact that more than 50 per cent of the cases in each of our three samples end up incarcerated in the CDC for a new conviction for a serious criminal charge that warranted incarceration in the state penal system.

TABLE 6.4. Means of background characteristic variables, by sample

Variable	*Sample*		
	1981–2 (N=1,989)	*1986–7 (N=1,443)*	*1991–2 (N=1,434)*
Ethnicity			
White	0.36	0.28	0.20
Hispanic	0.25	0.33	0.34
African-American	0.36	0.37	0.41
Other	0.02	0.02	0.06
Family background characteristics			
Family violence	0.17	0.18	0.23
Parental alc./drug dependence	0.27	0.34	0.42
Parental criminality	0.20	0.28	0.33
Sibling criminality	0.39	0.38	0.43
Lack of supervision/neglect	0.35	0.43	0.65
Ineffective control	0.60	0.77	0.86
Subject characteristics			
Physical abuse	0.15	0.20	0.22
Sexual abuse	0.01	0.03	0.05
Drug abuse	0.69	0.86	0.72
Gang member/association	0.29	0.51	0.74
Previous violent behavior	0.80	0.86	0.88
School dropout	0.55	0.39	0.87

Note: All variables are binary (dummy) variables and the means represent the percentage of cases coded as 1 (which indicates the presence of the characteristic).

the CYA for the sample stay. All of the variables in Table 6.4 are binary or dummy variables, and thus the means displayed in the table represent the proportion of the sample coded as 1 (which was used to indicate the presence of the characteristic) on the variable. Again attention here focuses on providing a description of the cases, and not explaining the presence and/or significance of the differences between the samples. As a general comparison of the differences between the samples, we note that the overall picture of the results regarding our data (excluding the ethnicity variables) indicates that, in terms of the background characteristics, the 1986–7 sample came into the CYA with a 'more troubling past' than did the 1981–2 sample. Similarly, the 1991–2 sample came into the CYA with a 'more troubling past' than did the 1986–7 sample. For some of the 'troubling characteristics', the greatest change occurred between the 1981–2 and 1986–7 samples, while for other such characteristics the greatest change was between the 1986–7 and 1991–2 samples.

The first set of results we report here pertains to the ethnicities of the wards that we have classified here into four broad categories: White, Hispanic, African-American, and 'Other' (which is primarily composed of individuals of Asian descent). In the 1981–2 sample, White and African-American wards each consist of about 35 per cent of the sample, the Hispanics comprise 25 per cent, and the remaining 2 per cent were in the 'Other' category. In the other two samples, the percentage of White wards decreased in each sample (28% of the 1986–7 sample and 20% of the 1991–2 sample). The Hispanic wards made up 33 and 34 per cent of the 1986–7 and 1991–2 samples, respectively. The percentage of cases that were African-American also increased over the two samples, constituting 37 per cent (1986–7) and 41 per cent (1991–2) of these samples, respectively. The percentage of cases in the 'Other' category was stable between 1981–2 and 1986–7 (2%), but increased to 6 per cent in the 1991–2 sample.

The next set of data in Table 6.4 concerns what we have previously termed 'troubling characteristics' concerning the ward's family environment. About 20 per cent of each sample appears to have been raised in a family setting in which there were reported acts of family violence and (roughly speaking) around one-third of the wards in each sample had one or more parents with a reported drug or alcohol dependence problem (27% in 1981–2; 42% in 1991–2). There is also some evidence of relatively high rates of criminal activity of both parents (20–33%) and siblings (around 40% in all three samples), and a substantial number of the wards were raised in family settings reportedly characterized by either a lack of supervision or neglect of the ward (35–65%). It was even more likely that the wards in the samples were reported to have been beyond the control of their parents/guardians (60% in 1981–2; 77% in 1986–7; 86% in 1991–2).

The final set of data presented in Table 6.4 relates to some of the other 'troubling characteristics' in the social backgrounds of the subjects. Around 20 per cent of the wards were reported to have been subject to physical abuse/extreme punishment when they were growing up, and about 5 per cent or less of the cases in each sample had reportedly been sexually abused. The recorded drug abuse patterns also speak to a major problem affecting a great majority of the wards in each sample. About 70–80 per cent of the wards in these samples were reported to have had a history of drug abuse problems in their backgrounds, with some of these wards addicted to heroin, cocaine/crack, and sniffing paint.

Indeed, one case in the 1991–2 sample was already a heroin and methamphetamine addict at the precocious age of 10, after having been introduced to these drugs at age 9 by an uncle. The estimates of drug abuse patterns reported in Table 6.4 are right near the estimated percentage of the CYA population with a drug abuse problem (70–80%) based on a detailed questionnaire/interview with a sample of CYA wards (see Haapanen and Ingram 2000; Wilson *et al.* 2001). Our data indicate that there was a precipitous increase in the percentage of each sample that was either reported to be a gang member or was a known 'associate' of gang members, and this increase (from roughly 30% in 1981–2 to 75% in 1991–2) coincides with the documented proliferation of street gangs and the explosion in gang-related homicides occurring in the period between the early 1980s through the early 1990s (Klein 1995; Maxson 1999). Lastly, a considerable number of the wards in these samples had already dropped out of school prior to their incarceration for the sample stay period.[6] This was especially true for the 1991–2 sample—87 per cent of the wards in this sample had already dropped out of school at the time of their incarceration.

Variables Related to the Sample Stay

A summary description of the variables related to the sample stay is presented in Table 6.5. As we have seen in Table 6.1, there was a dramatic difference between our three samples in terms of the percentage of the cases committed from the juvenile court. This, of course, is a direct result of the legislation passed in the early 1980s (as described in Chapter 4) that put constraints on the CYA as a sentencing alternative for young adults between the age of 18 and 21. The majority of each sample was in the CYA for a first commitment (60–80%), but the 1986–7 and 1991–2 samples had a larger number of parole violator admissions than did the 1981–2 sample. Recommitment wards were the least prevalent admission type (at around 5–10% of each sample). The average age at admission for the sample stay was about age 18, and on average the wards were between the ages of 19.5 and 20 years old when they were released from the CYA.

[6] Some of the cases had voluntarily dropped out or had just stopped attending without formally withdrawing. Other cases had been formally expelled from the school district in which they resided, sometimes due to an arrest for possession of a loaded firearm on school grounds.

TABLE 6.5. Means of variables related to sample stay at CYA, by sample

Variable	*Sample*		
	1981–2 (N = 1,989)	*1986–7 (N = 1,443)*	*1991–2 (N = 1,434)*
Juvenile court commitment	0.54	0.75	0.91
Admission status			
First commitment	0.79	0.58	0.70
Parole violator	0.11	0.36	0.26
Recommitment	0.09	0.06	0.04
Age at admission	18.34	18.58	17.88
Age at release	19.45	20.10	19.67
Length of stay (in months)	13.43	18.28	21.48
Commitment offense			
Violent	0.42	0.39	0.40
Property	0.53	0.48	0.39
Drug	0.02	0.08	0.16
Other	0.03	0.05	0.04
County (of commitment) region			
Los Angeles	0.40	0.45	0.41
Bay Area	0.20	0.19	0.14
Southern California (not LA)	0.19	0.12	0.15
Northern/Central California	0.22	0.24	0.30
Number of DDMS infractions	1.09	1.92	2.01

Note: All variables are binary (dummy) variables except for age at admission, age at release, length of stay and number of DDMS infractions. For the binary variables, the means represent the percentage of cases coded as 1 (which indicates the presence of the characteristic).

There was a large increase in the average length of stay between the three samples (as noted in Chapter 4). The average offender in the 1991–2 sample was incarcerated about 21.5 months, whereas the average ward in the 1981–2 sample was incarcerated for 13 months. The majority of the wards were committed to the CYA for either a violent (40%) or property crime (40–50%). There was an increase in the percentage of wards committed for a drug offense (2% in 1981–2 and 16% in 1991–2), which is arguably a consequence of the 'War on Drugs' movement that began in the early 1980s.[7] Most of the wards in these samples came from either

[7] Some of the drug arrests that resulted in the commitment to the CYA involved small amounts of drugs such as a few individually packaged 'rocks' of crack cocaine, while other commitments involved large amounts of narcotics. For example, one case

Los Angeles county (40%) or from Northern/Central California (22–30%) counties such as Sacramento, Fresno, and Kern. The remaining cases were either from counties in the Bay Area (14–20%) such as Alameda, San Francisco, and San José or from counties in Southern California (excluding Los Angeles) such as San Diego, Ventura, and San Bernardino (12–19%). Finally, the wards in these three samples were written up for an average of 1.1, 1.92, and 2.02 DDMS infractions, respectively, during their sample stay at the CYA. The increasing infraction counts over time is probably the result of two characterizations of these samples already noted: the increasing average amount of time served mandated by YA Parole Board over time and the increase in gang membership among clients served by the YA over time. Those two characteristics tend to increase the chances for fights and assault among wards, and many of these fights and assaults reported among the 1991–2 sample were described as 'gang related.'

Mortality Experiences

Attention is now turned to the mortality experiences of the members of the three samples. Table 6.6 presents the frequencies of death events in each of the samples and decomposes the major types of death into 'High Risk' and 'Other Types.'[8] The 'High Risk' death types included homicide, suicide, drug overdose, AIDS, and auto accident deaths.

Of the 4,866 individuals in the three samples, 329 (6.8%) were found to be deceased at some point in the post-release period, with 152 (7.6%), 98 (6.8%), and 79 (5.5%) deaths occurring in the 1981–2, 1986–7, and 1991–2 samples, respectively. Even more importantly, about 80 per cent or more of the deaths were found to

was arrested for selling one and a half pounds of black tar heroin to undercover officers, another was arrested with 55 'balloons' of heroin, while another case was arrested while in possession of $36,000 worth of crack cocaine, an automatic firearm, and $5,000 in cash.

[8] The major type of death was obtained from the ICD9 and ICD10 (1999 deaths) codes. The ICD9 codes for firearm homicides included codes E965.0–E965.4 and E970. The ICD9 non-firearm homicides included codes: E960–E964, E965.5–E969, and E971–E978. The homicide deaths in the 1999 DSMF file were identified using ICD10 'group codes' 338–346, while group code 340 was used to determine the firearm homicides.

TABLE 6.6. Frequency and type of death, by sample

Death type	*Sample*								
	1981–2 (N = 1,989)			*1986–7 (N = 1,443)*			*1991–2 (N = 1,434)*		
	n	*% of deaths*	*% of sample*	*n*	*% of deaths*	*% of sample*	*n*	*% of deaths*	*% of sample*
All death types	152	100.0	7.6	98	100.0	6.8	79	100.0	5.5
'High-risk' deaths	117	77.0	5.9	83	84.7	5.8	69	87.3	4.8
Homicide	62	40.8	3.1	60	61.2	4.2	61	77.2	4.3
Firearm	51	33.6	2.6	51	52.0	3.5	58	73.4	4.0
Non-firearm	8	5.3	0.4	8	8.2	0.6	2	2.5	0.1
Legal intervention	3	2.0	0.2	1	1.0	0.1	1	1.3	0.1
Suicide	8	5.3	0.4	5	5.1	0.3	3	3.8	0.2
Drug overdose	22	14.5	1.1	11	11.2	0.8	3	3.8	0.2
AIDS	13	8.6	0.7	4	4.1	0.3	0	0.0	0.0
Auto accident	20	13.2	1.0	8	8.2	0.6	5	6.3	0.3
Other types of death	35	23.0	1.8	15	15.3	1.0	10	12.7	0.7

be in the 'High Risk' death types categories. That is, the majority of the deaths in the sample were not the result of 'natural causes', but rather most were the result of high-risk activities. Descriptions of four of the deaths in the 1991–2 sample can help describe the high-risk nature of some of these deaths.

Case 1: During an armed robbery, decedent was shot in the head while in a shoot-out with an armed security guard.
Case 2: Decedent choked on own vomit during a drug overdose.
Case 3: Decedent shot execution-style with the muzzle pressed against forehead. Decedent was killed for testifying against the homicide perpetrator (fellow gang member).
Case 4: Decedent lost control of motorcycle at a high rate of speed.

Perhaps the most striking feature of Table 6.6 concerns the homicide event totals—of the 329 deaths, 183 of them (or 56%) were homicide victims! Furthermore, there was a considerable disparity across the samples in terms of the percentage of deaths that were attributable to homicide. Consider that the 1991–2 sample had ten less years of exposure and roughly 550 fewer wards than the 1981–2 sample, and yet the 1991–2 sample accrued almost the exact same count number of homicides as did the 1981–2 sample. In the 1981–2 sample, 40.8 per cent (n = 62) of the deaths were attributed to homicide, whereas in the 1991–2 sample 77.2 per cent (n = 61) of the deaths were reported as the result of homicide. The 1986–7 sample fell nearly in the middle of the other two samples—61 per cent (n = 60) of the deaths in this sample were classified as the result of homicide. Of the 183 homicide events in all three samples, 160 of them (or 87%) were the result of gunshot wounds.

The extent of homicide mortality in these three samples should not be taken lightly. To make a comparison concerning the heightened risk of mortality among the samples, consider that the homicide rate peaked in California in 1993 at 12.9 homicide events for every 100,000 individuals. Thus, to obtain 183 homicide events in the general population, one would have needed a sample of about roughly 1.4 million people for that year. Granted the three samples analyzed herein were followed over time, but the fact that 183 homicide events were recorded in a sample of only 4,866 individuals is in our view, an extreme homicide rate under any circumstances.

TABLE 6.7. Summary of variables related to adult incarceration experiences, by sample

Variable	*Sample*		
	1981–2 (N = 1,989)	*1986–7 (N = 1,443)*	*1991–2 (N = 1,434)*
%with at least 1 CDC stay	65.1%	68.9%	52.3%
Maximum strike status			
Second Striker %	12.7%	11.7%	9.1%
Third Striker %	3.3%	2.1%	0.6%
Among those with at least 1 CDC stay			
Avg. no. of CDC stays	2.5	2.1	1.6
Avg. length of stay (in months)	25.5	22.2	19.5
Median length of stay (in months)	16.3	14.5	13.8
Average age at admission	27.6	26.2	23.7
Average age at first admission	24.2	24.2	22.8
Avg. no. of total years incarcerated in CDC	5.4	3.9	2.5
Median no. of total years incarcerated in CDC	4.4	3.2	2.0

Note: Length of stay was calculated as of 30 June 2000, if they were still incarcerated at that point.

Adult Incarceration Experiences

Finally, Table 6.7 presents summary information regarding the entrances of sample cases into the California Department of Corrections (CDC). Again, the different amounts of exposure time between the samples should be kept in mind when interpreting the results in Table 6.7. As can be seen in the table, a sizeable percentage of each of the samples had been incarcerated in the CDC at least once as of 30 June 2000—65 per cent of the 1981–2 sample, 69 per cent of the 1986–7 sample, and 52 per cent of the 91–2 sample. As of 30 June 2000, 13 per cent of the 1981–2, 12 per cent of the 1986–7, and 9 per cent of the 1991–2 samples, respectively, had been sentenced as 'Two Striker' under California's 'Three Strikes and You're Out' programme. A larger percentage (3.3%) of the 1981–2 sample had been sentenced as a 'Third Strike' case than either the 1986–7 sample (2.1%) or the 1991–2 sample (0.6%). This is not surprising, since the selection mechanisms built-into the 'Three Strikes' law in California put older individuals with convictions in their past at the greatest risk of being sentenced as a

'Three Strike' case. Thus, we would expect the 1981–2 sample to have the most individuals sentenced as a third strike case, since they have had a longer time period over which to accrue such a legal status.

Limiting the sample to only those individuals who had at least one 'stay' (or incarceration) in the CDC, we next generated some variables for these specific individuals. The average number of entrances among those with at least one CDC entrance was 2.5 (for the 1981–2 sample), 2.1 (for the 1986–7 sample), and 1.6 (for the 1991–2 sample). The average length of stay ranged from 20 to 25 months, while the median length of stay ranged from 14 to 16 months.[9] The average age of all admissions ranged from 23.7 (1991–2) to 27.6 (1981–2), and the average age at first admission was 24.2 in both the 1981–2 and 1986–7 samples, and 22.8 in the 1991–2 sample. The cumulative average number of years spent incarcerated in the CDC (as of 30 June 2000) was 5.4 years in the 1981–2 sample, 3.9 years in the 1986–7, and 2.5 years in the 1991–2 sample, with the median cumulative number of years incarcerated ranging from 2 to 4.4 years. Among those who were incarcerated at least once (and taking into account the differing amounts of exposure time in each sample), the median number of cumulative years incarcerated was just under one-quarter (about 0.24) of the total post-release period in each sample.

Summary

The main point we hope to have conveyed in this chapter is that the wards in our samples constitute a group of very serious offenders. To put it bluntly, when it comes to accumulating a record for serious crime (for any comparable period of time), the members of the samples from the other studies we have reviewed here appear not to be 'from the same league' as the members of our samples. Not surprisingly, many of the wards in our samples had led seriously troubled lives on a number of fronts and appear to have faced a myriad of major problems (besides the problems associated with

[9] The distribution of length of stay is right-skewed due to the effects of the 'lifers' (those sentenced to life) and those individuals incarcerated for long periods of time. Thus, we have presented both the median and the mean lengths of stay as of 30 June 2000.

their criminal activity). Drawing on a term from medical sociology, considering their crime, social problems (e.g. drug abuse, school dropout), and mortality risk simultaneously, the individuals in these three samples could be accurately characterized as having serious *co-morbidity* problems. In other words, while these individuals frequently engage in a wide variety of crimes throughout their life course, crime is not the only problem in the lives of these wards. Many of the individuals in these samples appear to have been raised in rather chaotic family environments, had serious academic difficulties and educational deficits, and many of them (especially in the 1991–2 sample) were raised in violent neighborhoods that were entrenched in gang activity. For many of the individuals in these samples, their stay at the CYA as a juvenile/young adult was a mere prelude to an accumulation of additional serious problems in adulthood, including future incarceration in the CDC for some and, unfortunately, a much higher than average risk of death and homicide compared to others in the general population.

Having now completed a summary description of the data, we next turn the focus of attention to the two main substantive chapters of this study. In the next chapter, we focus on the relationship between age and crime within latent classes of serious youthful offenders.

7

Age and Crime among Latent Classes of Serious Youthful Offenders

In the first chapter of this study it was noted that one of the foremost controversies in contemporary theoretical criminology concerns how to simultaneously explain the sources of both continuity and change in criminal behavior over time. The 'paradox of persistence' was described as a descriptive empirical finding that highlights the importance of the processes of both continuity and discontinuity in criminal offending patterns across the life course. We also detailed how the crux of the dispute between three different broad theoretical paradigms (i.e. population heterogeneity, state dependence, and the dual taxonomy approach) centers largely on predicted differences regarding the degree to which criminal propensity is stable/instable across the life course. The explanation as to why criminal propensity is either stable/instable (or a mixture of both properties) is of fundamental importance to the discipline of criminology because it has important theoretical implications for explaining two of the robust or 'brute facts' of criminology: (1) the reported inverse relationship between age and crime; and (2) the reported positive association between past and subsequent criminal activity. We examine the topic of the association between past and subsequent criminal activity in Chapter 8, but first we investigate in this chapter the empirical relationship between age and crime within latent classes of offenders (that are homogeneous with respect to their criminal activity across the life course).[1] We presented four hypotheses in Chapter 3 that address the relationship between age and crime. They included investigating: (1) whether there are multiple types of offenders, even on the high end of the criminal propensity continuum; (2) whether there are specifically

[1] The results of this chapter are also critical for Chapter 8. We make use of the latent class results presented in this chapter in several of the analyses in Chapter 8.

only two different offender types corresponding to the 'adolescent-limited' and 'life-course-persistent' groups; (3) whether there exists an 'adolescent-limited' offender type in the high-risk samples employed here; and, finally, (4) whether there are stable between-group differences among latent classes across the age range. The theoretical importance and empirical motivation for the analyses in this chapter can be found in the summaries of Chapters 2 and 3, respectively.

Accordingly, we now present a series of analyses in this chapter that address hypotheses 1–4 using the three samples of 'high-risk' offenders. This chapter has six main sections. In the first section, we present a descriptive summary of the aggregate age–crime relationship within the three samples. In the second section, we describe the process through which we arrived at the optimal number of latent classes for each sample. The optimal number of latent classes will provide evidence regarding the empirical support in these data for hypotheses $\mathbf{H_1}$ and $\mathbf{H_2}$ described in Chapter 3. The third section of this chapter contains a statistical test of Gottfredson and Hirschi's hypothesis that there is uniformity in the shape of the age–crime curves of different latent classes by testing the statistical significance of allowing the magnitude of the age parameters to vary across the latent classes (hypothesis $\mathbf{H_4}$ in Chapter 3). The final three sections present substantive evidence concerning the hypotheses for our three different samples.

As discussed in Chapter 3, the results presented in this chapter are derived from use of the semiparametric mixed Poisson model developed by Nagin and Land (1993). Using the final analytic samples constructed for each of the three CYA samples, the following model was (1) estimated on each of our three samples:

$$\ln\left(\lambda^{j}_{it}\right) = (\beta_0 + \bar{\varepsilon}_j) + \left((age_{it}/10) * \beta^{j}_{\text{age}}\right) + \left(((age^2_{it})/100) * \beta^{j}_{\text{age}^2}\right). \tag{1}$$

Models allowing up to eight latent classes were tested, and the BIC statistic along with empirical testing assessing whether the solutions are global maximums were used to select the optimal number of latent classes or components in the mixture distribution (discussed in further detail below). The finite mixture models employed in this study were estimated using the software program Latent GOLD, Version 2.0.9 (Vermunt and Magidson 2000).

Descriptive Summary of the Age–Crime Relationship

Prior to examining the heterogeneity with respect to the age–crime trajectories that exist within our serious youthful chronic offender samples, we first present an overall 'baseline' description of the age–crime relationship. Figure 7.1 presents the aggregate age–crime curve in the three samples.[2]

As seen in Figure 7.1, the overall shape replicates the robust shape of the aggregate age–crime curve, with rapidly increasing arrest rates in adolescence, a peak arrest rate during adolescence, and then a decline in the arrest rate through adulthood. It is informative to note that the trend of the age–crime curves is amazingly similar across the three samples, which is the type of finding that originally sparked the age-invariance argument of Gottfredson and Hirschi. In fact, the three samples are nearly identical up through about age 15, after which there is more variability from sample to sample; still the overall pattern is relatively robust from sample to sample.[3]

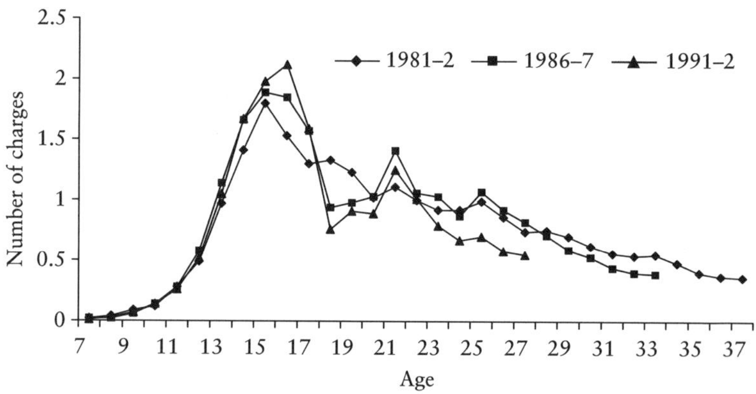

FIGURE 7.1. Aggregate age–crime curve, by sample.

[2] We have only graphed the curves up through the last age at which at least 50 per cent of the sample was available (at-risk) for estimation (see Appendix B).

[3] The dip in the rate between the ages of 18 and 20 for the 1986–7 sample and the 1991–2 sample probably: (1) partially reflects the fact that only ages during which the offenders were incarcerated in the CYA for the *entire* 'age year' during sample stay were excluded from being at-risk; and (2) partially reflects the increased parole revocation rates for those two samples compared to the 1981–2 sample. Unfortunately, determining the precise cause of the dip is impossible because we do not have access on the incarcerations in the CYA for parole revocations. That is, if a ward's

The peak age of arrest in these three samples actually peaks earlier than the typical aggregate age–crime curve computed using overall population-level data (as presented in Figure 1.1), but this is not surprising given that the samples are composed of known chronic youthful offenders who by definition were active at an early age in life. For example, in the 1981–2 sample, the peak age of arrest was age 15 (1.8 arrest charges). The peak age was also age 15 in the 1986–7 sample (1.89 arrest charges), and the peak age was 16 in the 1991–2 sample (2.12 arrest charges). In the final age category presented in Figure 7.1 (which is the last age at which at least 50% of the sample was available), the average number of arrest charges was 0.36 at age 37 (1981–2 sample), 0.33 at age 33 (1986–7 sample), and 0.55 at age 27 (1991–2 sample). It is interesting to note that the 1991–2 sample experienced a more rapid decline in their arrest rates compared to the other two samples, and this is the sample that would have been most likely to have benefited from both the crime rate and corresponding arrest rate declines of the mid- to late 1990s. Thus, in the aggregate, the age–crime curve for these three samples resembles the overall aggregate age–crime curve (albeit with an earlier peak). Our attention now turns to examining whether there are diverse, heterogeneous age–crime trajectories among different 'offender types' (or latent classes) concealed or masked within the overall age–crime curve (computed for the sample as a whole). In the next section, we discuss the selection of the optimal number of latent classes.

Selecting the Optimal Number of Latent Classes

As described in Appendix A, models with varying numbers of points of support are not nested within each other, and thus alternative methods (besides the likelihood ratio test) of determining the number of mixture components have been recommended. Following the lead of D'Unger *et al.* (1998) and Nagin (1999),

parole was revoked after the date of release on the sample stay, we did not have access to the exact dates of the subsequent incarcerations in the CYA for the parole revocation, and thus some individuals would appear to be at-risk when they really were incarcerated in the CYA for the entire age-year. It is probably the joint interaction between those two possibilities that is largely responsible for the drop. It is our contention that the drop is artifactually the result of complex at-risk processes, especially when you note the trend is back 'on track' at age 20.

we use the Bayesian Information Criterion (BIC) statistic for selecting the appropriate number of groups in the mixing distribution.

However, the selection of the optimal number of points of supports for the mixing distribution is also complicated by the fact that mixture models are known to often have a problem with 'local solutions' (i.e. a unique global solution is not always achieved) (Cameron and Trivedi 1998; Goodman 1974; Vermunt and Magidson 2000; Wedel and Kamakura 1998). This issue concerns whether the likelihood function is unimodal (i.e. globally concave) or multimodal. In brief, the local solution problem arises from the fact that it is possible for the model's numerical algorithm to converge to multiple local maxima. Following the recommendations of Wedel and Kamakura (1998), Cameron and Trivedi (1998), Greene (2000), and Vermunt and Magidson (2001), we tested extensively for the presence of local solutions through the use of 'multiple sets of starting values' coupled with multiple (10) runs of the estimation procedure. We describe this local solution problem and the testing process below, but first we briefly describe the method of estimation employed in generating the results presented herein.

Method of Estimation and Global/Local Solutions

The parameters for the semiparametric mixed Poisson models were obtained via a maximum likelihood (ML) estimation routine employing the Newton-Raphson algorithm.[4] The ML estimation routine that maximizes the likelihood function is

$$\ln L = \sum_i n_i \ln f(\mathbf{y}_i \mid \mathbf{X}_i, \boldsymbol{\theta}), \tag{2}$$

where $\boldsymbol{\theta}$ is a vector of estimated model parameters, $\mathbf{y}_i$ and $\mathbf{X}_i$ are vectors of dependent and independent variables, respectively, for the ith vector pattern, and n_i is the number of cases with the given i^{th} vector pattern.

In equation (2), $f(\mathbf{y}_i \mid \mathbf{X}_i, \boldsymbol{\theta})$ is the Poisson probability density function for covariate pattern i given the estimated parameter values contained in vector $\boldsymbol{\theta}$. The estimation task is to find a set of

[4] Further detailed information on using maximum likelihood (ML) estimation methods for finite mixture (latent class) models is available in Haberman (1988) and Vermunt and Magidson (2000), and the maximum likelihood method is described generally in Greene (2000). This presentation draws heavily on the exposition of ML methods in Vermunt and Magidson (2000: 162–8).

estimates, denoted as $\hat{\boldsymbol{\theta}}$, for the parameter vector $\boldsymbol{\theta}$ such that partial derivatives of the log-likelihood function with respect to $\boldsymbol{\theta}$ are equal to zero:

$$\frac{\partial \ln L}{\partial \hat{\boldsymbol{\theta}}} = 0. \tag{3}$$

In this study, the estimates were obtained using the Newton-Raphson (NR) algorithm, which is an iterative, gradient-based method of optimization. The NR method is an iterative, gradient-based method of optimization (Greene 2000):

$$\boldsymbol{\theta}^{v} = \boldsymbol{\theta}^{v-1} - \varepsilon \mathbf{H}^{-1}\mathbf{g}, \tag{4}$$

where v denotes the current j^{th} iteration, $\mathbf{g}$ is the gradient vector containing the first-order derivatives of the log-likelihood function evaluated at $\boldsymbol{\theta}^{v-1}$ (i.e. at the prior iteration of the algorithm), ε is a scalar number known as the 'step' size, and $\mathbf{H}$ is the Hessian matrix (or observed information matrix) that contains the second-order derivatives. The elements of the gradient vector, denoted as- g_r, are equal to

$$g_r = \sum_i n_i \frac{\partial \ln f(\mathbf{y}_i|\mathbf{X}_i, \boldsymbol{\theta})}{\partial \theta_r}, \tag{5}$$

and the elements of the Hessian matrix are:

$$H_{rs} = \sum_i n_i \frac{\partial^2 \ln f(\mathbf{y}_i|\mathbf{X}_i, \boldsymbol{\theta})}{\partial \theta_r \partial \theta_s'}. \tag{6}$$

The asymptotic variance-covariance matrix of the maximum likelihood estimates, which are the final estimates $\hat{\boldsymbol{\theta}}$ that solve equation (3) above, are calculated by inverting the Hessian matrix (the negative of the matrix of second derivatives of the log-likelihood function with respect to the estimated parameters)

$$V\left(\hat{\boldsymbol{\theta}}\right) = \mathbf{H}^{-1} = -\left[\frac{\partial^2 \ln L\left(\hat{\boldsymbol{\theta}}\right)}{\partial \hat{\boldsymbol{\theta}}\, \partial \hat{\boldsymbol{\theta}}'}\right]^{-1}. \tag{7}$$

Finally, *convergence* of the algorithm occurs when the sum of the absolute relative changes in the parameter estimates, or

$$\sum_r \left| \frac{\hat{\theta}_r^{v} - \hat{\theta}_r^{v-1}}{\hat{\theta}_r^{v-1}} \right|, \tag{8}$$

meets a prior defined tolerance criterion whereby the absolute change in the parameters meets the convergence criterion. In this study, we use a very 'tight' convergence criterion: 1e-10 (or 0.0000000001).

The local solution problem arises because the condition defined in equation (3), can often be satisfied with several different solutions such that a minor change in any one of the estimated parameters leads to a degradation of the log-likelihood value. The algorithm only distinguishes that a maximum has been reached, but it cannot determine whether the solution is a global or local maximum solution.[5] The distinction between the two is that a local solution is the best solution in a particular *area* of the parameter space, whereas a global solution is the best solution in *the* parameter space.

Maximizing a likelihood function is often characterized in a non-statistical way as climbing a mountain and perhaps this non-statistical description can be used to clarify the problems of local solutions. Imagine that you have to climb a mountain blindfolded ten times and you have to place a flag at the top of the mountain when you think you are at the top (i.e. maximized the likelihood function).[6] You climb the mountain using some pre-defined 'step' sizes that take you, according to your exact step rule (i.e. the numerical algorithm), up the mountain to a specific location. If you started climbing from the same spot every time you climbed the mountain (i.e. use the same starting values), you will always end up at the exact same spot because you take 'steps' according to a very specific rule. Your ten flags will all be at the same spot simply because that is where your 'step rules' tell you the top of the mountain is located, not because it actually is the top of the mountain. If, however, you started your climb up the mountain from a different location each time (i.e. use different starting estimates) and you ended up at the same location each time regardless of where you started your ascent (i.e. same likelihood value and same model parameter estimates regardless of the value of the starting estimates), you would be more confident that you had actually reached the top of the mountain (i.e. attained a global solution).

[5] Our results suggest that local solutions may be a problem with the higher-order latent class models (e.g. 7-class, 8-class models).

[6] Of course, this is an oversimplification of the problem because of the actual dimensionality of the likelihood function, but the imagery accurately conveys the nature of the problem.

If on the other hand, you placed your flags at multiple sites (i.e. attained multiple local solutions), you would not be able to tell if you had actually reached the top of the mountain, nor would you be confident that you really know where the top of the mountain is located (i.e. what the true global solution is assuming there is one). The only thing you would know was that at certain sites on the mountain peak, your 'step' size calculations indicated to you that if you took any other steps, you would start going 'down the mountain' again (i.e. a degradation of the log-likelihood value). Our approach to the possible problem of local solutions is to climb the 'likelihood mountain' several times and see if we land at the same location each and every time.

The testing for global/local solutions process was as follows. Initially, 50 sets of random starting estimates were generated. These 50 sets of starting estimates were then run through 20 iterations of the EM algorithm.[7] Next, the top 10 per cent of the starting seeds with the largest log-likelihoods at this point were then run through an additional 40 iterations of the EM algorithm. Finally, the set of starting estimates with the largest log-likelihood value at this point was then entered into the ML algorithm, which either ended in convergence (i.e. a solution) or the maximum number of iterations (set at 150) was reached without convergence and algorithm stoops. This entire process was repeated ten times for each point of support model (except for the 1 point of support model which was only run once).[8] Thus, the 2 points of support model was run ten times, the 3 points of support model was run 10 times, and so on. The final

[7] The EM (expectation maximization) algorithm (Dempster, Laird, and Rubin 1977) was used in this step of the process because the EM algorithm is extremely stable and fast when the model is far away from the optimum. The NR algorithm, on the other hand, is inefficient and computationally burdensome (because of the calculation of the Hessian matrix) when far away from the optimum, but is extremely efficient and accurate when near the optimum (Greene 2000; Vermunt and Magidson 2001; Wang, Cockburn, and Puterman 1998).

[8] One might wonder why we chose to run the models ten separate times. Our initial testing of the problem indicated the five separate runs did not always identify local solutions, but ten separate runs caught all of the local solutions we encountered. The computational burden of even running the models ten times was quite severe, especially since this entire process was repeated three separate times (once for each sample). In total, the actual computer time for estimating the models ten times on each of the three samples was about 200 hours. This entire process had to be repeated all over again for the models presented in Chapter 8 because they involved a different specification.

solutions of the models were then compared in order to evaluate if the same unique solution was generated with each run of the model. Models with more than one solution (i.e. local solutions) were identified through this extensive model testing procedure.

The Optimal Number of Latent Classes in the Three Samples

To determine the optimal number of latent classes, we jointly used the BIC statistic and the testing for the local/global solutions described above. The rule, in short, was the model that resulted in the largest (or least negative) BIC value in the presence of only a single solution would be chosen as the optimum number of latent classes. Models with more than one (local) solution were not considered as possible models.

The results of fitting the 1-class through 8-class semiparametric mixed Poisson models for all three samples, according to the specification of equation (1), are presented in Table 7.1. The results of the local/global testing indicated that in all three samples the 7-class and 8-class models were prone to multiple local maxima solutions that varied from one solution to another.[9] In all three samples, however, the 6-class models generated the same unique solution all ten times they were estimated. Further, and as shown in Table 7.1, the 6-class model in all three samples had the largest BIC value, and thus the 6-class models were determined to be the models with the optimal number of latent classes for each of the three samples. Note also that the addition of a sixth point of support increased the BIC value by 427.84 in the 1981–2 sample, 190.66 in the 1986–7 sample, and 183.75 in the 1991–2 sample.

The results presented so far allow for an examination of the empirical support for the hypotheses H_1 and H_2 delineated in Chapter 3. The empirical evidence in this study (for all three samples) supports hypothesis, H_1, which predicts that there are multiple, distinct offender groups on the high-end of the criminal propensity continuum. These results support the contentions of Cohen and Vila (1996) and D'Unger *et al.* (1998) that the far end of the continuum appears to have far greater heterogeneity than previously thought.

[9] Examination of the estimates from the local solutions indicates that these models were 'weakly identified', meaning that two or more of the points of support were not very different from one another. See Note 4 of Chapter 8 for a discussion of weak identification.

TABLE 7.1. BIC values for the semiparametric mixed Poisson models, by sample

Number of latent classes	*Log-likelihood*	*BIC*	*Change in BIC*
1981–2 sample			
1	– 82,026.06	– 82,037.45	—
2	– 77,059.40	– 77,085.99	4,951.46
3	– 75,404.98	– 75,446.75	1,639.23
4	– 74,100.77	– 74,157.74	1,289.01
5	– 73,509.48	– 73,581.63	576.10
6	– 73,066.44	– 73,153.79	427.84
7	MS	MS	—
8	MS	MS	—
1986–7 sample			
1	– 52,620.27	– 52,631.18	—
2	– 49,806.40	– 49,831.86	2,799.32
3	– 49,024.08	– 49,064.09	767.78
4	– 48,347.17	– 48,401.73	662.35
5	– 48,032.93	– 48,102.03	299.70
6	– 47,827.72	– 47,911.38	190.66
7	MS	MS	—
8	MS	MS	—
1991–2 sample			
1	– 39,923.26	– 39,934.16	—
2	– 37,952.46	– 37,977.89	1,956.27
3	– 37,376.58	– 37,416.55	561.34
4	– 36,984.44	– 37,038.95	377.60
5	– 36,748.70	– 36,817.75	221.20
6	– 36,550.41	– 36,634.00	183.75
7	MS	MS	—
8	MS	MS	—

Note: 'MS' indicates multiple solutions were found, with no clear global solution. *The* model that has the least negative value of the BIC statistic is the favored model.

Empirically, the results presented so far also appear to shed considerable doubt on Moffitt's hypothesis (H_2) that there are only two discrete offender groups within even just the serious youthful offender population.[10] The BIC statistics in all three samples favored a 6-class model, and the positive increase in the magnitude of the BIC statistics between the models that only allow for two

[10] Importantly, regardless of whether one assumes a 3-class, 4-class, 5-class, or 6-class model, the evidence rejects the notion that there are only two latent classes or offender typologies present in the population; this appears to be the case even here among just the serious youthful offenders population.

TABLE 7.2. Parameter estimates from the 6-class semiparametric mixed Poisson model, by sample

	Sample		
	1981–2	*1986–7*	*1991–2*
Random effects			
Class 1	–4.860	–8.473	–7.346
	(36.06)	(28.28)	(24.10)
Class 2	–3.057	–5.062	–17.921
	(34.18)	(27.02)	(16.67)
Class 3	–5.771	–3.378	–8.321
	(33.60)	(16.52)	(32.57)
Class 4	–8.624	–24.448	–5.877
	(16.54)	(18.57)	(16.48)
Class 5	–22.006	–7.073	–39.014
	(23.36)	(25.84)	(17.57)
Class 6	–4.000	–4.082	–4.887
	(29.71)	(22.35)	(17.11)
Age effects			
Class 1 age	3.989	9.6355	7.554
	(33.53)	(28.36)	(21.16)
Class 1 age sq.	–0.813	–2.6269	–1.905
	(31.47)	(27.36)	(18.85)
Class 2 age	3.651	4.5456	21.464
	(41.34)	(26.71)	(16.56)
Class 2 age sq.	–0.884	–0.9924	–6.217
	(41.87)	(25.55)	(15.95)
Class 3 age	6.870	4.5163	9.876
	(35.45)	(19.06)	(34.78)
Class 3 age sq.	–1.881	–1.2677	–2.603
	(35.19)	(18.98)	(33.55)
Class 4 age	7.691	32.0432	8.141
	(13.90)	(18.24)	(19.12)
Class 4 age sq.	–1.882	–10.2455	–2.553
	(13.02)	(17.64)	(20.55)
Class 5 age	29.199	7.9416	52.885
	(23.39)	(28.31)	(17.40)
Class 5 age sq.	–9.375	–1.9275	–17.518
	(22.86)	(28.11)	(16.92)
Class 6 age	3.592	3.7658	4.753
	(31.73)	(22.89)	(16.25)
Class 6 age sq.	–0.666	–0.7319	–1.004
	(28.96)	(20.09)	(13.81)
N (observations)	1,989	1,443	1,434
N (panel observations)	60,453	37,390	29,385

Note: Absolute values of t-statistics are in parentheses.

latent classes (corresponding to the hypothesized number of discrete groups in the Moffitt theory) and those that allow for six latent classes were indeed quite large (3,932.2 in the 1981–2 sample; 1,920.5 in the 1986–7 sample; and 1,343.9 in the 1991–2 sample). Finally, it is important to note that Keribin (1997) and Wang, Cockburn, and Puterman (1998) both demonstrate that that the BIC statistic identifies the optimal number of components (points of support) in the mixing distribution with a high degree of precision.

The resulting parameter estimates for the 6-class models are presented in Table 7.2. Due to the fact that this model is full of non-linear terms, it is difficult to substantively interpret the parameter estimates of this model (as presented in Table 7.2). Below, we present a substantive presentation of each model's estimates by graphically depicting the offending trajectories, but for now we make several comments regarding these parameter estimates. First, it is apparent from the signs of the age and age-squared coefficients of each latent class that there was a significant non-linear relationship between age and crime for all six latent classes in each of the samples. There was no latent class in any of the samples that was found to offend at a relatively constant rate across age in the 'spirit' that describes the 'life-course-persistent' offender group. The age and age-squared parameter estimates for all of the latent classes were significantly different from zero (and indicative of a significant quadratic relationship). Moffitt (1993: 695) explicitly argues that age is not a predictor of the offending trajectory of the 'life-course-persistent' group. These results then are highly inconsistent with the notion that there is a group of offenders whose offending behavior is not significantly variable over the age distribution observed in our samples.

Statistically Testing the Age-Invariance Hypothesis

In this section, we present results from statistical tests of Gottfredson and Hirschi's age-invariance hypothesis. As depicted in Table 7.2, the nature of the age coefficients seem to be highly variable over the latent classes—this drives at the core of the age-invariance hypothesis. It does not appear from the results presented in Table 7.2 (in any of the three samples) that the age and age-squared variables in each latent class are hovering in the neighborhood of a common value shared by all of the latent classes. The nature of the relationship between age and crime appears to be highly variable across the different latent classes. For example, the estimate of the age parameter in the first latent class in the 1981–2 sample was 3.99, whereas the estimate of the age parameter in the fifth latent class was 29.20. The results presented thus far are inconsistent with the invariance hypothesis of Gottfredson and Hirschi asserting that there is uniformity in the shape of the age–crime curves across the six latent classes (hypothesis $\mathbf{H}_4$ in Chapter 3); however, a more formal statistical test is required to adequately judge the empirical validity of their hypothesis. Below we will now formally test this hypothesis.

Recall that Gottfredson and Hirschi (1990) argue in favor of a robust relationship between age and crime—while groups differ on their mean offending rate, the actual shapes of the trajectories are identical. In other words, the shapes of the age–crime curves are invariant. This predicted relationship corresponds to a specification of the finite mixture model that allows the latent classes to have intercept values that vary over the latent classes, but the age parameters (i.e. age and age squared) must share a common (invariant) value. This hypothesis can be evaluated without re-estimating the model by using the Wald statistic to test the equality of each set of age coefficients across the latent classes via a linear constraint (Long 1997; Powers and Xie 2000; Vermunt and Magidson 2000). The Wald statistical test that the age coefficients are identical across the latent classes tests the null hypothesis

$$\mathrm{H}_0 : \mathbf{Q}\boldsymbol{\beta} = \mathbf{r}, \tag{9}$$

where $\boldsymbol{\beta}$ is a vector of regression parameters, $\mathbf{Q}$ is a matrix of constraints, and $\mathbf{r}$ is a vector of constants (Long 1997: 89–90). The null hypothesis of equation (9) can be tested using the Wald statistic that is calculated as

$$W = \left(\mathbf{Q}'\hat{\boldsymbol{\beta}} - \mathbf{r}\right)'\left(\mathbf{Q}\hat{\mathbf{H}}^{-1}\mathbf{Q}'\right)^{-1}\left(\mathbf{Q}'\hat{\boldsymbol{\beta}} - \mathbf{r}\right), \tag{10}$$

where $\mathbf{H}$ is the Hessian matrix with elements described above in equation (6). The Wald statistic is chi-square distributed with degrees of freedom equal to the number of imposed constraints (Long 1997).

TABLE 7.3. Wald statistics testing the equality of the estimated parameters across the six latent classes, by sample

Parameter tested	*Wald statistic*	*Degrees of freedom*	*p-value*
1981–2 sample			
Intercept	533.63	5	0.0000
Age	635.07	5	0.0000
Age-squared	791.36	5	0.0000
1986–7 sample			
Intercept	566.49	5	0.0000
Age	593.53	5	0.0000
Age-squared	737.72	5	0.0000
1991–2 sample			
Intercept	456.94	5	0.0000
Age	477.84	5	0.0000
Age-squared	545.66	5	0.0000

Table 7.3 presents the results generated from calculating the Wald statistic testing the constraint that the parameter estimates for (1) the intercept, (2) the age variable, and (3) the age-squared variable were equal across the six latent classes. As shown in Table 7.3, the hypotheses that the age and age-squared parameter estimates were equal across all six latent classes were resoundingly rejected in all three samples. We say 'resoundingly' because of the size and significance of the Wald statistics shown in Table 7.3. For comparative purposes, note that a chi-square value of 16.75 (with 5 degree of freedom) is significant at the 0.005 level. The smallest value of the Wald statistic shown in Table 7.3 for either the age or age-squared variables is 477.84 (for the age variable in the 1991–2 sample), which is extremely large compared to the value of 16.75. Thus, the intercepts for each of the classes were found not to be equal to an overall constant value (the inequality expectation would be consistent with the prediction of Gottfredson and Hirschi). We reiterate that the estimated age parameters for both the age and the age-squared variables in all three samples were found to be highly inconsistent with the invariance hypothesis, which specifies that they all be equal to the same value. Thus, in all three samples, there is strong statistical evidence that fails to confirm the hypothesis (H_4) that the age–crime curves among the latent classes are invariant. The curves differ not only with respect to their mean

rate, but they also differ (significantly) with respect to the developmental shape or nature of their age–crime curve.[11]

Thus far, we have presented statistical evidence testing hypotheses H_1, H_2, and H_4. The obtained evidence testing these three hypotheses supports hypothesis H_1, but fails to support hypotheses H_2 and H_4. However, as students of statistics learn very early, there is a difference between statistical significance and substantive importance (especially when dealing with large samples). Accordingly, we now turn to a substantive-based approach for examining these hypotheses. This substantive, graphically based method also allows us to address hypothesis H_3 concerning the existence of an 'adolescent-limited' (AL) offender type within these samples. The numerical focus to this point has not allowed for the determination of whether there was an AL offender group in each or in any of the three samples.

The substantive approach we employ here makes use of the assignment of each individual in the sample to a particular latent class using the posterior assignment probabilities (described in Appendix A) that indicate the probability that each latent class has generated the individual's observed longitudinal pattern of offending. This assignment of each individual to a latent class allows for a descriptive summary and graphical depiction of how substantively different the latent classes are with respect to their observed overall rate of offending and their longitudinal offending patterns. In the next three sections (one section for each of our three samples) we make use of these posterior assignment probabilities—each individual in the sample was 'assigned' to the latent class to which he had the highest probability of belonging. After each individual was assigned to a particular latent class, the individual's membership in the latent class was considered unique and distinct. Next, summary characteristics and longitudinal offending trajectories depicting the relationship between age and crime within each of the latent classes were computed using both the offending histories of the individuals

[11] For comparative purposes, we did re-estimate the semi-parametric mixed Poisson model according to the specification that constrained all of the estimated age parameters to be equal across the six latent classes. Comparisons of the log-likelihood values for these models compared to the log-likelihood values from the models where the estimated age parameters were allowed to vary across the latent classes indicated the same conclusion reached above—there is a significant improvement in the fit of the model when the estimated age parameters are allowed to vary across the latent classes.

assigned to that latent class (i.e. observed offending characteristics) and the parameter estimates from the model (predicted offending characteristics). The results of these procedures allow for a substantive look at the differences between the latent classes in each sample, including their overall mean rate of offending (by the end of the follow-up period) and the nature of their trajectories across the age distribution.

The basic plan for the description of the results within each of our samples is as follows. First, there is a description of the percentage of each sample assigned to each latent class and a description of the posterior assignments probabilities. Next, the basic descriptive features of the offending patterns of the latent classes are discussed (e.g. age at first arrest, mean number of arrest charges). Then the observed and predicted offending trajectories across the age range are graphed and compared. The examination of the shape of the arrest trajectories will allow for a graphical examination of whether there is an AL offender group in these samples (H_3 in Chapter 3), as well as whether between-group differences are maintained across the age range (H_4). Finally, a descriptive analysis is undertaken to examine what role, if any, adult incarceration time may have had on the decline in criminal offending among these three groups of serious youthful offenders.

Results for the 1981–2 Sample

The first section of 'substantive' results presented here is for the 6-class semiparametric mixed Poisson model of the 1981–2 sample. The analyses that will follow for the 1986–7 and 1991–2 samples are procedurally exact replications of the same processes employed here for the 1981–2 sample.[12]

[12] Because it is not relevant to the substantive goals of this chapter, we have not presented a description of the background characteristic variables (described in Chapter 6) within each of the latent class to compare if any of the variables distinguish among the latent classes. Tables containing summary descriptions of the background characteristic variables within each of the latent classes are available on the Internet (see Appendix C). Given that these background characteristics are descriptive of the wards as of the time they were incarcerated in the CYA on the sample stay (and the wards were of varying ages at that point), and especially since the variables were measured after all of the trajectories were already in motion, these tables are presented there merely for descriptive purposes. It is interesting to note, however, that there are few variables that have any numerically distinguishing values across the latent classes.

Latent Class Assignment Percentages and Posterior Probabilities

To begin our analyses, we present a description of the percentages of each sample that were assigned to a given latent class and a corresponding description of the nature of the assignment probabilities (for assignment to that particular latent class) for those individuals assigned to each latent class. In the results that follow, all of the latent classes were named as LC1, LC2, . . . , LC6 according to their rank-ordered estimated prevalence in the sample (e.g. LC number, where the number simply represents the rank-ordered *estimated* prevalence of that latent class based on the estimates of the model).

The percentages of (estimated and actual) cases assigned to each latent class (Panel A) and a summary description of the posterior assignment probabilities (Panel B) are presented in Table 7.4. As found in Panel A, the maximum probability assignment rule

TABLE 7.4. Summary descriptions of latent class assignment percentages and posterior assignment probabilities: 1981–2 sample

Panel A: Group assignment percentages

Latent class	*Estimated %*	*Assigned*	
		%	N
LC1	26.25	26.09	519
LC2	20.49	20.26	403
LC3	20.16	20.81	414
LC4	12.22	12.27	244
LC5	10.80	10.81	215
LC6	10.09	9.75	194

Panel B: Posterior assignment probabilities

Latent class	*Mean*	*Percentiles*		
		25th	*50th*	*75th*
LC1	0.92	0.88	0.99	1.00
LC2	0.91	0.86	0.98	1.00
LC3	0.88	0.82	0.97	1.00
LC4	0.89	0.84	0.97	1.00
LC5	0.93	0.94	1.00	1.00
LC6	0.92	0.92	1.00	1.00

resulted in the following percentage of cases being assigned to each latent class: 26 per cent (LC1; n = 519); 20 per cent (LC2; n = 403); 21 per cent (LC3; n = 414); 12 per cent (LC4; n = 244); 11 per cent (LC5; n = 215); and 10 per cent (LC6; n = 194). Thus, there are no latent classes that contain an overwhelming percentage of the cases, but rather the latent class with the largest percentage of cases assigned to it (LC1) only had 26 per cent of the sample in it. Also found in Table 7.4 (under the 'Estimated %' column) is a model-based estimate of the percentage of cases that were expected to belong to each latent class; the obtained estimate is from the theta vector described in Appendix A. The reader will note that there is a considerable degree of congruence between the estimated percentage of the sample and the actual percentage of the sample that was assigned to the latent class. In fact, the largest discrepancy was less than 1 per cent (0.65% in LC3).

Panel B contains a summary description of the posterior assignment probabilities. Each row of the panel pertains to a description of the assignment probabilities for the individuals who were assigned to that latent class. As is evident in the table, the average assignment probabilities were quite high, and the lowest average probability was only 0.88. Indeed, four of the latent classes had average assignment probabilities of 0.91 or greater. The lowest median probability value for any of the latent classes was 0.97, and thus over 50 per cent of the sample members were assigned to the latent class that had a 0.97 probability or greater of having generated the individual's longitudinal offending pattern.

Summary Arrest Charge Information

Next we turn our attention to a descriptive summary of the arrest charge histories of the individuals assigned to each latent class. Table 7.5 summarizes the arrest histories for each latent class, including the average observed number of total arrest charges (at the end of the follow-up period on 30 June 2000), the predicted average number of arrest charges (based on the estimates from the semi-parametric mixed Poisson model), the observed number of serious arrest charges, and the average age at first arrest. To briefly recap the descriptive results presented earlier in Chapter 6, the 'average individual' in the 1981–2 sample accumulated 22.8 arrest charges by the end of the follow-up period, accrued 12.51 relatively serious arrest charges (as defined in Chapter 6), and was first arrested at an

TABLE 7.5. Summary arrest charge information, by latent class: 1981–2 sample

Latent class	*Mean total arrest charges*		*Obs. mean serious arrest charges*	*Average age at first arrest*
	Observed	*Predicted*		
LC4	5.59	5.83	3.92	17.24
LC5	11.59	11.47	6.99	13.57
LC1	18.83	18.89	11.06	15.51
LC3	20.48	20.45	12.23	13.06
LC2	36.35	35.96	19.04	12.26
LC6	44.10	43.83	20.35	14.26

age of 14.22 years old. We have chosen to present the information in Table 7.5 rank-ordered by the mean observed number of arrest charges (from lowest to highest) because this will make the presentation of some of the other information in the table clearer to the reader.

In Table 7.5, a significant amount of between-class heterogeneity in the average number of arrest charges is obvious. The mean number of arrest charges varied from 5.59 all the way up to 44.10. LC6, the smallest latent class (10% of the sample), was the latent class that had the highest average number of arrest charges. LC4 (11%), on the other hand, had the smallest average arrest charge total. Thus, there was a difference of roughly 39 arrest charges between the latent classes with the highest and lowest arrest charge total. The largest latent class, LC1 (26%), had about an average number of arrest charges (18.83), a little below the overall number of arrest charges for the entire sample (22.8). The other arrest charge totals for the remaining three latent classes were 11.59 (LC5; 11%), 20.48 (LC3; 21%), and 36.35 (LC2; 20%), respectively. Clearly the average arrest charge total presented in Chapter 6 is not very representative of the arrest charge averages of most of the individual latent classes.

The results presented in Table 7.5 also indicate that the average number of predicted arrest charges (based on the model estimates presented in Table 7.2) for each of the latent classes was fairly accurate (in comparison with the observed average). For example, the model predicted members in the LC4 latent class would have 5.83 arrest charges, and they were observed on average to have 5.59. Similarly, the members of the LC6 latent class were predicted to have 43.83 arrest charges on average, and they were observed to have 44.1 arrest charges. Overall then, the model appears to do a fairly accurate job at predicting the total number of arrest charges by the end of the follow-up period.

It is significant to note that for most of the six latent classes, a little over half of their arrest charges were for relatively serious offenses. It is especially significant that in the LC6 latent class, the individuals in this sample were arrested on average for over 20 serious arrest charges. Thus, it is not simply the case that this is a latent class composed of chronic, non-serious offenders (for all of these offenders are regarded by most people as very serious offenders). Nonetheless, roughly 50–60 per cent of the observed arrest charges in each latent class were for relatively serious offenses. The latent class with the highest percentage of serious offenses was the LC4 latent class (who had the lowest number of actual charges), with roughly 70 per cent of their arrest charges having been composed of relatively serious offenses.

Finally, it is significant to note several items about the average age at first arrest across the latent classes. First, there is a considerable degree of heterogeneity between the classes with respect to their average age of onset (as measured by their first arrest). LC2 had the youngest average age of onset (12.26 years old), whereas LC4 had the oldest average age of onset (17.24). Second, there is little semblance, however, to the rank ordering of average age at first arrest with respect to the average number of arrest charges (after noting that the latent class with the oldest average age had the lowest arrest charge total). The latent class with an average age at first arrest exactly equal to the overall average for the sample as a whole was the latent class with the highest average arrest charge total. One of the classes with an average age of onset that ranked third in terms of the youngest average age (and right around the onset of adolescence) was the latent class that had the second lowest number of arrest charges.

The reader will recall from the discussions in Chapters 2 and 6 that age of onset is a critical variable in criminological research because it is often used as a proxy variable for criminal propensity in that it is reported that individuals with a younger age of onset *tend* to have higher rates of criminal activity throughout life. The fact that the rank orderings of the age of onset variable are not the reverse-identical of the average number of arrest charges is already a possible indication of a significant amount of between-group differences in their trajectories of arrest. They should be reverse-identical if between-group differences were stable across time. For if one group is offending earlier than another, they should also be expected to offend later and at a higher rate if the between-group differences persist across time. Given the statistical results presented earlier that tested (and failed to confirm) the hypothesis that the estimated age parameters were equal, this would be the finding one would have expected.

In the next section of results we present the predicted and observed trajectories for each of the latent classes in order to more conclusively address and examine the issue of the stability of between-group differences across the age range. From the graphical depiction of the nature of the arrest trajectories of each of the latent classes, the question of the magnitude of the substantive differences in the nature of the growth and offending trajectories should become much more apparent once we have completed this process.

Predicted and Observed Trajectories of Arrest

In this section, we present and examine two figures: Figure 7.2 contains the predicted arrest trajectories (on the basis of the model parameters) for the six latent classes and Figure 7.3 contains the actual observed arrest trajectories of the 1981–2 sample.[13]

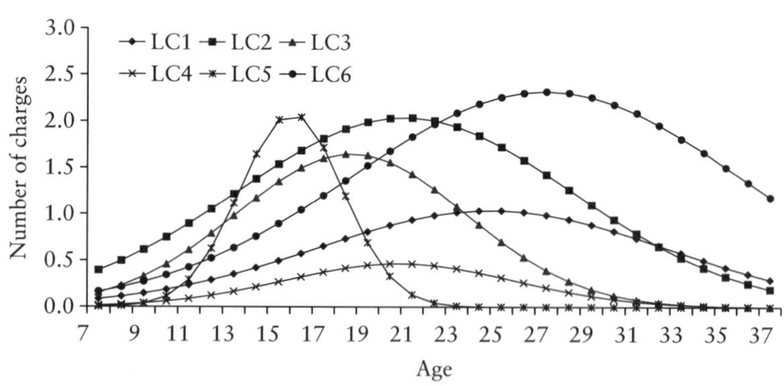

FIGURE 7.2. Predicted arrest trajectories: Six-class model of the 1981–2 sample.

[13] Similar to Figure 7.1, we have only graphed the curves up through the last age at which at least 50 per cent of the sample was available (at-risk) for estimation.

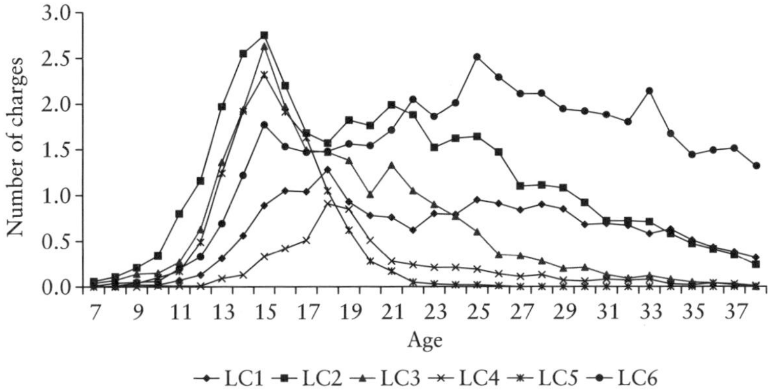

FIGURE 7.3. Observed arrest trajectories: Six-class model of the 1981–2 sample.

The observed arrest trajectories presented in Figure 7.3 were generated by averaging the arrest charge totals at each age for all of the individuals assigned to the particular latent class at risk at that age.

On the whole, we note that for the 1981–2 sample, the predicted trajectories tend to slightly overestimate the arrest rates at the younger ages, undercut the peak ages, and slightly over-predict during the early twenties when the dip in the arrest rates occur (as described in Note 3).[14] Again, the most likely reason for the arrest dip *in the early twenties* is probably an artefact of a drop in 'at-risk' time due to incarceration (e.g. for both new offenses and parole revocations) during this short period of time. The average observed number of charges appear to be back 'on track' with the predicted number of charges by the mid-twenties. In sum, however, the predicted trajectories do a fairly accurate job of tracking the arrest charges at each age for each of the latent classes, and a good

[14] The reason the predicted trajectory undercuts four of the actual observed peaks (LC1, LC2, LC3, and LC4) is that the rate of increase in the arrest during early adolescence is much faster than the corresponding decline in adulthood (which is much more drawn out over time) for these four latent classes. Mathematically speaking, such a trend makes it extremely difficult to accurately model the arrest rate at each and every age, and the model favors undercutting the peak rate because there are simply more data points during adulthood (when the decline is slower). On average, though, it is important to remember that the model does an excellent job of predicting the final number of arrest charges.

job at predicting the mean number of arrests by the end of the follow-up period as shown in Table 7.5.

Before describing the trajectories in Figures 7.2 and 7.3, it is important to point out to our readers that our goals for the description of the offending trajectories are focused on addressing several key issues of this chapter: (1) whether there are offender groups in the population with distinct arrest trajectories; (2) whether there is an 'adolescent-limited' group in the serious youthful offender population; and (most importantly) (3) whether between-group arrest differences are maintained across time. It is critical to note at this point that the substantive implications of both the predicted and observed arrest trajectories are identical, even if the peak ages are not always identical. For the reader interested in the comparison of the observed and predicted arrest trajectories for each latent class, we refer you to the graphical depictions available via the Internet (see Appendix C).

We begin our discussion of Figures 7.2 and 7.3 by noting that it is readily apparent from the trajectories in both figures that there are groups with very distinct arrest trajectories across the age distribution studied here. The LC4 latent class, for example, had a very low-rate of arrests across time, whereas LC6 had a very high rate. Thus, these offender groups are not only statistically different (as the results presented earlier indicated), but there are also significant substantive differences between these offender groups as well (which we discuss below).

The substantive nature of the arrest trajectories presented in Figures 7.2 and 7.3 lend support to hypothesis H_1 that there are multiple offender groups in the serious youthful offender population, and thus these results fail to support hypothesis H_2 predicting that there are only two distinct offender groups. There is simply more heterogeneity (even within this select segment of the offender population) than that which is expected on the basis of the predictions of Moffitt's dual taxonomy theory (1993, 1997).

Second, note that the arrest trajectory of the LC5 latent class clearly follows an 'adolescent-limited' (AL) trajectory. This group of offenders (in terms of both their actual and observed rates) had a rapid increase in their rate of arrest once onset began (which on average was when they were 13.57 years old), and then there was a nearly identical decrease in their arrest rate after their peak age. By their early twenties, this group appears to have largely desisted from offending. In fact, for the individuals assigned to this trajectory, there were only a handful of arrests between the ages of 21 through 26. From ages 27 through 42, there was not even a single arrest charge for the offenders assigned to this latent class. Thus, the (predicted and observed) arrest trajectories of the LC5 latent class clearly lend support to hypothesis H_3 that there is an AL offender group in the very serious youthful offender population.

Finally, it is also clear from Figures 7.1 and 7.2 that the trajectories of the offender groups depicted clearly differ not only with respect to their average rate of arrest, but that they are also substantively different in terms of the growth and decline of their arrest trajectories over time. In other words, the between-group differences in arrests are not stable over time. By virtue of the fact that there is an AL group, this conclusion is relatively straightforward (i.e. notice how this trajectory cuts across all of the other arrest trajectories). But, it is important to note that even were we to exclude the AL latent class from our analysis, we would still observe a lack of stable between-group differences among the remaining classes. The between-group differences in our sample are largely maintained up through age 15, but after age 15 (and throughout adulthood), there is a clear failure to maintain these between-group differences in arrests. For example, note that the LC1 latent class had a much lower and later peak age of arrest in comparison with the LC3 latent class, but at about age 25 the LC1 latent class was predicted (and observed) to have a higher arrest rate than did the LC3 latent class. In fact, by their mid-thirties, the LC1 latent class had a rate of arrest very similar to that of LC2, even though during earlier ages the arrest rate of LC2 was much higher than was the arrest rate of the LC1 latent class. Similarly, notice that the LC6 latent class, which had both the highest rate of arrest during adulthood and the highest average arrest charge total overall (see Table 7.5), fell right in the middle of both the observed and predicted arrest trajectories all the way through age 16. Shortly thereafter, however, this latent class assumed the rank of the group with the highest arrest rate at the later adult ages.

In short, the arrest trajectories depicted in Figures 7.2 and 7.3 fail to confirm the assertion that between-group differences in arrests are maintained across time. Thus, at this point in our analyses we have accrued neither substantive nor statistical evidence to support the contention that the relationship between age and crime is 'invariant' across the latent classes.

The Adult Prison Experiences of the Latent Classes

In this final section for the 1981–2 sample, we present some descriptive evidence concerning the adult prison experiences of the latent classes in this sample. The reason for this presentation is that a rival hypothesis for the failure of the maintenance of the between-group differences in recidivism is that members of the various groups had distinctively different prison experiences. For example, it could be argued that the AL group was less likely to have been arrested from their mid-twenties through the end of the follow-up period in 2000 because they were incapacitated in prison and were thus denied the opportunity to offend against the non-institutionalized public. We warn the reader in advance that the evidence we present here to assess such possibilities is merely descriptive and therefore suggestive, rather than conclusive.

Table 7.6 presents a brief summary description of the adult incarceration experiences for each of the latent classes in the 1981–2 sample, including the percentage of each latent class that had at least one 'stay' in the CDC (California Department of Corrections), the percentage that was incarcerated at the end of the follow-up period, and among those who had at least one stay, the average number of CDC stays, and the median years spent incarcerated in the CDC.

TABLE 7.6. Summary of variables related to adult incarceration experiences, by latent class: 1981–2 sample

Variable	*Latent class*					
	LC1	*LC2*	*LC3*	*LC4*	*LC5*	*LC6*
% with at least 1 CDC stay	73.03	88.83	71.74	21.72	15.81	89.18
% still incarcerated on 30 June 2000	13.87	21.34	16.43	5.74	5.58	6.19
Among those with at least 1 CDC stay:						
Avg. number of CDC stays	2.39	3.08	2.02	1.64	1.21	2.85
Median number of total years incarcerated in CDC	4.02	5.26	5.36	2.92	4.25	3.01

As depicted in Table 7.6, there is a marked difference in the percentage of each latent class that has at least one incarceration in the CDC. The AL group (LC5) has the lowest percentage (15.81%), whereas the LC2 and LC6 latent classes have the highest percentages (both around 89%). Not surprisingly, the results in Table 7.6 show the stochastic nature of the process through which offenders end up incarcerated in the prison system—the higher the number of criminal arrests (during adulthood), the higher the rate of entrance into prison (see, e.g., Canela-Cacho, Blumstein, and Cohen 1997). Further, the mean number of stays in the CDC and the median number of years incarcerated in the CDC obviously also are highly correlated with the number of criminal arrests during adulthood. The latent classes that had the most active arrest records during adulthood (LC1, LC2, LC3, LC6) also tended to have the highest mean number of prison entrances and spent the most amount of time incarcerated.

Again, the results presented in Table 7.6 appear to indicate the obvious in that they demonstrate that those who were most frequently arrested as adults were the ones who were most likely to be sentenced to prison and to have the longest prison stays. We suspect, however, that such findings do not offer confirmation for the notion that the causes of the between-group differences in arrest rates *over the entire age distribution* were due merely to differential adult incarceration rates and lengths of prison stays. For example, if the rates of arrest which decline in adulthood were purely a function of time spent incarcerated in prison, then why do the LC1 and LC3 latent classes have the same percentage that make a transition into prison and nearly the same median amount of time incarcerated for those that had at least one stay (differing only by about one year in total out of a possible 18 years of exposure time after release from the CYA), yet vastly different rates of arrest decline in adulthood? If incapacitation effects explained arrest differentials between the two latent classes, you would expect the two groups to have similar declines in arrest rates since their imprisonment experiences are substantively similar. Furthermore, the 'adolescent-peaked' group (LC5) had the lowest rate of prison entrance, yet this group had the most dramatic decline in the adult arrest patterns. Again, it is, of course, highly suggestive to contend that adult prison experiences were not driving the differences in the arrest rates between the latent classes over the entire age distribution.

Results for the 1986–7 Sample

In this section, we present the 'substantive' results for the 6-class semiparametric mixed Poisson model of the 1986–7 sample. These analyses are procedural replications of the same processes employed for the 1981–2 sample.

Latent Class Assignment Percentages and Posterior Probabilities

Our analysis of data for the 1986–7 sample begins with a presentation of the percentage of cases assigned to each latent class and a descriptive summary of the posterior probabilities of assignment to the latent class.

Table 7.7 contains two panels: Panel A presents the estimated and actual group assignment percentages and Panel B contains a summary description of the posterior assignment probabilities. Similar to the results reported for the 1981–2 sample, there are no latent classes

TABLE 7.7. Summary descriptions of latent class assignment percentages and posterior assignment probabilities: 1986–7 sample

Panel A: Group assignment percentages

Latent class	*Estimated %*	*Assigned*	
		%	*N*
LC1	27.08	27.58	398
LC2	23.23	23.08	333
LC3	15.09	14.62	211
LC4	12.58	13.03	188
LC5	11.88	11.78	170
LC6	10.13	9.91	143

Panel B: Posterior assignment probabilities

Latent class	*Mean*	*Percentiles*		
		25th	*50th*	*75th*
LC1	0.87	0.80	0.95	0.99
LC2	0.86	0.77	0.95	0.99
LC3	0.82	0.66	0.88	0.99
LC4	0.93	0.92	0.99	1.00
LC5	0.85	0.77	0.94	1.00
LC6	0.88	0.82	0.96	1.00

that contain an overwhelming majority of the cases. Using the maximum probability assignment rule (i.e. each case was assigned to the latent class to which they had the highest probability of belonging), the following percentage of cases was assigned to each specific latent class: 28 per cent (LC1; n = 398); 23 per cent (LC2; n = 333); 15 per cent (LC3; n = 211); 13 per cent (LC4; n = 188); 12 per cent (LC5; n = 170); and 10 per cent (LC6; n = 143).

There is also a model-based estimate of the percentage of cases that were expected to belong to each latent class found in Table 7.7. Comparing the estimate of the percentage to the actual assigned percentage in each latent class, we find a considerable degree of similarity between the two.

Panel B of Table 7.7 contains a summary description of the posterior assignment probabilities. Although not as high as the assignment probabilities found in Table 7.4 for the 1981–2 sample, the average assignment probabilities for the 1986–7 sample were still quite high. Most of the average assignment probabilities ranged between 0.85 and 0.93. The latent class with the lowest average assignment probability was LC3, which had an average assignment probability of 0.82. Looking at the medians (50th percentiles) presented in Panel B of Table 7.7, we find that the median values for most latent classes were very high.

Summary Arrest Charge Information

In this section we present a descriptive summary of the arrest histories of the individuals in the 1986–7 sample assigned to each latent class. Table 7.8 presents the observed and predicted mean

TABLE 7.8. Summary arrest charge information, by latent class: 1986–7 sample

Latent class	*Mean total arrest charges*		*Obs. mean serious arrest charges*	*Average age at first arrest*
	Observed	*Predicted*		
LC4	9.45	9.46	5.37	14.27
LC1	14.55	14.59	8.52	14.03
LC2	18.31	18.41	9.91	14.63
LC3	27.62	27.19	14.99	11.29
LC6	35.87	35.46	16.61	13.59
LC5	36.19	35.75	17.95	13.40

number of arrest charges, the mean number of observed relative serious arrest charges (as defined in Chapter 6), and the average age at first arrest for each of the latent classes. As discussed earlier in Chapter 6, the 'average individual' in the 1986–7 sample was arrested for 21.33 total charges, of which 11.29 were for serious offences. The average individual in this sample was first arrested when he was 13.7 years old. Similar to the results presented for the 1981–2 sample, we report the information in Table 7.8 rank-ordered by the mean observed number of arrest charges (from lowest to highest).

As expected, given the findings presented above for the 1981–2 sample, there is a considerable amount of heterogeneity in the average number of total arrest charges accumulated in each latent class for the 1986–7 sample as well. The mean number of total arrest charges varied from a low of 9.45 in the LC4 latent class (which accounted for 13% of the sample), while the highest average number of arrest charges was 36.19 in the fifth latent class (LC5; 12% of sample). The sixth latent class, LC6 (10%), was not far behind the LC5 latent class in terms of their average arrest charge total. The LC6 latent class averaged 35.87 total arrest charges. The difference in the mean number of arrest charges between the latent classes with the highest and lowest arrest charge averages was nearly 27 arrest charges. The latent class (LC1) with the largest percentage of the sample assigned to it (27%) had an average of 14.55 arrest charges. This is well below the overall average number of arrest charges for the sample as a whole (21.33). In the remaining two latent classes, the average arrest charge totals were 18.31 (LC2; 13%) and 27.62 (LC2; 15%), respectively.

The 'Predicted' charge column in Table 7.8 contains the model-based predicted number of total arrest charges based on the estimates from the semiparametric mixed Poisson model. Comparing this average total to the observed average total for each latent class, we find that the model was fairly accurate, on average, in predicting the sum number of arrest charges in each of the latent classes. For example, the model predicted the LC4 latent class would have 9.46 arrest charges, and the individuals assigned to this latent class were observed to have on average, 9.45 total arrest charges. Overall, the model does a fairly accurate job at predicting the total number of arrest charges for the various latent classes by the end of the follow-up period in the 1986–7 sample. This is the same conclusion we reached for the 1981–2 sample.

Again, as in the 1981–2 sample, relatively serious offences comprised a substantial portion of the arrest charges for individuals in each of the latent classes in the 1986–7 sample. The latent class with the lowest percentage of relatively serious charges was the LC6 latent class. The LC6 latent class was arrested, on average, for 35.87 charges, and this latent class averaged 16.61 serious charges (or 46%). Overall though, in each latent class roughly one-half of the arrest charges were for relatively serious offences.

Just as we have found heterogeneity between the latent classes with regard to the average total number of arrest charges, we also find heterogeneity between the latent classes in terms of their average age at first arrest. The LC3 latent class had the youngest average age at first arrest—they averaged their first arrest at the precocious age of 11.29 years old. The LC6 and LC5 latent classes both averaged their first arrest at around 13.50 years old, while the LC1, LC2, and LC4 latent classes were, on average, about 14 years old when they were first arrested.

Similar to the findings for the 1981–2 sample, there is no apparent pattern of reverse-ordering of the average ages at first arrest and the rank-orderings (from lowest to highest) of the total arrest charges for the 1986–7 sample. For example, note that the latent class with the youngest average age at first arrest (LC3) did not accumulate the highest average number of arrest charges. Similarly, the latent class with the oldest average age at first arrest (LC2) also did not accumulate the lowest number of average arrest charge totals. Indeed the two latent classes with highest average arrest charge totals (LC5 and LC6) both had average ages at first arrest that were nearly identical to the average age of arrest for the sample as a whole (13.68 years old). Again, these results are consistent with those presented earlier that tested (and failed to confirm) the hypothesis that the estimated age parameters were equal across the latent classes in this sample (Table 7.3). This finding is inconsistent with the age-invariance hypothesis promulgated by Gottfredson and Hirschi (1990). To more definitively investigate the substantive differences in the arrest trajectories of these latent classes, we present in the next section a graphical depiction of the observed and predicted arrest trajectory for each latent class.

Predicted and Observed Trajectories of Arrest for the 1986–7 Sample

Similar to the analysis of data for the 1981–2 sample, we present two figures that help describe the arrest trajectories for the 1986–7 sample. Figure 7.4 contains the predicted trajectories and Figure 7.5 depicts the actual observed trajectories for the six latent classes in the 1986–7 sample. The observed arrest trajectories presented in Figure 7.5 were generated by averaging the arrest charge totals at each age for all of the individuals in a given latent class that were at risk at that age.

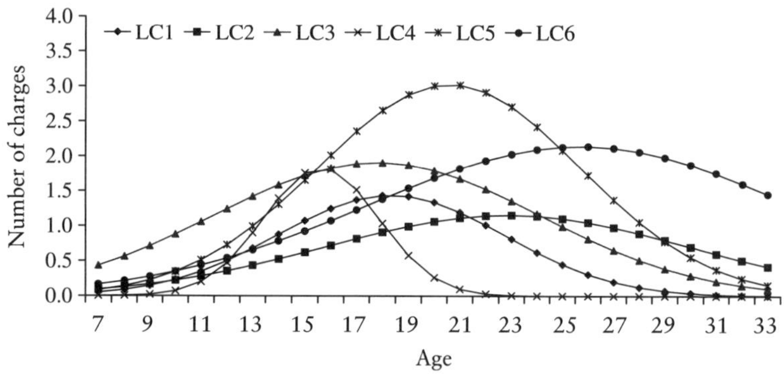

FIGURE 7.4. Predicted arrest trajectories: Six-class model of the 1986–7 sample.

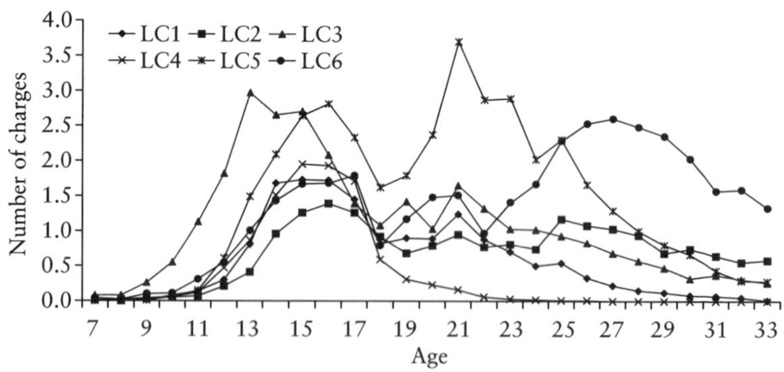

FIGURE 7.5. Observed arrest trajectories: Six-class model of the 1986–7 sample.

Similar to the results presented for the 1981–2 sample, the predicted trajectories here also tend to slightly overestimate the arrest rates at the younger ages, undercut the peak ages of arrest, and slightly over-predict arrests during the early twenties. Again, the most probable reason for the dip in arrests *during the early twenties* is that it appears to be a 'time at risk' artefact due to an unmeasured drop in the 'at risk' time as a result of the increased likelihood of incarceration (for both new offenses and parole revocations) during this age period (see Note 3 of this chapter). It is important to note, that whatever the cause of the drop, the observed number of charges appear to be back 'on track' with the predicted number of charges by the time the 1986–7 sample reaches its mid-twenties.

As in the description of the results for the 1981–2 sample, we focus our discussion of the trajectories represented in Figures 7.4 and 7.5 around the key issues of the age–crime relationship identified earlier. Due to the fact that it is easier to see the differences in the predicted trajectories (because of the natural 'smoothing' that occurs in the predictions), we focus our discussion on the trajectories that are presented in Figure 7.4. The substantive implications of both the predicted and observed trajectories, however, are identical, and the fact that the peak ages of arrest are not always identical in the two figures is immaterial to the main focus of our study.

First, in both of the figures it is clear (although it is clearer in Figure 7.5) that the latent classes have qualitatively distinct arrest trajectories. For example, the LC5 latent class had a very high peak rate of arrest, whereas the LC2 latent class had a much lower peak rate. Again, we find that the nature of the trajectories presented in these figures lends substantive support to the first hypothesis ($\mathbf{H_1}$) that there are multiple offender groups in the serious youthful offender population. Also, these results appear to contradict the second hypothesis ($\mathbf{H_2}$) that there are only two distinct offender groups in this population. It would be very hard to imagine that all of these different arrest trajectories could be adequately described using only two trajectories (which would be one step beyond Figure 7.1). There is simply too much heterogeneity between these latent classes in terms of both their mean rate of offending and the developmental nature of their arrest trajectories to fully capture this heterogeneity with only two latent classes.

Second, we also find once again that there is an 'adolescent-limited' offender group (LC4) in the serious youthful offender population. The trajectory of the LC4 latent class clearly follows such a trajectory, with a rapid increase in their arrest rate during early adolescence and then a nearly identical decrease in the arrest rate on the other side of their peak age (age 16). By their early twenties, this group (like the LC5 latent class in the 1981–2 sample) appears to have largely desisted from offending. For the individuals assigned to this trajectory, there were only a handful of arrests between the ages of 21 through 26. From ages 27 through 37, there was not even a single arrest charge for the offenders assigned to this latent class (who were followed through those ages). Thus, the arrest trajectory of the LC4 latent class lends support to third hypothesis (H_3) that there is an 'adolescent-limited' offender group in the serious youthful offender population.

Finally, the arrest trajectories depicted in both Figures 7.4 and 7.5 provide additional evidence against the age-invariance hypothesis put forth by Gottfredson and Hirschi. Whether you look at the observed or the predicted arrest trajectories in these figures, it is clear that the trajectories depicted do not maintain their differences over time. Parallel to the findings discussed above for the 1981–2 sample (and excluding the 'adolescent-limited' group), there appears to be more stability in the differences among the arrest trajectories during the early ages studied here (through age 15) compared to the later ages in the distribution. The reader can observe a significant change in the between-group differences in arrests throughout adulthood in these figures. For example, note that the LC3 latent class had the highest arrest rate during the early ages studied here (through about age 15), but then by the late twenties there were four latent classes with higher predicted (and observed) arrest trajectories. By itself, the mere presence of an 'adolescent-limited' (AL) trajectory poses a serious problem to the age-invariance hypothesis. The arrest trajectory of the AL group is simply incompatible with the age-invariance argument because this arrest trajectory of the AL offender group (LC4) drops right across the (predicted and observed) arrest trajectories of several of the other arrest trajectories (e.g. LC1, LC2, LC6). Further evidence against the age-invariance hypothesis can be gleaned from the arrest trajectory for the LC2 latent class. This latent class had the lowest arrest rate through age 19, but by age 33 it had the second highest arrest rate. Finally, still another observed arrest trajectory that is problematic for the age-invariance hypothesis is that of the LC6 latent class. The LC6 latent class displayed an offending trajectory that was midway between the other arrest trajectories through about age 17 (both in terms of the observed and predicted trajectory). By the end of the follow-up period, however, this latent class had the highest arrest trajectory (both predicted and observed).

Overall then, the trajectories depicted in Figures 7.4 and 7.5 fail to support the notion that between-group differences in arrest trajectories over the age distribution are similar across time. In sum, as in the 1981–2 sample, the results to this point in our analyses have provided both substantive and statistical evidence that fails to confirm the notion that the relationship between age and crime is 'invariant' across the latent classes in our study.

The Adult Prison Experiences of the Latent Classes

In this final section of results for the 1986–7 sample, we again present some descriptive evidence concerning the adult prison experiences of the latent classes. Table 7.9 includes the percentage of each latent class that had at least one 'stay' in the CDC, the percentage that was incarcerated at the end of the follow-up period and those who had at least one stay, the average number of CDC stays and the median years spent incarcerated in the CDC. Like the results observed for the 1981–2 sample, Table 7.9 depicts a striking difference in the percentage of each latent class that had at least one entrance into the CDC. The percentages range from 14.4 per cent

TABLE 7.9. Summary of variables related to adult incarceration experiences, by latent class: 1986–7 sample

Variable	*Latent class*					
	LC1	*LC2*	*LC3*	*LC4*	*LC5*	*LC6*
% with at least 1 CDC stay	64.14	78.62	84.88	14.44	92.22	80.43
% still incarcerated on 30 June 2000	11.62	9.75	13.66	5.35	17.37	6.52
Among those with at least 1 CDC stay:						
Avg. number of CDC stays	1.74	2.07	2.229	1.15	2.6	2.29
Median number of total years incarcerated in CDC	4.01	2.71	4.19	4.35	3.48	2.06

(LC4) all the way up to 92.2 per cent (LC5). The mean number of stays in the CDC (among those who had at least one stay) varied from 1.15 (LC4) to 2.6 (LC5), while the median number of total years incarcerated (among those incarcerated at least once) ranged for 2.06 (LC6) to 4.35 (LC4).

For our purposes here, however, again we note that the results presented in Table 7.9 do not (in our opinion) appear to support the interpretation that the differences in arrest trajectories were most likely the result of incapacitation effects *over the entire age distribution*. For example, again we find that the AL offender group (which experienced the most abrupt change in arrests) had an extremely low-rate of entrance into the CDC (which makes sense given their relative lack of arrests during their adult years). And we note that LC5 and LC6 both had extremely high rates of entrance into the CDC, yet their arrest trajectories did not respond in identical manners.

To look at this finding a different way, the reader can examine the percentage of cases that make a CDC entrance for the LC1 and LC3 latent classes. Sixty-four per cent of the LC1 latent class had at least one stay in the CDC (and those 64% spent around four years in the CDC according to the median), whereas 85 per cent of the LC3 latent class made a transition into the CDC (and also spent a median length of four years there). Thus, 20 per cent more of the LC3 latent class made a transition into the CDC compared to LC1, but the decline during adulthood for these two arrest trajectories was virtually identical. If incapacitation effects were causing the arrest trajectories to fall at different rates, then it seems reasonable to believe that the LC3 trajectory should have fallen at a much faster rate than did the arrest trajectory of the LC1 latent class. Stated differently, why would the arrest trajectories of these two latent classes change at the same rate when they had different rates of exposure to the CDC if incapacitation effects were primarily responsible for the decline in arrests?

In sum, when you consider that the group with the most significant and fastest drop in arrests had the lowest prison entrance rates, or that the two groups with the same change in arrest trajectories have vastly different CDC experiences, the conclusion that differential incarceration rates were causing the between-group arrest differences to be reduced does not seem reasonable to us, given the descriptive results depicted in Table 7.9.

Results for the 1991–2 Sample

This final analysis section presents the 'substantive' results of the 6-class semiparametric mixed Poisson model for the 1991–2 sample.

Latent Class Assignment Percentages and Posterior Probabilities

Table 7.10 presents the estimated and actual group assignment percentages (Panel A), and this table also summarizes the posterior assignment probabilities (Panel B). Using the maximum probability assignment rule, the following percentages of cases were assigned to each latent class: 28 per cent (LC1; n = 396); 24 per cent (LC2; n = 344); 16 per cent (LC3; n = 224); 15 per cent (LC4; n = 211); 11 per cent (LC5; n = 159); and 7 per cent (LC6; n = 100). The model-based estimate of the percentage of cases that were expected to belong to each latent class can also be found in Table 7.10. Looking at both the estimated and actual assigned

TABLE 7.10. Summary descriptions of latent class assignment percentages and posterior assignment probabilities: 1991–2 sample

Panel A: Group assignment percentages

Latent class	*Estimated %*	*Assigned*	
		%	N
LC1	27.67	27.62	396
LC2	23.2	23.99	344
LC3	15.85	15.62	224
LC4	14.78	14.71	211
LC5	10.65	11.09	159
LC6	7.85	6.97	100

Panel B: Posterior assignment probabilities

Latent class	*Mean*	*Percentiles*		
		25th	*50th*	*75th*
LC1	0.84	0.74	0.91	0.98
LC2	0.82	0.69	0.87	0.96
LC3	0.86	0.79	0.94	0.99
LC4	0.82	0.65	0.91	0.99
LC5	0.89	0.79	0.96	1.00
LC6	0.87	0.76	0.96	1.00

percentages, we again find a remarkable degree of similarity between the two percentages.

The summary description of the posterior assignment probabilities can be found in Panel B of Table 7.10. The average assignment probabilities for all of the latent classes were between 0.82 and 0.89. Given that there are significantly fewer 'age years' (or data points) included in the data of the 1991–2 sample compared to the previous two samples, it is not surprising that the posterior assignment probabilities are not as high in this sample (i.e. the more 'trials' in the data, the more information there is to compute the posterior probabilities). The two latent classes with the lowest average assignment probabilities for the 1991–2 sample were the LC2 and LC4 latent classes, both of which had average assignment probabilities of 0.82. An examination of the medians (50th percentiles) presented in Panel B of Table 7.10 indicates that most latent classes had median assignment probabilities that were fairly high—the lowest median probability value was 0.87.

Summary Arrest Charge Information

At the outset, we note here that many of the substantive findings of this section concerning the overall nature of the arrest patterns of the latent classes are, in fact, substantively identical to the findings noted above in both the 1981–2 and 1986–7 samples. Therefore, some of the findings will not be discussed in as much detail here as those presented previously.

A descriptive summary of the arrest charge histories of the individuals assigned to each latent class for the 1991–2 sample can be found in Table 7.11. The information presented in Table 7.11

TABLE 7.11. Summary arrest charge information, by latent class: 1991–2 sample

Latent class	*Mean total arrest charges*		*Obs. mean serious arrest charges*	*Average age at first arrest*
	Observed	*Predicted*		
LC5	9.43	9.63	5.50	13.88
LC2	11.36	11.42	6.37	14.54
LC1	13.06	13.03	7.23	14.22
LC4	19.12	18.78	10.20	11.35
LC6	27.26	26.53	12.87	13.90
LC3	28.57	28.10	13.18	13.13

includes the average observed number of total arrest charges (at the end of the follow-up period on 30 June 2000), the predicted average number of arrest charges based on the estimates from the semiparametric mixed Poisson model, the observed number of relatively serious arrest charges, and the average age at first arrest. To briefly review our previous description of the overall arrest patterns for the sample as a whole (from Chapter 6), the 'average individual' in the 1991–2 sample accumulated 16.56 arrest charges by the end of the follow-up period, of which 8.59 of those were relatively serious arrest charges (as defined in Chapter 6). The 'average' individual in this sample was first arrested at an age of 13.64 years old. As in the two previous sample results sections, the information depicted in the descriptive arrest history (Table 7.11) is rank-ordered by the mean number of observed arrest charges (from lowest to highest).

The results displayed in Table 7.11 speak to a significant amount of between-group (or between-class) heterogeneity in the average number of arrest charges. This finding was expected given the earlier findings obtained for both the 1981–2 and 1986–7 samples. The mean number of total observed arrest charges varied from a low of 9.43 in the LC5 latent class (which accounted the 11% of the sample), while the highest average number of arrest charges was 28.57 for LC3 (16% of sample). As in the 1986–7 sample, there were two latent classes with very high arrest charge totals—the sixth latent class, LC6 (7%), was not far behind the LC3 latent class in terms of their average arrest charge total (27.26). Overall though, there was a difference of over 19 arrest charges between the latent classes with the highest and lowest arrest charge averages. The LC1 latent class with the largest percentage of the sample assigned to it (28%) had an average of 13.06 arrest charges. The average arrest charge totals in the remaining two latent classes were 11.36 (LC2; 24%) and 19.12 (LC4; 15%). As in the two previous samples, the average arrest charge totals within each latent class indicate that the average number of arrest charges calculated for the sample as a whole is not very representative of the average number of arrest charges found in each of the distinct latent classes.

The 'Predicted' column in Table 7.11 contains the model-based predicted number of total arrest charges based on the estimates from the semiparametric mixed Poisson model. Comparing the averages in the two columns, we find again that the model-based prediction was fairly accurate in predicting the overall average number of arrest charges in each of the latent classes. As in the earlier samples, about 50 per cent of the arrest charges in each latent class were composed of relatively serious arrest charges (the percentages ranged from 46% to 58%).

Once again we find between-class heterogeneity in our sample with respect to the average age at first arrest (Table 7.11). The youngest average age at first arrest was found in the LC4 latent class—they averaged their first arrest at the early age of 11.35 years old. The LC3, LC5, and LC6 latent classes averaged their first arrest when they were about 13 years old, while the LC1 and LC2 latent classes were about 14 years old when they were first arrested by law-enforcement authorities.

Also consistent with the findings from the two previous samples, Table 7.11 fails to depict a neat, reverse-ordering of the average ages at first arrest on the basis of the rank-orderings (from lowest to highest) of the total arrest charges among the latent classes. That is, the latent class with the youngest average age at first arrest (LC4) did not accumulate the highest average number of arrest charges, while the latent class with the oldest average age at first arrest also did not accumulate the lowest number of average arrest charge totals. We again find here that the two latent classes with highest average arrest charge totals (LC3 and LC6) both had average ages at first arrest that were nearly identical to the average age of arrest for the sample as a whole (which is 13.64 years old).

These results support the previously stated conclusion from earlier samples that the estimated age parameters were not equal across the latent classes in 1991–2 sample (Table 7.3), and once again these findings are inconsistent with the age-invariance hypothesis promulgated by Gottfredson and Hirschi (1990). In the next section we again present the graphical depiction of the observed and predicted arrest trajectory for each latent class to better investigate the substantive differences in the arrest trajectories of these latent classes.

Predicted and Observed Trajectories of Arrest

As in the prior section, the findings here replicate those noted above in the 1981–2 and 1986–7 samples. Similar to the findings observed for the two prior samples, the predicted trajectories for the latent classes in the 1991–2 sample here also tend to slightly overestimate the arrest rates at the younger ages, undercut the peak ages, and slightly over-predict during the early twenties. And once again, regardless of the causes of the drop in arrests, the observed number of charges are back 'on track' with the predicted number of charges once the sample members reach their mid-twenties.

Once again, due to the fact that it is easier to see the differences in the predicted arrest trajectories (because of the natural 'smoothing' that occurs in the predictions), we focus our discussion here on the predicted trajectories in Figure 7.6. However, we again note that it is important to recall that the substantive implications of interest to us in this study do not depend on whether one uses the predicted or observed arrest trajectories.

First, both Figures 7.6 and 7.7. indicate that the latent classes have qualitatively distinct arrest trajectories (although this depiction is clearer in Figure 7.6). For example, the LC3 latent class has a very high peak rate of offending, whereas the LC2 latent class has a peak rate that is roughly one-half of the peak rate of the LC3 latent class. The nature of the trajectories presented in these figures lends further substantive support to the first hypothesis (H_1) that there are multiple offender groups in the serious youthful offender population. However, these results again contradict the second hypothesis examined in this study (H_2). Our analyses show that there are more than two distinct offender groups in our samples. Important differences in the developmental nature of the offending

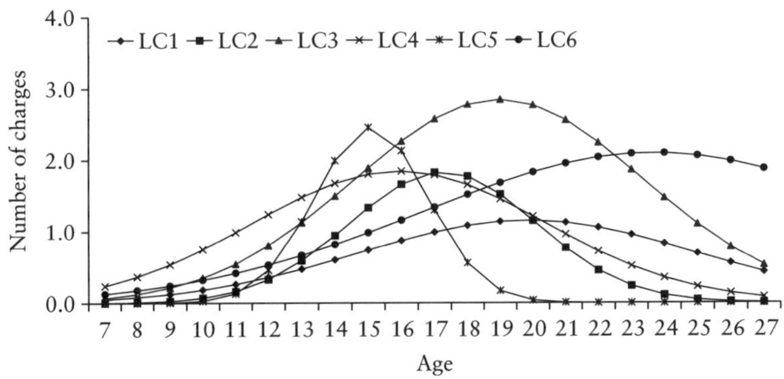

FIGURE 7.6. Predicted arrest trajectories: Six-class model of the 1991–2 sample.

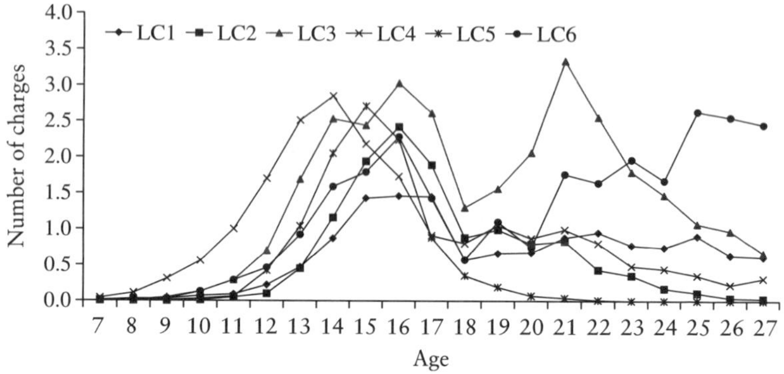

FIGURE 7.7. Observed arrest trajectories: Six-class model of the 1991–2 sample.

trajectories would be lost if we limited even this select portion of the offender population to contain only two distinct latent classes.

Second, once again we find an 'adolescent-limited' offender group (LC4) in the serious youthful chronic offender population. Thus, this offender group was uncovered in all three of the samples used in this study. The trajectory of the LC4 latent class clearly follows an 'adolescent-limited trajectory'; as there is a rapid increase in their arrest rate during early adolescence and a nearly identical decrease in the arrest rate on the other side of their peak age (age 16). By their early twenties, this group (like the AL groups in the two earlier samples) had largely desisted from offending. There were only a handful of arrests between ages 20 through 22 for the individuals in the LC4 latent class, and from ages 23 through 31, there was not even a single arrest charge for the offenders assigned to this latent class (that were followed through the specified age distribution). Thus, once again we find support for the third hypothesis (H_3) regarding the presence of an AL offender group in the serious youthful offender population.

Finally, the trajectories depicted in both Figures 7.6 and 7.7 provide additional evidence against the 'age-invariance' hypothesis of Gottfredson and Hirschi (1990). Whether using Figure 7.6 (predicted trajectories) or Figure 7.7 (observed trajectories), there are visible differences in the trajectories of the latent classes in terms of not only their mean rate of offending, but also in the developmental nature of their trajectories as well. Once again we find that (excluding the 'adolescent-limited' group) there was considerable stability in the differences among the trajectories during the early ages (through about age 15). However, there was a significant breakdown in the preservation of between-group differences all the way through the adult years studied here. For example, the LC4 latent class had the highest arrest rate during the early ages, but by the late twenties, three of the other latent classes had higher predicted (and observed) arrest trajectories than did LC4. Further, the presence of this offender group in the data (LC5) poses a serious problem to the age-invariance hypothesis because the arrest trajectory of the AL offender group plunges right across all of the other (observed and predicted) arrest trajectories in the 1991–2 sample. Overall, the trajectory patterns shown in Figures 7.6. and 7.7. reject the notion that between-group differences are maintained across time. In sum, as in the two previous samples, both the statistical and substantive results provide evidence that fails to confirm the hypothesis that the relationship between age and crime is 'invariant' across the latent classes.

The Adult Prison Experiences of the Latent Classes

Finally, Table 7.12 presents a brief summary description of the adult incarceration experiences for each of the latent classes in the 1991–2 sample. Once again, we find that there were varying levels of entrance into the CDC across the six latent classes. Table 7.12 reports that 9 per cent of the AL offender group (LC5) made at least

TABLE 7.12. Summary of variables related to adult incarceration experiences, by latent class: 1991–2 sample

Variable	*Latent Class*					
	LC1	*LC2*	*LC3*	*LC4*	*LC5*	*LC6*
% with at least 1 CDC stay	51.40	46.78	80.72	59.72	9.43	62.24
% still incarcerated on 30 June 2000	7.38	10.23	9.42	11.37	1.26	6.12
Among those with at least 1 CDC stay:						
Avg. number of CDC stays	1.57	1.41	1.64	1.54	1.07	1.79
Median number of total years incarcerated in CDC	1.90	2.29	2.07	2.53	2.44	1.60

one transition into the CDC, whereas 81 per cent of the LC3 latent class was incarcerated at least once in the CDC over the age distribution period studied here. Among those who were incarcerated in the CDC, the average number of stays ranged from 1.07 (LC5) to 1.79 (LC6), while the median number of years institutionalized ranged from 1.60 (LC6) to 2.53 (LC4).

The results presented in Table 7.12 for the 1991–2 sample lead us to the same conclusion we arrived at for the two previous samples. Again we find here no clear (or robust) indication that incapacitation effects *over the entire age distribution studied here* are responsible for the failure of the different latent classes to support the age-invariance hypothesis (again, see Note 4). The group that poses the greatest difficulty for the hypothesis proposed by Gottfredson and Hirschi (because of its rapid, early decline compared to the other trajectories) is the group with the smallest percentage of its members that were eventually incarcerated (LC5). The other groups, which had much slower rates of change (the kind of change that would be expected when the members were not 'incapacitated'), were the groups that had the highest prison entrance rates. Again, we find no evidence here to suggest that our results indicate that incapacitation effects are responsible for group differences in the relationship between age and crime over time.

It is important to note that our conclusion here dovetails with the results of the Piquero *et al.* (2001) study that examined the adult arrest patterns for a sample of 272 CYA wards and employed the use of 'offset terms' in the finite mixture model in order to account for differences in street time. As Piquero *et al.* (2001: 68) noted, 'the general shape of the arrest trend appears to be robust to controls for exposure time.'

Summary and Discussion

The purpose of this chapter was to critically examine the relationship between age and crime among latent classes of serious youthful offenders. This chapter began with a summary description of the different explanations for the shape of the age–crime curve that were presented in Chapter 2 of this study. Recall that Chapter 2 presented a detailed description of the theories of Gottfredson and Hirschi (1990), Sampson and Laub (1993) and Moffitt (1993). The distinction between these theories is critical because each makes different assertions regarding the stability of individual differences in crime across time, and similarly each theory has a different explanation for the observed aggregate age–crime curve. In Chapter 3, we reviewed the extant literature on studies of the age–crime curve (within homogeneous latent classes of offenders) and concluded that there were several current limitations with the previous studies on this topic that necessitated further research. With those theoretical and empirical issues in mind, our study set out to investigate four hypotheses related to the age–crime curve using three large, random samples of serious youthful offenders. The first two hypotheses noted in Chapter 3 were:

H_1: There are multiple groups or latent classes of offenders with distinct offending trajectories even on the high-end of the criminal propensity continuum where the serious youthful offenders are located.
H_2: There are more than two groups of offenders with distinctly different trajectories even on the high-end of the criminal propensity continuum.

The semiparametric mixed Poisson model of Nagin and Land (1993) was used to empirically create the latent classes for the three samples. In all three samples, the BIC statistic favoured the finite mixture model with six components in the mixing distribution. Thus, the results for all three samples indicated significant support for the first hypothesis, $\mathbf{H_1}$, that there are multiple, distinct offender groups on the high-end of the criminal propensity continuum. These results support the previous descriptive (rather than empirical) contentions of Cohen and Vila (1996) and D'Unger *et al.* (1998) that the far end of the continuum has far greater heterogeneity than was previously specified.

Our empirical findings also provide evidence that appears to contradict the theoretical claims of Moffitt (1993) that there are only two discrete offender groups (i.e. the evidence does not support hypothesis H_2). The BIC statistics in all three samples favoured a 6-class model. Furthermore, the positive increase in the magnitude of the BIC statistics between the models that only allow for two latent classes (corresponding to the hypothesized number of discrete groups in Moffitt's theory) and those that allow for six latent classes were indeed quite large.

Further support for the notion that there are more than two groups in the offender population was provided after assigning each individual to the latent class to which they had the greatest probability of belonging. Examination of both the observed average total arrest charges and the observed and predicted arrest trajectories in each latent class indicated that there was simply too much heterogeneity in the population (both in terms of the mean rates of offending and the developmental shapes of the arrest trajectories) to be adequately and sufficiently accounted for with only two latent classes. Examination of the latent class parameter estimates indicated further evidence contrary to the dual taxonomy theory of Moffitt (1993). No latent class in any of the samples was found to offend at a relatively constant rate across the age distribution in the hypothesized 'spirit' of the 'life-course-persistent' offender group—the age and age-squared parameter estimates for all of the latent classes were found to be significantly different from zero (and indicative of a quadratic relationship). This contradicts Moffitt's (1993: 695) explicit contention that age is not a predictor of the offending trajectory in the 'life-course-persistent' group. Further, the graphical results presented in this chapter also failed to lend support to the existence of an offender group that offends across the age span at a relatively constant and persistent rate independent of age as claimed by Blumstein and his colleagues. This finding was found to be valid even among this select group of serious youthful offenders where presumably, if there were such a 'life-course persistent' group, it should have been identified.

The third hypothesis examined in this chapter was:

H_3: There is an 'adolescence-limited' (peaked) group even in samples of serious youthful offenders.

The examination of the predicted and observed arrest trajectories provided overwhelming support for the presence of an AL offender group in the serious youthful offender population. In all three samples, a latent class offender group was identified that was clearly arrested in an AL pattern. Importantly, for the final 16 age-years in the 1981–2 sample, the final 11 age-years in the 1986–7 sample, and the final 9 age-years in 1991–2 sample, not a single individual assigned to the AL offender groups was arrested for even a single charge. This is an impressive finding given that 10%, 13%, and 11% of the 1981–2, 1986–7, and 1991–2 samples, respectively, were assigned to this offender group and is extremely notable given the proclivity that the members of these samples have displayed for getting arrested.

However, we also want to address recent critical commentaries regarding the latent classes that result from the application of the semiparametric methods of Nagin and Land (1993). Recall that the semiparametric models are based on the idea that a *continuous* distribution of unobserved heterogeneity can be *approximated* by a discrete multinomial probability distribution. This approximation element has been the topic of discussion, with a central concern focusing on the possibility of reifying latent classes as actual distinct groups in the population (see Laub and Sampson 2003; Sampson and Laub 2003; Eggleston, Laub, and Sampson 2004; Nagin 2004; Sampson, Laub, and Eggleston 2004). Sampson and Laub were especially worried about the reification of any identified offender group for both policy and theoretical reasons, as some of the theoretical offender groups could easily be used to promote historically seductive public policies (e.g. incapacitation). We fully agree with the potential dangers of 'reading' too much into any identified group (especially in the absence of any replication across samples of the identified group) and especially with respect to the dangers of extrapolation. Yet, the fact that we have three separate samples allows us to be more confident in making a claim that there is a cluster of individuals in the population that share a similar adolescent-limited developmental trajectory.[15] Finding that group in three independently gathered samples poses a problem for the suggestion that this pattern was merely a temporal anomaly. Still, drawing on the admonitions of Sampson and Laub (2003; Laub and Sampson 2003; Sampson, Laub, and Eggleston 2004; Eggleston, Laub, and Sampson 2004) and Nagin (2004), we want to caution the reader that simply because we have uncovered the presence of a group with an offending trajectory that *retrospectively* can be identified as being distributed in an adolescent-limited style does not indicate either (1) that membership in that latent class can be *prospectively predicted* nor (2) that they are under a distinct, unique theoretical regime. Indeed, our comparisons of the subject

[15] It is interesting to note that the LC4 latent class of the 1981–2 sample did not show up in either the 1986–7 sample or the 1991–2 sample. As discussed in Chapter 4, legislation passed in 1982 removed the CYA as a potential sentencing alternative (in place of sentencing to the CDC) for young adult offenders who had been convicted of serious (e.g. Index) offenses. Nonetheless, the results of the models fit with the changes in the sentencing patterns that removed the LC4 type of offender from the CYA population.

characteristics across the latent classes indicated that very few variables have any numerically distinguishing values across the latent classes (these results are available via the Internet; see Appendix C). Nonetheless, the existence of the adolescent-limited group (whether 'real' or as a 'heuristic device') in each of the three samples also calls into question the next hypothesis we tested:

H_4: The age–crime curve is invariant among the latent classes of serious youthful offenders. Between-group differences will not vary across time.

The results presented in this chapter *for all three samples* send a vigorous signal indicating a failure to find support for the H_4 hypothesis. The age-invariance hypothesis was first statistically tested using the (linear constraint) Wald statistic that tests the restriction of constraining each age parameter to be equivalent across the latent classes. The statistical evidence strongly rejected the null hypothesis of no difference in the estimated age parameters across the latent classes within all three samples.

Next, the age-invariance hypothesis was tested by examining the stability/instability of between-group differences in terms of the observed and predicted arrest trajectories of the latent classes. The results in all three samples provided further resounding evidence of a breakdown in the maintenance of between-group differences across time. In all three of the samples, the maintenance of between-group differences in arrests was relatively strong only through mid-adolescence. Soon thereafter, however, there was a considerable amount of change in the between-group differences in arrests throughout the remainder of the adult years studied here. Indeed, the mere presence of the 'adolescent-limited' offender group poses in our judgement, an insurmountable hurdle for the age-invariance hypothesis, especially since this latent class was shown to have the lowest incarceration rates in adult prison, and because mortality data was used to exclude deceased individuals from being considered in the at-risk population at ages subsequent to their death. Therefore, the rapid decline in arrests cannot be argued to be simply a consequence of the differential effects of incapacitation and/or mortality. Thus, the group that at one point consistently had one of the highest arrest rates (at around age 15–16), just several years later had the lowest arrest rate. Arrest records indicate that individuals in this group appear to have officially terminated their offending activity. This finding is completely incompatible with the hypothesis that the relationship between age and crime is invariant.

Indeed, the findings in this chapter resonate extremely well with the earliest study to examine the relationship between age and crime within discrete latent classes of offenders: 'explanations of the age–crime curve are not easily reduced to summary statements about average population tendencies' (Nagin and Land 1993: 358). According to the results presented in this chapter, this appears to be the case even within the serious youthful offender population.

Before concluding this chapter, several final comments seem to be in order. First, it is clear from the results presented here that longitudinal data are absolutely necessary for examining the causes of crime contrary to the claims of Gottfredson and Hirschi. Lacking longitudinal data, one would tend to lose sight of the fact that even within these samples of persistent offenders, there exists a group of individuals who only appear to have high rates of criminal activity during adolescence. In fact, if you took a cross-section of these offenders at around age 15, you would find that the 'adolescent-limited' offenders appear to be among the highest rate offenders in the samples. However, if you took the cross-section during their early twenties, these same offenders would be the lowest rate offenders (at a rate near or equal to zero) in the three samples. Of course, the connection that these are the same individuals at two distinct points in time could only be deduced with longitudinal data. Gottfredson and Hirschi (1987*a*) were, however, correct in their contention that there are high costs associated with the collection of longitudinal data (which the authors of this study know all too well), but we would argue that it is clear from the results presented in this chapter that an adequate and complete understanding of the over time criminal behavior of these individuals could not be accomplished through the use of cross-sectional data only. For example, many criminologists will probably be surprised by the existence of an 'adolescent-limited' offender group within the CYA offender population, given that the CYA wards are renowned for their excessive failure rates upon exit from the CYA institutions, and their persistence in offending through adulthood (see, e.g., Haapanen 1990; Piquero *et al.* 2001). Without longitudinal data, one would completely lose sight of the fact that even among this population of high-rate serious offenders, there is such an 'adolescent-limited' offender group. Of course, as Tittle

(1988: 76) has noted, 'whether longitudinal data are preferred over cross-sectional is something like asking whether hammers or saws are more useful to carpenters.' Forced to choose between the alternatives, it depends on what the carpenter is trying to build. Cross-sectional data have their strengths and weaknesses, as do longitudinal data, but favoring one at the complete expense of the other in the abstract would be a serious error equal only to deciding that only quantitative or qualitative analyses should be undertaken to best understand criminal behavior.

Second, the findings in this study clearly indicate a significant amount of heterogeneity in the propensity to offend within this 'at-risk' population, a fact that is important for both theoretical and public policy reasons. Our findings indicate that it would be dangerous to think of this population as being 'relatively homogeneous' as some researchers have noted (Ge, Donnellan, and Wenk 2001: 750). As a whole, serious youthful offenders are an elusive class of offenders because they are relatively rare in the population of lawbreakers (Cernkovich, Giordano, and Pugh 1985). Researchers, however, should keep in mind that even within this segment of the offending population there is a considerable amount of heterogeneity. The offenders from the serious youthful offender population undoubtedly will always stand out when (assuming they are actually sampled by chance) they are found in general population samples. As the results obtained here clearly indicate, just because these offenders 'stand out' compared to non-offenders or low-rate offenders in the general population, does not mean they then 'stand together' when you actually examine the longitudinal offending patterns of a large sample of such offenders. There simply is much more heterogeneity in this population than has previously been acknowledged.

Finally, the results obtained in this study suggest the limited utility of the dual offender typology employed by Moffitt. This is potentially problematic because of the tendency of some contemporary criminological researchers to investigate the tenets of this theoretical perspective after dividing the sample into two groups (which are then labeled as 'life-course-persistent' and 'adolescent-limited') on the basis of age of onset alone (see, e.g., Aguilar *et al.* 2000; Cernkovich and Giordano 2001; Dean, Brame, and Piquero 1996; Ge, Donnellan, and Wenk 2001; Klevens *et al.* 2000; Piquero *et al.* 1999; Scholte 1999; Mazerolle *et al.* 2000; Piquero and Brezina 2001).

The results presented in this study indicate that it was not the age of onset that differentiated the 'adolescent-limited' offender group from the other offender groups, but rather it was the unique developmental nature of their arrest trajectory. Given that there appears to be more offender groups in the population than simply two (and that age of onset appears to be a questionable method of separating out the two groups), analyses and interpretations based on this dual taxonomy distinction might appear to be helpful heuristic devices, but in practice they may be: (1) of questionable theoretical import, and (2) potentially misleading to policy makers. If populations/samples cannot be neatly and discretely divided into two groups by arbitrarily dividing them on the basis of age of onset (and the results obtained herein indicate), then such a process is likely to do nothing other than reify the dual offender categories as if they actually exist within the offending population.

8

On the Relationship of Past to Subsequent Criminal Activity

Just as the last chapter critically examined one of the most robust findings in criminology—the supposed invariance in the age–crime relationship, here the relationship between past and subsequent criminal activity (another robust finding in criminology) will be explored. As Brame, Bushway, and Paternoster (1999: 600) note: 'The strong positive association between past and subsequent criminal offending is one of the most agreed, yet least well understood facts about law breaking behavior. Individuals who have offended in the past are most likely to offend in the future. There is little doubt or ambiguity about the validity of this claim. *Still, it is not clear why this association exists*' (emphasis added). In other words, the fact that there is a positive association between criminal offending at two (or more) points in time is really not in question; what is at issue, however, is the aetiological significance of this association.

As presented in explicit detail in Chapter 2, there are three broad aetiological expositions that assert unique alternative explanations for this recurrently documented positive association: (1) population heterogeneity; (2) state dependence; and (3) mixed theories of crime. Each of these explanations has substantively different predictions about the causal significance of the link between past and future offending, including spuriousness (population heterogeneity theories), a significant positive association between past and subsequent criminal activity for all offender types (state dependence theories), and, depending on the specific offender type, both spuri ousness and causal significance (dual taxonomy theories).

Our review of the extant literature on this topic in Chapter 3 indicated that there are several limitations in the previous literature that highlight the need for additional analyses such as that to be undertaken here. Recall that in Chapter 3 we discussed two key possible limitations of this research. First, there are questions regarding the validity of the observed state dependence effects identified in prior studies due to the possible consequences of violations in the assumptions of the statistical models employed in these studies. Second, there are also questions regarding whether population heterogeneity processes 'rule the day' in high-risk samples such as those employed in our study.

In view of these two possible limitations in previous research, we now present a series of analyses that aim to examine whether there are any state dependence effects within our three parole release samples of what can only be described as 'very high-risk' offenders. This chapter contains three main sections, with one main section of results dedicated to each of the three parole release samples. In this chapter we will employ the use of the multi-method approach advocated by Bushway, Brame, and Paternoster (1999), which is essentially the 'compare and contrast strategy' recommended by Heckman and Singer (1984). More specifically, we will test the robustness of any observed association of past and subsequent criminal behavior by employing several different methods of analysis.

As described in the final section of Chapter 5, we will proceed through four stages of analysis for each of the three parole release samples employed in our study. In the first stage of analysis, we employ the Poisson finite mixture models to estimate the magnitude of the state dependence parameter while non-parametrically controlling for the unobserved heterogeneity. Stage two of the analysis will contain a presentation of the results from the parametric random effects model, where the unobserved heterogeneity is assumed to follow a specific parametric distribution (the beta distribution) and where the age parameters are assumed to apply equally to all individuals. In stage three of the analysis, we incorporate the latent class indicators from the results obtained in Chapter 7. The use of these indicators will allow us to address two important questions. First, we ask if the incorporation of the set of latent class indicators in the analysis removes the presence of unobserved heterogeneity. This question will be answered by comparing the results of the parametric random effects model that includes the latent class indicators to the results of the negative binomial (NB1) model with the latent class indicators. Second, we ask if allowing the estimates of the age parameters to vary over the obtained latent classes improves the estimation of the state dependence parameter. Finally, stage four of our analysis examines the effect of the state dependence parameter estimate calculated within each of the obtained latent classes by themselves. The results of our analyses will be presented separately for the 1981–2 sample, the 1986–7 sample, and finally for the 1991–2 sample, respectively. It bears repeating that differentiating state dependence processes from population heterogeneity processes with respect to the relationship between past and subsequent criminal activity is a methodologically complicated task, a point that should not be underemphasized (Nagin and Paternoster 2000). We have included technical comments and footnotes when necessary and relevant in order to clarify the presentation of our results to the reader.

Results for the 1981–2 Sample

For the 1981–2 sample, we describe each analytical stage in detail as well as the rationale supporting its use. The analyses that will follow for the 1986–7 and 1991–2 samples are exact replications of the same analytical processes employed here for the 1981–2 sample, and thus will not be described in the same detail as given to the 1981–2 parole release sample.

Stage One—The Semiparametric Mixed Poisson Model

We begin our analyses by employing the semiparametric mixed Poisson model developed by Nagin and Land (1993; Land and Nagin 1996; Land, McCall, and Nagin 1996; Nagin 1999). Again, this model controls for persistent individual differences through the non-parametric 'points of support' approach identified in the previous chapter. The only assumption this model makes with respect to the distribution of unobserved heterogeneity in the sample is that it can be approximated using a discrete, multinomial distribution. The random effects, in other words, are assumed to have been drawn from $j = 1, 2, 3, \ldots, J$ discrete groups. This model is an excellent model to begin the presentation of results for two reasons. First, a model with one point of support corresponds, in fact, to a standard Poisson model that assumes no stochastic variation and no unobserved heterogeneity, and thus provides an excellent baseline model for subsequent comparisons. Second, by specifying models with increasing numbers of points of support, we can numerically observe the effects that the improved control for unobserved heterogeneity has on the various magnitudes of the state dependence effects.

The specification used in the semiparametric models in this chapter is similar to the specification of these models employed in Chapter 7, with the exception that the model specifications in this chapter also include a binary indicator of arrest in the prior period (arr_{t-1}).

The formal specification employed in this chapter is:

$$\ln\left(\lambda^{j}_{it}\right) = (\beta_0 + \bar{\varepsilon}_j) + \left((age_{it}/10) * \beta^{j}_{age}\right) + \left(((age^2_{it})/100) * \beta^{j}_{age^2}\right) + \left(arr_{t-1} * \beta_{arr_{t-1}}\right). \quad (1)$$

This specification allows for both latent class-specific (or group-specific) intercepts and age coefficients, but the effect of the regression coefficient that estimates the state dependence relationship between the binary variable (indicating arrest in the prior period) and the mean offending rate in the current period, denoted as $\hat{\beta}_{arr_{t-1}}$ in equation (1) above, was constrained to be equal across the latent classes. This assumption is relaxed in stage four below.

The same process for fitting and testing the semiparametric mixed Poisson model with varying numbers of 'points of support' described in Chapter 7 was also employed here. Similar to the results presented in Chapter 7, the 7-class and 8-class models in the 1981–2 sample were again prone to local solutions. The 6-class model, however, generated the same unique solution all ten times it was estimated. Further, and as shown in Table 8.1, the 6-class model had the largest BIC value (i.e. the least negative value), and thus this model was determined to be the model with the optimal number of latent classes. The 6-class model had the least negative BIC value of −72,391.62, whereas the BIC value for the 5-class model was only −72,670.64). However, since interest in this chapter also lies in changes in the magnitude of the state dependence coefficient, we also present the solutions for all the models up through the 6-class model in Table 8.1. Thus, the optimal number of latent classes in this chapter was used to end the presentation of model results (i.e. results from the 7-class solutions are not presented), rather than to present only the solutions from that model.

TABLE 8.1. Investigation of state dependence effects with semiparametric random effects Poisson model: 1981–2 sample (N = 1,989; panel observations = 60,453)

	Points of support					
	1	*2*	*3*	*4*	*5*	*6*
Random effects						
Class1	−2.978	−3.015	−3.867	−4.994	−4.986	−4.663
	(74.58)	(60.35)	(46.80)	(39.50)	(38.09)	(35.58)
Class 2	—	−5.560	−2.911	−3.523	−2.756	−2.733
		(38.81)	(36.26)	(22.81)	(32.17)	(30.18)
Class 3	—	—	−15.229	−3.067	−5.603	−5.374
			(24.63)	(26.99)	(26.68)	(28.23)
Class 4	—	—	—	−14.855	−19.289	−21.242
				(18.71)	(23.35)	(21.75)
Class 5	—	—	—	—	−3.771	−8.840
					(29.59)	(14.55)
Class 6	—	—	—	—	—	−3.689
						(28.17)
Age effects						
Class 1 age	2.511	2.664	3.715	3.962	3.903	3.716
	(64.71)	(57.98)	(43.78)	(36.41)	(34.77)	(33.59)
Class 1 age-squared	−0.585	−0.577	−0.923	−0.842	−0.814	−0.766
	(67.92)	(58.48)	(42.61)	(35.33)	(34.33)	(32.99)
Class 2 age	—	5.943	2.625	4.059	3.067	3.103
		(34.88)	(39.32)	(24.41)	(36.27)	(34.65)
Class 2 age-squared	—	−1.657	−0.544	−1.083	−0.752	−0.762
		(33.77)	(39.91)	(23.05)	(37.45)	(36.07)
Class 3 age	—	—	9.056	2.764	6.430	6.221
			(23.65)	(32.97)	(27.90)	(29.06)
Class 3 age-squared	—	—	−5.935	−0.555	−1.780	−1.722
			(22.87)	(35.46)	(28.37)	(29.30)
Class 4 age	—	—	—	18.535	24.515	28.031
				(17.57)	(22.88)	(21.67)
Class 4 age-squared	—	—	—	−5.743	−7.727	−9.059
				(16.67)	(22.43)	(21.29)
Class 5 age	—	—	—	—	3.152	7.784
					(30.03)	(12.17)
Class 5 age-squared	—	—	—	—	−0.586	−1.896
					(27.91)	(11.29)
Class 6 age	—	—	—	—	—	3.127
						(28.75)
Class 6 age-squared	—	—	—	—	—	−0.579
						(26.48)
State depen. effects						
Arr_{t-1}	0.857	0.618	0.545	0.470	0.439	0.404
	(86.28)	(61.07)	(53.43)	(45.50)	(42.38)	(38.82)
Log-likelihood	−78,225.72	−75,155.540	−73,945.49	−73,047.13	−72,594.68	−72,300.470
BIC	−78,240.91	−75,185.92	−73,991.06	−73,107.9	−72,670.64	−72,391.62

Note: Absolute values of t-statistics are in parentheses.

Table 8.1 presents the results of the 1- through 6-class semi-parametric mixed Poisson models. Interest here focuses exclusively on the regression coefficient, $\hat{\beta}_{\mathrm{arr}_{t-1}}$, found in the row identified as, 'Arr_{t-1}'. This estimate represents the state dependence relationship between the binary variable indicating arrest in the prior period (arr_{t-1}) and the mean offending rate in the current period (age). The first column in Table 8.1 contains the parameter estimates from the 1-class model. The estimate of the state dependence parameter was 0.857, which was highly significant with a t-statistic of 86.28. This t-statistic offers empirical support for the fifth hypothesis addressed in this study indicating a statistically significant positive association between past and subsequent offending behaviour for the members of this sample. Again, this model corresponds to a standard Poisson regression model with no stochastic variation and under the assumption of complete homogeneity with respect to criminal propensity (which as was already shown in Chapter 7 to be an erroneous assumption).

The next column in Table 8.1 presents the results from a two-class model that assumes there are two latent classes in the population. The resulting parameter estimate of the state dependence relationship in this model was 0.618 (t-statistic = 61.07), which, in comparison with the estimate from the one-class model, represents a 27.9 per cent decrease in the magnitude of the parameter estimate.[1] The next column corresponds to a 3-class model (which allows three additional parameters—an intercept and two additional age parameters), and here again we observe a decline in the magnitude of the state dependence parameter estimate from 0.618 (2-class) to 0.545 in this model. The estimate was still highly significant in this model with an estimated t-statistic of 53.43. Allowing for four points of support further reduced the parameter estimate to 0.470 (t-statistic = 45.50), while allowing for five points of support reduced it even further to 0.439 (t-statistic = 42.38). Lastly, the final state dependence estimate in the 1981–2 sample was 0.404

[1] Ideally, one would like to conduct a formal statistical test concerning whether the difference is equal to 0. However, since the statistical theory underlying such a test presumes that the samples on which the parameter estimates are calculated are independent, there is no formal test available (Paternoster *et al.* 1997). The problem is that the covariance between the two estimated coefficients is unknown and it cannot be assumed to be zero (since the samples on which they are both estimated are the exact same samples).

when we allowed for six points of support (which can be found in the last column in Table 8.1).

Three findings at this point in our analysis are especially important to note. First the state dependence parameter is positive, and well above zero even in the 6-class model. The positive parameter estimate in the final model indicates that even after controlling for persistent individual differences (through the points of support approach), individuals who were arrested at a prior age had a higher mean number of arrest charges at the next observed age in comparison with the individuals who were not arrested at the immediately observed prior age. Second, the state dependence parameter estimate is not only positive, but it is still highly significant with an associated t-value of 38.82 in the 6-class model. In other words, having been arrested at a prior age appears to have *significantly* increased the rate of criminal activity at the next age, a finding that is entirely consistent with the state dependence position of Sampson and Laub (1993) and incompatible with the pure population heterogeneity explanation espoused by Gottfredson and Hirschi (1990). This result supports the seventh hypothesis examined in this study and refutes our sixth hypothesis. That is, after controlling for persistent individual differences in criminal propensity, the association between past and subsequent offending behaviour appears to have been reduced in magnitude, but is still positive and statistically significant. Third, controlling for persistent individual differences was found to be critical in terms of calculating the precise numerical estimate of the state dependence parameter. In the standard Poisson model (1 point of support model), the parameter estimate was 0.86, whereas controlling for the significant individual differences reduced this estimate to 0.40, which amounts to a 53 per cent reduction in the absolute magnitude of the effect. Clearly, the results for the 1981–2 sample derived from this model lend support to the 'mixed' model approach used by Sampson and Laub to explain the relationship between past and subsequent criminal activity. Both population heterogeneity and state dependence explanations appear to make significant contributions towards explaining the relationship between criminal offending at the two age periods.

As noted in Chapter 7, the semiparametric mixed Poisson model contains a number of non-linear terms that make it difficult to substantively interpret the parameter estimates from this model.

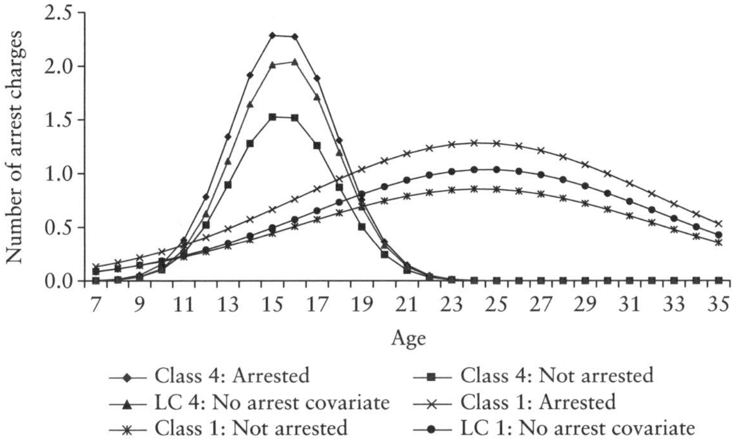

FIGURE 8.1. Predicted mean arrest charges, by arrest status at prior age: 1981–2 sample.

To aid in understanding the substantive importance of the state dependence parameter estimate in the 6-class model found in Table 8.1, we generated predicted arrest trajectories for two of the latent classes in this model. Figure 8.1 presents the predicted offending trajectories for the first and fourth latent classes in the 6-class model in Table 8.1. This figure contains six predicted trajectories, three for each class. Two of the trajectories represent the predicted trajectories for each of the two latent classes that were presented in Chapter 7 in which there was no covariate in the model indicating arrest at the prior age (these two trajectories are labeled 'No arrest covariate' in Figure 8.1).[2] The other two trajectories for each latent class that are presented in Figure 8.1 represent the predicted mean arrest charge for cases who (1) were arrested at the prior age (labeled 'Arrested' in Figure 8.1) and (2) were not

[2] These two predicted trajectories are the exact trajectories presented in Chapter 7. Note that in Chapter 7 the adolescent-peaked trajectory in the 1981–2 sample was labelled 'LC5' because it was the latent class that ranked 5th in prevalence. This adolescent peaked trajectory in this chapter was the fourth latent class in Table 8.1 because it ranked 4th in prevalence (i.e. with respect to how many people are estimated to belong to the latent class). In Chapter 7, 'LC5' had 215 cases (10.81%) assigned to it, whereas in the 6-class model of Table 8.1, the adolescent-peaked group had 222 cases (11%) assigned to it. The 7 additional cases were enough to make it rank fourth in prevalence.

arrested at the prior age (labelled 'Not arrested'). The two trajectories 'borrowed' from the results presented in Chapter 7 lie in between the other two trajectories for each latent class. This is because the effect of having been arrested at a prior age was 'averaged' out in the model presented in Chapter 7 (which did not have a covariate controlling for this effect).

Nonetheless, an important conclusion derived from Figure 8.1 is that not only is there a statistically significant difference between the mean arrest rates of those who were and were not arrested at a prior age (i.e. the difference is not zero), but more importantly there is a *substantively important difference* in their mean offending rates as well.[3] For example, for the adolescent-limited trajectory depicted in Figure 8.1, there is a difference (between those who were and were not arrested at the prior age) of about 0.75 arrest charges (on average) between the ages of 15 and 18. Again, recall that the descriptive presentation of the arrest histories of these individuals in Chapter 6 indicated that over half of all of their arrest charges were for serious criminal offences, and thus this difference is substantively meaningful. Hence, many of the criminal offences for which these individuals were arrested were not trivial matters, and thus differences between mean offending rates could have extremely important implications in terms of their costs to victims, offenders, and the larger society as well.

Before moving on to stage two of the analysis, it is interesting to note that the decrease in the magnitude of the state dependence parameter estimate that occurs with each additional point of support became smaller as we added additional points of support to the model. For example, the addition of a second class resulted in a decrease of 0.239 in the state dependence parameter estimate (i.e. $0.857 - 0.618 = 0.239$), whereas going from the 3-class model to a 4-class model resulted in a decrease of 0.075, and going from a 5- to 6-class model resulted in a change of only 0.035 in the parameter estimate. These results are entirely consistent with how the 'point of

[3] We want to be clear that in Figure 8.1 the expected arrest rate changes significantly depending on whether the individual was arrested in the prior year. The expected arrest rate of an individual assigned to one of the latent classes depicted in the figure 'zig zags' back and forth from the 'Arrested' to the 'Not arrested' depending on whether they were arrested in the prior year. In other words, individuals do not exclusively follow either the 'Arrested' or 'Not arrested' trajectories presented in the figure.

support' methods approximate the mixing distribution. Eventually the extraction of an additional point of support results in two or more of the points of support becoming similar, which is what eventually results in the model failing to reach convergence (or leading to local solutions with weak identification). Mathematically, the new additional point of support becomes too similar to one of the other points of support, and this causes the model to 'blow-up' because the Hessian matrix becomes singular (i.e. two columns of the matrix are linearly dependent) and cannot be inverted.[4] Substantively, however, the fact that the change in the state dependence parameter estimate became smaller as the higher-order points of support were added to the model was a clear indication that the heterogeneity in the mixing distribution was well approximated with the finite number of points of support.

Stage Two—The Parametric Random Effects Negative Binomial Model

Attention is now turned towards the typical approach employed in previous research to control for individual differences—the parametric random effects model. In this stage, we employ the use of the parametric random effects negative binomial model and estimate the following model:

$$\ln(\lambda_{it}) = \beta_0 + \left((age_{it}/10)*\beta_{\text{age}}\right) + \left(((age_{it}^2)/100)*\beta_{\text{age}^2}\right) + \left(arr_{t-1}*\beta_{\text{arr}_{t-1}}\right) + \varepsilon_{it}. \quad (2)$$

Again, here we are interested in the regression coefficient, $\hat{\beta}_{\text{arr}_{t-1}}$, that estimates the state dependence relationship between the binary

[4] Wedel and Kamakura (1998) found that this is also one of the principal causes of local solutions. The local solution models differ from non-convergence models in that the local solution models are still able to obtain estimates (i.e. the Hessian matrix can still be inverted and standard errors can still be calculated), but they indicate a 'weak identification' of the model, since the 'points of support' are not clearly separated or well-defined. Indeed, our investigation of the local solutions in the release samples analyzed in this chapter indicated that this is what was precisely occurring in these cases. The local solutions were 'weakly identified' meaning that two or more of the points of support were not very different from one another. It is important to note that in these 'local solution' models, the estimate of the state dependence parameter hovered in the general vicinity of the estimated parameter estimate from the 6-class model. This lends further support to the conclusion that the 6-class models described in this chapter are sufficient to account for the distribution of unobserved heterogeneity among our data.

variable indicating arrest in the prior period (arr_{t-1}) and the mean offending rate. Unlike the semiparametric model, this model assumes that the distribution of unobserved heterogeneity follows a very specific, mathematically tractable parametric distribution, which in the current model is the beta distribution. To the degree that the unobserved heterogeneity is distributed in the population according to the assumed distribution, the random effects model is more efficient than is the semiparametric model. The random effects models have most likely been used more frequently to control for unobserved heterogeneity because these models have been readily available in canned software packages commonly used by social scientists (e.g. SAS, Stata, LIMDEP). The complexity of the finite mixture models and a lack of available software have thus limited the use of such models to control for unobserved heterogeneity. Here we will compare the estimates of the state dependence effect from this model using the parametric specification of the unobserved heterogeneity to those estimates obtained in the first stage using the non-parametric specification of the random effects.

The results from the random effects negative binomial model are found in the first column of Table 8.2 (under the Model 1 column heading). This model involves the estimation of four regression coefficients—an intercept, age, age-squared, and the state dependence parameter. To test for the presence of significant unobserved heterogeneity, we performed a 'boundary-value likelihood ratio' that compares the random effects negative binomial model against the NB1 negative binomial model (Gutierrez, Carter, and Drukker 2001), which is the nested model of the random effects negative binomial model.[5] This statistical test, which tests the significance of the r and s ancillary parameters, resulted in a χ^2_{01} value of 391.28 (p-value = 0.000), which clearly indicates the presence of significant unobserved heterogeneity. The estimate of the state dependence

[5] Similar to the discussion of testing the negative binomial model against the Poisson model, the null hypothesis here concerning the absence of individual-specific effects is also on the boundary of the parameter space. The null hypothesis, $\alpha_I = 0$, is on the boundary of the parameter space because there can be an absence of individual-level effects, but they cannot be negative. Therefore, the appropriate statistical test is a boundary-value likelihood ratio test (Self and Liang 1987; Gutierrez, Carter, and Drukker 2001). As shown by Self and Liang (1987), this test statistic is a 50:50 mixture (χ^2_{01}) of (1) a chi-square distribution with a point mass at zero (χ^2_0) and (2) a chi-square distribution with 1 degree of freedom (χ^2_1).

TABLE 8.2. Investigation of state dependence effects with parametric random effects and NB1 negative binomial models: 1981–2 sample

	Model			
	1	*2*	*3*	*4*
Overall intercept	−3.834	−4.590	−3.993	−17.869
	(65.13)	(68.70)	(60.36)	(23.94)
Latent class indicators				
LC1	—	0.553	0.553	13.199
		(16.10)	(16.10)	(17.45)
LC2	—	1.023	1.023	14.873
		(29.91)	(29.91)	(19.78)
LC3	—	0.543	0.543	12.913
		(15.38)	(15.38)	(17.01)
LC4	—	−0.493	−0.493	10.472
		(10.45)	(10.45)	(12.57)
LC6	—	1.165	1.165	13.875
		(32.40)	(32.40)	(18.21)
Age effects				
Age	2.792	2.956	2.956	23.490
	(49.22)	(52.51)	(52.51)	(24.36)
Age sq	−0.643	−0.678	−0.678	−7.540
	(50.88)	(54.14)	(54.13)	(24.55)
LC1 * age	—	—	—	−19.811
				(20.44)
LC1 * age-squared	—	—	—	6.797
				(22.09)
LC2 * age	—	—	—	−20.245
				(20.93)
LC2 * age-squared	—	—	—	6.768
				(22.01)
LC3 * age	—	—	—	−17.959
				(18.43)
LC3 * age-squared	—	—	—	6.055
				(19.59)
LC4 * age	—	—	—	−17.299
				(16.84)
LC4 * age-squared	—	—	—	6.060
				(19.06)
LC6 * age	—	—	—	−20.091
				(20.67)
LC 6 * age-squared	—	—	—	6.902
				(22.41)
State depen. effects				
Arr_{t-1}	0.770	0.615	0.615	0.402
	(48.67)	(40.57)	(40.57)	(27.27)
Ancillary parameters				
ln(r)	2.627	15.903	—	—
ln(s)	3.123	16.499	—	—
ln(alpha)	—	—	0.596	0.475
Log-likelihood	−63,700.517	−62,157.225	−62,157.225	−59,971.658

Note: Absolute values of t-statistics are in parentheses. Latent class indicator variables are from the results presented in Chapter 6.

effect in the random effects model was 0.770 (t-statistic = 48.67), which is considerably larger in magnitude than the estimate from the semiparametric model. In fact, this estimate from the random effects model is nearly twice as large in magnitude as the estimate from the 6-class mixed Poisson model. Although, it should be noted that both models are compatible in the sense that they each indicate a positive, significant, and substantively important effect of having been arrested at the prior age on the mean offending rate at the subsequent age. Still, there is a large discrepancy in the effect between the two models, which indicates a need for additional methods of calculating the estimate of this parameter in order to test its methodological robustness. Thus, in the third stage of this analysis, we will use a method of calculating the state dependence parameter that has not previously been utilized in the empirical literature.

Stage Three—Incorporating Latent Class Indicator Variables

In the third stage of our analysis, we employ the use of both the random effects negative binomial model and the standard negative binomial model, and estimate both of these models using the following specification:

$$\begin{aligned}\ln(\lambda_{it}) = \beta_0 + \mathbf{X}_{\mathrm{LCV}}\boldsymbol{\beta}_{\mathrm{LCV}} + \left((age_{it}/10)*\beta_{\mathrm{age}}\right)\\ + \left(((age_{it}^2)/100)*\beta_{\mathrm{age}^2}\right) + \left(arr_{t-1}*\beta_{\mathrm{arr}_{t-1}}\right) + \varepsilon_{it}, \qquad (3)\end{aligned}$$

where $\mathbf{X}_{\mathrm{LCV}}$ is a matrix of binary variables indicating latent class membership (with the adolescent-limited group, denoted as LC5 in Chapter 7, used as the reference group) and $\boldsymbol{\beta}_{\mathrm{LCV}}$ is a column vector of regression coefficients for the latent class indicators.

Again, the latent class indicator variables employed in this stage of the analysis are from the results of the semiparametric mixed Poisson models that were presented in Chapter 7. These latent class variables then *are not* from the results presented in stage one of this chapter (i.e. Table 8.1). This stage of analysis allows us to address two previously unanswered and important questions that we raised earlier. First, does including the set of binary latent class indicator variables remove the underlying unobserved heterogeneity that was found in the random effects model just presented in stage two? Second, this stage of the analysis addresses whether the state dependence effects uncovered in stage two *over-estimate* the genuine state dependence effect because the age effects in the random effects model were controlled through the use of only two parameters that are assumed to be common to all individuals in the sample. The reader will recall that in Chapter 7 it was determined that allowing the age parameters to vary over the latent classes resulted in a significant improvement to the model fit. This indicates that all individuals in the sample do not follow the same trajectory of offending across the age distribution. Bushway, Brame, and Paternoster (1999) found that models that allowed for 'time trend' or age effects significantly reduced the effect of the state dependence variable, but these authors did not test to determine if it was also sensitive so as to allow the age parameters to vary over the latent classes. Presumably, the under-estimation of the age effects among the most frequent offenders will cause an over-estimation in the state dependence parameter because the state dependence parameter will then naturally absorb the 'unaccounted for' age effects.

Model 2 of Table 8.2 presents the results of fitting a random effect negative binomial model with 5 latent class indicator variables included in the specification—the 'adolescent-limited' group, denoted as LC5 in Chapter 7, was used as the omitted reference group here. To test for the presence of significant unobserved heterogeneity in this model, we again performed a 'boundary-value' likelihood ratio test that compares the log-likelihood value from this model against the log-likelihood value of the NB1 negative binomial model (which is the negative binomial model with constant dispersion). This statistical test resulted in a χ^2_{01} value of 0.0 (p-value = 1.000), which indicates that the log-likelihood of the random effects model identically matched the log-likelihood from the NB1 negative binomial model, and more importantly, clearly indicates a lack of individual-level heterogeneity. For comparative purposes, we present the estimates from the NB1 negative binomial model in the Model 3 column of Table 8.2. In both of these models, one can see that (with the exception of the overall intercept term) all of the parameter estimates presented in Models 2 and 3 of Table 8.2 are identical. This indicates that the individual-specific effects have been removed through the incorporation of the 5 latent class indicator variables. Importantly, note that the t-statistics for the latent class indicator variables are all highly significant, indicating that there are highly significant differences in the mean offending rates of the 5 latent classes and the omitted reference group, the 'adolescent-limited' group. With respect to the state dependence variable indicating an arrest at the prior age, the resulting parameter estimate in Model 3 (which is identical in Model 2 as well) was 0.615 (t-statistic = 40.57). Thus, the parameter estimate from the NB1 model with the latent class indicator variables is smaller than the estimate from the random effects model presented in Model 1 of Table 8.2, but it still is much larger than the estimate that resulted from the semiparametric model.

The NB1 model presented in Model 4 of Table 8.2 adds 10 parameters to the specification of the NB1 model presented in Model 3.[6] These additional parameters, which are interaction variables between each of the latent class indicator variables and the two age variables, allow each latent class to have its own set of regression coefficients for the age parameters. The overall age parameters (the 'age' and 'age-squared' variables in Table 8.2) now represent the age parameters for the omitted reference group, the 'adolescent-limited' (LC5) group. The latent class * age interaction variables in Model 4 represent the latent class-specific age coefficients (expressed in terms of deviations from the age coefficients of the omitted group, the 'adolescent-limited' group). All of the latent class * age interaction variables were highly significant, indicating that that age coefficients for each of the latent class variables were significantly different from the age coefficients of the 'adolescent-limited' group. The latent class indicator variables were also still highly significant in Model 4.

More importantly, however, the state dependence parameter estimate recovered in Model 4 is almost identical in magnitude to the parameter estimate from the semiparametric mixed Poisson model. The estimate in Model 4 of Table 8.2 was 0.402, whereas it was 0.404 in the 6-class model of Table 8.1. Thus, after accounting for the latent class-specific effects of the age coefficients, we were able to nearly recover the identical parameter estimates of the state dependence effect. Had we simply applied the random effects estimator and not accounted for class-specific temporal shifts in the

[6] The NB1 standard negative binomial model was employed here because the comparison of Models 2 and 3 indicated a complete lack of individual-specific effects once the latent class indicators are included in the specification. Since the NB1 model is a much simpler model in comparison with the random effects version, the NB1 model is used for Model 4.

mean offending rate, we would have significantly overestimated the magnitude of the state dependence parameter by almost twice its estimated value. As Bushway, Brame, and Paternoster (1999: 53) note, 'clearly, then, it is possible for very general temporal shifts in the probability of offending activity to masquerade as genuine state dependence effects.' We would further add that not only do general temporal shifts masquerade as state dependence effects, but so too do group-specific shifts.

Stage Four—Latent Class-Specific Models

In the fourth analytical stage, we estimate separate NB1 negative binomial models on each latent class by itself.[7] The results presented up to this point have relied on a single estimate of the state dependence parameter, but for both theoretical and mathematical reasons, it is possible that the estimates calculated so far are not representative of the state dependence relationships *within each latent class itself*. Mathematically, the results calculated so far may simply be an 'average' estimate that may reflect large effects in some latent classes and small/non-existent effects in other latent classes. Recall that the dual taxonomy theory of Moffitt (1993) specifically hypothesizes the state dependence effects vary over her two hypothetically discrete offender groups, with an especially pronounced effect predicted to occur among the 'adolescent-limited' group and a muted or non-existent effect proposed among the 'life-course-persistent' group that is dominated by a static aetiological explanation. Sampson and Laub's (1993) theory, on the other hand, does not hypothesize that the state dependence process only affects specific types of offenders, but rather their general theory (i.e. the same causal structure is at work for all individuals) specifies that the state dependence process should be found in all latent classes. According to Sampson and Laub then, the state dependence process is unconditional, whereas it is a conditional process according to Moffitt. Of course, the effect does not causally exist in any latent

[7] These NB1 models were tested against the parametric random effects negative binomial models using the boundary-value likelihood ratio tests. In all 6 of the models, the null hypothesis of no individual-level effects could not be rejected. Similar to the results described in stage three, the resulting χ^2_{01} was equal to 0.00 in all 6 tests (p-value = 1.00), which indicates that the log-likelihood values for the NB1 model (which ignores individual differences) were all identical to the log-likelihood values of the random effects models.

class according to the theory proposed by Gottfredson and Hirschi (1990).

By estimating models on each latent class separately, we are able to test for differential effects of the state dependence variable within each of the latent classes. The specification for this stage of analysis will be identical to the specification noted above in the second stage of analysis, and will include the following covariates: age, age-squared, and the binary indicator of arrest at the previous age. In other words, it is identical to the specification of equation (2), except here the standard negative binomial model is used and it is estimated for each latent class separately (see Note 9). Again, the latent classes represented in Table 8.3 are from the analyses presented in Chapter 7 and are not the latent classes presented in Table 8.1 of this chapter. In Chapter 7, we presented results that indicated the fifth latent class, 'LC5', in the 1981–2 sample clearly offended in an 'adolescent-limited' pattern. Further, we also saw that 'LC6' and 'LC2' were the highest rate offenders, with an average of 44.10 and 36.35 arrest charges, respectively. LC4 had the lowest offending rate, and had, on average, a later age of onset (according to their arrest histories) in comparison with the other latent classes, but the offending

TABLE 8.3. Investigation of state dependence effects with NB1 negative binomial models: 1981–2 sample, latent class-specific models

	Latent class					
	LC1	*LC2*	*LC3*	*LC4*	*LC5*	*LC6*
Overall intercept	−4.769	−2.983	−4.920	−7.454	−17.983	−3.879
	(36.79)	(28.90)	(31.77)	(19.67)	(22.04)	(23.71)
Age effects						
Age	3.731	3.270	5.472	6.149	23.630	3.323
	(32.69)	(31.43)	(32.01)	(16.61)	(22.23)	(23.39)
Age-squared	−0.754	−0.776	−1.471	−1.472	−7.586	−0.624
	(31.85)	(32.66)	(33.77)	(17.01)	(22.59)	(21.77)
State depen. effects						
Arr_{t-1}	0.383	0.365	0.433	0.508	0.399	0.437
	(13.58)	(13.47)	(12.71)	(6.08)	(6.13)	(11.79)
Ancillary parameters						
ln(alpha)	0.247	0.597	0.466	0.174	0.414	0.691
Log-likelihood	−15,809.220	−17,070.52	−11,667.37	−3,183.097	−3,143.458	−9,043.450
N (panel)	16,299	12,123	12,341	7,675	5,977	6,038
N (observations)	519	403	414	244	215	194

Note: Absolute values of t-statistics are in parentheses. The 6 latent classes are from the results presented in Chapter 6.

of this group was observed to extend into the early thirties (albeit at a comparatively low-rate). The results of these latent class-specific models are presented in Table 8.3.

Overall, the results in Table 8.3 clearly speak to the robustness of the estimated state dependence effect calculated within each latent class in the 1981–2 sample. In all of the latent classes, the estimate is positive, significant, and substantively large. Furthermore, the estimates in all of the latent classes were generally in the immediate region of the overall parameter estimate (0.40) recovered in the 6-class model of Table 8.1 and Model 4 of Table 8.2. The largest effect estimated in any of the samples was in the fourth latent class, LC4. In this latent class, the estimated state dependence parameter was 0.508. The latent class with the lowest rate was LC2 (parameter estimate = 0.365; t-statistic = 13.47).

Indeed, there is not even a hierarchical ranking of the magnitude of the state dependence parameter according to the rate or 'style' of offending. The lowest-rate latent class, LC4 had the largest parameter estimate, but the latent class with the highest rate of offending (LC6) had the second largest parameter estimate (0.437). The parameter estimate for the 'adolescent-limited' group was nearly identical to the overall estimate presented in Tables 8.1 and 8.2, and was very close in magnitude to the effect calculated in the first latent class, LC1. A test of significant differences between each of the parameter estimates failed to generate any support for the hypothesis of differential effects across the latent classes.[8] Instead, the overall estimate seems to accurately represent all of the latent classes in the 1981–2 sample. These results are compatible with the theoretical predictions of Sampson and Laub (1993), run counter to those of Moffitt (1993), and fail to support the eighth hypothesis ($\mathbf{H}_8$) examined in this study. Recall that this hypothesis predicts the association between past and subsequent offending behaviour will be non-significant for the 'life-course-persistent' (high criminal propensity) group(s), while the effect should be substantial and

[8] The method used here to test for significant differences between two coefficients is described in Clogg, Petkova, and Haritou (1995), Brame *et al.* (1998), and Paternoster *et al.* (1998). The test statistic is calculated as $z = (\theta_1 - \theta_2)/\sqrt{(SE(\theta_1))^2+(SE(\theta_2))^2}$. Bonferonni adjustments were applied when calculating the p-values to adjust for the fact the multiple comparisons were being made. The same method of testing for significant differences between the latent-class specific state dependence estimates is employed in the analyses of both the 1986–7 and 1991–2 samples.

significant for the 'adolescent-limited' or what could also be called the 'adolescent-peaked' group. Our analysis finds that the 'adolescent-limited' group had a state dependence parameter estimate that was both very similar to the overall estimate and similar to the estimates calculated in the other latent classes as well.

Results for the 1986–7 Sample

Our attention is now turned to the analysis of the data for the 1986–7 parole release sample. The four-stage analytical approach undertaken here for this data set will be identical to the approach presented above for the 1981–2 sample.

Stage One—The Semiparametric Mixed Poisson Model

We start again with a presentation of the results from the semiparametric mixed Poisson model. The local solution testing this model was completed for the 1986–7 sample and indicated that both the 7-class and 8-class models were again found to be prone to multiple local solutions that varied from one solution to another. Similar to the results for the 1981–2 sample, the 6-class model generated the same unique solution all ten times this model was estimated. Furthermore, and as shown in Table 8.4, the 6-class model had the largest BIC value (i.e. least negative value), and thus the 6-class model was selected as the model with the optimal number of latent classes. The 6-class model had a BIC value of –47,723.16, whereas the BIC value for the 5-class model was only –47,874.92. Again, since interest in this chapter also focuses on changes in the size of the state dependence coefficient, the solutions for all models up through the 6-class model are presented in Table 8.4.

Table 8.4 presents the results for the 1- through the 6-class semiparametric mixed Poisson models. The first column contains the 1-class semiparametric mixed Poisson model, which again is equivalent to the estimation of a standard Poisson regression model. The estimate of the state dependence parameter in the 1-class model that assumes complete homogeneity was 0.619. This estimate was highly significant with a t-statistic calculated at a value of 51.58 (which, as was the case for the 1981–2 sample, supports hypothesis 5 of this study predicting a significant positive association between past and subsequent offending behaviour). The next column allows for two latent classes in the population, and here we find that this

TABLE 8.4. Investigation of state dependence effects with semiparametric random effects Poisson model: 1986–7 sample (N = 1,443; panel observations = 37,390)

	Points of support					
	1	*2*	*3*	*4*	*5*	*6*
Random effects						
Class1	−3.953	−3.998	−7.785	−5.837	−6.922	−7.912
	(69.61)	(53.39)	(33.40)	(37.97)	(30.94)	(19.17)
Class 2	—	−6.860	−4.523	−4.701	−4.763	−4.971
		(38.95)	(39.54)	(32.35)	(26.00)	(22.73)
Class 3	—	—	−4.640	−4.416	−4.510	−2.987
			(34.80)	(31.89)	(33.90)	(6.15)
Class 4	—	—	—	−19.854	−23.4311	−23.5408
				(18.51)	(16.98)	(16.56)
Class 5	—	—	—	—	−4.533	−6.750
					(20.95)	(23.38)
Class 6	—	—	—	—	—	−4.115
						(11.30)
Age effects						
Class 1 age	3.883	3.945	9.009	6.405	7.983	8.9379
	(65.27)	(54.04)	(31.55)	(37.79)	(30.61)	(21.31)
Class 1 age-squared	−0.956	−0.902	−2.580	−1.716	−2.222	−2.4507
	(66.28)	(53.37)	(30.00)	(36.51)	(29.54)	(21.87)
Class 2 age	—	7.881	5.2303	4.025	4.191	4.378
		(37.06)	(42.23)	(31.37)	(24.92)	(23.49)
Class 2 age-squared	—	−2.238	−1.3438	−0.811	−0.921	−0.9575
		(35.83)	(40.74)	(29.47)	(23.60)	(23.03)
Class 3 Age	—	—	3.986	5.177	5.326	3.8543
			(33.45)	(35.79)	(36.78)	(6.15)
Class 3 age-squared	—	—	−0.8199	−1.304	−1.361	−1.078
			(31.79)	(36.09)	(36.04)	(5.78)
Class 4 age	—	—	—	25.708	30.515	30.8176
				(18.40)	(16.79)	(16.15)
Class 4 age-squared	—	—	—	−8.161	−9.753	−9.8903
				(18.08)	(16.43)	(15.59)
Class 5 age	—	—	—	—	4.066	7.5113
					(21.50)	(24.82)
Class 5 age-squared	—	—	—	—	−0.799	−1.8336
					(19.82)	(23.93)
Class 6 age	—	—	—	—	—	3.6824
						(12.44)
Class 6 age-squared	—	—	—	—	—	−0.7174
						(12.31)
State depen. effects						
Arr_{t-1}	0.619	0.411	0.345	0.295	0.266	0.245
	(51.58)	(33.80)	(27.98)	(23.92)	(21.37)	(19.18)
Log-likelihood	−51,270.407	−49,227.309	−48,628.149	−48,057.750	−47,802.170	−47,635.868
BIC	−51,284.956	−49,256.407	−48,671.795	−48,115.946	−47,874.915	−47,723.162

Note: Absolute values of t-statistics are in parentheses.

simple adjustment has a large impact on the estimate of the state dependence parameter. In the 2-class model, the estimate of the state dependence parameter was reduced to 0.411 (t-statistic = 33.80). Allowing for another additional point of support further reduced the state dependence parameter estimate to 0.345 (t-statistic = 27.98). Next, allowing for four points of support reduced the estimate even further to 0.295 (t-statistic = 23.92), while allowing for five points of support reduced it to 0.266 (t-statistic = 21.37). Finally, the sixth point of support reduced the state dependence parameter estimate further to its final value of 0.245 (t-statistic = 19.18).[9]

Thus, accounting for the persistent individual differences in the 1986–7 sample by allowing for 6 points of support and class-specific age parameters reduced the magnitude of the state dependence parameter estimate from 0.619 (1-class model) to 0.245 (6-class model). This amounts to about a 60 per cent reduction in the absolute size of the state dependence parameter. Yet, even after accounting for persistent individual differences, there was still a highly significant positive effect between prior and subsequent offending (which fails to support our sixth hypothesis while offering empirical support for our seventh hypothesis in this study).

To aid in the substantive interpretation of this parameter estimate, we predicted the arrest trajectory for the sixth latent class. This latent class is the same latent class labelled 'LC6' in the 1986–7 results presented in Chapter 7—this group had the highest arrest charge total of any group with members averaging over 36 total arrest charges. We have also included the predicted trajectory for this group that was generated in Chapter 7 with no control for arrest status at the prior age (labeled as 'No arrest control' in Figure 8.2). Once again, the 'No arrest control' trajectory (extracted from the results in Chapter 7) falls in between the estimated arrest rate for the cases that were not arrested at the prior age ('Not arrested') and the estimated rate for the cases that were arrested at the prior age ('Arrested'). At the peak of their predicted offending rate, the cases that had been arrested at the prior age were estimated to be arrested for, on average, an extra 0.75 arrest

[9] The estimates of the state dependence parameter in the local solution models of both the 7-class and 8-class models mixed Poisson model had the value of the parameter hovering at just above around 0.23.

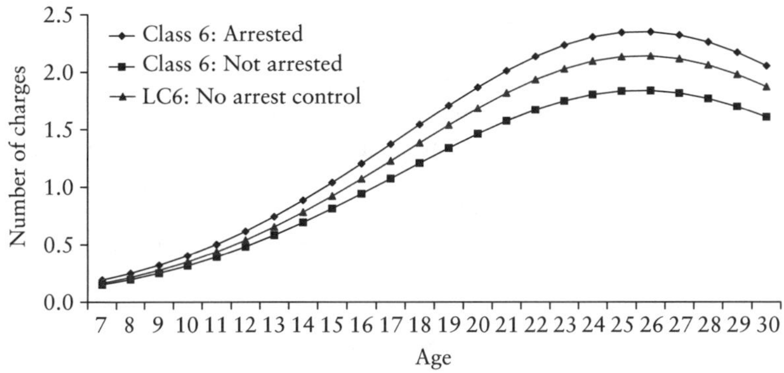

FIGURE 8.2. Predicted mean arrest charges, by arrest status at prior age: 1986–7 sample.

charges. Thus, even though the size of the state dependence parameter estimate decreased by over 60 per cent after controlling for persistent individual differences in criminal propensity, the remaining parameter estimate still had a significant positive substantive implication for the arrest rates of the cases. Again, since these individuals are consistently arrested for serious offences, we would argue that the state dependence parameter estimate in the 6-class model still implies a substantively important difference even though the magnitude of the effect was much smaller than was estimated in the model with no control for persistent individual differences in criminal propensity.

Similar to the results generated for the 1981–2 sample, the results from the 1986–7 sample employing the semiparametric mixed Poisson model clearly support the 'mixed' position. Also, similar to the 1981–2 results, the addition of a second latent class to the model (or a second point of support) had the largest effect on the reduction of the magnitude of the state dependence effect (a decrease of 0.208), whereas the change that resulted from adding another point of support to the 5 points of support model was considerably smaller (a reduction of 0.021; i.e. $0.266 - 0.245 = 0.021$).

Stage Two—The Parametric Random Effects Negative Binomial Model

In this stage we present, for the 1986–7 sample, the results from the parametric random effects negative binomial model and compare the estimate of the state dependence parameter in this model with the estimate from the semiparametric mixed Poisson model. Model 1 in Table 8.5 contains the resulting parameter estimates from the application of this model to our second parole release sample. Before discussing the results with respect to the state dependence parameter estimate, we note that the boundary-value likelihood ratio test for the presence of significant unobserved heterogeneity (that tests the significance of the r and s ancillary parameters) resulted in a χ^2_{01} value of 96.84 (p-value = 0.000). This finding indicates the presence of significant unobserved heterogeneity in the data. The estimate of the state dependence parameter in the parametric random effects model (with only a single set of age parameters) is found in the first column of Table 8.5. As reported, the state dependence estimate in this model was 0.598, which was nearly identical in magnitude to the estimate generated in the 1-class semiparametric (Poisson) model that has no controls for persistent individual differences. Thus, as with the 1981–2 sample, the random effects model for the 1986–7 data also significantly overestimates the state dependence parameter in comparison with the final estimate we arrived at in the 6-class semiparametric model (which was 0.245). Comparing the estimate of the state dependence parameter in the parametric model to the estimate in the 6-class semiparametric model, we see the parametric model's estimate is nearly twice as large. This is a very large discrepancy between the estimates of these two models.

Stage Three—Incorporating Latent Class Indicator Variables

In the third stage of analysis for these data, we again employ the use of the random effects and standard (NB1) negative binomial models, and build on the model specification used in Model 1 of Table 8.5. Model 2 in Table 8.5 is a parametric random effects model that also includes a set of binary latent class indicators. Model 3 is the NB1 negative binomial model (that does not include individual specific effects as in Model 2). The latent class indicator variables employed in Models 2 through 4 of this stage are from the results of the semiparametric mixed Poisson models presented in Chapter 7. The 'adolescent-limited' group, denoted as LC4 in the Chapter 7 analysis of the 1986–7 data, was used as the omitted reference group in these models.

TABLE 8.5. Investigation of state dependence effects with parametric random effects & NB1 negative binomial models: 1986–7 Sample

	Model			
	1	*2*	*3*	*4*
Overall intercept	−4.755 (57.64)	−5.726 (62.91)	−5.091 (56.07)	−21.033 (20.93)
Latent class indicators				
LC1	—	0.534 (12.82)	0.534 (12.82)	13.375 (13.03)
LC2	—	0.753 (18.20)	0.753 (18.20)	16.131 (15.83)
LC3	—	1.066 (25.15)	1.066 (25.15)	17.938 (17.65)
LC5	—	1.273 (29.70)	1.273 (29.70)	14.420 (14.01)
LC6	—	1.247 (28.75)	1.247 (28.75)	17.022 (16.60)
Age effects				
Age	4.014 (46.32)	4.246 (49.46)	4.246 (49.46)	27.101 (21.17)
Age sq	−0.983 (46.62)	−1.037 (49.76)	−1.037 (49.76)	−8.571 (21.30)
LC1 * age	—	—	—	−18.663 (14.37)
LC1 * age-squared	—	—	—	6.310 (15.52)
LC2 * age	—	—	—	−22.798 (17.68)
LC2 * age-squared	—	—	—	7.636 (18.91)
LC3 * age	—	—	—	−23.193 (17.98)
LC3 * age-squared	—	—	—	7.495 (18.53)
LC5 * age	—	—	—	−19.914 (15.34)
LC5 * age-squared	—	—	—	6.845 (16.88)
LC6 * age	—	—	—	−23.534 (18.20)
LC6 * age-squared	—	—	—	7.877 (19.48)
State depen. effects				
Arr_{t-1}	0.598 (31.71)	0.465 (25.29)	0.465 (25.29)	0.248 (13.90)
Ancillary parameters				
ln(r)	3.254	15.742	—	—
ln(s)	3.870	16.377	—	—
ln(alpha)	—	—	0.635	0.627
Log-likelihood	−41,852.752	−41,035.307	−41,035.306	−41,615.098

Note: Absolute values of t-statistics are in parentheses. Latent class indicator variables are from the results presented in Chapter 7.

Comparing the results of Models 2 and 3, we find that the two models generate identical parameter estimates and solutions. The boundary-value likelihood ratio test comparing these two models generates a χ^2_{01} value of 0.001 (p-value = 1.000), which indicates that including just the set of five binary indicators removes the presence of significant unobserved heterogeneity (which was previously found to be significant in stage two). The state dependence parameter estimate in Model 3 was 0.465, which is smaller than the estimate from the parametric random effects model presented in Model 1 of Table 8.5, but is still much larger than the estimate that we obtained in the 6-class finite mixture model (0.245). Thus, while the indicator variables do remove the presence of significant individual-level heterogeneity, the indicator variables by themselves do not allow for the recovery of the same parameter estimate found in the 6-class mixture model.

In Model 4 of Table 8.5, we next added a set of interaction variables between the latent class indicator variables and the age and age-squared variables to the model. In this part of the analysis, we are interested in determining whether the state dependence effects uncovered in stage two is *over-estimated* because the age effects in the random effects model (Model 2) were controlled through the use of only two parameters assumed to be common to all individuals in the sample. Our presumption is that the underestimation of the age effects among the most frequent offenders will cause an overestimation in the state dependence parameter. We believe this will occur because this parameter will absorb the unaccounted for 'age effects' in the most 'active' latent classes.

The NB1 model presented in Model 4 adds 10 parameters to the specification of the NB1 model found in Model 3. These additional parameters allow each latent class to have its own set of regression coefficients for the age parameters. Thus, if the overestimation of the state dependence parameter is a consequence of erroneously modelling the age effects with only two parameter estimates, we should find a state dependence estimate in Model 4 that is similar to the point estimate found in the 6-class semiparametric model. The parameter estimates for this model are found in the fourth numerical column of Table 8.5. First, note that all of the latent class $*$ age interaction variables in Model 4 were highly significant, which indicates that the offending trajectories of these 5 latent classes were significantly different from the offending trajectory of the 'adolescent-limited' group. Again, all of the latent class indicator variables were also still highly significant in Model 4.

More important for our concerns here, allowing for latent class-specific age parameters resulted in the successful recovery of essentially the exact same state dependence parameter estimate found in the semiparametric mixed Poisson model in Table 8.4. The state dependence parameter estimate in Model 4 of Table 8.5 was 0.248, whereas the estimate found in the 6-class model of Table 8.4 was 0.245. Identical to the previous findings in the 1981–2 sample, we find once again that the calculation of the estimate of the state dependence parameter in the 1986–7 sample is very sensitive to the accurate estimation of the 'age effects' in these data.

Stage Four—Latent Class-Specific Models

Next, we present the results from the models estimated on each latent class by themselves. Recall, that one of the main theoretical reasons for estimating the state dependence effect within the latent classes was to determine if (1) the 'adolescent-limited' group had a much larger state dependence effect and (2) if there was a minimal state dependence effect in the 'life-course persistent' group. In Chapter 7, the 'adolescent-limited' group was the fourth latent class, and hence it was labelled 'LC4'. The two classes with the highest arrest rates were the fifth and sixth latent classes (averaging 36.2 and 35.9 arrest charges, respectively). The fifth latent class had a higher and earlier peak rate of offending (3 arrest charges at about age 20), whereas the sixth latent class did not reach their peak age of offending until their late twenties (where it peaked at about 2 arrest charges). The results of estimating NB1 negative binomial models on each of the latent classes separately are found in Table 8.6.[10]

As depicted in Table 8.6, the estimated state dependence effects were positive in all six of the latent classes, however, in the fifth latent class, the estimate was not statistically significant at the 0.05 level (t-statistic = 1.81; p-value = 0.070). This latent class represented just under 12 per cent of the sample, and thus a significant,

[10] In an identical finding to the 1981–2 sample, the boundary-value likelihood ratio tests of these NB1 models against the parametric random effect models (which allow for individual-level effects) resulted in a failure to reject the null hypothesis of no individual-level effects for all six latent classes.

TABLE 8.6. Investigation of state dependence effects with NB1 negative binomial models: 1986–7 sample, latent class-specific models

	Latent class					
	LC1	*LC2*	*LC3*	*LC4*	*LC5*	*LC6*
Overall intercept	−7.803	−4.951	−3.096	−20.238	−6.717	−3.836
	(33.93)	(28.07)	(18.62)	(18.94)	(27.13)	(17.86)
Age effects						
Age	8.575	4.311	3.918	26.046	7.415	3.394
	(33.58)	(25.55)	(20.50)	(19.01)	(29.24)	(16.99)
Age-squared	−2.300	−0.938	−1.078	−8.253	−1.774	−0.664
	(34.26)	(24.57)	(21.61)	(19.26)	(29.19)	(15.22)
State depen. effects						
Arr_{t-1}	0.229	0.269	0.239	0.386	0.080	0.388
	(5.95)	(7.34)	(5.76)	(5.06)	(1.81)	(8.24)
Ancillary parameters						
ln(alpha)	0.288	0.341	0.518	0.555	0.713	0.699
Log-likelihood	−8,708.972	−9,389.148	−7,153.637	−2,375.699	−6,178.243	−5,611.288
N (panel)	10,207	9,068	5,326	4,610	4,336	3,843
N (observations)	398	333	211	188	170	143

Note: Absolute values of t-statistics are in parentheses. Latent class indicator variables are from the results presented in Chapter 7.

positive state dependence effect was estimated in the latent classes representing over 88 per cent of the 1986–7 parole release sample. For the first three latent classes, the estimated state dependence relationships ranged from 0.229 to 0.269 and were very similar to the overall effect of 0.245. For the fourth and sixth latent classes, the estimated state dependence relationships were of a slightly greater magnitude (both estimated at just over 0.38). The 95 per cent confidence intervals for the state dependence parameter estimates of these two latent classes, however, both overlapped with the 95 per cent confidence intervals for the first three latent classes. Indeed, a test of significant differences between the parameter estimates of the two latent classes with the largest effects and the parameter estimates of the first three groups (which had smaller estimates) failed to reject the null hypothesis indicating no differences. In other words, taking into account sampling variation, the hypothesis that the five significant state dependence coefficients were not significantly different from one another could not be rejected. Taken as a whole, and with the exception of the one latent class with a non-significant positive effect, the overall state dependence effect seemed to accurately represent the vast majority of the latent classes in the sample. Thus, the results for the 1986–7 sample also fail to support Moffitt's hypothesis that the state dependence effects are much greater in the 'adolescent-limited' offender group relative to the 'life-course-persistent' group (hypothesis eight of this study).

Results for the 1991–2 Sample

Stage One—The Semiparametric Mixed Poisson Model

The presentation of results for our third sample begins again with the estimation of the semiparametric mixed Poisson model. The same process followed for the first two samples when fitting and testing the semiparametric mixed Poisson model with varying numbers of 'points of support' was also employed here with the 1991–2 sample. Consistent with both the 1981–2 and 1986–7 samples, the local solution testing indicated that both the 7-class and 8-class models were prone to multiple local solutions. The 6-class model in this sample also generated the same unique solution all ten times this model was estimated. As shown in Table 8.7, the least negative BIC statistic again favoured the 6-class model (BIC = – 36,533.44) over the 5-class model (BIC = – 36,691.35).

Results for the 1- through 6-class semiparametric mixed Poisson models are presented in Table 8.7. The first column contains the 1-class Poisson model. The estimate of the state dependence parameter from the 1-class model (that assumes complete homogeneity) was 0.553, which was highly significant with a t-statistic of 40.25. Adding an additional point of support (i.e. two latent classes), we again find a large impact on the estimate of the state dependence parameter. In the 2-class model, the estimate of the state dependence parameter was reduced to 0.375 (t-statistic = 27.00). Allowing for 3 points of support reduced the state dependence parameter estimate further to 0.319 (t-statistic = 22.79), while adding an additional point of support (4-class model) again reduced the estimate to 0.262 (t-statistic = 18.51). With five points of support, the state dependence parameter estimate was 0.229 (t-statistic = 15.71), and finally, the final estimate from the six point of support model was 0.206 (t-statistic = 14.38).[11]

[11] The estimates of the state dependence parameter in the local solution models of both the 7-class and 8-class models mixed Poisson model had the value of the parameter at just over 0.20.

TABLE 8.7. Investigation of state dependence effects with semiparametric random effects Poisson model: 1991–92 sample (N = 1,434; panel observations = 29,385)

	Points of Support					
	1	*2*	*3*	*4*	*5*	*6*
Random effects						
Class1	−6.004	−10.5233	−7.454	−7.978	−10.749	−7.177
	(70.12)	(32.62)	(37.13)	(27.71)	(4.46)	(21.78)
Class 2	—	−5.5445	−5.582	−7.303	−5.149	−17.245
		(42.14)	(32.51)	(26.04)	(15.19)	(14.28)
Class 3	—	—	−25.906	5.741	−7.172	−7.877
			(19.24)	(33.94)	(17.73)	(29.46)
Class 4	—	—	—	−25.443	−30.308	−5.701
				(20.37)	(5.78)	(15.03)
Class 5	—	—	—	—	−6.070	−38.839
					(5.24)	(15.74)
Class 6	—	—	—	—	—	−4.793
						(15.59)
Age effects						
Class 1 age	6.5983	12.8995	8.695	8.269	12.070	7.353
	(66.64)	(32.82)	(34.75)	(23.80)	(3.72)	(18.54)
Class 1 age-squared	−1.7859	−3.8711	−2.465	−2.142	−3.321	−1.867
	(66.29)	(31.07)	(32.30)	(21.31)	(3.29)	(16.24)
Class 2 age	—	5.9493	5.970	9.349	4.758	20.636
		(42.30)	(33.90)	(28.16)	(14.05)	(13.92)
Class 2 age-squared	—	−1.494	−1.449	−2.786	−1.049	−6.011
		(41.41)	(32.61)	(27.52)	(9.68)	(13.31)
Class 3 age	—	—	33.783	6.166	8.363	9.264
			(18.56)	(34.81)	(16.12)	(31.00)
Class 3 age-squared	—	—	−10.7928	−1.482	−2.174	−2.445
			(17.69)	(32.17)	(13.96)	(29.88)
Class 4 age	—	—	—	32.970	39.928	7.780
				(19.71)	(5.09)	(17.25)
Class 4 age-squared	—	—	—	−10.453	−12.872	−2.445
				(18.83)	(4.51)	(18.64)
Class 5 age	—	—	—	—	8.261	52.794
					(5.83)	(15.54)
Class 5 age-squared	—	—	—	—	−2.596	−17.584
					(6.27)	(15.12)
Class 6 age	—	—	—	—	—	4.586
						(14.61)
Class 6 age-squared	—	—	—	—	—	−0.976
						(12.63)
State depen. effects						
Arr_{t-1}	0.553	0.375	0.319	0.262	0.229	0.206
	(40.25)	(27.00)	(22.79)	(18.51)	(15.71)	(14.38)
Log-likelihood	−39,101.26	−37,583.21	−37,113.93	−36,811.490	−36,618.66	−36,446.22
BIC	−39,115.8	−37,612.28	−37,157.54	−36,869.64	−36,691.35	−36,533.44

Note: Absolute values of t-statistics are in parentheses.

To review the results from the initial step in this analysis, we reiterate that, like the results for the two previous parole release samples, accounting for the persistent individual differences in the 1991–2 sample significantly reduced the magnitude of the state dependence parameter estimate. The reduction of this parameter estimate from 0.553 (1-class model) to 0.206 (6-class model) represents a 63 per cent reduction in the absolute size of the state dependence parameter. But even after accounting for the unobserved heterogeneity (e.g. persistent differences), the state dependence parameter was still highly significant. This finding fails to offer empirical support for hypothesis 6 which predicts that, after controlling for persistent individual differences in criminal propensity, the association between past and subsequent criminal activity will be reduced to statistical non-significance. However, the fact that this association (though reduced in magnitude) was still positive and statistically significant offers support for H_7 of our study.

Similar to the procedures for the analyses of data from our two earlier samples, we also predicted an arrest trajectory for the fourth latent class in Table 8.7 in order to show the substantive implications of the state dependence estimate. This latent class corresponds to the 'LC4' latent class presented in the results section for the 1991–2 sample in Chapter 7. As can be seen in Figure 8.3, the estimated arrest rate at a given age for the cases that were not arrested at the prior age ('Not arrested') were predicted to be significantly

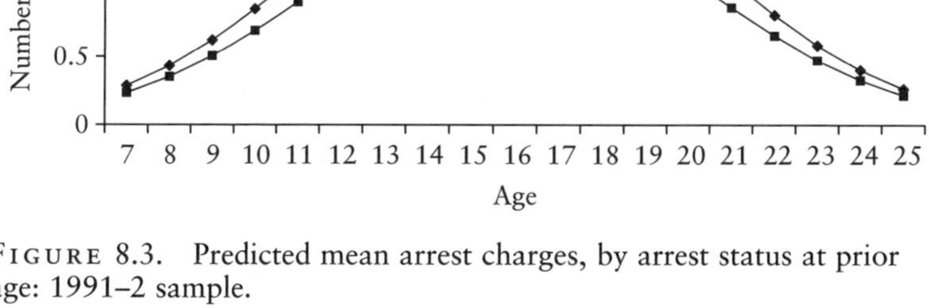

FIGURE 8.3. Predicted mean arrest charges, by arrest status at prior age: 1991–2 sample.

lower than the estimated rate for the cases that were arrested at the prior age ('Arrested'). At the peak of their predicted offending rate, the cases that had been arrested at the prior age were estimated to have been arrested for, on average, an additional 0.50 arrest charges. Thus, in spite of the fact that there was a significant decrease in the state dependence parameter estimate after controlling for persistent individual differences in criminal propensity, again we find that the remaining parameter estimate still had a significant substantive implication for the arrest rates.

Thus, as with the earlier samples, the results generated for the 1991–2 sample from the semiparametric mixed Poisson model also clearly support the 'mixed' position of Sampson and Laub. First, there was significant population heterogeneity in the propensity to commit criminal acts, and accounting for these differences was critical for estimating the genuine magnitude of the state dependence parameter. Second, even after controlling for the unobserved heterogeneity in the propensity to commit criminal acts, there was still a significant, positive, and substantively important relationship between the mean offending rate at a given age and whether an individual was arrested at the prior age. Similar to the results for the 1981–2 and 1986–7 samples then, the simple adjustment of moving from a 1-class model to the 2-class model (in the 1991–2 sample) had the largest effect on the reduction of the magnitude of the state dependence effect (a decrease of 0.178), whereas the change that resulted from moving from a 5-class model to a 6-class model was considerably smaller in size (a reduction of 0.023). Again, the fact that speed of decline in the magnitude of the state dependence parameter had significantly tapered-off was a substantive indication that the mixing distribution (i.e. distribution of unobserved heterogeneity) was adequately approximated with 6-points of support.

Stage Two—The Parametric Random Effects Negative Binomial Model

Moving on to the second stage of the analysis for the 1991–2 sample, here we present results from the parametric random effects negative binomial model. Again, we compare the resulting estimate of this model to the estimate of the state dependence parameter presented above in the semiparametric mixed Poisson model. The results from the random effects model are presented in the first column of Table 8.8 (under Model 1). In this model, the boundary-value

TABLE 8.8. Investigation of state dependence effects with parametric random effects and NB1 negative binomial models: 1991–2 sample

	Model			
	1	*2*	*3*	*4*
Overall intercept	−6.797	−7.622	−6.989	−32.806
	(55.29)	(58.35)	(53.46)	(19.50)
Latent class indicators				
LC1	—	0.539	0.539	25.906
		(11.71)	(11.71)	(15.27)
LC2	—	0.347	0.347	16.957
		(7.26)	(7.26)	(9.71)
LC3	—	1.103	1.103	24.856
		(23.58)	(23.58)	(14.62)
LC4	—	0.779	0.779	27.603
		(16.17)	(16.17)	(16.26)
LC6	—	1.054	1.054	27.744
		(20.43)	(20.43)	(16.18)
Age effects				
Age	6.679	6.982	6.982	44.231
	(46.54)	(49.20)	(49.20)	(19.79)
Age sq	−1.795	−1.873	−1.873	−14.603
	(45.79)	(48.41)	(48.41)	(19.84)
LC1 * age	—	—	—	−37.304
				(16.60)
LC1 * age-squared	—	—	—	12.888
				(17.46)
LC2 * age	—	—	—	−25.533
				(11.11)
LC2 * age-squared	—	—	—	9.248
				(12.31)
LC3 * age	—	—	—	−34.981
				(15.54)
LC3 * age-squared	—	—	—	12.174
				(16.47)
LC4 * age	—	—	—	−37.240
				(16.53)
LC4 * age-squared	—	—	—	12.443
				(16.79)
LC6 * age	—	—	—	−39.522
				(17.49)
LC 6 * age-squared	—	—	—	13.627
				(18.40)
State depen. effects				
Arr_{t-1}	0.533	0.417	0.417	0.188
	(25.08)	(20.02)	(20.02)	(9.33)
Ancillary parameters				
ln(r)	4.093	15.937	—	—
ln(s)	4.761	16.570	—	—
ln(alpha)	—	—	0.634	0.461
Log-likelihood	−32,072.642	−31,520.064	−31,520.063	−30,094.455

Note: Absolute values of t-statistics are in parentheses. Latent class indicator variables are from the results presented in Chapter 7.

likelihood ratio test for the presence of significant unobserved heterogeneity (that tests the significance of the *r* and *s* ancillary parameters) once again indicated the presence of significant heterogeneity ($\chi^2_{01} = 14.34$; p-value = 0.000). Turning our attention now to the estimate of the state dependence parameter in the parametric random effects model (with only a single set of age parameters), we find that the state dependence estimate in this model was 0.533. This estimate is nearly identical in magnitude to the estimate generated in the 1-class semiparametric Poisson model (which makes no correction for persistent individual differences). Once again we find that the parametric random effects model significantly overestimates the state dependence parameter in comparison with the final estimate we arrived at in the 6-class semiparametric model (which was 0.206). Indeed, the estimate from the parametric random effects model is more than twice the size of the estimate from the 6-class semiparametric model. We contend that this is a serious discrepancy in the magnitude of the effect and highlights the critical need for the multi-method approach employed herein.

Stage Three—Incorporating Latent Class Indicator Variables

In an effort to further investigate the discrepancy between the estimates of the state dependence parameter in the Model 1 of Table 8.8 and the estimate from the 6-class model in Table 8.7, we again employ the use of the random effects and standard (NB1) negative binomial models. We build on the model specification used in Model 1 of Table 8.8 by including the set of binary latent class indicator variables. Model 2 is a parametric random effects model that includes the set of binary latent class indicators from the results presented in Chapter 7, and Model 3 is the NB1 negative binomial model. To be consistent with the specification used in the two earlier samples, the 'adolescent-limited' group, denoted as LC5 in the Chapter 7 analyses, was used as the omitted reference group in these models.

Comparing the results of Models 2 and 3 in Table 8.8, we again find that the two models produce identical solutions. A boundary-value likelihood ratio test comparing these two models (χ^2_{01} value = 0.001; p-value = 1.000) indicates that including the set of five binary indicators removed the presence of significant unobserved heterogeneity (which was previously found to be significant in stage two). Again, we find here that the models with the binary latent class indicator variables produce a smaller estimate of the state dependence effect than does the parametric random effects model presented in Model 1 of Table 8.8. The effect in Model 3, however, was still much larger (almost twice the size) than was the estimate we arrived at earlier with the 6-class finite mixture model (0.206). Thus, while the indicator variables do once again remove the presence of significant individual-level heterogeneity, the estimate of the state dependence parameter is still significantly larger than it should be.

The specification used in Model 4 incorporates a set of interaction variables between the latent class indicator variables and the age and age-squared variables. The fourth numerical column of Table 8.8 contains the parameter estimates for this model. All of the latent class * age interaction variables in Model 4 were highly significant, which indicates that the offending trajectories of the 5 latent classes were significantly different from the 'adolescent-limited' group. Note the massive increase in the log-likelihood value (+1426) that resulted from adding these ten parameters to the model.

For the purposes of this study, however, the fundamental importance of allowing for latent class-specific age parameters in the model is that it permits the successful recovery of a state dependence parameter estimate similar to that found in the semiparametric mixed Poisson model of Table 8.7. The state dependence parameter estimate in Model 4 of Table 8.12 was 0.188, whereas the estimate from the 6-class semiparametric model (of Table 8.7) was 0.206. In all three of our parole release samples, the calculation of the estimate of the state dependence parameter was extremely sensitive to the accurate estimation of the 'age effects' in the data. We reiterate that if the age effects are not adequately modelled, the state dependence covariate will absorb the effects, and the state dependence effect will appear to be significantly larger than it actually is.

Stage Four—Latent Class-Specific Models

The next stage of the analyses pertains to the models estimated on each latent class by themselves. Interest in these models concerns whether the overall estimate of the state dependence effect is generally reflective of the state dependence relationship found within each latent class. In particular, we focus on the magnitude of the effect within the 'adolescent-limited' group given the theoretical argument of Moffitt (1993). Recall that in Chapter 7 that the 'LC5'

TABLE 8.9. Investigation of state dependence effects with NB1 negative binomial models: 1991–2 sample, latent class-specific models

	Latent class					
	LC1	*LC2*	*LC3*	*LC4*	*LC5*	*LC6*
Overall intercept	−7.097	−16.653	−7.711	−5.079	−31.815	−4.870
	(29.71)	(31.74)	(26.64)	(19.24)	(17.69)	(13.97)
Age effects						
Age	7.096	19.678	9.033	6.794	42.914	4.532
	(27.37)	(31.85)	(27.56)	(19.90)	(17.94)	(12.77)
Age-squared	−1.759	−5.636	−2.368	−2.101	−14.199	−0.949
	(26.17)	(32.01)	(27.04)	(20.45)	(18.15)	(11.00)
State depen. effects						
Arr_{t-1}	0.140	0.054	0.192	0.257	0.314	0.364
	(3.62)	(1.14)	(4.38)	(5.25)	(3.69)	(5.55)
Ancillary parameters						
ln(alpha)	0.155	0.198	0.788	0.508	0.486	0.722
Log-likelihood	−8,193.382	−5,400.409	−6,520.795	−5,151.611	−1,772.791	−2,984.292
N (panel)	8,469	6,930	4,598	4,160	3,068	2,160
N (observations)	396	344	224	211	159	100

Note: Absolute values of t-statistics are in parentheses. The 6 latent classes are from the results presented in Chapter 7.

latent class exhibited an 'adolescent-limited' offending style. The two classes with the highest arrest rates were the third and sixth latent classes. Each of these latent classes averaged around 27–28 arrest charges. The third latent class had an earlier and higher peak rate of arrest, whereas the sixth latent class did not reach its peak age of arrest until individuals were in their late twenties. The results from the NB1 negative binomial models estimated on each of the latent classes separately are found in Table 8.9.[12]

As indicated in Table 8.9, the estimates of the state dependence effects in all six of the latent classes were positive, but for the second latent class the estimate was not statistically significant at the .05 level (t-statistic = 1.14; p-value = 0.254). This latent class had 344 individuals (24%) in the sample assigned to it, and thus a significant, positive state dependence effect was estimated in the latent classes representing over 75 per cent of the 1991–2 parole release sample. For the latent classes with significant positive estimates, the values

[12] In an identical finding to the 1981–2 sample, the boundary-value likelihood ratio tests of these NB1 models against the parametric random effect models (which allow for individual-level effects) resulted in a failure to reject the null hypothesis of no individual-level effects for all six latent classes.

ranged from 0.140 to 0.364. The two latent classes with the largest estimates were the fifth (0.314) and sixth (0.364) latent classes, but the 95 per cent confidence intervals for the state dependence parameter estimates of these two latent classes completely overlapped with the 95 per cent confidence intervals for the other three latent classes with significant estimates. Furthermore, a test of significant differences between the parameter estimates of each of the two latent classes with the largest effects and the parameter estimates of the other three groups failed to reject the null hypothesis of no differences. Similar to the previously obtained results for the 1981–2 and 1986–7 samples then, after making allowances for sampling variation, the hypothesis that the five significant state dependence coefficients were all equal could not be rejected. Excluding the one latent class with a non-significant positive effect, the results in their entirety indicated that the overall effect seemed to accurately represent the state dependence relationship in the vast majority of the latent classes in the sample. The evidence here, as in the two previous samples, fails to confirm the hypothesis that the state dependence effects in the 'adolescent-limited' offender group are more pronounced (i.e. the evidence thus fails to confirm hypothesis 8 of this study).

Summary and Discussion

The purpose of this chapter was to carefully examine the positive association between past and subsequent offending. More specifically, the substantive focus of this chapter concerned the nature of the relationship between criminal activities at adjacent ages while controlling for persistent individual differences. In direct response to the calls for further investigations of this key theoretical issue by Bushway, Brame, and Paternoster (1999), Brame, Bushway, and Paternoster (1999), and Nagin and Paternoster (2000), this study set out to examine four hypotheses concerning the relationship between past and subsequent criminal offending behaviour using data collected on three samples of serious youthful offenders. The first hypothesis examined is this study was:

H_5: There will be a statistically significant positive association between past and subsequent offending behaviour.

The results presented in this chapter clearly support this hypothesis. Ignoring individual differences in the propensity to offend, the relationship between criminal offending at adjacent ages was found to be positive and highly significant. The estimate of this relationship was 0.857 (t-statistic = 86.28) in the 1981–2 sample, 0.619 (t-statistic = 51.58) in the 1986–7 sample, and 0.553 (t-statistic = 40.25) in the 1991–2 sample. The results relevant to this hypothesis were important for establishing a baseline estimate of the relationship between past and subsequent offending in these three samples.

Again, the theoretical dispute regarding the results relevant to our fifth hypothesis centres not on the existence of the relationship (all parties to this theoretical dispute agree on the existence of a significant positive association), but rather on the substantive interpretation of this observed relationship. The next three hypotheses that guided the research in this chapter centred on the dispute among the three aforementioned theoretical perspectives over this issue:

H_6: After controlling for persistent individual differences in criminal propensity, the association between past and subsequent offending will be reduced to a non-significant level (Gottfredson and Hirschi).

H_7: After controlling for persistent individual differences in criminal propensity, the association between past and subsequent offending behaviour will be reduced in magnitude but will still be positive and statistically significant (Sampson and Laub).

H_8: The association between past and subsequent offending behaviour will be non-significant for the 'life-course-persistent' group(s), while the effect should be substantial and significant for the 'adolescent-limited' group (Moffitt).

The obtained results presented in this chapter overwhelmingly support the seventh hypothesis (**H_7**) and largely fail to support the hypotheses delineated as **H_6** and **H_8**. After accounting for the population heterogeneity in the propensity to engage in criminal activities non-parametrically in the semiparametric mixed Poisson model of Nagin and Land (1993), the estimates of the state dependence relationship in this chapter were 0.404 (t-statistic = 38.82), 0.245 (t-statistic = 19.18), and 0.206 (t-statistic = 14.59) in the 1981–2, 1986–7, and 1991–2 samples, respectively. The estimates from the parametric random effects negative binomial model (after properly accounting for the age effects in the data) were 0.402 (t-statistic = 0.402), 0.248 (t-statistic = 13.90), and 0.188 (t-statistic = 9.33) in the 1981–2, 1986–7, and 1991–2 samples, respectively. Thus, after accounting for persistent unobserved heterogeneity in the propensity to engage in criminal activities (as measured by arrest data) through both parametric and non-parametric methods, there was still a significant positive relationship between having been arrested at the prior age and the frequency of arrest at the current age. Results such as these clearly support H_7 and explicitly fail to support H_6. That is, even after accounting for population heterogeneity in criminal propensity within the three samples, there was still a significant positive relationship between criminal activity patterns at adjacent ages. Statistical tests for unaccounted individual differences failed to reject the null hypothesis of no individual-specific effects, and thus the remaining state dependence effects uncovered in the models cannot be simply argued to be spuriously due to persistent unobserved differences.

We wish to emphasize again that it was found here to be absolutely critical for researchers to adequately control for the differences in criminal propensity when estimating the relationship between past and subsequent criminal activity. There was a very large decrease in the magnitude of the state dependence relationship after controlling for persistent individual differences. In fact, recall that there was a consistent 50–60 per cent reduction of the magnitude of the state dependence parameter between the initial baseline estimate (from the 1-class semiparametric mixed Poisson model) that makes no allowances for individual differences in the propensity to commit criminal acts and the final estimates arrived at after accounting for the unobserved heterogeneity (and age effects). Clearly then, accounting for individual differences is critically important when examining the relationship between past and subsequent criminal activity, even within these three samples of serious chronic offenders. Even after doing so, however, it should be kept in mind that there still remained a significant positive relationship between criminal offending at adjacent ages in the final models presented in this chapter. Graphs of the predicted arrest rates for those who had and had not been arrested at the prior age were used to display the final estimates. Again these graphs implied that there was a substantively meaningful and important relationship between these covariates, even if they were significantly reduced from those obtained from initial estimates.

With respect to H_8 examined in this study, the results of the models estimated within each latent class failed to uncover significant differential state dependence effects that were stronger in the 'adolescent-limited' group. There were two latent classes found to have positive state dependence effects that failed to attain statistical significance (at conventional levels). For the other 16 latent classes with significant positive effects, however, the class-specific state dependence estimates were not found to be significantly different from one another after taking possible chance sampling variation into account. The significant positive effects in the three 'adolescent-limited' groups were found not to be of a significantly greater magnitude when compared with the significant estimates in the other 13 latent classes. Thus, the evidence examined in this study failed to support H_8. The latent classes that most closely resembled (in a relative sense at least) the 'life-course-persistent' group (i.e. their criminal offending extended further into adulthood) also had significant positive estimates that were very close to the estimates found within the 'adolescent-limited' groups. No evidence was found in any of the three samples indicating that the state dependence effects were more pronounced in the adolescent-limited group. The state dependence effect uncovered in the data appeared to be a *general* effect that applied to all offender types, and not to just a specific offender type such as the adolescent-limited group. The fact that similar positive (significant) state dependence effects were found in 16 of the 18 latent classes sheds a degree of empirical doubt on the dual taxonomy perspective proposed by Moffitt (1993). This evidence appears to lend further empirical support to the major tenets of the (mixed) theory of Sampson and Laub (1993), who argue that the state dependence effect should be robust across offender types (i.e. apply to all offenders), rather than any specific type of offender (as claimed in Moffitt's theory).

The results presented in this chapter also resonate with a significant methodological theme on this topic. Previous research has discussed how reliable conclusions regarding the importance of state dependence processes (versus population heterogeneity) are contingent on the proper specification of the underlying mixing distribution (distribution of unobserved heterogeneity). This is the benefit of the multi-method approach—to the degree one can replicate a finding across various methods that make different and/or more/less stringent assumptions, the tenability of the finding(s) become more reliable. The use of a single method of analysis leaves the results of a study in a 'grey' area, where conclusions often will undoubtedly (and justly) be viewed with a healthy degree of scepticism (Bushway, Brame, and Paternoster 1999; Nagin and

Paternoster 2000). Results shown to be robust across different methods and model specifications, however, should be given greater credence.

In addition, the results obtained in this study clearly speak to the need to not only apply the multi-method approach, but also of the need to adequately model the 'age effects' in these data. Recall that the results for all three samples clearly showed both an overwhelming change in the nature of criminal offending patterns across the age distribution as well as a considerable degree of heterogeneity in the offending patterns among the latent classes. The findings obtained here were not indicative of a common trajectory that was merely differentiated in terms of the mean arrest rate. There was considerable heterogeneity in the nature of the estimated age parameters among the latent classes. The results of the analyses presented in this chapter clearly indicate that a failure to accurately capture the age effects within a sample of data will lead to a severe overestimation of the estimated state dependence effect. According to the results presented herein, this point is of fundamental importance from a methodological standpoint because it highlights the need for researchers to think critically about the proper specification necessary to accurately model age effects. For example, we re-estimated the semiparametric mixed Poisson model and constrained all of the age parameters to be equal across the latent classes such that

$$\ln\left(\lambda_{\mathrm{it}}^{\mathrm{j}}\right) = (\boldsymbol{\beta}_0 + \bar{\varepsilon}_j) + \left((age_{it}/10) * \boldsymbol{\beta}_{\mathrm{age}}\right) + \left(\left((age_{it}^2)/100\right) * \boldsymbol{\beta}_{\mathrm{age}^2}\right) + \left(arr_{t-1} * \boldsymbol{\beta}_{\mathrm{arr}_{t-1}}\right). \quad (4)$$

The estimates of the state dependence relationship from these models were nearly identical to the those estimated in the parametric random effects models where the age affects were only accounted for through the use of two overall terms (i.e. Model 1 of Tables 8.2, 8.5, and 8.8). The estimates from these semiparametric models were 0.60 (1981–2), 0.43 (1986–7), and 0.42 (1991–2) respectively, which are almost identical to the most comparable random effects specification. These coefficients still represent an over-estimation of the state dependence effects compared to that obtained when the age effects were properly modeled. Thus, while agreeing that the multi-method approach is a very important technique that should be adhered to when addressing this topic of research, simply reproducing the results across the different methods still does not mean the estimates are correct. We could accurately reproduce the nearly identical 'overestimates' of the state dependence parameter in both the parametric and semiparametric approaches to the mixing distribution. The methodological contribution that the results presented in this study suggest is that it is critical to ensure that the age parameters are adequately modeled in the data because unaccounted for variation in the age parameters appears to be quite adept at masking genuine state dependence effects (Bushway, Brame, and Paternoster 1999). Had we not accounted for the diverse age effects across the latent classes, the estimates of the state dependence parameter would have *doubled* in magnitude (in both the parametric and semiparametric mixed Poisson models). Without the flexibility of the semiparametric mixed Poisson model of Nagin and Land (1993), this realization would never have come about. The only way to account for the temporal shifts in the mean arrest rates was to either: (1) implicitly allow the age effects to vary across the latent classes as in the semiparametric mixed Poisson model specified in equation (1); or (2) to have access to the latent class indicators which could be interacting with the overall age parameters. Thus, although Bushway, Brame, and Paternoster (1999) note that 'the addition of time controls to random effects models is a very simple task,' accounting for the class-specific effects cannot be accomplished in the parametric random effect models by themselves. Therefore, results obtained from these models should be viewed with more than a healthy degree of scepticism. The direct benefit of the semiparametric mixed Poisson model is that its flexibility allows for building the variation in the age parameters directly into the specification. Perhaps this is only a problem for high-rate groups such as those studied here, but more than likely, it may be problematic any time there are significant differences in the age parameters and the estimated age parameters do not accurately reflect the actual age parameters in the high rate groups. Thus, the results obtained here indicate, quite emphatically, that the state dependence variable will absorb the effect of unaccounted for temporal, age-based variation that is unaccounted for in the model.

For the most part, however, the evidence presented in this chapter overwhelmingly favors the *mixed* position advocated by Sampson and Laub (1993) that allows for the general importance of both population heterogeneity and state dependence processes. The association between past and subsequent criminal activity cannot be simply argued to be a spurious artifact of population heterogeneity in criminal propensity. Yet at the same time, a large portion of the obtained relationship did appear to be a consequence of heterogeneity in the propensity to engage in criminal acts (i.e. the evidence does not favor either the pure population heterogeneity or pure state dependence positions). Thus, in general, the results obtained in this chapter simply do not appear here to resonate with the strong static explanations embodied in the static population heterogeneity theories such as those offered by Gottfredson and Hirschi (1990) or Wilson and Herrnstein (1985).

To bring these results back into perspective with the overarching theme under which this study has been framed—the dual processes of continuity and discontinuity (change) of criminal offending patterns across the life course—the results in this chapter clearly lend empirical support to the idea that both continuity and change are necessary for explaining the etiology of criminal offending across the life course; this appears to be true even within the serious offender population (with a dependent variable based on arrest data). In the final chapter to follow, we conclude by considering the general overarching theme of this study and the implications of the results presented in this study for critical policy issues facing our contemporary criminal justice system.

9

Looking Backward and Forward

We began this study by discussing three critically important questions: (1) how stable are individual differences in the propensity to commit criminal acts across the life course; (2) are there two (or more) discrete groups of offenders with distinct age–crime curves concealed within the aggregate age–crime curve; and (3) does the relationship between offending at one age period and a subsequent age period endure when time-stable individual differences in criminal propensity are controlled? We noted how questions one and two could be assessed with multivariate analyses of the age–crime curves of different latent classes of offenders and that question three could be assessed through a series of multivariate analyses of the relationships between the arrest rates of individuals at adjacent ages within these different latent classes. This led to complicated but necessary statistical analyses in two substantive chapters (7 and 8). Given that the results of each substantive chapter have been previously summarized, reviewed, and discussed, this final chapter will focus on our general theoretical and substantive conclusions, possible directions for future research, and the policy implications that follow from our analyses.

Theoretical and Substantive Implications

In a nutshell, the old adages, 'you can't unscramble eggs' and 'a leopard never changes its spots,' describe the fundamental overarching issue addressed in this study—the relevance of stability and change in criminal behavior over the life course. What have we learned here by confining our study of these issues to the serious chronic offender population? Recall that our study examined the competing predictions of three broad theoretical frameworks regarding the possibility of behavioral change over the life course for serious criminal offenders; all were derivative hypotheses of the same fundamental question: how stable or inflexible are individual differences in the propensity to engage in criminal/antisocial activities across the life course for these individuals? Or stated differently, is behavioral *change* possible in the lives of serious criminal offenders? Each perspective makes different predictions regarding the relationship between age and crime and the relationship between past and subsequent criminal activities.

Our study examined these two primary issues in Chapters 7 and 8, respectively, by addressing (1) whether the relationship between age and crime was invariant across different latent classes (i.e. stable) or whether there were variable between-class differences over time (i.e. change over time) and (2) whether or not past criminal activity was related to subsequent criminal activity after controlling for persistent individual differences. The findings presented in these two chapters provided resounding support for the notion that behavioral change is extremely relevant on both counts. With respect to the first source of change (the relationship between age and crime), between-group differences were shown to be highly variable over time; between-group differences were invariant only through early adolescence, and then during adulthood such differences were largely *unstable* and variable. With respect to the second question of behavioral change (the relationship between past and subsequent criminal behavior), we found that even after accounting for persistent unobserved heterogeneity in the propensity to engage in criminal activities (through both parametric and non-parametric statistical methods), a significant positive relationship between having been arrested at a earlier age and the frequency of arrest at the observed later age period persists. In other words, something about being arrested must influence—or change—these offenders' lives, propelling them to further subsequent arrests given that we controlled for their propensity to reoffend. These substantive results broadly imply that behavioral *change matters significantly* in the lives of offenders, and *even* in the lives of the most persistent serious youthful offenders in the population (who arguably would be the most prone to stability in the spirit of Moffitt's 'life-course-persistent offender' type). It is important to remember that these substantive findings were documented across three independent samples. Thus, the observed findings lend considerable credence to the notion that behavioral change in the patterns of criminal arrest across the life course is not only possible, but is indeed also one of the 'brute facts of criminology' (to borrow Gottfredson and Hirschi's statement).

In our judgement, there are three main substantive conclusions to be drawn from this study that are related to both the over-arching theme of continuity/discontinuity in criminal arrest patterns and that are important for any aetiological explanation of criminal offending patterns across the life course. First, the findings in this study inform what Sampson and Laub (1992) have referred to as the overstatement and/or misinterpretation of antisocial behaviors across the life course (see also Loeber and Stouthamer-Loeber 1998). Our results clearly indicate that the continuity of arrest patterns will be much stronger when the measurement periods are closer together in time. That is, greater stability (including between-group stability) is displayed within shorter (e.g. two years) compared to longer periods of time. Indeed, the vast majority of the available data sets in criminology typically measure incidents of crime and arrest over very short periods of time. As noted by Cohen and Vila (1996: 147), 'consistency of behavior might depend on the time scale selected for analysis.' The empirical results of this study indicate a considerable amount of support for this contention. Continuity in arrests for crime appears to be much stronger when the measurement points are closer together in time. Discontinuity (change), on the other hand, is much more apparent in empirical studies when long-term criminal offending patterns are examined. Longer-term data, such as presented here, provide more rigorous examinations of the balance between continuity and discontinuity in criminality, the latter of which only appears to emerge in more extended data. Furthermore, the results presented herein demonstrate that some segments of the age-span display more continuity in behavioural patterns (e.g. early to mid-adolescence) than do other segments of the age-span (e.g. adulthood). Thus, while it is important for criminological theory to recognize the continuity in behavioral crime patterns over time, our data validate the importance of the possible temporal nature of this continuity.

Second, the findings observed herein indicate a significant amount of heterogeneity in the longitudinal arrest patterns of serious youthful offenders, suggesting a preference for panel designs over cross-sectional research when studying criminal behavior. Examination of both the observed average total arrest charges and the observed and predicted arrest trajectories of each latent class identified in our study indicated a significant amount of heterogeneity even in this select extreme segment of the offender population. Thus, our results bolster the contention of Sampson and Laub (1992, 1993; Laub and Sampson 2001) that far more heterogeneity in longitudinal criminal arrest and offending patterns exists than previously thought. It is important to specifically highlight that the type of heterogeneity of which we speak here is heterogeneity in the patterns of criminal offending over extended periods of the life course. As clearly shown in the graphical depiction of the arrest trajectories discussed in Chapter 7, there are periods of time when the distinctions between the arrest trajectories of the various latent classes were blurred or even non-existent. Over more extended periods of time, however, the crime trajectories of different latent classes were vastly distinct.

Third (and related to the second point noted above), large variations in criminal arrest patterns appear during adulthood that cannot be simply argued as the long-term consequences of childhood propensities (Sampson and Laub 1992). As recently noted by LeBlanc and Loeber (1998: 131), 'against the backdrop of [relative] continuity, studies also show large within-individual changes in offending, a point understated in the invariance hypothesis suggested by Gottfredson and Hirschi (1987*a*).' The findings presented in Chapter 7 indicate varying rates of developmental change in the arrest trajectories of the identified latent classes. For the most part, the latent classes appear to have discontinued their antisocial activities at very different paces and ages (see also Cernkovich and Giordano 2001). That is, among the different identified latent classes, the 'desistence process' did not begin at the same age, nor did it take place at the same relative pace. The results obtained in this study thus seem to add further empirical support to bolster the contention of Sampson and Laub that 'intra-individual change is widespread even among a large group of individuals labeled as serious, persistent youthful offenders. These chronic offenders possess all of the risk characteristics that many researchers believe to be enduring and stable traits across the life course' (Laub and Sampson 2001: 58).

In sum, the main theoretical and substantive implications of this study suggest that the processes of both continuity and change (discontinuity) are important in any aetiological explanation of criminal offending patterns across the entire life course (see also Paternoster *et al.* 1997). Ignoring either of these processes, or viewing them as polar opposites on a continuum will lead to inadequate explanations of criminal behavior (see also Horney, Osgood, and Marshall 1995). Given the critical nature of both processes of continuity and change, we now move to discussing how future research must use this knowledge to next unpack the precise causal nexus behind each of these processes over the life course. Unfortunately, it is at this point in our study where the limits of our data preclude their usefulness for examining such issues.

Suggestions for Future Research

Our data clearly direct the field of criminology away from the static theoretical perspectives that claim the existence of a population of offenders who will always persistently offend regardless of their age or life circumstances. Instead, research should be directed towards understanding the kinds of change in offenders' lives that contribute to either their persistence or discontinuation of criminal offending (see Laub and Sampson 2003; Sampson and Laub 2003).

As discussed in Chapter 2, our study is not able to test the specific causal structures of a particular theory or set of theories, but rather our goal was to evaluate the empirical validity of the longitudinal implications of three leading criminological theoretical perspectives. Overall, our data failed to empirically validate several of the implications of Moffitt's 'dual taxonomy' theory. We have in our study, three independently selected samples of what Moffitt would label 'life-course-persistent offenders', those whom would be predicted to continue their offending throughout their lifetimes. Instead, we found that these samples of serious offenders could be empirically classified into six groups, each with a different arrest rate trajectory across time. However, the arrest rates in each of these six latent classes proved not to be as 'persistent' as predicted by Moffitt; the arrest rate of each latent class declined with age, albeit at different rates. Further, age was a highly significant predictor of offending behavior in all of the latent classes. However, our examination of the predicted and observed arrest trajectories provided overwhelming support for the presence of an 'adolescent-limited' offender group in this population (which is an interesting result given the nature of our samples), but our examination of the state dependence processes in Chapter 8 did not reveal evidence indicating that state dependence is more important for this group. This is contrary to the theoretical arguments of Moffitt concerning this group. We conclude, therefore, that the analyses of our data overall have failed to validate the empirical expectations of Moffitt's dual taxonomy perspective.

Our analyses also failed to support the age-invariance hypothesis promulgated by Gottfredson and Hirschi. That is, we found little support for the confirmation of this hypothesis after adolescence. Therefore, longitudinal research may be much more valuable in the study of the relationship between age and crime than these researchers acknowledge. What should not be lost on the readers of our study, however, is the confirmation found here for several contentions of Gottfredson and Hirschi's 'general theory of crime'. For example, we did find support for one of their 'brute facts' of criminology that—even among the most persistent offender groups in the population—offense rates do eventually decline with age. By the mid-to-late twenties, the vast majority of the latent classes identified in our samples had begun to demonstrate a declining arrest trajectory, and some have even largely ceased their offending (as measured by arrests). The strong relationship between age and crime demands a theoretical explanation and further empirical examination addressing the aetiological explanation of this 'brute fact.' We also found support for several other contentions of Gottfredson and Hirschi such as the high mortality rate of high-rate offenders and the generality of offending in criminal patterns (i.e. offenders engage in a wide variety of offenses). While we cannot support their age-invariance hypothesis, we believe it would be a serious mistake to dismiss the theory altogether. This particular hypothesis is only one part of what is a much more expansive and complex theory.

In the end, the examination of the issues addressed in this study have led us to the tentative conclusion that, overall, the evidence obtained here is perhaps most consistent with the predictions implied from Sampson and Laub's (1993), age-graded social control theory. The findings in our study have shown (1) that behavioral change is evident among serious chronic offenders, (2) that the heterogeneity in criminal propensity among the chronic offender population is often underreported, and (3) that there is considerable post-adolescent heterogeneity in the arrest rates of offenders that cannot be explained purely as a consequence of earlier individual differences.

We cannot however speak to Sampson and Laub's proposed labeling effect as the best explanation for this pattern of crime continuity observed in our data. They believe that youths who are seriously delinquent accumulate social disadvantage as they age, making it increasingly more difficult for them to exit from a life of crime. This loss of 'social capital' is generated most directly by sanctions such as arrest, conviction, and incarceration by watchful social control agents who scrutinize their every move. Being officially labeled and stigmatized as a serious delinquent serves to further reduce future educational and employment opportunities. Chronic offenders thus become trapped in a vicious cycle in which crime leads to failure in conventional activities that in turn exacerbates further delinquency. As they grow older, however, most of these young men will gain access to other sources of achievement and social satisfaction—a job, a girlfriend and/or wife, and in many cases, children. When chronic offenders become attached to such barriers to crime and delinquency, they become less dependent on delinquent peer-groups for support and reinforcement.

Admittedly the data limitations do not permit us to assess if or to what degree such constraints on criminal behaviour impact the members of our samples over time. Nor do these data allow us to speculate as to whether continuity in arrest rates observed during adolescence and early adulthood among our samples were the result of labeling, exposure to definitions favorable to crime, lack of legitimate opportunity, sub-cultural reinforcement of criminal conduct, weak social bonds, or the absence of fear at the prospect of being caught and punished for criminal activity. Such data limitations raise the issue of possible avenues for future research that could better inform the specific causal structures of change in criminal behavior.

The data sets employed in our study, and the findings observed herein, cannot be used to answer the four critical questions raised by Nagin and Paternoster (2000) that they believe are of crucial importance for understanding the population heterogeneity-state dependence debate: (1) what are the specific causal mechanisms underlying the individual differences in the propensity to commit criminal acts; (2) what are the specific positive and negative salient life events that lead individuals both into and out of the criminal lifestyle; (3) what are the specific causal processes underlying the desistence process; and (4) what processes determine both the availability of pro-social opportunities and whether an individual will take advantage of these opportunities?

Such questions, along with the empirical results of our study, suggest a critical need for the discipline of criminology to engage in further research to determine both the theoretical and empirical aetiological mechanisms driving the change (see also Bushway *et al.* 2001; Laub and Sampson 2001). Particularly critical is determining why offenders who have shown a pronounced proclivity (albeit a varying one) to engage in criminal activities for a significant segment of their lifespan would begin to decrease their offending in adulthood? As is evident here in the lives of even the most serious offenders in the population, positive behavioural change does occur, and it occurs earlier for some individuals/groups than for others. Given the record numbers of Americans under some form of custody in the criminal justice system, identifying the theoretical and public policy implications requires further research on the causes and nature of pro-social behavioral change among the serious offender population.

Finally, even though it is clear that many of the serious chronic offenders within our samples appear to follow a path of 'desistence', we have no idea exactly what kind of lives they actually lead in their thirties, forties, and thereafter. Information of this sort is sadly lacking and little is known on this topic (Laub and Sampson 2001). Do the majority of these individuals lead highly marginalized lives full of alcohol and drug abuse problems, unemployment, and marital discord as Gottfredson and Hirschi (1990) have suggested? Unfortunately, questions such as this cannot be answered with the data sets we have utilized.

Laub and Sampson (2003), however, have recently updated the longitudinal records for many of the surviving members from the Glueck's original sample of seriously delinquent youths through the age of 70. Their study suggests that many of these individuals led troubled lives even though crime rates eventually declined by the middle adult years for all groups of offenders identified in their study. In fact, the results of our study dovetail nicely with some of the results of the recent work of Laub and Sampson (2003; Sampson and Laub 2003) in several ways, including: the presence of a significant amount of heterogeneity in the long-term offending patterns of serious young offenders; that measured covariates do not effectively distinguish offenders in different latent classes; that the age-invariance assumption is violated over the long-term, especially in adulthood, and that adult offending patterns are not simply the long-term outcomes of differences present early in life; and finally that even though our data naturally lends itself to finding the life-course-persistent offender, the notion of differential 'life-course desisters' seems more descriptively accurate.

Having discussed the theoretical and empirical implications of our research and some possible directions for future research, we conclude this study with a discussion of how the role of change in offenders' lives can inform the public policy debates struggling with this same relationship between age and crime.

Public Policy Implications

The nature of the age–crime relationship has profound implications regarding the practical utility of contemporary criminal justice policies. Over the past three decades in the United States, the public's outrage about serious crime and the government's response to their outrage have resulted in an increase in both the probability of offenders being sentenced to prison after conviction and in the length of time served while in custody (Blumstein and Beck 1999; Donziger 1996; Irwin and Austin 1997). This increased punitiveness against convicted criminals is the direct result of the get 'tough on crime' attitude that has swept this country since the late 1960s (Caplow and Simon 1999).

The interaction effect between the increased probability of imprisonment and the increased length of time served for felony convictions has led to a phenomenal increase in the number of offenders imprisoned over the last thirty years (Blumstein and Beck 1999; Caplow and Simon 1999). In 2000 there were nearly 2 million adults in prison in the United States (Bureau of Justice Statistics 2001). Between 1970 and 2000, for example, the adult (prison) incarceration rate in the United States nearly quintupled, increasing from 96 per 100,000 adult residents in 1970 to 478 per 100,000 in 2000 (Bureau of Justice Statistics 2000). Indeed by mid-year 2000, one out of every 142 Americans was incarcerated in either prison or jail, compared to one out of every 218 in 1990 and one out of every 320 in 1985 (Bureau of Justice Statistics 1995, 2001).

Conservative policy makers in particular, have long maintained that putting more people in prison for longer periods of time would have both deterrent and incapacitation effects that would substantially reduce crime. Such beliefs were certainly apparent among California policy makers during the period covered in our study when the state's imprisonment rate quadrupled. Much of the political leadership in California for what would turn out to be the largest prison expansion program in the country would be provided by Governor George Deukmejian, who would build ten new prisons during his administration (1982–90). Deukmejian and his successor Governor Pete Wilson would both earn well-deserved reputations as leaders for sentence reform policies aimed at both adult and juvenile offenders that incarcerated more people for far longer periods of time than any of the other political administrations in the state's history. In Chapter 4, for example, we described how a CYA ward's average length of stay increased significantly over this time period. The post-release recidivism rates of wards paroled under this policy change, however, appear to have been unaffected by the increase in the length of institutionalization over time. Our analysis indicated that the recidivism rates of each of the three cohorts (subjected to increasingly severe treatment, respectively) were virtually identical. Twelve months after release on parole, roughly 50 per cent of each of the three cohorts had been rearrested, while after three years, about 75 per cent of each cohort was apprehended for the commission of a new offence. Thus, while such policies may have successfully served the ambitions of politicians and bureaucrats and satiated public outrage, they did not appear to contribute much to public safety once these wards were released on parole.

As a result of the concern over high recidivism rates among serious offenders, several states, most notably California, have enacted tough new statutes like the one commonly known as 'Three Strikes and You're Out,' introduced in 1994 during Governor Wilson's administration. These statutes are proactive crime control policies mandating the incarceration of individuals who repeatedly commit most of the serious crimes in society—the chronic, or career, offenders (the same population that our study examines). The primary goal of such programs is to selectively identify those offenders deemed to present the greatest risk to society and to remove these individuals away from the general public by incarcerating them for longer periods of time.

In California, the basic content of the 'Three Strikes' law requires that defendants with two prior 'violent' or 'serious' felonies (i.e. those who have already accumulated two strikes), are to be sentenced to a mandatory term of 25 years to life in prison after conviction of *any* third felony, even if it is non-violent. Furthermore, this law mandates that any second-strike felony offense receive double the prison time it would receive were it a first offense.

Sustained petitions against juveniles, however, do not count as 'strikes' under California's 'Three Strikes' law until the juvenile reaches the age of 16. Once a juvenile reaches age 16, however, sustained petitions for the commission of 'violent' or 'serious' offenses (felonies) are then counted as 'strikes' against them. This fact has the potential effect of increasing the age at which chronic, youthful offenders are typically sentenced for their 'third-strike' offense. Thus, it is conceivable that many youthful, chronic offenders will not accumulate their 'third strike' until after they reach the age of about 25, because they may be required to serve considerable time periods for their first and/or second offenses after conviction.

Our finding that each of the six latent classes of serious chronic offenders tended to 'age out' of serious crime suggests the potential for heavy financial and social implications associated with incarcerating such individuals for extended periods of time under a 'Three Strikes' policy. For example, using national statistics on the costs of constructing and maintaining prisons, Irwin and Austin (1997) calculated the cost per additional prisoner (including both supervision costs and the amortized prison construction costs) in 1997 to be $39,000 per year. In total, the 30-year cost of adding space for just one additional prisoner was estimated to be over $1 million dollars (Irwin and Austin 1997: 139).

Beyond financial cost, consider the relationship between age and crime uncovered here and its implications for the use of prisons, especially 'draconian crime control policies' such as 'Three Strikes.' If the offending rate of a 'high risk' individual is not constant over his or her criminal career, but actually declines with age (as we find in our study), then sentencing such 'high-rate' serious offenders to very long prison terms, perhaps just at a point when their offending rates are sharply declining does not seem to be a socially efficient or cost-effective crime control policy (see also Haapanen 1990; Ezell and Cohen 1997). Despite the contentions of certain criminologists, we found no evidence of a group of 'life-course-persistent' serious offenders where age does not predict their behaviour. The notion that such groups exist is well represented in the criminological literature and is very seductive when considering crime control policies (Laub and Sampson 2003; Sampson and Laub 2003). As described earlier in this chapter, however, much of Gottfredson and Hirschi's initial critique and reaction towards the criminal career approach of Blumstein and his colleagues was specifically directed at selective incapacitation policies, and how these polices completely disregard the relationship between age and crime (see Gottfredson and Hirschi 1986, 1990; Hirschi and Gottfredson 1986, 1988). Our study both validates and extends this argument by detailing the declining criminal offending patterns across three samples and within each of the latent classes within those samples.

The crime prevention prospects of selective incapacitation policies appear 'murky' when we consider the different implications of the processes of state dependence and population heterogeneity theories with respect to the practical utility of effectively and efficiently preventing crime. According to the population heterogeneity perspective, criminal propensity once formed *is not malleable*. Thus, from the perspective of Gottfredson and Hirschi (1990), any intervention with a lasting impact on the criminal propensity of an individual must involve the efficacy of early child-rearing practices prior to the approximate age of 8 (see Hirschi 1995). As Gottfredson and Hirschi (1990: 272) pointedly state: 'Apart from the limited benefits that can be achieved by making specific criminal acts more difficult [e.g. target hardening], policies directed toward enhancement of the ability of familial institutions to socialize children are the only realistic long-term state policies with potential for substantial crime reduction.'

Imprisonment according to some researchers, for example, will have neither an enduring beneficial (deterrent) nor negative (criminogenic) effect on the individual after release because it has nothing to do with the source of criminal propensity, and thus cannot alter it (Nagin and Farrington 1992*b*). Furthermore, as Gottfredson and Hirschi note, any potential beneficial impacts of criminal justice programs are more likely to be a function of selection bias effects with respect to who is placed in what programmes. In other words, high-rate (low self-control) offenders get placed in certain (restrictive, secure) programs, while low-rate offenders get placed in other programs, and the differential success rates claimed by supporters of these various programs will be entirely dependent on such selection bias effects.

From the perspective of Sampson and Laub, however, programs that serve to strengthen an individual's bond to society, rather than weakening it, have the possibility to bring about considerable positive change in the criminal propensity of offenders. Given that the state dependence perspective views criminal propensity as malleable across the life course, this perspective asserts that it is possible for criminal justice policies to ultimately change the probability of future criminal behavior through assisting the development of positive life events (see Laub *et al.* 1995). Unfortunately, however, policies regarding positive life events in adulthood are arguably extremely difficult or impractical to implement in practice.

Nonetheless, critics often note that the current 'get tough on crime' policies often simply serve to further isolate the individual and cut off possible future (positive) opportunities for change. Recall, for example, Sampson and Laub's, argument that imprisonment has criminogenic effects because of its deleterious impact on the prospects of stable employment during adulthood, especially since many of the 'escape routes' for convicted felons have been increasingly shut-off as available paths to evade the criminal lifestyle. 'Although there is considerable state-by-state variation, licensing boards bar ex-offenders from virtually hundreds of other occupations [besides being a barber], including apprentice electrician, billiards operator, and plumber' (Sampson and Laub 1997: 148; see also Laub *et al.* 1995). Making prisons even more hostile environments through the removal of educational opportunities, job training, and visitation hours also does not appear to be good policy from a state dependence theoretical perspective. Reintegrating the offender into society and establishing bonds with conventional persons rather than further isolating them is seen as the key to bringing about change in the lives of these individuals according to many adherents with a state dependence perspective (see also Braithwaite 1989). As Laub *et al.* (1995: 103) assert, 'it is critical that individuals have the opportunity to reconnect to institutions such as family, school, and work after a period of incarceration.'

Given the above discussion, what are the policy implications for the state of California that may be said to flow directly from our study? First, given the extremely high parole failure rates reported in Chapter 6, the pessimist who reads this study will conclude that the benefits of institutional placement in the CYA appear to be very discouraging, at least in the short-term. Upon reflection, however, perhaps we never should have expected low or even moderate recidivism rates among our three samples of serious chronic offenders. Assume for the moment that the CYA is stocked with dedicated employees, who by and large work very hard to rehabilitate and support wards under their supervision, and that the available programmes provide a variety of educational, treatment, training, and supervisory services and opportunities for wards. Why shouldn't we expect low failure rates? To begin, we would do well to remember that these wards represent the worst 5 per cent of the youthful offender population in the state. The case history records of these serious chronic offenders are considerably worse than any we have previously seen. For this and other groups of active offenders, we find no consistent evidence to support the commonly held expectation that policy changes which increase the severity of punishment and the average length of sentence will significantly deter the likelihood of subsequent criminal behavior. The 'get tough on crime' movement began largely in the mid-1970s as a justification for establishing an increase in the severity of sentencing decisions because of the failure of the rehabilitation programmes (in vogue during the 1960s) that were supposed to reduce recidivism rates. The changes in policy and parole decisions in the 1980s and early 1990s that have had the effect of increasing the average length of institutional stay of CYA wards do not appear to have improved the subsequent post-release behavior of parolees as is well documented in Chapter 6. The simplest explanation for this finding is that the menu of education, treatment, training, and supervisory services in place (assuming wards could get in these programs) could not overcome or appreciably reduce the existing powerful social forces influencing offenders to continue their criminal offending behavior.

The optimist who reads our study, however, will be intrigued by the long-term relationship observed here between age and crime. While we have found little evidence to support Gottfredson and Hirschi's notion that the relationship between age and crime is invariant, we also found no support for the idea that the frequency of serious criminal behavior does not decline with age among active offenders. Instead we have observed support for a 'brute fact' of criminology that the arrest trajectories for every latent class derived from our active offender samples eventually declined with age. While we have no direct evidence to support Sampson and Laub's explanation for this phenomenon, the timing of the desistence patterns among our samples is consistent with the possibility that the processes of developing and strengthening social bonds could be at work here. Recall that Gottfredson and Hirschi, on the other hand, speculate an alternative hypothesis for this observed behavioral pattern of desistence—maturational reform. They argue (1990) that desistence is nothing more than behavioral change that comes with maturation; desistence cannot be explained through traditional conceptual schemes employed by criminologists. It is only when you apply their substantive distinction between 'crime' and 'criminality' to the basic facts about crime that you are able to understand and explain the relationship between age and crime (for more on their explanation of desistence over time, see Gottfredson and Hirschi 1990: 136–41).[1] Our data do not allow for an informed opinion of which of the above explanations is most appropriate to account for the pattern of desistance observed over time in our study, but clearly this issue is in need of considerable attention in the field of criminology.

The serious criminal offences that are of the greatest concern to society (e.g. Index crimes) were found here to have been most frequently committed by members of our samples when they were relatively young (e.g. ages 14–22). That is, the data presented in this study showed a marked relationship between age and crime even for the serious criminal offenses that are the intended targets of selective incapacitation policies such as 'Three Strikes.' In fact, over time, the individuals who recidivated in these samples became increasingly more likely to have been arrested for a drug-related offense as they aged than for any other type of offence. For example, the members of the 1981–2 sample accrued 166 robbery charges in 1983. In 1999 they accrued only 18 arrest charges for robbery offences. For drug-related offences, on the other hand, they accrued

[1] If it is maturational change, then an obvious question that needs to be addressed concerns why certain groups of offenders experience rapid periods of maturational reform (e.g. the adolescent-limited offender) while others experience slow maturational processes. Given the results of our study, if it is 'maturational change,' it appears that maturational change processes vary considerably in the population.

396 charges in 1983 and still accrued 299 charges for such offenses in 1999. Because of their long histories of past involvement in serious crime, however, these individuals become prime candidates for selective incapacitation as 'third strike' offenders at the approximate point in the age–crime curve where most no longer appear to pose a grave danger to public safety. The trends in our data suggest that the decline in crime with age is going to continue in the coming years, which (extrapolating to the general population of criminal offenders) indicates that there are going to be a fair number of offenders in prison who appear to pose relatively little danger to society. If many of these individuals no longer represent a serious danger to society because they have 'aged out' of, or are in the final stages of aging out of serious felony crimes, then there are potentially enormous social and economic costs to be accrued for treating them outside the community at later ages.

As in life, 'there are no free lunches' when it comes to building and maintaining a massive prison industrial complex. In order to finance the massive increases in state prison populations, legislatures have certainly been forced to divert money from discretionary line items in state budgets—education, welfare, medical care, mental health services, and child care. The fear among critics of 'get tough' crime policies is that money is being diverted away from the very institutions that have traditionally played a crucial role in either preventing some individuals from engaging in serious crime in the first place, or in helping individuals to desist from the criminal lifestyle. Ironically, the worry here is that higher incarceration rates may serve to set in motion a spiraling effect that in the long term could push crime rates to rise rather than decline. If true, this unintended consequence of harsh crime policy would confirm Dante's well-cited admonition that 'the road to hell is paved with good intentions.'

Appendix A
Technical Description of the Employed Methodology

The dependent variable of this study (arrest counts) has two properties associated with it that must be appropriately taken into account in any statistical model: (1) it is a non-negative count variable and (2) the data structures contain multiple observations per case (i.e. there is a lack of independence). We deal with each of these issues below.

Modelling a Count Variable: The Poisson and Negative Binomial Regression Models

Given that the dependent variable is a non-negative count variable, the methods of analysis employed must take into account the discrete nature of this variable.[1] If we were to apply standard OLS linear regression models that assume a continuous, normally distributed dependent variable as opposed to a skewed count dependent variable such as that used here, it would produce biased, inefficient, and inconsistent estimates of the covariates included in the model specification, as well as possibly predicting a negative number of events (King 1988; Long 1997). For these reasons, two general regression models based on a probability distribution that explicitly takes into account the discrete nature of count variables have been proposed: (1) the Poisson regression model and (2) the negative binomial regression model.

The Poisson Regression Model

To begin, let us allow y_{it} to denote the observed event count of the ith individual ($i = 1, \ldots n$) at time (age) t ($t = 7, 8, 9, \ldots, T_i$), where T_i = max (age_i). The univariate Poisson probability distribution function is specified as

$$\Pr(Y_{it} = y_{it}) = \frac{e^{-\lambda_{it}} \lambda_{it}^{y_{it}}}{y_{it}!}, \qquad y_{it} = 0, 1, 2, \ldots \tag{1}$$

[1] This discussion of the Poisson model and generalizations of it draw heavily on the detailed treatments of these methods in Hausman, Hall, and Griliches (1984), Cameron and Trivedi (1986, 1998), Hardin and Hilbe (2001), and especially Land, McCall, and Nagin (1996). Excellent discussions of the statistical issues involved in modelling continuity and change are available in Brame, Bushway, and Paternoster (1999) and Bushway, Brame, and Paternoster (1999).

where $\Pr(Y_{it} = y_{it})$ indicates the probability that the random variable (Y_{it}) takes on the observed value (Y_{it}) for the ith individual at time t, and λ is the non-negative Poisson parameter representing the mean rate of event occurrence at time t (Land, McCall, and Nagin 1996).[2] The Poisson distribution, which is a one-parameter probability distribution, makes a strong assumption regarding the relationship between the mean and variance of the random variable (Y_{it}). This assumption, known as the *equidispersion* assumption, assumes that the mean and the variance are equal:

$$\mathrm{E}(Y_{it}) = \mathrm{var}(Y_{it}) \equiv \lambda_{it}. \tag{2}$$

More generally, the expected value of a count variable such as this could be written as

$$E(Y_{it}) = \mathrm{var}(Y_{it}) \equiv \lambda_{it}\sigma^2, \tag{3}$$

where σ^2 is the *dispersion parameter* constrained to be greater than or equal to zero (King 1989). A count variable is said to exhibit equidispersion and to be Poisson-distributed if $\sigma^2 = 1$, but if $0 \leq \sigma^2 < 1$ then the variable is said to be *underdispersed,* and if $\sigma^2 > 1$ then the variable is said to *overdispersed* (King 1989; Land, McCall, and Nagin 1996; Lindsey 1993, 1995). Overdispersion is a very common property among dependent variables utilized in social science data, whereas underdispersion is rare (King 1989).

The important point to make here is that overdispersion implies a significant substantive fact critically relevant to this study: there is unexplained variation in accounting for why some subjects have greater or fewer total arrests (events) than do other subjects. Stated differently, there is more heterogeneity in the mean event rate *among the individuals* than would be expected according to the Poisson distribution. One possible way to account for why some individuals have a higher mean arrest rate than others is to specify a Poisson regression model whereby a set of measured covariates are included through the equality

$$\ln(\lambda_{it}) = \mathbf{X}_{it}\boldsymbol{\beta}, \tag{4}$$

or equivalently

$$\lambda_{it} = \exp(\mathbf{X}_{it}\boldsymbol{\beta}), \tag{5}$$

[2] See Appendix A in King (1988) for a mathematical proof that event count data that meet a few modest assumptions about the data generation process can be shown to arise from a Poisson process.

where $\mathbf{X}_{it}$ is a matrix of measured covariates on individual i at time t, and $\boldsymbol{\beta}$ is a column vector of regression coefficients relating the covariates to the mean arrest rate.[3]

According to Land, McCall, and Nagin (1996), inclusion of measured covariates in the model specification now leads to a conditional expectation function whereby the expected mean and variance of the event count are conditional on the **X** matrix such that

$$E(Y_{it}|\mathbf{X}_{it}) = \text{var}(Y_{it}|\mathbf{X}_{it}) = \lambda_{it} = \exp(\mathbf{X}_{it}\boldsymbol{\beta}). \tag{6}$$

Similar to the deterministic relationship stated above in equation (2), equation (6) still implies a deterministic relationship, only now it is a conditional deterministic relationship (conditional on the measured covariates), whereas before it was an unconditional deterministic relationship (Hausman, Hall, and Griliches 1984).[4] However, conditional on the observed covariates, the observed relationship is still nonstochastic.

As noted by Land, McCall, and Nagin (1996), the equidispersion assumption of the Poisson regression model is an unrealistic expectation in many social science data sets, and furthermore the failure to satisfy the equidispersion assumption leads to underestimated standard errors and inflated t-ratio tests of significance (see also Dean 1998; Hardin and Hilbe 2001). In other words, applying a Poisson regression model to data that cannot satisfy the equidispersion assumption can cause a covariate to appear to be a significant predictor of the outcome variable, when in fact it is not. In that situation, the statistical significance is spurious, due to the consequences of overdispersion. For this reason, methods that 'scale' the relationship between the mean and variance were sought (Hardin and Hilbe 2001). The primary method that is used in the presence of significant overdispersion in a Poisson regression model is to estimate a negative binomial regression model.

The Negative Binomial Regression Model

As stated in Chapter 3, it is unrealistic to assume that every factor related to a dependent variable will be measured and included in all data sets, and thus there will always be some inherent variability (e.g. overdispersion) in the event counts between individuals that must be accounted for (Lindsey 1993, 1995; Land, McCall, and Nagin 1996). In the absence of

[3] The logarithmic *link function* is used to link the linear systematic component, denoted as $\mathbf{X}\boldsymbol{\beta}$, to the response variable (Nelder and Wedderburn 1972; McCullagh and Nelder 1989; Hardin and Hilbe 2001) in order to ensure that that event rate is predicted to be non-negative (Land, McCall, and Nagin 1996).

[4] Hardin and Hilbe (2001: 128) show the mean (first derivative) and variance (second derivative) functions of the Poisson distribution are identical.

the measured covariates that explain the discrepancy, this variation is usually accounted for as *stochastic* or *random variation* in the dependent variable. Indeed, the precise reasoning behind fitting a negative binomial regression model (instead of a Poisson regression model) is to include stochastic variation in the event count (Hausman, Hall, and Griliches 1984; Cameron and Trivedi 1986; Land, McCall, and Nagin 1996).[5] The negative binomial regression model is specified as

$$\ln(\lambda_{it}) = \mathbf{X}_{it}\boldsymbol{\beta} + \varepsilon_{it}, \tag{7}$$

or

$$\lambda_{it} = \exp(\mathbf{X}_{it}\boldsymbol{\beta}) \bullet \exp(\varepsilon_{it}), \tag{8}$$

where $\exp(\boldsymbol{\varepsilon})$is distributed as $\Gamma(1, \alpha)$. The α parameter is known as the dispersion parameter and plays a defining role in scaling the relationship between the mean and the variance as shown in equation (9) below. The inclusion of the gamma distributed error term allows for unexplained variation in $1\text{n}(\lambda_{it})$ (Land, McCall, and Nagin 1996). This unexplained variation can be thought of as having been produced in one of two ways: (1) through the effects of an omitted exogenous variable(s) (Gourieroux, Monfort, and Trognon 1984*a*, 1984*b*) or (2) through inherent stochastic variation (Hausman, Hall, and Griliches 1984). The negative binomial model is known in the statistical literature as a *parametric mixed Poisson* regression model because a parametric mixing distribution (i.e. the gamma distribution) has been incorporated into the Poisson model.

There are two general formulations of the negative binomial model (Cameron and Trivedi 1986, 1998; Hardin and Hilbe 2001): (1) NB1 that specifies a linear mean-variance relationship; and (2) NB2 that specifies a quadratic mean-variance relationship. These models both consider the variance as a function of the mean (or Poisson parameter) such that

$$\text{var}(Y_{it}|\mathbf{X}_{it}) = \lambda_{it} + \alpha\lambda_{it}^{p}, \tag{9}$$

where p is equal to 1 in the NB1 formulation of the negative binomial models and p is equal to 2 in the NB2 formulation. The NB1 and NB2 models are both Poisson-gamma mixture models, but each model provides a different specification of the mean-variance relationship. The log-likelihood functions for the NB1 and NB2 models are presented in Cameron and Trivedi (1998) and Hardin and Hilbe (2001).

[5] The gamma distribution is the 'conjugate distribution' for the Poisson distribution, which allows for a closed form solution that is analytically tractable (Lindsey 1995). Assuming the heterogeneity is normally distributed does not lead to an analytically tractable solution (Cameron and Trivedi 1998; Land, McCall, and Nagin 1996).

NB2 is the more commonly used negative binomial model because it is the model that was first programmed into software packages such as LIMDEP (Greene 1998) and Stata (StataCorp. 2001) that were commonly used to model count data. As demonstrated by Land, McCall, and Nagin (1996), under the assumption that exp($\boldsymbol{\varepsilon}$)is distributed as $\Gamma(1, \alpha)$ and that $\boldsymbol{\varepsilon}$ is independent of **X**, the probability of observing the count y_{it} for the ith individual at time t in the NB2 model is:

$$\Pr(Y_{it} = y_{it}) = \int_0^{\infty} \Pr[Y_{it} = y_{it}, \lambda_{\text{it}}] f(\lambda_{\text{it}})\, d\lambda_{it} \tag{10}$$

$$= \left(\frac{\Gamma(y_{it} + v)}{y_{it}!\Gamma(v)}\right)\left(\frac{v}{v + \lambda_{\text{it}}}\right)^{v}\left(\frac{\lambda_{it}}{v + \lambda_{\text{it}}}\right)^{y_{it}}, \tag{11}$$

where $\lambda_{it} = \exp(\mathbf{X}_{it}\boldsymbol{\beta})$,$\Gamma(\cdot)$ is the gamma distribution, $v = 1/\alpha$, and $\alpha \geq 0$ (see also Cameron and Trivedi 1986). Estimates of α and $\boldsymbol{\beta}$ are obtained using maximum likelihood methods (Hausman, Hall, and Griliches 1984; Cameron and Trivedi 1998; Land, McCall, and Nagin 1996). Under this specification, the mean and variance are (Cameron and Trivedi 1986, 1998; Land, McCall, and Nagin 1996):

$$E(Y_{it}|\mathbf{X}_{it}) = \exp(\mathbf{X}_{it}\beta) = \lambda_{it} \tag{12}$$

and

$$\text{var}(Y_{it}|\mathbf{X}_{it}) = \lambda_{it}(1 + \alpha\lambda_{\text{it}}) = \lambda_{it} + \alpha\lambda_{it}^2. \tag{13}$$

Thus, the expected number of events is still equal to λ_{it}(or $\exp(\mathbf{X}_{it}\boldsymbol{\beta})$), but the variance is no longer constrained to be equal to the mean; there is now a quadratic relationship between the mean and variance.

Under the NB1 model, a change is made to equation (11): $v = \lambda/\alpha$ instead of $v = 1/\alpha$ (Cameron and Trivedi 1998; Long 1997). The mean and variance under the NB1 specification are:

$$E(Y_{it}|\mathbf{X}_{it}) = \exp(\mathbf{X}_{it}\beta) = \lambda_{it} \tag{14}$$

and

$$\text{var}(Y_{it}|\mathbf{X}_{it}) = \lambda_{it}(1 + \alpha\lambda_{\text{it}}) = \lambda_{it} + \alpha\lambda_{it}. \tag{15}$$

Thus, the expected number of events is still equal to λ_{it}, but the variance is now linearly related to the mean through the dispersion parameter.

Cameron and Trivedi (1998) recommend choosing between the NB1 and NB2 model on the basis of the log-likelihood values. The model with the larger (less negative) log-likelihood value is favored, since they both are estimated using the same number of parameters.[6] Substantively, however, the importance of the negative binomial model (whether specified as NB1 or NB2) is that individuals with identical values on the included covariates now have gamma distributed expected event counts, rather than being equal to the same conditional mean rate (as in the Poisson model).

In fact, the Poisson model is nested in the negative binomial model (Cameron and Trivedi 1986, 1998; Hardin and Hilbe 2001; Land, McCall, and Nagin 1996; Long 1997). The boundary or limiting case corresponds to $\alpha = 0$, under which the negative binomial model becomes the Poisson model. For example, if $\alpha = 0$ in equation (9), then we arrive back at the initial equidispersion assumption of the Poisson regression model found in equation (6). As Land, McCall, and Nagin (1996: 398) note, 'this circumstance corresponds to the limiting case where all individuals have the same λ_i, conditional on $\mathbf{X}_i$, which is precisely the assumption of the Poisson regression model.'

Of course, α as increases in size, so does the overdispersion of the data (Hardin and Hilbe 2001), and thus testing for the presence of significant overdispersion often becomes a primary task when modelling count data. The standard statistical test for assessing overdispersion involves testing the null hypothesis $H_N : \alpha = 0$ against its alternative, $H_A : \alpha > 0$. Because the Poisson model is a nested version of the negative binomial model, the test for significant overdispersion is frequently accomplished via a likelihood ratio test that compares the log-likelihood values of the negative binomial regression and Poisson regression models. The likelihood ratio test statistic is calculated as twice the difference in likelihood values, and this test statistic is distributed as χ^2 with one degree of freedom. While this is how the test for overdispersion has been calculated in the past, currently it is recognized that this form of the likelihood ratio test is incorrect in this particular situation. More specifically, because the dispersion parameter has to be greater than or equal to 0, the null hypothesis sits on the boundary of the parameter space (Self and Liang 1987; Gutierrez, Carter, and Drukker 2001). Because the null hypothesis is on the boundary of the parameter space, a critical regularity condition is violated—'the null parameter space is no longer interior to the full parameter space, and thus the result which states that the likelihood ratio test statistic tends towards χ_1^2 [chi-square with one degree of freedom] in distribution is untrue' (Gutierrez, Carter, and Drukker 2001: 16). As shown by Self and Liang

[6] The negative binomial models presented in Chapter 8 were estimated using both the NB1 and NB2 specifications. The NB1 specifications always had larger log-likelihood values, and thus the NB1 versions are the ones presented in Chapter 8. It should be noted, however, that the NB2 models generated identical substantive conclusions to those reached with the NB1 models.

(1987), the correct test statistic is a 50:50 mixture (χ^2_{01}) of (1) a chi-square distribution with a point mass at zero (χ^2_0) and (2) a chi-square distribution with 1 degree of freedom (χ^2_1). P-values calculated according to this $50:50$ χ^2_{01} mixture corresponds, in fact, to one-half the p-value calculated using only the upper tail area of the chi-square distribution with 1 degree of freedom.[7]

Land, McCall, and Nagin (1996) note that the negative binomial regression model is a significant generalization of the Poisson model because it accommodates overdispersion in count data while simultaneously keeping the suitable features necessary to model count data. However, Land, McCall, and Nagin (1996) also note that the negative binomial regression is also a restrictive model because it assumes that the heterogeneity is gamma distributed in the population, which maybe an arbitrary assumption. If this assumption is incorrect, the standard errors of the regression coefficients will be spuriously deflated leading to inflated t-ratios.

More importantly, however, the negative binomial regression model, in its most basic form (as specified in this section), completely ignores the dependence among observations when it is applied to panel data. This is significant because serial dependence among observations is known to be a significant cause of overdispersion in count data (Lindsey 1993, 1995; Winkelmann 1995, 1997; Dean 1998; Pickles 1998). Recall that overdispersion substantively implies that the model fails to account for why some subjects have greater or fewer total arrest events than other subjects, or stated differently, there is more heterogeneity in the outcome variable *among the individuals* than would be expected according to the probability distribution.

In the presence of panel data, the negative binomial model specified here is often referred to as a 'naïve pooling' model (Burton, Gurrin, and Sly 1998; Hardin and Hilbe 2001) because it *naively* treats the panel data set as a *pooled* sample consisting of N*T independent individuals rather than as simply N independent individuals each with T (or T_i if unbalanced) dependent observations (Hamerle and Ronning 1995). For example, the negative binomial model expressed above treats the extra variation as resulting purely from transient stochastic variation, rather than allowing a main component of the extra variation to be caused *explicitly* by the stochastic dependence between the observations within the N individuals (Cameron and Trivedi 1998; Dean 1998; Lindsey 1993). Within each individual, each 'draw' (i.e. for a given 'age' record) of the random effect from the gamma distribution is completely independent of the other draws for that individual (i.e. for the other 'age' records of that individual). Stated more emphatically, the standard version of the negative binomial model (that ignores the panel structure of the data) does not control for persistent

[7] See the simulations of Gutierrez, Carter, and Drukker (2001) for an example.

unobserved heterogeneity, or as Hsiao (1986: 158) notes, 'statistical models developed for analyzing cross-sectional data essentially ignore individual differences.' The stochastic variation of the event counts for each individual's panel records is viewed as having been generated by chance—there is no serial dependence of the individual's records. A 'shortcoming of the negative binomial model is that it does not allow for firm [individual] specific effects so that serial correlation of the residuals (i.e., non-independence of the counts) may be a problem' (Hausman, Hall, and Griliches 1984: 922–3).

This failure to correct for the dependence among the observations is particularly critical for the topic of this study because the 'naïve pooled' negative binomial model completely ignores two possible sources of overdispersion in the data—population heterogeneity and state dependence—because it ignores the serial dependence within the data (Cameron and Trivedi 1998; Dean 1998; Hsiao 1986; Lindsey 1993, 1995). For example, if 'individuals who have experienced an event in the past are more likely to experience the event in the future than are individuals who have not previously experienced the event,' then this will induce overdispersion in the data (Heckman 1981*b*: 91). In such cases the key question is whether this overdispersion (which is a consequence of the serial dependence) is the result of a process of contagion/state dependence, population heterogeneity, or possibly both of these processes.[8] These two sources of overdispersion are the same two explanations discussed in Chapter 2 as fundamentally critical to our study (because they are rival hypotheses in explaining the relationship between past and future criminal activity). As Hamerle and Ronning (1995: 411–12) state, ignoring 'heterogeneity among cross-sections or time-series units [individuals] could lead to inconsistent or meaningless estimates of the structural parameters ... controlling for heterogeneity is in most applications a means to obtain consistent estimates of the systematic part of the model.'

For example, suppose in the pooled negative binomial model one were to find a significant association between a binary indicator of arrest at the previous age and arrest at the current age. In the standard negative binomial model, the process underlying this significant association would be indeterminable because the effects of persistent individual differences are left uncontrolled in this model. Lindsey (1993: 157) pointedly remarks, 'if a missing variable [underlying criminal propensity] can be assumed constant

[8] This issue has been raised not only in studies of criminal behaviour but also in studies of accidents (Bates and Neyman 1952; Greenwood and Yule 1920), unemployment (Heckman 1981*b*; Heckman and Borjas 1980), bouts of schizophrenia (Kessing, Olsen, and Andersen 1999) and emotional distress (Fischer *et al.* 1984; Robins 1966, 1978), and Medicare claims for Alzheimer's/dementia among the elderly (Taylor, Fillenbaum, and Ezell 2002).

over all events on a unit, but differs among units, this will yield stochastic dependence among the events on each unit,' and this missing variable will, in fact, 'induce an effect identical to apparent contagion' or state dependence.

It has been shown, however, that the unique structure of panel data can be exploited to investigate the above two critical sources of serial correlation of an outcome variable across waves or periods (Cameron and Trivedi 1998; Hamerle and Ronning 1995; Heckman 1981*a*; Hsiao 1986; Powers and Xie 2000). For example, in an early study investigating whether population heterogeneity or state dependence was driving overdispersion in accident data, Neyman (1965: 6) noted that the distinction between these two processes would be possible if 'one has at one's disposal data on accidents incurred by each individual separately for two periods of six months each.' Thus, with multiple waves or periods of data on a set of individuals, models can be estimated that attempt to disentangle the effects of population heterogeneity from those of state dependence by specifically incorporating sources of 'hidden' or unobserved heterogeneity into the model specification.

Accounting for Serial Dependence: Persistent Individual Differences

In this section, we discuss the two most common methods that are used to control for persistent individual differences in panel data: parametric random effects models and semiparametric random effects models.[9] Before presenting the technical aspects of each formulation, we first broadly compare the two different methods on the basis of how each model accounts for persistent unobserved heterogeneity.

In the parametric random effects model, the error term is specified to be composed of two components (Hamerle and Ronning 1995; Heckman 1981*a*; Hsiao 1986; Nagin and Paternoster 1991):

$$\varepsilon_{it} = \alpha_i + u_{it}, \qquad (16)$$

where α_i represents a persistent (time-stable) individual-specific component that is assumed to follow a specific parametric distribution and u_{it} is a stochastic component that follows some specified parametric distribution. Thus, the parametric random effects model assumes that the persistent

[9] Fixed effects estimators are not included here or employed in this study because fixed effects models with lagged values of the outcome variable prohibit inclusion of time trends or age effects (Bushway, Brame, and Paternoster 1999; Cameron and Trivedi 1998; Hamerle and Ronning 1995). Due to the incredibly strong relationship between age and crime (see Chapter 7), these models are clearly inappropriate for modeling crime data and therefore are not considered here.

unobserved heterogeneity follows a known, mathematically tractable parametric distribution that is specified by the user.

The semiparametric random effects model, on the other hand, makes no parametric assumption about the distribution of unobserved heterogeneity, but rather this method non-parametrically approximates the distribution of persistent unobserved heterogeneity via a set of discrete 'points of support'. The method only assumes that the distribution of unobserved heterogeneity can be approximated by a discrete multinomial probability distribution (Heckman and Singer 1984; Land, McCall, and Nagin 1996; Nagin 1999; Nagin and Land 1993).

Graphically speaking, this is an example of the classic approach in statistics of approximating a continuous distribution with a discrete distribution. This is often shown by taking a continuous distribution and graphing that distribution using a histogram (which uses a discrete number of 'bins' or bars). Using this analogy, the 'points of support' would be the histogram 'bins' propping-up the continuous distribution. Nagin and Land (1993), Land, McCall, and Nagin (1996) and Nagin (2004) all contain graphical representations of this process.

The distinction between these two methods can be viewed in the light of the tension in statistics that is ever-present between 'parametric' and 'non-parametric' methods (Bushway, Brame, and Paternoster 1999). Parametric methods are more restrictive methods, but if the parametric assumption is appropriate *in the population*, then this method of estimation will be more statistically efficient (i.e. it will have less variance from sample to sample). The non-parametric methods are less efficient if the true distribution is a (mathematically tractable) known continuous distribution, but since these methods do not assume that the mixing distribution follows a restrictive mathematical parametric form *a priori*, they can approximate any continuous distribution regardless of its shape.

As Nagin and Tremblay (1999: 1188) note, 'the cost of approximation is obvious. Approximations are just that—there is a loss of accuracy. Balanced against this are gains in generality and flexibility. Generally we have no empirical or theoretical basis for specifying the distribution of the growth curve parameters [random effects] within the population.' The choice of a parametric mixing distribution is generally made purely on the fact that the some distributions (e.g. conjugate distributions) make the model more mathematically tractable because they ensure that the marginal density of such models have a closed form solution (Cameron and Trivedi 1998). For example, in the standard (single record per individual) Poisson model, the gamma distribution is the conjugate distribution that allows for a closed form solution to the negative binomial regression model. Although in some situations the available mathematically tractable mixing distribution makes substantive sense, while in other cases this is unlikely to be true. Indeed, this was the precise reasoning of the thought behind the development of finite mixture models: a particular mixture distribution does not have to be used simply because it is mathematically tractable. The discrete mixture methods allow the data to *speak for themselves* with respect to the nature and extent of unobserved heterogeneity.

Parametric Random Effects Negative Binomial Model

The parametric random effects specification of the negative binomial model was first presented by Hausman, Hall, and Griliches (1984), who specified it as

$$\ln(\lambda_{it}) = \mathbf{X}_{it}\boldsymbol{\beta} + \varepsilon_{it}, \qquad \varepsilon_{it} = \alpha_i + u_{it}. \tag{17}$$

This specification differs from the negative binomial specification of equation (7) in the decomposition of the error term, which in the standard model is specified as $\varepsilon_{it} = u_{it}$. In the random effects formulation of the negative binomial model, the decomposition of the error term results in one component, α_i, representing the fixed, individual-specific component, and one component, u_{it}, representing the transitory stochastic variation. Substantively this model allows for randomness both between-individuals and within-individual across time (or age) (Hausman, Hall, and Griliches 1984: 927).[10] The random effects negative binomial model yields a negative binomial model for the ith group that has constant dispersion within the ith group, but the dispersion varies randomly between groups. According to this model,

$$\Pr(Y_{it} = y_{it}|\delta_i) = \left(\frac{\Gamma(\lambda_{\text{it}} + y_{it})}{\Gamma(\lambda_{\text{it}})\Gamma(y_{it} + 1)}\right)\left(\frac{1}{1 + \delta_{\text{i}}}\right)^{\lambda_{it}}\left(\frac{\delta_{\text{i}}}{1 + \delta_{\text{i}}}\right)^{y_{it}}. \tag{18}$$

Further, in this the model the ratio $1/(1 + \delta_i)$ is assumed to be randomly distributed according to the beta distribution, with the r and s parameters of the beta distribution, $B(r, s)$, estimated from the data at-hand.[11] This results in the following joint probability of events counts for the ith group

[10] The Poisson random effects model for panel data, which generally assumes gamma distributed heterogeneity, only allows for the individual-specific component (which accounts for between-individual differences) (Cameron and Trivedi 1998; Hamerle and Ronning 1995; Hausman, Hall, and Griliches 1984).

[11] This model was estimated using Stata Version 7 (StataCorp. 2001). The distribution of dispersion (noted here) programmed into Stata is the inverse of the Hausman, Hall, and Griliches (1984) method, which is just a technical preference of StataCorp. Regardless of the whether δ is estimated using the parameterization employed by Hausman, Hall, and Griliches (1984), or the inverse parameterization employed in Stata, the resulting solutions are identical.

(Hausman, Hall, and Griliches 1984):

$$\Pr(Y_{i1} = y_{i1}, Y_{i2} = y_{i2}, \ldots, Y_{in_i} = y_{in_i}) \tag{19}$$

$$= \int_0^{\infty} \prod_{t=1}^{n_i} pr[Y_{it} = y_{it}|\delta_i] f(\delta_i)\, d\delta_i \tag{20}$$

$$= \left(\frac{\Gamma(r+s)\Gamma\left(r + \sum_{t=1}^{n_i} \lambda_{\text{it}}\right)\Gamma\left(s + \sum_{t=1}^{n_i} y_{\text{it}}\right)}{\Gamma(r)\Gamma(s)\Gamma\left(r + s + \sum_{t=1}^{n_i} \lambda_{\text{it}} + \sum_{t=1}^{n_i} y_{\text{it}}\right)} \right) \prod_{t=1}^{n_i} \frac{\Gamma(\lambda_{it} + y_{it})}{\Gamma(\lambda_{it})\Gamma(y_{it} + 1)}, \tag{21}$$

where $n_i = T_i$ or $\max(t)$ for the ith individual, and the log-likelihood for equation (21) is (StataCorp. 2001: 393)

$$\begin{aligned} \ln L = {} & \sum_{i=1}^{n} \ln \Gamma(r+s) + \ln \Gamma\left(r + \sum_{t=1}^{n_i} \lambda_{\text{it}}\right) + \ln \Gamma\left(s + \sum_{t=1}^{n_i} y_{\text{it}}\right) \\ & - \ln\Gamma(r) - \ln(s) - \ln\Gamma\left(r + s + \sum_{t=1}^{n_i} \lambda_{\text{it}} + \sum_{t=1}^{n_i} y_{\text{it}}\right) \\ & + \sum_{t=1}^{n_i} [\ln \Gamma(\lambda_{\text{it}} + y_{it}) - \ln \Gamma(\lambda_{\text{it}}) - \ln(y_{it} + 1)] \end{aligned} \tag{22}$$

The beta distribution is a flexible distribution because it has two parameters (Greene 2000), but it should be remembered that the beta distribution is used in the negative binomial random effects model precisely because it produces a mathematically tractable expression that allows the unobserved random effects to be integrated out without encountering serious numerical complications. Instead of assuming that the unobserved heterogeneity is distributed according to the beta distribution, we next discuss the semi-parametric formulation whereby a discrete set of nonparametric 'random effects' are used to account for unobserved heterogeneity. This method also allows us to investigate the nature of the age–crime relationship within latent classes of serious youthful offenders.

The Semiparametric Mixed Poisson Model

Before describing the technical aspects of the semiparametric mixed Poisson model, we first present a non-technical discussion of the semiparametric mixed Poisson model.[12] In brief, the model assumes that the distribution of

[12] It should be noted here that while this discussion centres on the Poisson version of the finite mixture model, the finite mixture model is a general class of models that extends far beyond the formulation of the model on the basis of the Poisson distribution. Finite mixture models can be estimated for any distribution in the exponential or multivariate exponential family (see Nagin 1999; Vermunt and Magidson 2000; and Wedel and Kamakura 1998).

unobserved heterogeneity can be 'segmented' into a finite number of discrete groups—each of the groups are internally homogeneous with respect to the nature of the unobserved heterogeneity within the group, but there is significant heterogeneity between the groups. According to Nagin and Land (1993) (see also Land, McCall, and Nagin 1996), the simplest specification of this model is

$$\ln\left(\lambda^{\mathrm{j}}_{\mathrm{it}}\right) = (\boldsymbol{\beta}_0 + \varepsilon_j) + \mathbf{X}_{it}\boldsymbol{\beta}, \tag{23}$$

where $\boldsymbol{\beta}_0$ is the overall constant of the model, $\bar{\varepsilon}_j$ is a constant term that is specific to the jth discrete group or latent class ($j = 1, 2, \ldots, J$), $\mathbf{X}_{it}$ is a matrix of measured covariates on individual i at time t, and $\boldsymbol{\beta}$ is a column vector of regression coefficients.[13] Cameron and Trivedi (1998: 129) refer to this model as a *random intercept model* because each latent class has a separate constant or intercept parameter assigned to it. The effects of the regression coefficients are constrained to be equal across the groups, and the latent classes differ only with respect to their 'location parameter'. Nagin and Land (1993) describe this model as producing 'constant shifts' in the mean rate. That is, the trajectories of each class are identical in shape, but they differ in the mean location of the trajectory. It bears noting that this is the precise specification that corresponds to Gottfredson and Hirschi's hypothesis concerning the robust nature of the relationship between age and crime—groups differ on their mean offending rate, but the actual shapes of the trajectories are identical.

The bare essence of this finite mixture model is that the finite number of intercept coefficients—there is a separate intercept coefficient for each group or 'point of support'—represent the 'average contribution' of persistent unobserved heterogeneity to the expected Poisson rate for 'individuals possessing levels of unobserved heterogeneity in the immediate vicinity of the jth point of support' (Nagin and Land 1993: 338). This model was subsequently referred to as semiparametric in nature because it 'combines a parametric specification of the regression component of the model with a nonparametric specification of the error term' (Land and Nagin 1996: 170).

Nagin and Land (1993) also present a more general form of the mixture model

$$\ln\left(\lambda^{\mathrm{j}}_{\mathrm{it}}\right) = (\boldsymbol{\beta}_0 + \bar{\varepsilon}_j) + \mathbf{X}_{it}\boldsymbol{\beta}^j \tag{24}$$

where $\boldsymbol{\beta}^j$ is a vector of group-specific regression coefficients. By permitting the regression coefficients to vary across the latent classes, this model allows for full heterogeneity not just in the 'location', but also in the nature

[13] The latent classes or groups are also commonly referred to as the mixture 'components' (Cameron and Trivedi 1998) and 'segments' (Wedel and Kamakura 1998).

of each latent class's offending trajectory over time. It is also possible for some of the regression coefficients to be constrained so that they are equal across the latent classes, while also simultaneously allowing other coefficients to vary across the latent classes. Wedel *et al.* (1993) refer to this type of model as a model with random effects in both the intercept and slope parameters. For example, consider the case where the **X** matrix contains two variables: age and age-squared. By permitting the age coefficients (i.e. growth parameters) to vary across the latent classes, this specification of the mixed model not only allows for heterogeneity in the mean event rate at a given time t, but also for the developmental shape of the trajectories (Nagin 1999; Nagin and Tremblay 1999).

Before concluding this discussion of these finite mixture models, it may be helpful to discuss briefly the more technical side of these models.[14] Let us begin by denoting individual i's longitudinal offending sequence as the vector $\mathbf{Y}_i = [y_{i1}, y_{i2}, \ldots, y_{iTi}]$, and allow m_j to denote a random variable indicating the proportion of the data set estimated to belong to the jth point of support. The random variable m_j is postulated as a draw from a 'super-population'—the super population is an additive 'mixture' of J discrete populations (Cameron and Trivedi 1998: 128). It is important to note that all of the model parameters in the finite mixture model are jointly estimated, including the proportion of the data set that is estimated to belong to the jth point of support. The estimated proportion belonging to each latent class is calculated using the logit function

$$m_j = \frac{\exp(\Theta_j)}{\sum\limits_j \left[\exp(\Theta_j)\right]}, \tag{25}$$

where the following constraints are imposed: $m^j \geq 0$ and. $\sum_j m^j = 1$. The probability of observing y_{it} events for individual i in time period t in group j is

$$f(y_{it}; \lambda_j), \tag{26}$$

where $f(\bullet)$ is the Poisson density function, and the probability of the entire sequence of individual i at the jth point of support is (Land *et al.* 1996)

$$P^j(Y_i|\Theta^j) = \prod_t f(y_{it}; \lambda_j)\cdot \tag{27}$$

Now the unconditional probability of observing individual i's longitudinal sequence can be calculated by aggregating the likelihood function

[14] Readers interested in further details than presented here are referred to Land, McCall, and Nagin (1996), Land and Nagin (1996), Nagin (1999), Nagin and Land (1993), Roeder *et al.* (1999), Wedel *et al.* (1993), and Wedel and Kamakura (1998).

(i.e. aggregating the conditional likelihoods) for individual i over the j points of support according to

$$P(Y_i) = \sum_j m^j \bullet P^j(Y_i|\Theta^j), \quad m^j \geq 0, \quad \sum_j m^j = 1, \tag{28}$$

which is simply the probability of Y_i at the each of the jth point of supports multiplied by the proportion of the population estimated at that point of support and then summed over the J points of support (Land, McCall, and Nagin 1996). The log-likelihood function of this model is

$$\ln L = \sum_i \ln(P(Y_i)) = \sum_i \ln\left(\sum_j m^j \bullet P^j(Y_i|\Theta^j)\right). \tag{29}$$

Of course, a key issue related to the finite mixture model concerns the number of points of supports/latent classes/groups to include in the mixture (D'Unger *et al.* 1998).[15] In other words, how does one decide how many points of support to include in the model? Unfortunately, a finite mixture model with $J = 2$ mixture components is not nested in the model with $J = 3$ components, and therefore a likelihood ratio test statistic cannot be used to determine the number of components in the mixture distribution 'because there is not a unique way of obtaining the null hypothesis from the alternative hypothesis' (D'Unger *et al.* 1998; Ghosh and Sen 1985; Land, McCall, and Nagin 1996: 424; Nagin 1999; Titterington, Smith, and Makov 1985). More specifically, one is prevented from calculating the appropriate degrees of freedom for the likelihood ratio test.

Given this problem with the likelihood ratio test, alternative methods of determining the number of mixture components have been recommended. For example, D'Unger *et al.* (1998) propose the use of the Bayesian Information Criterion (BIC) statistic as a basis of selecting the appropriate number of groups in the mixing distribution (see also Nagin 1999). The BIC statistic is calculated as:

$$\text{BIC} = \log(L) - 0.5 * \log(N) * (k) \tag{30}$$

where $\log(L)$ is the model log-likelihood value, N is the sample size, and k is the number of estimated parameters. The BIC statistic rewards parsimony because each additional fitted parameter results in a 'penalty' proportional to the log of the sample size (Kass and Raftery 1995; Raftery 1995; Nagin 1999). In short, the BIC statistic follows the principle of 'Occam's Razor' and values parsimony; nonetheless, the substantive goal

[15] To connect this issue back to the 'urn schemes' discussion in Chapter 2, this issue is directly related to the 'total number of urns in the population' (Nagin and Paternoster 2000: 120).

of the BIC statistic is the same as the likelihood ratio statistic—find the best model with the fewest number of parameters. The model that has the least negative value of the BIC statistic is the favored model (Nagin 1999).

The selection of the optimal number of points of supports for the mixing distribution is complicated by the fact that mixture models are known to often have a problem with 'local solutions' (i.e. a unique global solution is not always achieved) (Cameron and Trivedi 1998; Goodman 1974; Vermunt and Magidson 2000; Wedel and Kamakura 1998). This issue concerns whether the likelihood function is unimodal or multimodal—it is possible for the model's algorithm to converge to a local maximum, which is not a true global solution. Simulations by Wedel and Kamakura (1998) indicate that the probability of a local solution increases (1) as the number of mixture components increases; (2) as the number of parameters estimated increases (e.g. including a large number of covariates); (3) when the mixture components are not well separated, resulting in *weak identification* of the model (i.e. the model is 'overparameterized' and the estimated groups are not that dissimilar); and (4) when using the Poisson and binomial probability distributions. Several authors have recommend testing for the presence of local solutions through the use of multiple sets of starting values in order to test for the presence of local solutions (see, e.g., Cameron and Trivedi 1998, Greene 2000; Vermunt and Magidson 2000; Wedel and Kamakura 1998). In this study, we follow the recommendations of D'Unger *et al.* (1998) and Nagin (1999) and guide the selection of the optimum number of mixture components using the BIC statistic. We also undertake extensive testing for the presence of local solutions.

While the finite mixture model is a method of controlling for unobserved heterogeneity, depending on the goals of a particular analysis, each individual can be 'assigned' to the latent class to which the individual has the highest probability of belonging. Analyses can then be conducted using either the latent class membership variables (the set of J binary variables indicating whether the individual was assigned to the jth latent class) or within each of the 'latent classes' (i.e. using only the individuals assigned to a particular latent class) (Nagin and Paternoster 2000). For example, graphs of the offending trajectories depicting the relationship between age and crime within each of the latent classes could then be computed. Another alternative is to include the set of J binary variables in regression models as variables that control for persistent unobserved heterogeneity (see Laub *et al.* 1998 for an example).

Thus, often times one of the key steps of the application of finite mixture models is to sort the individuals in the sample into the latent class for which they have the highest probability of belonging. As shown in Nagin (1999), the *posterior probability* of membership in the jth latent class for individual i is calculated as

$$\hat{P}(j|Y_i) = \frac{\hat{P}(Y_i|j)\hat{m}_j}{\sum_j \hat{P}(Y_i|j)\hat{m}_j}. \tag{31}$$

This probability represents the estimated probability (based on the model coefficients) of observing individual i's longitudinal sequence (i.e. their longitudinal record of arrest charges), $\mathbf{Y}_i$, given membership in the jth latent class, and the estimated proportion of the population in latent class j. These J probabilities are calculated after model estimation based on the maximum likelihood estimates of the model (i.e. on the basis of an *ex post facto* comparison); heuristically, each individual's observed trajectory is compared against the predicted trajectory of each latent class, and they are then assigned to the latent class that is most similar to their observed trajectory. The posterior probabilities provide substantive information on the precision of group assignment, with probabilities larger in magnitude indicating more precision in the assignment of individuals to a particular latent class. The posterior probabilities 'are among the most useful products of the group-based modeling approach' (Nagin 1999: 149) because they allow for the assignment of each individual to a particular latent class, which then allows for simple graphical and tabular analyses of the characteristics of the members of the latent classes and their offending behaviors (Nagin 2004).

Appendix B

APPENDIX B. Percentage of cases 'at risk' of arrest at each age, by sample

Age	*Sample*					
	1981–2		*1986–7*		*1991–2*	
	N	%	N	%	N	%
7	1,989	100.00	1,443	100.00	1,434	100.00
8	1,989	100.00	1,443	100.00	1,434	100.00
9	1,989	100.00	1,443	100.00	1,434	100.00
10	1,989	100.00	1,443	100.00	1,434	100.00
11	1,989	100.00	1,443	100.00	1,434	100.00
12	1,989	100.00	1,443	100.00	1,434	100.00
13	1,989	100.00	1,443	100.00	1,434	100.00
14	1,984	99.75	1,440	99.79	1,426	99.44
15	1,965	98.79	1,428	98.96	1,405	97.98
16	1,941	97.59	1,372	95.08	1,317	91.84
17	1,905	95.78	1,274	88.29	1,193	83.19
18	1,850	93.01	1,175	81.43	1,053	73.43
19	1,863	93.67	1,241	86.00	1,197	83.47
20	1,883	94.67	1,332	92.31	1,323	92.26
21	1,926	96.83	1,397	96.81	1,353	94.35
22	1,963	98.69	1,401	97.09	1,368	95.40
23	1,957	98.39	1,407	97.51	1,381	96.30
24	1,955	98.29	1,405	97.37	1,374	95.82
25	1,948	97.94	1,407	97.51	1,333	92.96
26	1,934	97.23	1,394	96.60	1,236	86.19
27	1,927	96.88	1,387	96.12	999	69.67
28	1,917	96.38	1,378	95.50	656	45.75
29	1,904	95.73	1,366	94.66	338	23.57
30	1,898	95.42	1,339	92.79	197	13.74
31	1,891	95.07	1,261	87.39	126	8.79
32	1,879	94.47	1,049	72.70	62	4.32
33	1,867	93.87	751	52.04	10	0.70
34	1,841	92.56	474	32.85	—	—
35	1,739	87.43	263	18.23	—	—
36	1,553	78.08	184	12.75	—	—
37	1,243	62.49	113	7.83	—	—
38	896	45.05	51	3.53	—	—
39	529	26.60	—	—	—	—
40	252	12.67	—	—	—	—
41	89	4.47	—	—	—	—
42	25	1.26	—	—	—	—
43	6	0.30	—	—	—	—
Total Panel observ.	60,453		37,390		29,385	

Appendix C

The following resources are available at the web site noted below:

Offenses Seriousness Hierarchy and Categorization of Offense Type
Cumulative Ages of Onset of First Criminal Arrest
Means of Background Characteristic Variables, by Latent Class
Observed and Predicted Arrest Trajectories, by Latent Class
California Youth Authority Resources

Website Location: http://people.vanderbilt.edu/~mike.ezell/oupbook.htm

References

Agnew, Robert (1992). 'Foundation for a General Strain Theory of Crime and Delinquency'. *Criminology*, 30: 47–87.

Aguilar, Benjamin, Sroufe, L. Alan, Egeland, Byron, and Carlson, Elizabeth (2000). 'Distinguishing the Early-Onset/Persistent and Adolescence-Onset Antisocial Behavior Types: From Birth to 16 Years'. *Development and Psychopathology*, 12: 109–32.

Akers, Ronald (1985). *Deviant Behavior: A Social Learning Approach*. Belmont, Calif.: Wadsworth.

——(1991). 'Self-Control as a General Theory of Crime'. *Journal of Quantitative Criminology*, 7: 201–11.

Allison, Paul D. (1995). *Survival Analysis using the SAS System*. Cary, NC: SAS Institute.

Ayers, Charles D., Williams, James Herbert, Hawkins, J. David, Peterson, Peggy L., Catalano, Richard F., and Abbott, Robert D. (1999). 'Assessing Correlates of Onset, Escalation, Deescalation, and Desistance of Delinquent Behavior'. *Journal of Quantitative Criminology*, 15: 277–306.

Baltes, P. and Nesselroade, J. (1984). 'Paradigm Lost and Paradigm Regained: Critique of Dannefer's Portrayal of Life-Span Developmental Psychology'. *American Sociological Review*, 49: 841–6.

Barlow, Hugh (1991). 'Explaining Crimes and Analogous Acts, or Will the Unrestrained Grab at Pleasure Whenever They Can'. *Journal of Criminal Law and Criminology*, 82: 229–42.

Bates, G. and Neyman, J. (1952). 'Contributions to the Theory of Accident Proneness. II: True or False Contagion'. *University of California Publications in Statistics*, 1: 255–75.

Beccaria, Cesare (1963). *On Crimes and Punishment*. Trans. Henry Paolucci. Indianapolis: Bobbs-Merrill.

Becker, Gary S. (1968). 'Crime and Punishment: An Economic Approach'. *Journal of Political Economy*, 76: 169–217.

Benson, Michael L. (2002). *Crime and the Life Course*. Los Angeles: Roxbury Publishing Company.

Bernard, Thomas J. and Ritti, R. Richard (1991). 'The Philadelphia Birth Cohort and Selective Incapacitation'. *Journal of Research in Crime and Delinquency*, 28: 35–54.

Bernberg, Jon Gunnar and Krohn, Marvin D. (2003). 'Labeling, Life Chances, and Adult Crime: The Direct and Indirect Effects of Official

Intervention in Adolescence on Crime in Early Adulthood'. *Criminology*, 41: 1287–1318.

Blumstein, A. and Beck, Allen J. (1999). 'Population Growth in U.S. Prisons, 1980–1996', in M. Tonry and J. Petersilia (eds.), *Crime and Justice: A Review of Research*. Chicago: University of Chicago Press, pp. 17–61.

——and Cohen, J. (1979). 'Estimation of Individual Crime Rates from Arrest Records'. *Journal of Criminal Law and Criminology*, 70: 561–85.

——(1987). 'Characterizing Criminal Careers'. *Science*, 237: 985–91.

——and Farrington, D. (1988*a*). 'Criminal Career Research: Its Value for Criminology'. *Criminology*, 26: 1–36.

——and Farrington, D. (1988*b*). 'Longitudinal and Criminal Career Research: Further Clarifications'. *Criminology*, 26: 57–74.

——Roth, J., and Visher, C. A. (1986). *Criminal Careers and 'Career Criminal'*. Washington, DC: National Academy Press.

Bolen, Jane (1972). 'The California Youth Authority 1941–1971: Structure, Policies and Practices', School of Social Work, University of Southern California.

Braithwaite, John (1989). *Crime, Shame and Reintegration*. Cambridge, UK: Cambridge University Press.

Brame, Robert and Piquero, Alex R. (2003). 'Selective Attrition and the Age–Crime Relationship'. *Journal of Quantitative Criminology*, 19: 107–27.

——Bushway, Shawn, and Paternoster, Raymond (1999). 'On the Use of Panel Research Designs and Random Effects Models to Investigate Static and Dynamic Theories of Criminal Offending'. *Criminology*, 37: 599–641.

——Paternoster, Raymond, Mazerolle, Paul, and Piquero, Alex R. (1998). 'Testing for the Equality of Maximum-Likelihood Regression Coefficients between Two Independent Equations'. *Journal of Quantitative Criminology*, 14: 245–61.

Britt, C. L. (1992). 'Constancy and Change in the U.S. Age Distribution of Crime: A Test of the "Invariance Hypothesis"'. *Journal of Quantitative Criminology*, 8: 175–87.

Bureau of Justice Statistics (1995). *Prisoners in 1994*. Washington, DC: US Government Printing Office.

——(2000). *Sourcebook of Criminal Justice Statistics*. Washington, DC: US Government Printing Office.

——(2001). *Prisoners in 2000*. Washington, DC: US Government Printing Office.

Burton, Paul, Gurrin, Lyle, and Sly, Peter (1998). 'Extending the Simple Linear Regression Model to Account for Correlated Responses: An

Introduction to Generalized Estimating Equations and Multi-Level Mixed Modeling'. *Statistics in Medicine*, 17: 1261–91.

Bushway, Shawn, Brame, Robert, and Paternoster, Raymond (1999). 'Assessing Stability and Change in Criminal Offending: A Comparison of Random Effects, Semiparametric, and Fixed Effects Modeling Strategies'. *Journal of Quantitative Criminology*, 15: 23–61.

——Piquero, Alex R., Broidy, Lisa M., Cauffman, Elizabeth, and Mazerolle, Paul (2001). 'An Empirical Framework for Studying Desistance as a Process'. *Criminology*, 39: 491–515.

California Department of Justice (1999). *Crime and Delinquency in California, 1998*. Sacramento: California Department of Justice.

——(2000). *Crime and Delinquency in California, 1999*. Sacramento: California Department of Justice.

——(2001). *Crime and Delinquency in California, 2000*. Sacramento: California Department of Justice.

California Youth Authority (1971). *An Analysis of Institution Lengths of Stay by Selected Variables*. Sacramento: Department of the Youth Authority.

——(1981). *Analysis of Institutional and Parole Lengths of Stay, 1980*. Sacramento: Department of the Youth Authority.

——(1991). *Length of Stay of Youth Authority Wards Institutionalized and on Parole during 1990*. Sacramento: Department of the Youth Authority.

——(1999). *Length of Stay of Youth Authority Wards*. Sacramento: Department of the Youth Authority.

——(2001). *Annual Report 2001: Program Description and Statistical Summary*. Sacramento: Department of the Youth Authority.

Cameron, A. Colin and Trivedi, Pravin K. (1986). 'Econometric Models Based on Count Data: Comparisons and Applications of Some Estimators'. *Journal of Applied Econometrics*, 1: 29–53.

——(1998). *Regression Analysis of Count Data*. Cambridge: Cambridge University Press.

Canela-Cacho, Jose, Blumstein, Alfred, and Cohen, Jacqueline (1997). 'Relationship between the Offending Frequency of Imprisoned and Free Offenders'. *Criminology*, 35: 133–71.

Caplow, Theodore and Simon, Jonathon (1999). 'Understanding Prison Policy and Population Trends', in M. Tonry and J. Petersilia (eds.), *Crime and Justice: A Review of Research*. Chicago: University of Chicago Press, pp. 63–120.

Caspi, Avshalom, Lynam, D., Moffitt, Terrie E., and Silva, P. A. (1993). 'Unraveling Girls' Delinquency: Biological, Dispositional, and Contextual Contributions to Adolescent Misbehavior'. *Developmental Psychology*, 29: 19–30.

Caspi, Avshalom and Moffitt, Terrie E. (1992). 'The Continuity of Maladaptive Behavior: From Description to Understanding in the Study of Antisocial Behavior', in D. Cicchetti and D. Cohen (eds.), *Manual of Developmental Psychopathology*. New York: Wiley, pp. 472–511.

——and Moffitt, Terrie E. (1993). 'When Do Individual Differences Matter? A Paradoxical Theory of Personality Coherence'. *Psychological Inquiry*, 4: 247–71.

Cernkovich, Stephen A. and Giordano, Peggy C. (2001). 'Stability and Change in Antisocial Behavior: The Transition from Adolescence to Early Adulthood'. *Criminology*, 39: 371–410.

——and Pugh, M. D. (1985). 'Chronic Offenders: The Missing Cases in Self-Report Delinquency Research'. *Journal of Criminal Law and Criminology*, 76: 705–32.

Chung, Ick-Joong, Hill, Karl G., Hawkins, J. David, Gilchrist, Lewayne D., and Nagin, Daniel S. (2002). 'Childhood Predictors of Offense Trajectories'. *Journal of Research in Crime and Delinquency*, 39: 60–90.

Cline, H. F. (1980). 'Criminal Behavior over the Life Span', in O. Brim and J. Kagan (eds.), *Constancy and Change in Human Development*, Cambridge, Mass.: Harvard University Press, pp. 641–74.

Clogg, Clifford C., Petkova, Eva, and Haritou, Adamantios (1995). 'Statistical Methods for Comparing Regression Coefficients between Models'. *American Journal of Sociology*, 100: 1261–93.

Cohen, Lawrence E. (1987). 'Throwing Down the Gauntlet: A Challenge to the Relevance of Sociology for the Etiology of Criminal Behavior'. *Contemporary Sociology*, 16: 202–5.

——and Land, Kenneth C. (1987). 'Age Structure and Crime: Symmetry Versus Asymmetry and the Projection of Crime Rates through the 1990s'. *American Sociological Review*, 52: 170–83.

——and Vila, Bryan J. (1996). 'Self-Control and Social-Control: An Exposition of the Gottfredson–Hirschi/Sampson–Laub Debate'. *Studies on Crime and Crime Prevention*, 5: 125–50.

Coleman, James S. (1988). 'Social Capital in the Creation of Human Capital'. *American Journal of Sociology*, 94: 95–120.

——(1990). *Foundations of Social Theory*. Cambridge, Mass.: Harvard University Press.

Collin, A. Colin and Trivedi, Pravin K. (1996). 'Count Data Models for Financial Data', in G. Maddala and C. Rao (eds.), *Handbook of Statistics*, Volume 14, *Statistical Methods in Finance*. Amsterdam: North-Holland.

Dannefer, Dale (1984). 'Adult Development and Social Theory: A Paradigmatic Reappraisal'. *American Sociological Review*, 49: 100–16.

——(1987). 'Aging as Intracohort Differentiation: Accentuation, the Matthew Effect, and the Life Course'. *Sociological Forum*, 2: 211–36.

Dean, Charles W., Brame, Robert, and Piquero, Alex R. (1996). 'Criminal Propensities, Discrete Groups of Offenders, and Persistence in Crime'. *Criminology*, 34: 547–74.

Dean, Charmaine B. (1998). 'Overdispersion', in P. Armitage and T. Colton (eds.), *Encyclopedia of Biostatistics*. Chichester, NY: John Wiley & Sons, pp. 3226–32.

Dempster, A. P., Laird, N. M., and Rubin, D. B. (1977). 'Maximum Likelihood Estimation from Incomplete Data via the EM Algorithm (with Discussion)'. *Journal of the Royal Statistical Society, Series B*, 39: 1–38.

DeMuro, Paul, DeMuro, Anne, and Lerner, Steve (1988). *Reforming the California Youth Authority*. Bolinas, Calif.: Common Knowledge Press.

Dobrin, Adam (2001). 'The Risk of Offending on Homicide Victimization: A Case Control Study'. *Journal of Research in Crime and Delinquency*, 38: 154–73.

Donziger, Steven R. (ed.) (1996). *The Real War on Crime*. New York: Harper Collins.

D'Unger, Amy V., Land, Kenneth C., and McCall, Patricia L. (2002). 'Gender Differences in Age Patterns of Delinquent/Criminal Careers: Results from Poisson Latent Class Analysis of the Philadelphia Cohort Study'. *Journal of Quantitative Criminology*, 18: 349–76.

——and Nagin, Daniel S. (1998). 'How Many Latent Classes of Delinquent/Criminal Careers? Results from Mixed Poisson Regression Analyses'. *American Journal of Sociology*, 103: 1593–1630.

Durkheim, Émile ([1897] 1951). *Suicide*. Trans. J. Spaulding and G. Simpson. Repr. New York: Free Press.

Eggleston, Elaine P., Laub, John H., and Sampson, Robert J. (2004). 'Methodological Sensitivities to Latent Class Analysis of Long-Term Criminal Trajectories'. *Journal of Quantitative Criminology*, 20: 1–26.

Elder, Glen H., Jr (1985). 'Perspectives on the Life Course', in Glen H. Elder, Jr, *Life Course Dynamics*. Ithaca, NY: Cornell University Press, pp. 23–49.

——(1992). 'The Life Course', in E. F. Borgatta and M. L. Borgatta (eds.), *The Encyclopedia of Sociology*. New York: Macmillan, pp. 1120–30.

——(1996). 'Human Lives in Changing Societies: Life Course and Developmental Insights', in R. B. Cairns, Glen H. Elder, and E. J. Costello (eds.), *Developmental Science*. Cambridge: Cambridge University Press, pp. 31–62.

——and O'Rand, Angela M. (1995). 'Adult Lives in a Changing Society', in K. S. Cook, G. A. Fine, and J. S. House (eds.), *Sociological Perspectives in Social Psychology*. Boston: Allyn & Bacon, pp. 452–75.

Elliot, Delbert S. (1994). 'Serious Violent Offenders: Onset, Developmental Course, and Termination—The American Society of Criminology 1993 Presidential Address'. *Criminology*, 32: 1–21.

Ezell, Michael E. and Cohen, Lawrence E. (1997). 'Age, Crime, and Crime Control Policies: A Longitudinal Analysis of Youthful, Serious, Chronic Offenders with Implications for the "Three Strikes" Legislation'. *Studies on Crime and Crime Prevention*, 6: 169–99.

Farrington, David P. (1983). *Further Analyses of a Longitudinal Survey of Crime and Delinquency*. Final Report to the National Institute of Justice. Washington, DC: National Institute of Justice.

—— (1986). 'Age and Crime', in M. Tonry and N. Morris (eds.), *Crime and Justice: An Annual Review of Research*. Chicago: University of Chicago Press, pp. 189–250.

—— (1989). 'Self-Reported and Official Offending from Adolescence to Adulthood', in M. Klein (ed.), *Cross-National Research in Self-Reported Crime and Delinquency*. Dordrecht: Kluwer, pp. 399–423.

—— (1997). 'Human Development and Criminal Careers', in M. Maguire, R. Morgan, and R. Reiner (eds.), *The Oxford Handbook of Criminology*. Oxford: Clarendon Press, pp. 361–408.

—— (2003). 'Developmental and Life-Course Criminology: Key Theoretical and Empirical Issues—The 2002 Sutherland Award Address'. *Criminology*, 41: 221–556.

—— Loeber, Rolf, Elliot, Delbert S., Hawkins, David, Kandel, Denise B., Klein, Malcolm W., McCord, Joan, Rowe, David C., and Tremblay, Richard E. (1991). 'Advancing Knowledge about the Onset of Delinquency and Crime', in Benjamin B. Lahey and Alan E. Kazdin (eds.), *Advances in Clinical Child Psychology*, Volume 13. New York: Plenum, pp. 283–342.

Fergusson, David M., Horwood, L. John, and Nagin, Daniel S. (2000). 'Offending Trajectories in a New Zealand Birth Cohort'. *Criminology*, 38: 525–51.

Fischer, M., Rolf, J. E., Hasazi, J. E., and Cummings, L. (1984). 'Follow-up of a Pre-School Epidemiological Sample: Cross Age Continuities and Predictions of Later Adjustment with Internalizing and Externalizing Dimensions of Behavior'. *Child Development*, 55: 137–50.

Ge, Xiaojia, Donnellan, M. Brent, and Wenk, Ernst (2001). 'The Development of Persistent Criminal Offending in Males'. *Criminal Justice and Behavior*, 28: 731–55.

Geerken, Michael R. (1994). 'Rap Sheets in Criminological Research: Considerations and Caveats'. *Journal of Quantitative Criminology*, 10: 3–21.

Ghosh, J. K. and Sen, P. K. (1985). 'On the Asymptotic Performance of the Log-Likelihood Ratio Statistic for the Mixture Model and Related Results', in L. M. LeCam and P. A. Olshen (eds.), *Proceedings of the*

Berkeley Conference in Honor of Jerry Neyman and Jack Kiefer, Volume 2. Monterey, Calif.: Wadsworth, pp. 789–806.

Gibbons, Don C. (1982). *Society, Crime, and Criminal Behavior*. Englewood Cliffs, NJ: Prentice Hall.

Gladstone, Mark and Rainey, James (1999). 'Abuse Reports Cloud Youth Authority'. *Los Angeles Times*, 24 December, A1.

Glueck, Sheldon and Glueck, Eleanor (1950). *Unraveling Juvenile Delinquency*. Cambridge, Mass.: Harvard University Press.

——(1968). *Delinquents and Nondelinquents in Perspective*. Cambridge, Mass.: Harvard University Press.

Goodman, L. A. (1974). 'Exploratory Latent Structure Analysis Using Both Identifiable and Unidentifiable Models'. *Biometrika*, 61: 215–31.

Gottfredson, Michael R. and Hirschi, Travis (1986). 'The True Value of Lambda Would Appear to be Zero: An Essay on Career Criminals, Criminal Careers, Selective Incapacitation, Cohort Studies, and Related Topics'. *Criminology*, 24: 213–33.

——(1987*a*). 'The Methodological Adequacy of Longitudinal Research on Crime'. *Criminology*, 25: 581–614.

——(1987*b*). *Positive Criminology*. Newbury Park, Calif.: Sage Publications.

——(1988). 'Science, Public Policy, and the Career Paradigm'. *Criminology*, 26: 37–55.

——(1990). *A General Theory of Crime*. Stanford, Calif.: Stanford University Press.

Gourieroux, C., Monfort, A., and Trognon, A. (1984*a*). 'Pseudo Maximum Likelihood Methods: Theory'. *Econometrica*, 52: 681–700.

——(1984*b*). 'Pseudo Maximum Likelihood Methods: Applications to Poisson Models'. *Econometrica*, 52: 701–29.

Gove, Walter R. (1985). 'The Effect of Age and Gender on Deviant Behavior: A Biopsychological Perspective', in A. S. Rossi (ed.), *Gender and the Life Course*. New York: Aldine de Gruyter, pp. 115–44.

Grasmick, Harold G., Tittle, Charles R., Bursik, Robert J., Jr, and Arneklev, Bruce J. (1993). 'Testing the Core Empirical Implications of Gottfredson and Hirschi's General Theory of Crime'. *Journal of Research in Crime and Delinquency*, 30: 5–29.

Greenberg, David F. (1977). 'Delinquency and the Age Structure of Society'. *Contemporary Crises*, 1: 189–224.

——(1985). 'Age, Crime, and Social Explanation'. *American Journal of Sociology*, 91: 859–66.

Greene, William H. (1998). *LIMDEP, Version 7.0*. Belport, NY: Econometric Software.

——(2000). *Econometric Analysis*, 4th edn. Upper Saddle River, NJ: Prentice Hall, Inc.

Greenwood, M. and Yule, G. U. (1920). 'An Inquiry into the Nature and Frequency Distributions Representative of Multiple Happenings with Particular Reference to the Occurrence of Multiple Attacks or of Repeated Accidents'. *Journal of the Royal Statistical Society*, 83: 255–79.

Gutierrez, Roberto G., Carter, Shana, and Drukker, David M. (2001). 'On Boundary-Value Likelihood-Ratio Tests'. *Stata Technical Bulletin*, 60: 15–20.

Haapanen, Rudy (1990). *Selective Incapacitation and the Serious Offender: A Longitudinal Study of Criminal Career Patterns*. New York: Springer-Verlag.

——and Britton, Lee (2002). 'Drug Testing for Youthful Offenders on Parole: An Experimental Evaluation'. *Criminology and Public Policy*, 1: 217–44.

——and Ingram, Wes (2000). *California Youth Authority Mental Health and Substance Abuse Treatment Needs Assessment: Description and Preliminary Findings*. Sacramento, Calif.: California Youth Authority.

Haberman, S. J. (1988). 'A Stabilized Newton-Raphson Algorithm for Log-Linear Models for Frequency Tables Derived by Indirect Observation', in C. Clogg (ed.), *Sociological Methodology 1988*. San Francisco: Jossey-Bass, pp. 193–211.

Hagan, John and Palloni, Alberto (1988). 'Crimes as Social Events in the Life Course: Reconceiving a Criminological Controversy'. *Criminology*, 26: 87–100.

Hamerle, Alfred and Ronning, Gerd (1995). 'Panel Analysis for Qualitative Variables', in G. Arminger, C. C. Clogg, and M. E. Sobel (eds.), *Handbook of Statistical Modeling for the Social and Behavioral Sciences*. New York: Plenum Press, pp. 401–52.

Hardin, James and Hilbe, Joseph (2001). *Generalized Linear Models and Extensions*. College Station, Tex.: Stata Corporation.

Hausman, Jerry, Hall, Bronwyn H., and Griliches, Zvi (1984). 'Econometric Models for Count Data with an Application to the Patents–R&D Relationship'. *Econometrica*, 52: 909–39.

Heckman, James J. (1981*a*). 'Statistical Models for Discrete Panel Data', in C. F. Manski and D. Mcfadden (eds.), *Structural Analysis of Discrete Data with Econometric Applications*. Cambridge, MA: MIT Press, pp. 147–78.

——(1981*b*). 'Heterogeneity and State Dependence', in S. Rosen (ed.), *Studies in Labor Markets*. Chicago: University of Chicago Press, pp. 91–139.

——(1981*c*) 'The Incidental Parameters Problem and the Problem of Initial Conditions in Estimating a Discrete Time-Discrete Stochastic Process', in C. F. Manski and D. McFadden (eds.), *Structural Analysis of Discrete Data with Econometric Applications*. Cambridge, MA: MIT Press, pp. 179–95.

——and Borjas, J. George (1980). 'Does Unemployment Cause Future Unemployment? Definitions, Questions and Answers from a Continuous Time Model of Heterogeneity and State Dependence'. *Economica*, 47: 247–83.

——and Singer, Burton (1984). 'A Method for Minimizing the Impact of Distributional Assumptions in Econometric Models for Duration Analysis'. *Econometrica*, 52: 909–38.

Hindelang, M. J., Hirschi, Travis, and Weis, J. G. (1979). 'Correlates of Delinquency: The Illusion of Discrepancy between Self-Report and Official Measures'. *American Sociological Review*, 44: 995–1014.

——(1981). *Measuring Delinquency*. Beverly Hills, Calif.: Sage Publications.

Hirschi, Travis (1969). *Causes of Delinquency*. Berkeley: University of California Press.

——(1995). 'The Family', in J. Q. Wilson and J. Petersilia (eds.), *Crime*. San Francisco: Institute for Contemporary Studies Press, pp. 121–40.

——and Gottfredson, Michael R. (1983). 'Age and the Explanation of Crime'. *American Journal of Sociology*, 89: 552–84.

——(1985). 'Age and Crime, Logic and Scholarship: Comment on Greenberg'. *American Journal of Sociology*, 89: 552–84.

——(1988). 'Toward a General Theory of Crime', in W. Buikhuisen and S. Mednick (eds.), *Explaining Criminal Behavior*. Leiden: E. J. Brill, pp. 8–26.

——(1993). 'Commentary: Testing the General Theory of Crime'. *Journal of Research in Crime and Delinquency*, 30: 47–54.

Horney, Julie, Osgood, D. Wayne, and Marshall, Ineke Haen (1995). 'Criminal Careers in the Short-Term: Intra-Individual Variability in Crime and its Relation to Local Life Circumstances'. *American Sociological Review*, 60: 655–73.

Hsiao, Cheng (1986). *Analysis of Panel Data*. Cambridge: Cambridge University Press.

Huizinga, D. and Elliott, D. S. (1986). 'Reassessing the Reliability and Validity of Self-Report Measures'. *Journal of Quantitative Criminology*, 2: 293–327.

Humes, Edward (1996). *No Matter How Loud I Shout*. New York: Touchstone.

Irwin, John and Austin, James (1997). *It's about Time: America's Imprisonment Binge*. Belmont, Calif.: Wadsworth Publishing Company.

Jeffrey, C. (1972). 'The Historical Development of Criminology', in H. Mannheim (ed.), *Pioneers in Criminology*. Montclair: Patterson-Smith.

Kass, Robert E. and Raftery, Adrian E. (1995). 'Bayes Factors'. *Journal of the American Statistical Association*, 90: 773–95.

Keribin, C. (1997). 'Consistent Estimation of the Order of Mixture Models (Working Paper #61)'. Université d'Evry-val d'Essonne, Laboratorie Analyse et Probabilité.

Kessing, Lars Vedal, Olsen, Elisabeth Wreford, and Andersen, Per Kragh (1999). 'Recurrence of Affective Disorder: Analysis with Frailty Models'. *American Journal of Epidemiology*, 149: 404–11.

King, Gary (1988). 'Statistical Models for Political Science Event Counts: Bias in Conventional Procedures and Evidence for the Exponential Poisson Regression Model'. *American Journal of Political Science*, 32: 838–63.

——(1989). 'Variance Specification in Event Count Models: From Restrictive Assumptions to a Generalized Estimator'. *American Journal of Political Science*, 33: 762–84.

Klein, Malcolm W. (1995). 'Street Gang Cycles', in J. Q. Wilson and J. Petersilia (eds.), *Crime*. San Francisco: Institute for Contemporary Studies, pp. 217–36.

Klevens, Joanne, Restrepo, Ofelia, Roca, Juanita, and Martinez, Adriana (2000). 'Comparison of Offending with Early- and Late-Starting Antisocial Behavior in Colombia'. *Criminology*, 44: 194–203.

Krisberg, Barry (2003). *General Corrections Review of the California Youth Authority*. San Francisco: National Council on Crime and Delinquency.

Lahey, Benjamin B., Goodman, Sherryl H., Waldman, Irwin D., Bird, Hector, Canino, Glorisa, Jensen, Peter, Regier, Darrel, Leaf, Philip J., Gordon, Rachel, and Applegate, Brooks (1999). 'Relation of Age of Onset to the Type and Severity of Child and Adolescent Conduct Problems'. *Journal of Abnormal Child Psychology*, 27: 247–60.

Lambert, D. (1992). 'Zero-Inflated Poisson Regression, with an Application to Defects in Manufacturing'. *Technometrics*, 34: 1–14.

Land, Kenneth C. (1992). 'Models of Criminal Careers: Some Suggestions for Moving Beyond the Current Debate'. *Criminology*, 30: 149–55.

——and Nagin, Daniel S. (1996). 'Micro-Models of Criminal Careers: A Synthesis of the Criminal Careers and Life Course Approaches via Semiparametric Mixed Poisson Regression Models, with Empirical Applications'. *Journal of Quantitative Criminology*, 12: 163–91.

——McCall, Patricia L., and Nagin, Daniel S. (1996). 'A Comparison of Poisson, Negative Binomial, and Semiparametric Mixed Poisson Regression Models'. *Sociological Methods and Research*, 24: 387–442.

——Nagin, Daniel S., and McCall, Patricia L. (2001). 'Discrete-Time Hazard Regression Models with Hidden Heterogeneity'. *Sociological Methods and Research*, 29: 342–73.

Lattimore, Pamela K., Linster, Richard L., and MacDonald, John M. (1997). 'Risk of Death among Serious Young Offenders'. *Journal of Research in Crime and Delinquency*, 34: 187–209.

Laub, John H. and Sampson, Robert J. (1988). 'Unraveling Families and Delinquency: A Reanalysis of the Gluecks' Data'. *Criminology*, 26: 355–79.
——(1993). 'Turning Points in the Life Course: Why Change Matters to the Study of Crime'. *Criminology*, 31: 301–25.
——(1998). 'The Long-Term Reach of Adolescent Competence: Socioeconomic Achievement in the Lives of Disadvantaged Men', in A. Colby, J. James, and D. Hart (eds.), *Competence and Character through Life*. Chicago: University of Chicago Press, pp. 89–112.
——(2001). 'Understanding Desistence from Crime', in M. Tonry (ed.), *Crime and Justice: An Annual Review of Research*. Chicago: University of Chicago Press, pp. 1–69.
——(2003). *Shared Beginnings, Divergent Lives: Delinquent Boys to Age 70*. Cambridge, Mass.: Harvard University Press.
——Nagin, Daniel S., and Sampson, Robert J. (1998). 'Trajectories of Change in Criminal Offending: Good Marriages and the Desistance Process'. *American Sociological Review*, 63: 225–38.
——Sampson, Robert J., Corbett, Jr, Ronald P., and Smith, Jinny S. (1995). 'The Public Policy Implications of a Life-Course Perspective on Crime', in H. D. Barlow (ed.), *Crime and Public Policy*. Boulder, Colo.: Westview Press, pp. 91–106.
Lauritsen, Janet L. (1998). 'The Age–Crime Debate'. *Social Forces*, 77: 127–55.
——(1999). 'Limitations in the Use of Longitudinal Self-Report Data: A Comment'. *Criminology*, 37: 687–94.
LeBlanc, M. and Loeber, R. (1998). 'Developmental Criminology Updated', in Michael Tonry and Mark H. Moore (eds.), *Crime and Justice: An Annual Review of Research*. Chicago: University of Chicago Press, pp. 115–98.
Legislative Analyst's Office (1994). *Crime in California*. Sacramento: State of California.
——(1995). *Juvenile Crime*. Sacramento: State of California.
——(1996). *Analysis of the 1996–97 Budget*. Sacramento: State of California.
——(2001). *Analysis of the 2001–02 Budget Bill*. Sacramento: State of California.
Lemert, E. M. (1972). *Human Deviance, Social Problems, and Social Control*. Englewood Cliffs, NJ: Prentice Hall.
Lerner, Steve (1982). *The CYA Report: Conditions of Life at the California Youth Authority*. Bolinas, Calif.: Common Knowledge Press.
——(1986). *Bodily Harm: The Pattern of Fear and Violence at the California Youth Authority*. Bolinas, Calif.: Common Knowledge Press.
——(1989). *The Good News about Juvenile Justice*. Bolinas, Calif.: Common Knowledge Press.

Lindsey, J. K. (1993). *Models for Repeated Measurements*. Oxford: Clarendon Press.

——(1995). *Modelling Frequency and Count Data*. Oxford: Clarendon Press.

Little Hoover Commission (1994). *The Juvenile Crime Challenge: Making Prevention a Priority*. Sacramento: State of California.

Loeber, Rolf (1982). 'The Stability of Antisocial and Delinquent Child Behavior: A Review'. *Child Development*, 53: 1431–46.

——and Farrington, David P. (1998). 'Conclusions and the Way Forward', in R. Loeber and D. P. Farrington (eds.), *Serious and Violent Juvenile Offenders*. Thousand Oaks, Calif.: Sage Publications, pp. 405–27.

——and LeBlanc, M. (1990). 'Toward a Developmental Criminology', in M. Tonry and N. Morris (eds.), *Crime and Justice: A Review of Research*. Chicago: University of Chicago Press, pp. 375–473.

——and Stouthamer-Loeber, Magda (1996). 'The Development of Offending'. *Criminal Justice and Behavior*, 23: 12–24.

——(1998). 'The Development of Juvenile Aggression and Violence: Some Common Misconceptions and Controversies'. *American Psychologist*, 52: 242–59.

——Farrington, David P., and Waschbusch, Daniel A. (1998). 'Serious and Violent Juvenile Offenders', in R. Loeber and D. P. Farrington (eds.), *Serious and Violent Juvenile Offenders*. Thousand Oaks, Calif.: Sage Publications, pp. 13–29.

Long, J. Scott (1997). *Regression Models for Categorical and Limited Dependent Variables*. Thousand Oaks, Calif.: Sage Publications.

Maddala, G. S. (1987). 'Limited Dependent Variable Models Using Panel Data'. *Journal of Economic Resources*, 22: 307–38.

Maltz, Michael D. (1984). *Recidivism*. Orlando: Academic Press.

——(1994). 'Deviating from the Mean: The Declining Significance of Significance'. *Journal of Research in Crime and Delinquency*, 31: 434–63.

Maxson, Cheryl L. (1999). 'Gang Homicide: A Review and Extension of the Literature', in M. Dwayne Smith and Margaret A. Zahn (eds.), *Homicide: A Sourcebook of Social Research*. Thousand Oaks, Calif.: Sage Publications, pp. 239–54.

Mazerolle, Paul, Brame, Robert, Paternoster, Ray, Piquero, Alex, and Dean, Charles (2000). 'Onset Age, Persistence, and Offending Versatility: Comparisons across Gender'. *Criminology*, 38: 1143–72.

McCord, Joan (1980). 'Patterns of Deviance', in S. Sells, R. Crandall, M. Roff, J. S. Strauss, and W. Pollin (eds.), *Human Functioning in Longitudinal Perspective*. Baltimore: Williams and Wilkins, pp. 157–65.

McCullagh, P. and Nelder, J. A. (1989). *Generalized Linear Models*. London: Chapman & Hall.

McDermott, Joan (1983). 'The Serious Juvenile Offender: Problems in Definition and Targeting', in James R. Kluegel (ed.), *Evaluating Juvenile Justice*. Beverly Hills, Calif.: Sage Publications, Inc., pp. 67–90.

McDermott, Shaun and Nagin, Daniel S. (2001). 'Same or Different? Comparing Offender Groups and Covariates over Time'. *Sociological Methods and Research*, 29: 282–318.

Moffitt, Terrie E. (1993). 'Adolescence-Limited and Life-Course-Persistent Antisocial Behavior: A Developmental Taxonomy'. *Psychological Review*, 100: 674–701.

——(1997). 'Adolescence-Limited and Life-Course-Persistent Offending: A Complementary Pair of Developmental Theories', in T. P. Thornberry (ed.), *Developmental Theories of Crime and Delinquency. Advances in Criminological Theory*, Volume 7. New Brunswick: Transaction Publishers, pp. 11–54.

Mullahy, J. (1986). 'Specification and Testing of Some Modified Count Data Models'. *Journal of Econometrics*, 33: 341–65.

Nagin, Daniel S. (1999). 'Analyzing Developmental Trajectories: A Semiparametric, Group-Based Approach'. *Psychological Methods*, 4: 139–57.

——(2004). 'Response to "Methodological Sensitivities to Latent Class Analysis of Long-Term Criminal Trajectories"'. *Journal of Quantitative Criminology*, 20: 27–35.

——and Farrington, David P. (1992*a*). 'The Stability of Criminal Potential from Childhood to Adulthood'. *Criminology*, 30: 235–59.

——and Farrington David P. (1992*b*). 'The Onset and Persistence of Offending'. *Criminology*, 30: 501–23.

——and Land, Kenneth C. (1993). 'Age, Criminal Careers, and Population Heterogeneity: Specification and Estimation of a Nonparametric, Mixed Poisson Model'. *Criminology*, 31: 327–62.

——and Paternoster, Raymond (1991). 'On the Relationship of Past to Future Participation in Delinquency'. *Criminology*, 29: 163–89.

——and Paternoster, Raymond (1993). 'Enduring Individual Differences and Rational Choice Theories of Crime'. *Law and Society Review*, 27: 467–96.

——and Paternoster, Raymond (1994). 'Personal Capital and Social Control: The Deterrence Implications of a Theory of Individual Differences in Criminal Offending'. *Criminology*, 32: 581–606.

——and Paternoster, Raymond (2000). 'Population Heterogeneity and State Dependence: State of the Evidence and Directions for Future Research'. *Journal of Quantitative Criminology*, 16: 117–44.

——and Tremblay, Richard E. (1999). 'Trajectories of Boys' Physical Aggression, Opposition, and Hyperactivity on the Path to Physically Violent and Nonviolent Juvenile Delinquency'. *Child Development*, 70: 1181–96.

Nagin, Daniel S., Farrington, David P., and Moffitt, Terrie E. (1995). 'Life-Course Trajectories of Different Types of Offenders'. *Criminology*, 33: 111–37.

Nelder, J. A. and Wedderburn, R. W. M. (1972). 'Generalized Linear Models'. *Journal of the Royal Statistical Society, Series B*, 135: 370–84.

Neyman, J. (1965). 'Certain Chance Mechanisms Involving Discrete Distributions', in G. N. Patil (ed.), *Classical and Contagious Discrete Distributions*. Calcutta: Statistical Publishing House, pp. 1–14.

Paternoster, Raymond and Brame, Robert (1997). 'Multiple Routes to Delinquency? A Test of Developmental and General Theories of Crime'. *Criminology*, 35: 49–84.

——and Farrington, David P. (2001). 'On the Relationship between Adolescent and Adult Conviction Frequencies'. *Journal of Quantitative Criminology*, 17: 201–25.

——Mazerolle, Paul, and Piquero, Alex (1998). 'Using the Correct Statistical Test for the Equality of Regression Coefficients'. *Criminology*, 36: 859–66.

——Dean, Charles W., Piquero, Alex, Mazerolle, Paul, and Brame, Robert (1997). 'Generality, Continuity, and Change in Offending'. *Journal of Quantitative Criminology*, 13: 231–66.

Patterson, Gerald R. (1995). 'Orderly Change in a Stable World: The Antisocial Trait as a Chimera', in J. M. Gottman (ed.), *The Analysis of Change*. Mahwah, NJ: Lawrence Erlbaum Associates, Inc., pp. 83–102.

——and Yoerger, Karen (1993). 'Developmental Models for Delinquent Behavior', in S. Hodgins (ed.), *Mental Disorder and Crime*. Newbury Park, Calif.: Sage Publications, pp. 140–72.

——DeBaryshe, Barbara B., and Ramsey, Elizabeth (1989). 'A Developmental Perspective on Antisocial Behavior'. *American Psychologist*, 44: 329–35.

——Reid, John B., and Dishon, Thomas J. (1992). *Antisocial Boys*. Eugene, Ore.: Castilia Publishing Co.

Pickles, A. (1998). 'Generalized Estimating Equations', in P. Armitage and T. Colton (eds.), *Encyclopedia of Biostatistics*. Chichester, NY: John Wiley & Sons, pp. 1626–36.

Piquero, Alex R. and Brezina, Timothy (2001). 'Testing Moffitt's Account of Adolescence-Delimited Delinquency'. *Criminology*, 39: 353–70.

——Farrington, David P., and Blumstein, Alfred (2003). 'The Criminal Career Paradigm: Background and Recent Developments', in M. Tonry (ed.), *Crime and Justice: A Review of Research*, Volume 30. Chicago: University of Chicago Press, pp. 137–83.

——MacIntosh, Randall, and Hickman, Matthew (2002). 'The Validity of a Self-Reported Delinquency Scale'. *Sociological Methods and Research*, 30: 492–529.

——Paternoster, Raymond, Mazerolle, Paul, Brame, Robert, and Dean, Charles W. (1999). 'Onset Age and Offense Specialization'. *Journal of Research in Crime and Delinquency*, 36: 275–99.

——Blumstein, Alfred, Brame, Robert, Haapanen, Rudy, Mulvey, Edward P., and Nagin, Daniel S. (2001). 'Assessing the Impact of Exposure Time and Incapacitation on Longitudinal Trajectories of Criminal Offending'. *Journal of Adolescent Research*, 16: 54–74.

Powers, Daniel A. and Xie, Yu (2000). *Statistical Methods for Categorical Data Analysis*. San Diego: Academic Press.

Raftery, Adrian E. (1995). 'Bayesian Model Selection in Social Research'. *Sociological Methodology*, 25: 111–64.

Rainey, James and Gladstone, Mark (1999). 'Another Try at Youth Justice Reform'. *Los Angeles Times*, 25 December, A1.

Riley, Mathilda White (1986). 'Overview and Highlights of a Sociological Perspective', in A. Sorensen, F. Weinert, and L. Sherrod (eds.), *Human Development and the Life Course: Multidisciplinary Perspectives*. Hillsdale, NJ: Lawrence Erlbaum, pp. 153–75.

Robins, Lee N. (1966). *Deviant Children Grown Up*. Baltimore: Williams & Wilkins.

——(1978). 'Sturdy Childhood Predictors of Adult Antisocial Behavior'. *Psychological Medicine*, 8: 611–22.

Roeder, Kathryn, Lynch, Kevin G., and Nagin, Daniel S. (1999). 'Modeling Uncertainty in Latent Class Membership: A Case Study in Criminology'. *Journal of the American Statistical Association*, 94: 766–76.

Rutter, Michael and Rutter, Marjorie (1993). *Developing Minds: Challenge and Continuity across the Life Span*. New York: Basic Books.

Sampson, Robert J. (1992). 'A General Theory of Crime'. *Social Forces*, 71: 545–6.

——(1998). 'Continuity and Discontinuity in Criminal Careers'. *Social Forces*, 76: 1149–50.

——(2000). 'Whither the Sociological Study of Crime?'. *American Sociological Review*, 26: 711–14.

——and Laub, John H. (1990). 'Crime and Deviance over the Life Course: The Salience of Adult Social Bonds'. *American Sociological Review*, 55: 609–27.

——and Laub, John H. (1992). 'Crime and Deviance in the Life Course'. *Annual Review of Sociology*, 18: 63–84.

——and Laub, John H. (1993). *Crime in the Making: Pathways and Turning Points through Life*. Cambridge, Mass.: Harvard University Press.

——and Laub, John H. (1996). 'Socioeconomic Achievement in the Life Course of Disadvantaged Men'. *American Sociological Review*, 61: 347–67.

Sampson, Robert J. and Laub, John H. (1997). 'A Life-Course Theory of Cumulative Disadvantage and the Stability of Delinquency', in T. P. Thornberry (ed.), *Developmental Theories of Crime and Delinquency. Advances in Criminological Theory*, Volume 7. New Brunswick: Transaction Publishers, pp. 133–61.

—— and Laub, John H. (2003). 'Life Course Desisters? Trajectories of Crime among Delinquent Boys Followed to Age 70'. *Criminology*, 41: 555–92.

—— and Laub, John H. and Eggleston, Elaine P. (2004). 'On the Robustness and Validity of Groups'. *Journal of Quantitative Criminology*, 20: 37–42.

Scholte, Evert M. (1999). 'Factors Predicting Continued Violence into Young Adulthood'. *Journal of Adolescence*, 22: 3–20.

Self, S. G. and Liang, K. Y. (1987). 'Asymptotic Properties of Maximum Likelihood Estimators and Likelihood-Ratio Tests under Nonstandard Conditions'. *Journal of the American Statistical Association*, 82: 605–10.

Shannon, Lyle W. (1988). *Criminal Career Continuity*. New York: Human Sciences Press.

—— (1991). *Changing Patterns of Delinquency and Crime: A Longitudinal Study in Racine*. Boulder, Colo.: Westview Press.

—— McKim, J. L., Curry, J. P., and Haffner, L. J. (1988). *Criminal Career Continuity: Its Social Context*. New York: Human Sciences Press.

Shavit, Yossi and Rattner, Arye (1988). 'Age, Crime, and the Early Life Course'. *American Journal of Sociology*, 6: 1457–70.

Skonovd, Norman (1986). *Youth Authority Institutional Length of Stay and Recidivism: California Juvenile Arrest Rates and Guidelines for Parole Consideration Dates*. Sacramento, Calif.: Department of the Youth Authority.

—— and Haapanen, Rudy (2000). *Predicting Parole Performance in the Era of Crack Cocaine*. Sacramento, Calif.: Department of the Youth Authority.

Snyder, H. (2002). *Juvenile Arrests 2000*. Washington, DC: Office of Juvenile Justice and Delinquency Prevention.

StataCorp. (2001). *Stata Statistical Software: Release 7.0*. College Station, Tex.: Stata Corporation.

State of California (1941). *California: Statutes and Amendments to the Codes. (Chapter 937)*. Sacramento: State of California.

—— (1993). *California Youth Authority Committee Report*. Sacramento: State of California.

—— (1996). *California Task Force to Review Juvenile Crime and the Juvenile Justice Response: Final Report*. Sacramento: State of California.

Steffensmeier, D. S. and Harer, M. D. (1987). 'Is the Crime Rate Really Falling? An "Aging" U.S. Population and Its Impact on the Nation's Crime Rate, 1980–1984'. *Journal of Research in Crime and Delinquency*, 24: 23–48.

——Allan, E. A., Harer, M. D., and Streifel, C. (1989). 'Age and the Distribution of Crime'. *American Journal of Sociology*, 94: 803–31.

Sutherland, Edwin H. and Cressey, Donald R. (1978). *Criminology*. 10th edn. Philadelphia: J. B. Lippincott.

Taylor, Donald H., Fillenbaum, Gerda G., and Ezell, Michael E. (2002). 'The Accuracy of Medicare Claims Data in Identifying Alzheimer's Disease'. *Journal of Clinical Epidemiology*, 55: 929–37.

Thornberry, Terence P. (1989). 'Reflections on the Advantages and Disadvantages of Theoretical Integration', in S. F. Messner, M. D. Krohn, and A. E. Liska (eds.), *Theoretical Integration in the Study of Deviance and Crime*. Albany: State University of New York Press, pp. 51–60.

——and Krohn, Marvin D. (2001). 'The Development of Delinquency, an Interactional Perspective', in Susan O. White (ed.), *Handbook of Youth and Justice*. New York: Kluwer Academic/Plenum Press, pp. 289–305.

Titterington, D. M., Smith, A. F. M., and Makov, U. E. (1985). *Statistical Analysis of Finite Mixture Distributions*. Chichester, UK: Wiley.

Tittle, Charles (1988). 'Two Empirical Regularities (Maybe) in Search of an Explanation: Commentary on the Age–Crime Debate'. *Criminology*, 26: 75–86.

——(1995). *Control Balance toward a General Theory of Deviance*. Boulder, Colo.: Westview Press.

——and Grasmick, Harold G. (1998). 'Criminal Behavior and Age: A Test of Three Provocative Hypotheses'. *Journal of Criminal Law and Criminology*, 88: 309–42.

Tolan, Patrick H. and Gorman-Smith, Deborah (1998). 'Development of Serious and Violent Offending Careers', in R. Loeber and D. P. Farrington (eds.), *Serious and Violent Juvenile Offenders*. Thousand Oaks, Calif.: Sage Publications, pp. 68–85.

Tolan, Patrick H. and Thomas, Peter (1995). 'The Implications of Age of Onset for Delinquency Risk II: Longitudinal Data'. *Journal of Abnormal Child Psychology*, 23: 157–69.

Tracy, Paul E. and Kempf-Leonard, Kimberly (1996). *Continuity and Discontinuity in Criminal Careers*. New York: Plenum Press.

Tracy, Paul E., Wolfgang, M. E., and Figlio, R. M. (1985). *Delinquency in Two Birth Cohorts, Executive Summary*. Washington, DC: US Government Printing Office.

——(1990). *Delinquency Careers in Two Birth Cohorts*. New York: Plenum Press.

Vermunt, Jeroen and Magidson, Jay (2000). *Latent GOLD User's Manual*. Belmont, Mass.: Statistical Innovations, Inc.

Vold, George B., Bernard, Thomas J., and Snipes, Jeffrey B. (1998). *Theoretical Criminology*. New York: Oxford University Press.

Walker, Samuel (1998). *Sense and Nonsense about Crime and Drugs.* Belmont, Calif.: Wadsworth Publishing Company.

Wang, Peiming, Cockburn, Iain M., and Puterman, Martin L. (1998). 'Analysis of Patent Data—A Mixed-Poisson-Regression-Model Approach'. *Journal of Business and Economic Statistics*, 16: 27–41.

Wedel, Michel and Kamakura, Wagner A. (1998). *Market Segmentation.* Boston: Kluwer Academic Publishers.

Wedel, W., DeSarbo, W. S., Bult, J. R., and Ramaswamy, V. (1993). 'A Latent Class Poisson Regression Model for Heterogeneous Count Data'. *Journal of Applied Econometrics*, 8: 397–411.

Weitekamp, E. G. M., Kerner, H. J., Schindler, V., and Schubert, A. (1995). 'On the "Dangerousness of Chronic/Habitual Offenders": A Re-Analysis of the 1945 Philadelphia Birth Cohort Data'. *Studies on Crime and Crime Prevention*, 4: 159–75.

West, D. J. and Farrington, D. P. (1973). *Who Becomes Delinquent?* London: Heinemann.

——(1977). *The Delinquent Way of Life*. London: Heinemann.

Wilson, James Q. and Herrnstein, Richard (1985). *Crime and Human Nature*. New York: Simon and Schuster.

Wilson, Jeffrey, Rojas, Neal, Haapanen, Rudy, Duxbury, Elaine, and Steiner, Hans (2001). 'Substance Abuse and Criminal Recidivism: A Prospective Study of Adolescents'. *Child Psychiatry and Human Development*, 31: 297–312.

Winkelmann, Ranier (1995). 'Duration Dependence and Dispersion in Count-Data Models'. *Journal of Business and Economic Statistics*, 13: 467–74.

——(1997). *Econometric Analysis of Count Data*. New York: Springer.

Wolfgang, M. E., Figlio, R. M., and Sellin, T. (1972). *Delinquency in a Birth Cohort*. Chicago: Chicago University Press.

Youthful Offender Parole Board (1988). 'Response to Reforming the California Youth Authority', in Paul DeMuro, Anne DeMuro, and Steve Lerner (eds.), *Reforming the California Youth Authority*. Bolinas, Calif.: Common Knowledge Press, pp. 53–56.

Zimring, Franklin E. (1998). *American Youth Violence*. New York: Oxford University Press.

——and Hawkins, Gordon (1994). 'The Growth of Imprisonment in California'. *British Journal of Criminology*, 34 (Special Issue): 83–96.

——and Hawkins, Gordon (1997). *Crime is not the Problem: Lethal Violence in America*. Oxford: Oxford University Press.

Zorn, Christopher J. (1998). 'An Analytic and Empirical Examination of Zero-Inflated and Hurdle Poisson Specifications'. *Sociological Methods and Research*, 26: 368–400.

Index